RETURNING LIFE

Methodology and History in Anthropology

Series Editors:

David Parkin, *Fellow of All Souls College, University of Oxford*

David Gellner, *Fellow of All Souls College, University of Oxford*

RETURNING LIFE

Language, Life Force and History
in Kilimanjaro

Knut Christian Myhre

berghahn
NEW YORK • OXFORD
www.berghahnbooks.com

First published in 2018 by

Berghahn Books

www.berghahnbooks.com

Library of Congress Cataloging-in-Publication Data

Names: Myhre, Knut Christian, 1971– author.
Title: Returning life : language, life force, and history in Kilimanjaro /
   Knut Christian Myhre.
Description: New York : Berghahn Books, 2017. | Series: Methodology
   & history in anthropology ; volume 32 | Includes bibliographical
   references and index.
Identifiers: LCCN 2017050584 (print) | LCCN 2017051665 (ebook) |
   ISBN 9781785336669 (eBook) | ISBN 9781785336652 |
   ISBN 1785336657?(hardback :?alk. paper)
Subjects: LCSH: Chaga (African people)—Tanzania—Social life and
   customs. | Chaga (African people)—Tanzania—Rites and
   ceremonies. | Ethnology—Tanzania—Kilimanjaro Region.
Classification: LCC DT443.3.W33 (ebook) | LCC DT443.3.W33 M94
   2017 (print) | DDC 305.800967826—dc23
LC record available at https://lccn.loc.gov/2017050584

British Library Cataloguing in Publication Data

A catalogue record for this book is available from the British Library

ISBN 978-1-78533-665-2 hardback
ISBN 978-1-80073-947-5 paperback
ISBN 978-1-78533-666-9 ebook

https://doi.org/10.3167/9781785336652

For Tove Myhre and
in memory of Knut Olav Myhre (1942–2017).

CONTENTS

ILLUSTRATIONS

PREFACE

In the dead of night in late October 2008, nearly a dozen Chagga-speaking men left their homesteads in Keni Ward of Rombo District, on the eastern slopes of Mount Kilimanjaro in northern Tanzania. The men are descendants of the area's last serving *mangi* or 'chief' Tengia, and belong to an agnatic descent group (*ukoo*) that traces its origins to Horombo, a man who allegedly united and ruled large tracts of Kilimanjaro in the late eighteenth and early nineteenth century. Although distant in time, Horombo remains a frequent topic of contemporary conversation in this area, and is the person for whom Rombo District is named as an administrative unit of the Republic of Tanzania.

After leaving our houses, a handful of us gathered first at one particular homestead (*kaa*), where Peter the officiating elder tossed curdled milk onto a bull-calf, so that it could be untethered and removed from the house.[1] The entire group then met by the road that circles the mountain, before we set off down the mountainside in the dark. Heading east, we crossed the international border with Kenya shortly after sunrise and proceeded to a nearby settlement, where a group of Kamba-speaking male elders expected us. Bringing along a large female goat (*mooma*) with full udders that revealed how it had recently borne kids, the Kamba elders accompanied us to an uncultivated place (*sakeu*) at the edge of the village. The place consisted of two small clearings surrounded by thick bush and shaded by a large overgrown acacia tree, which obscured the surrounding fields and nearby houses. Named Witini, the place is where Horombo's body purportedly was left behind, after he was killed in internecine warfare with people from nearby Taita. His men were unable to carry his large frame all the way back to the mountain, so Horombo's son cut off his head and brought it back to be buried at the homestead of one of his wives on the mountain, while his body remained beneath this tree in the plains.

Once we had removed some of shrubs and brush that had sprouted on the clearings, we gathered in a circle underneath the sprawling acacia tree. We watched in silence as Peter poured banana beer (*wari*) on the ground, while making the following statement:

> With this beer, Horombo, we request (*duiterewa*) something to eat, we request sufficient rain, not rain that kills. We request rain that will bring us something to eat, so that your children will not come to an end. We are coming to an end, *mangi*. The cattle and even the goats have nothing to eat. Just look, Horombo Ukoni, the people are finished, we are finished. We are exhausted from the heat (*muu*), we are completely exhausted. We request very much, you great one (*hai sha moombe*). It is indeed this we request, *mangi simba*. Do not give us rain that kills, but that brings us food. We request very much, you great one, the children are dying completely. We have dwelled for a long time (*dulekaa kasha*), but we have not forgotten you. The evangelicals said that we no longer place foods on the ground (*dutchasa se ku*), but this beer for remembering you, we are placing underneath your arm.

Peter then refilled his drinking gourd (*shori*) and poured more beer, while saying:

> Dwell here (*kaa haa*), *mangi*, you protect them, you bless them (*uwabariki*), those who have come to do this work here. When they climb back up, may the sun not bear down relentlessly on the place. Bring heat as normal and light rain as normal, so that we can get something to eat. We request very much, you great one, *hai*, my father, we request very much, Ukoni. At the homestead (*fo mrini*), we remember you. We remember you, *hai*, my father of the old days. Let us get rain.

Peter then poured a final round of beer that was accompanied with the words:

> I have returned life to you (*ngakuuriya moo*), Horombo Ukoni. We have reached the end. We have returned life to you. The banana trees have finished. We have nothing more to eat. We are exhausted, we are completely exhausted. We request very much, you great one, *hai*, Horombo Ukoni. I have returned life to you, *mangi*, I have returned life to you, great one, and to the owner of that banana garden (*monikihambaki*). I have returned life to all of you, sit and drink well. It is your grandchildren giving you this, your great-grandchildren are remembering you.

Peter's pouring of the beer occurred on the initiative of the Kenyan Kamba, who had crossed the border and climbed the mountain several times in the preceding months to complain of drought (*ukame*) and hunger (*njaa*) to Horombo's descendants. Like so many others in sub-Saharan Africa, both the people on the mountain and those in the plains derive their livelihoods from non-irrigated mixed agriculture, and therefore rely on rain for their existence. Accordingly, Peter stated that we had come to the plains to request rain that would bring food

and fodder, and abate the heat and relieve the sun that imperilled people, livestock and crops.

Once Peter was done, he yielded his place to the senior Kamba elder,
who poured their honey beer (*molatine*) next to our *wari*, while making
a strikingly similar request to Horombo in the Kamba language:

> You Olombo, we have come to pray to you, at least to bring us a little
> rain, the children are getting finished, even the cattle that we have,
> there is nothing, because are they going to eat soil? I mean, you (plural)
> can see, you (singular) can see how they look. So this is what I did, told
> them to read, to drink some alcohol with you and that is what we have
> prayed. So now this is what we have prayed – and we have prayed sev-
> eral times with nothing happening. Please we ask you Olombo, we have
> prayed, and the other person called the wife with no child (*Mūka ūte
> Mwana*), we ask that they too be there with you so that at least we can
> get something, no matter how small, for our cattle to eat. Forget even
> the people, people are in trouble, for all these years and everywhere,
> what shall they do, you and *Mūka ūte Mwana* drink, and bring us at
> least a small cloud that will stop above us as a promise that we shall see
> some fresh pastures. I mean, if it goes on like this how shall things look?
> We have come to pray to you. We have prayed, drink up. People who
> pray, there is, we have laid this prayer before you so that you (plural)
> may give us something no matter how small, at least, if the children get
> finished now, where shall we be? Drink, drink up Olombo, and all the
> other male elders. And if all the cattle are finished, what shall you eat?
> Drink. We have prayed and I shall give you food, the little we brought,
> so that you may eat just as it is, because if there is no food can people
> get fat? Drink. And those who haven't eaten anything drink. We have
> prayed to you (plural) at least that a small cloud comes from wherever
> and stops here, once it gathers it will have gathered, we shall, we shall
> not forget to thank you.

These acts in response to the heat and lack of rain were the inception
of a two-day event that took place for the first time in eight years. The
event began in the plains and continued on the mountain, where beer
and milk were poured on the ground multiple times, and a total of
three animals were butchered so their blood was spilled and the meat
shared.[2] Such acts have long formed part of a discourse on 'sacrifice'
that once occupied a central position in Africanist anthropology (de
Heusch 1985; Evans-Pritchard 1956; Lienhardt 1961; Ruel 1997).
However, the statements above do not address a transcendent being or
deity, and do not concern the sacred or the substitution of animal for
human life. Instead, they suggest a process of material transfers and
transformations that Peter enunciated in terms of 'dwelling' (*ikaa*)
and 'life' (*moo*), where foodstuffs are poured and placed on the ground
with the hope of receiving rain, so that they can get food and fodder to

continue their existence and be able to provide Horombo and the other deceased with similar substances in the future.

Notes

1. Most (but not all) names that occur in this book have been changed to anonymize the persons concerned.
2. The event is more closely described in chapter six.

ACKNOWLEDGMENTS

This book is based on several years of fieldwork among the Chagga-speaking people of Keni-Mengeni in Rombo District of Kilimanjaro Region. My first visit to the area was made in October–November 1998, while the bulk of the fieldwork was carried out between April 2000 and September 2001, and again between October 2006 and February 2007, and August and November 2008. Shorter trips were also made in April 2002, April 2003, November–December 2011 and October–November 2012.

During this time, I have accrued an immense debt of gratitude to all the people who willingly and patiently shared of their time, capacity and knowledge. While there is not room to name everyone here, I wish to thank Atali Nguvumali Buretta, who first enabled me to come to Keni and let me stay in his house during all my fieldwork visits. In Atali's absence from Rombo, the burden of my stay fell on Notiburga Nguvumali MaSway, who treated me like her own son and to whom I am accordingly indebted and devoted. Febro, Meki and Joyce have all since moved away, but I remember with fondness and gratitude our times together, and especially all the evenings we spent around MaSway's hearth. I am also grateful to Verani for his care and concern during his frequent trips to Rombo, and to him and his family for letting me stay with them whenever I passed through Moshi town. I also thank Oswald and Honesty, and their wives and children, along with the rest of the late Nguvumali's extended family and those of my mother's brothers at Shimbi. You received and accepted me in your midst, and I thank you with all my heart for your hospitality, help and companionship over all these years.

I also wish to thank one-time Ward Councillor Constantine Sebastian Shirima and the late Constantine Tengia Urio, who vouched for me at an early stage and were instrumental in affording access to their respective agnatic descent groups. Peter Mwanamangi August Urio and Teofuli Wilbert Urio have provided steadfast support and assistance for which I am exceedingly grateful. I also thank Aldegunda Hippolyt Shao for using her pedagogical skills to teach me the basics of the Rombo dialect, and enabling me to gather and trace the language to the best of my abilities. Last but not least, the quality and joy of this work owe an immense deal to Pastori Alois Samba, who has never failed to provide of his great skills and deep knowledge. I hope I do not presume too much by saying that Pasto remains my brother, and that I am humbled by and grateful for the affection and assistance accorded me by him and his extended family.

Away from Kilimanjaro, I thank the staff at the Evangelisch-Lutherisches Missionswerk Leipzig, the Tanzanian National Archives, and Rhodes House, Oxford, who facilitated my archival research. I moreover gratefully acknowledge financial support from the University of Oxford, the Research Council of Norway, the German Academic Exchange Service (DAAD), the Norwegian University of Science and Technology (NTNU), the Nordic Africa Institute, the University of Oslo, the Institute for Comparative Research in Human Culture, and St. Antony's College, Oxford. I also acknowledge receipt of research permits from the Tanzanian Commission for Science and Technology and thank *Africa*, the International African Institute, and Edinburgh University Press, as well as the *Journal of the Royal Anthropological Institute* and Wiley-Blackwell for allowing me to reprint portions of previously published texts. I am also grateful to the staff and editors at Berghahn for their efforts on my behalf and for making this an enjoyable undertaking.

A particular debt of gratitude is due to Wendy James, who not only trained me as a social anthropologist, but also alerted me to Bruno Gutmann and his ethnographic work, which has proved so decisive for my own. I furthermore thank David Anderson, Harri Englund and Bruce Kapferer for their interest in and support of my work, as well as David Parkin, who has never failed, least of all as a series editor.

The book has otherwise benefitted from conversations and discussions with Per Brandström, Giovanni da Col, René Devisch, Jean-Claude Galey, Wenzel Geissler, Maia Green, Thomas Håkansson, Penny Harvey, Kjell Havnevik, Martin Holbraad, Signe Howell, Kjersti Larsen, Morten Nielsen, Adam Reed, Knut Rio, Todd Sanders, Jan Ketil Simonsen, Tone Sommerfelt, Frode Storås, Aud Talle, Richard Vokes, Chris Wingfield, Cristoph Winter, Tom Yarrow and the reviewers for Berghahn. I also thank Nik Petek and Paul Lane for organizing the map, Neo Musangi for transcribing and translating the Kamba invocation that features in the preface, and Wenzel Geissler and Guy Tourlamain for their advice on my translations of German material. Needless to say, any mistakes or omissions remain my sole responsibility.

On a personal note, I am grateful to my parents, Tove and Knut, who have always supported my efforts even when it was less than clear what they were or where they were taking me. Sadly, my father passed away while this book was in production, so he did not get to see the finished result of which I am sure he would be proud. In love and appreciation, I dedicate this book to them.

Above all, I thank the love of my life, Katie, for keeping me company in Kilimanjaro, and for enduring the elation and anguish that this work entails. My greatest debt is due to you and our daughters Maia and Iben for the love, joy and encouragement you bestow, and that I can only hope to return.

NOTE ON LANGUAGE
AND ORTHOGRAPHY

Most of the vernacular terms that feature in this book belong to the Rombo version of the six dialects that are spoken on and around Mount Kilimanjaro. These dialects are currently classified as Northeast Savannah Bantu and are commonly grouped together as Chagga, even though they may differ considerably among themselves. The other vernacular terms that appear are from Swahili, which is the national language of Tanzania. As I explain later, nearly everyone in Rombo is fluent in both languages, which they alternate between and even use interchangeably in different settings. In accordance with this, I have not formally distinguished between the two languages in the text, but rely on the context to reveal when Swahili features rather than the Rombo dialect.

To enhance readability, I have refrained from using specialized orthography and diacritical markers in transcribing vernacular terms. The only exception is the *ng'* sound that features in both the dialects around the mountain and Swahili and that is pronounced like in the English *sing,* and the *lh* and the *ɽ* sounds that are used in Rombo and pronounced as an alveolar *l* and a retroflex *r,* respectively. When I quote vernacular terms from other ethnographic descriptions, I have endeavoured to reproduce their orthography and use of diacritical markers.

In addition to Chagga and Swahili, German terms also feature in the text, most commonly as they are used by the missionary-ethnographer Bruno Gutmann and his colleagues in their descriptions. These terms are only included to show and discuss how these early ethnographers rendered vernacular notions and practices that are of significance for my own ethnography. I have not formally distinguished these German terms either, but hope the reader will be able to tell them apart based on the contexts in which they occur.

INTRODUCTION

This book is a historical ethnography of the form life has for the Chagga-speaking people of Rombo District on the slopes of Mount Kilimanjaro. It is a language-oriented ethnography that takes as its focus the use of vernacular concepts and claims, and attends to how these entail, entangle and engage things and activities. The book is not concerned with matters of symbols or signification, or the ways in which words and statements name and represent objects and situations. Instead, it explores the constitutive relationships between the linguistic and non-linguistic, and investigates the mutuality between semantic, social and material phenomena.

At the heart of the book are notions and activities that featured prominently in the event that took place in the plains below Rombo in 2008. In particular, the account centres on the notion of *ikaa* that I translate as 'dwelling' and the different yet imbricating activities that take place in and around the homestead (*kaa*), which derives its term from this notion. As I will show, these activities transfer and transform 'life force' or 'bodily power' (*horu*) between humans, livestock and crops, which enables and constitutes their existence, capacity, health and well-being. Pursuing the different permutations of *horu*, the book shows how their transfers and transformations involve or engage a plethora of places, substances, conduits, beings and processes whose terms derive or unfold from the notions of *moo* or 'life'. By tracing and outlining these concepts, the book reveals how dwelling involves and concerns efforts to channel capacity in ways that realize life in a particular way.

My concern with vernacular concepts and claims is not an attempt to portray or propose a unique and distinct 'Chagga culture'. After all, it is now a commonplace in Africanist anthropology that broader social, political and economic processes embroil and connect even the most remote settings (Comaroff and Comaroff 1991, 1993, 1997; Ferguson 1999; Gupta and Ferguson 1997; Hutchinson 1996; Moore and Vaughan 1994; Piot 1999; Weiss 1996; West 2005). Indeed, it is perhaps the case to an even greater extent for Kilimanjaro than for most other places on the continent. At least, an important impetus for this insight emerged from Sally Falk Moore's (1986) 'time-oriented anthropology', which reveals the longstanding involvement of Kilimanjaro in regional trade, and details the political and economic transformations wrought by colonial rule and coffee cash-cropping for its banana-farming and livestock-rearing inhabitants. On that basis, Moore challenges and escapes the confines of bounded and bounding analytics, like 'society', 'culture' and 'tribe', and instead proposes a processual approach, where 'diagnostic events' and cases are described and combined so that an 'ethnography of the present' reveals the historical transformations and long-term effects of large-scale processes (Moore 1987, 1993, 2005a, 2005b). Unsurprisingly, Moore's conception has been formative for subsequent work in this area, where researchers draw on her analysis and extend her approach to explore the effects of missions, monetized economies and market conditions, as well as education, changing gender relations and the HIV/AIDS epidemic, for social life in Kilimanjaro (Hasu 1999; Pietilä 2007; Setel 1999; Stambach 2000).

In different yet related ways, these researchers unfold events into dynamics of longer reach and greater depth, and thus provide valuable material and conceptual contributions regarding the significance and impact of historical developments and the various phenomena they involve. It is nevertheless noteworthy that the notions of *ikaa, horu* and *moo* are not to be found in any of these studies. A perhaps obvious reason for this is the fact that Moore and her successors have opted to conduct their work through Swahili and English, rather than the Chagga vernacular.[1] It may also be that their preoccupations with larger-scale and longer-term dynamics eclipse the more mundane concepts of everyday life and regional interactions of a more immediate kind, like that which took place between people in the plains below Rombo in 2008. At the same time, it also seems that the interest for such dynamics has shifted anthropological attention away from issues such as settlement patterns, inheritance practices and bridewealth prestations that are central to these notions. Yet the main reason is probably the fact that these are elusive notions that are easily overlooked and even harder to grasp. Thus, Henrietta Moore (1999: 19) argues, 'All the societies of the region are concerned with the creative life forces of the world and their manifestations through fertility and reproduction. Yet, anthropologists, with some exceptions, have found it difficult to understand the nature of these life forces'. In line with her claim, it took me a while to discover the notions of *ikaa* and *horu*.

But at the time of the event in 2008, I had explored acts of pouring and placing beer, milk and meat on the ground as prestations of bodily power or life force, and I had investigated how *horu* is constitutive of people's capacity, health and well-being, and how it is transferred and transformed in the process of dwelling (Myhre 2006, 2007a, 2007b). Yet the notion of *moo*, which loomed large during the event in the plains, was first encountered – at least in that form – on that particular occasion. Nevertheless, these notions are not confined to that specific context, but concern a set of subtle and slippery concepts that are widespread in the area, yet receive little attention.

According to Moore, the prevalent life forces are overlooked by anthropologists due to a neglect of the practical and performative aspects of gender, and a disregard for the embodied character of agency and subjectivity. Her claim obviously relies on analytics that gained prominence since the 1970s and 1980s (Hirsch 2014; Merlan 2016), but it receives support from those scholars who do grapple with these phenomena. René Devisch (1993), for instance, relays how 'life-transmission processes' among the Yaka of southwestern Congo involve and concern combinations of 'agnatic life force' (*ngolu*) and 'uterine vital flow' (*mooyi*). Filip de Boeck (1994a: 271), meanwhile, describes how 'vital life-flow' (*mooy*) among the nearby Luunda 'constitutes the essential source of life, longevity, health and well-being', and 'is a relational force, with integrative and cohesive powers, connecting "male" and "female" processes of life-generation'. Reminiscent of how Peter, the descendant of a 'chief', addressed *mangi* Horombo, both argue that these forces are transposed metaphorically onto corporeal, social and cosmological fields that conjoin in the chiefly person, who derives his position and power from the capacity to articulate, mediate and embody opposing principles and provide a relationship to the regenerative forces that secure the fertility of persons and land (de Boeck 1994b; Devisch 1988).

These ideas are developed by Todd Sanders (2008), who explores how rainmaking is a matter of life and death among the Ihanzu of central Tanzania, which like other fertile and productive endeavours turns on the judicious combination of masculine and feminine forces. According to Sanders, these forces form part of a 'gender epistemology' that includes yet exceeds human bodies and their reproductive relations to encompass the seasons, spirits, positions, practices and paraphernalia that the Ihanzu hold for male and female. His perspective surpasses anthropological conceptions that privilege either the human body or a form of practice or field of experience, and promote one such as a model, metaphor, metonym or symbol for other areas and domains (Beidelman 1986, 1997; Broch-Due 1993; Feierman 1990; Harris 1978; Herbert 1993; Taylor 1992). In fact, it transcends such semantics altogether and thus also goes beyond those approaches that consider bodies and reproduction elements of broader metaphorical or symbolic relations (Comaroff 1985; Gausset 2002; H.L. Moore 1986; Weiss 1996). By contrast, Sanders considers how different phenomena *are* gendered and how they *are* combined to create particular effects that include rain.

In a similar vein, Wenzel Geissler and Ruth Prince (2010: 10) describe how gendered complementarity and generational sequence are central to a widespread notion of 'growth', 'in which the well-being of cosmic and social worlds, the fertility of the land and its inhabitants, people and animals, living and dead, form an interconnected whole, and in which seemingly disparate dimensions of growth are dependent upon one another'. Where earlier approaches to such notions attend to ritual, myth and symbolic systems, Geissler and Prince focus on everyday moments of material contact that the Luo-speaking people of western Kenya conceptualize in terms of 'touch'. As they point out, touch directs attention to boundaries and interfaces, and provides a view of how persons and things are brought into contact and into being through contested and ambivalent practices of social relations. In turn, this attends to how growth involves a care and concern for specific and valorized orientations and movements that unfold phenomena through time and space, in a different manner and through different relations than the ones emphasized by Sally Falk Moore and her followers in Kilimanjaro.

Another scholar wrestling with these ideas is Malcolm Ruel (1997: 117), who describes how the Kuria notion of *omooyo* means 'life', 'health' or 'well-being' in the abstract, yet concretely designates the gullet, windpipe or alimentary canal.[2] A cognate of Yaka *mooyi*, Luunda *mooy* and Chagga *moo*, the Kuria notion of *omooyo* forms part of a widespread series of Bantu-language words that in Ruel's view has been wrongly rendered as 'spirit', 'soul' and 'heart'. Instead, he argues, the notion concerns how life, health and well-being (*obohoro*) are effects of ungendered passages and processes that afford the movement and consumption of food, air, water and even speech. Indeed, these passages and processes extend beyond the person and the body to include other openings and pathways, such as the doorways and gateways of houses and homesteads through which *omohoro* flows (Ruel 1997: 120).[3] *Omooyo* therefore involves a relational and ecological conception of persons and life that differs and departs from the presuppositions of self-sufficiency and self-maintenance implied by its longstanding translations. Rendered properly, it provides a view of how life, health and well-being enter and emerge from parts of persons and the environment, and thus project *through* beings of different kinds.

The cognate character of *mooyi, mooy, omooyo* and *moo* problematize the assumptions and effects of enclosing analytics in a different way from the approaches of Sally Falk Moore and her followers. Rather than the reach, extent and impact of colonial and postcolonial developments, these notions reveal how vernacular values and meanings extend through time and space. They plumb other historical depths and recede towards a horizon within which they enmesh and facilitate interactions between peoples that may be considered distinct and separate in cultural or social terms (see Ruel 1997: 2). As such, it speaks to how the people from Rombo and the people from Kenya gathered and engaged across national, ethnic and linguistic boundaries for the common concern of rain and life. At the same time, the authors who engage these notions show how they make room for and call forth alternative conceptions that recast being and life in relational terms of forces, touch, passageways and openings. Indeed, their approaches can be plotted as a trajectory, where metaphorical connections give way to practical and material relations, which in turn yield to the movements of life through persons, things and the world at large.

This book extends this trajectory, as it describes how ungendered life force converts and conveys in different forms by means of different parts of persons through the everyday activities of dwelling. It moreover explores how the beings and entities that dwelling yields are transferred through the doorways of houses and along pathways in bridewealth prestations and marital relations, which extend persons through time and space. Conversely, burial practices consist of a protracted process, where these extensions are gathered to locate the deceased in a specific place. On this basis, the book investigates how the transfers and transformations of life force involve movements of extension and contraction, and processes of emplacement and displacement that actualize temporal and spatial orientations and relations of the kind that Peter invoked in his address. In this way, the book attends to how dwelling involves and engages places, substances, conduits, beings and processes from, through, along and by means of which *horu* converts and conveys. As these in turn derive their terms from *moo*, they reveal how life is an effect of the transfers and transformations of life force (*horu*) that occur through dwelling (*ikaa*) in and around the homestead (*kaa*). Cognates of the Kuria *omooyo* and *omohoro*, Chagga *moo* and *horu* hence concern how life emerges and results from material transfers and transformations that occur through parts of persons, houses, livestock and crops. The result is a view of *horu* as a uniform life force that exists between, acts upon and refracts through persons and things to yield all that the world contains.

Towards an Anthropological Concept of Life

To explore these notions and practices, I draw on Ludwig Wittgenstein's later philosophy. It might seem odd to engage a long-dead European philosopher to explore the character of dwelling and life in contemporary east Africa, and especially one whose chief contributions were to logic and the philosophies of language and mathematics. However, Wittgenstein's later philosophy emerged from an encounter with anthropology that occasioned a conception of language and meaning that speaks to concerns for pragmatics and performativity that have gained interest and influence in anthropology and related disciplines (see for instance Barad 2003; Latour 2005; Law 2009; Whyte 1997). Wittgenstein moreover attended specifically to ordinary language for which he developed a descriptive approach and attending tools that relate to and open for ethnographic enquiry. He even hinted at an 'ethnological approach' (CV: 45), and invoked and engaged a notion of 'life' that can shed light on the ideas and activities that are at play in Kilimanjaro.[4] The engagement finally gains support from Ruel's (1997: 3) contention that the notions and practices he describes as Kuria 'religion' could equally be considered a form of philosophy or a truth-system.

Wittgenstein's encounter with anthropology occurred in 1931, when he read James George Frazer's *The Golden Bough* with his student Maurice O'Connor Drury (1996: 134). The experience resulted in a set of critical remarks, where Wittgenstein took exception to Frazer's view that magic and religion are erroneous attempts to explain and influence the world, which in turn are in need of explanation, if not intervention. Wittgenstein's objection was that such explanation presupposes that the phenomena in question involve and rest on a hypothesis, which misconstrues the role they play in people's lives: 'Every explanation is after all an hypothesis. But a hypothetical explanation will be of little help to someone, say, who is upset because of love. – It will not calm him' (RFG: 123). Explanations and hypotheses moreover postulate underlying phenomena that account for the notions and practices in question, but these cannot resolve the meaning the latter have for those who use and engage in them. Wittgenstein pointed out: 'It was not a trivial reason, for really there can have been no *reason*, that prompted certain races of mankind to venerate the oak tree, but only the fact that they and the oak were united in a community of life, and thus that they arose together not by choice, but rather like the flea and the dog. (If fleas developed a rite, it would be based on the dog)' (RFG: 139). Wittgenstein therefore held: 'I believe that the attempt to explain is already therefore wrong, because one must only piece together what one *knows*, without adding anything, and the satisfaction being sought through the explanation follows of itself ... Here one can only *describe* and say: this is what human life is like' (RFG: 121).

These quotes show that Wittgenstein invoked 'life' in different ways in his remarks on Frazer, where it served as the ground for the phenomena in question and the object of their description. To further grapple with these issues, Wittgenstein adopted in his *Philosophical Investigations* (1953) the notion of 'form of life' (*Lebensform*), which already had a long and variegated history in German philosophy and scientific enquiry (Helmreich and Roosth 2010). 'Form of life' only appears a handful of times in Wittgenstein's book, where it is used in both the singular and the plural, and in indeterminate and determinate forms. Its scarce and apparently careless usage may obscure how this notion combines with other ideas and insights in Wittgenstein's effort to consider language not as an abstract system of representation, but as an integral part of human practice that grants privilege to description at the expense of explanation and theory (Allen and Turvey 2001; Bouveresse 2007; Glock 2001; Hacker 2001a).

Central in this regard is the concept of 'language-game' (*Sprachspiel*), which Wittgenstein coins to highlight how language embeds in non-linguistic practices: 'Here the term language-*game* is meant to bring into prominence the fact that the *speaking* of a language is part of an activity, or a form of life' (PI: §23). While *Lebensform* is borrowed from elsewhere, *Sprachspiel* is Wittgenstein's invention that aims to grasp how language is a practice where the meaning of a word is its use, and not the object to which it refers. It also attends to the diversity of uses that words have, and the overlapping and criss-crossing 'family resemblances' between their multiple meanings. These need not have any feature in common, but instead exist through a range of relationships: 'Instead of producing something common to all that we call language, I am saying that these phenomena have no one thing in common which makes us use the same word for all, – but that they are *related* to one another in many different ways. And it is because of this relationship, or these relationships, that we call them all "language"'

(PI: §65). It is because language consists of a multitude of relationships of different kinds that words and meanings must be considered and described in their concrete use: 'In order to see more clearly, here as in countless similar cases, we must focus on the details of what goes on; must look at them from close to' (PI: §51).

These ideas are particularly apposite for the notion of *horu*, which has a multiplicity of uses and imbricates with an array of activities, in what can be considered a diversity of language-games. *Horu* is in other words a family resemblance concept that both entails and forms part of a multiplicity of relationships that must be described in their detail. Moreover, *horu* is not some*thing*, but pertains to movements or interactions that manifest as beings of different kinds, which emerge, exist and evanesce as transformations of each other. In the different language-games played with this notion, *horu* therefore does not designate an object, but concerns the capacity of different beings to affect each other through the activities that constitute dwelling or *ikaa*.

However, the notion of language-game not only serves to embed language in other activities, it conversely captures how language-use entwines and concomitates non-linguistic actions. Thus, Wittgenstein says: 'I shall also call the whole, consisting of language and the actions into which it is woven, the "language-game"' (PI: §7). In the words of Avrum Stoll (2007: 103), 'a language-game is a slice of everyday human activity', where the use of language enables, entwines and entails other forms of action. Indeed, linguistic practice not only has bodily concomitants, but in a sense extends out of such activities: 'Language – I want to say – is a refinement, "in the beginning was the deed"' (CV: 31).[5] Or, as Wittgenstein stated in his remarks on Frazer, language forms part of 'the *surroundings* of a way of acting' (RFG: 147). These notes aim to grasp the multiple and variegated relationships that obtain between language and action and by extension the objects that these involve in concrete language-games. Along with Wittgenstein's equation between meaning and use, their result is that words and notions neither refer to nor index objects and practices, but rather contain and entail activities that entangle and engage things in specific language-games. Phrased in a different way, one can say that objects are gathered up in different ways in different language-games (see also Myhre 2012: 195–197), which hence involve a plethora of world-relations. These relations depart from epistemological and metaphysical perspectives, where persons confront and impute meaning to a world that is distinct from them and their description of it, and instead provide a view of how language and meaning involve and emerge from engagements and relations between persons and the world.

The relations that these notions involve entail that it is the language-game, rather than the word or proposition, that constitutes the semantic unit: 'Look on the language-games as the *primary* thing' (PI: §656). The relations require description to lay out the uses of words, along with the activities they entail and the objects these involve. In this way, description affords a 'surview' or 'overview' (*Übersicht*) of a particular portion of language of which it aims to provide a 'perspicuous representation' (*übersichtliche Darstellung*): 'The concept of perspicuous representation is of fundamental importance for us. It denotes the form of our representation, the way we see things ... This perspicuous representation brings about the understanding which consists precisely in the fact that we "see the connections". Hence the importance of finding *connecting links*. But the hypothetical connecting link should in this case do nothing but direct our attention to the similarity, the relatedness, of the *facts*' (RFG: 133).

The idea of perspicuous representation is the only element of the remarks on Frazer that Wittgenstein retained for his *Philosophical Investigations*. It became central for his endeavour to describe the 'conceptual topology' of a language that replaced the 'conceptual geology' of his earlier philosophy (Hacker 2001b), which gained no traction once 'nothing is hidden' (PI: §435). The emphasis on 'seeing connections' and 'finding connecting links', combined with the idea of family resemblance, could suggest that Wittgenstein conceives of language and meaning in terms of identity or commonality between phenomena. In truth, however, Wittgenstein is as concerned with difference and dissimilarity as with identity and similarity: 'The language-games are rather set up as *objects of comparison* which are meant to throw light on the facts of our language by way not only of similarities, but also of dissimilarities' (PI: §130). O'Connor Drury (1996: 157) accordingly recalled Wittgenstein arguing that, 'Hegel seems to me to be always wanting to say that things which look different are really the same. Whereas my interest is in showing that things which look the same are really different. I was thinking of using as a motto for my book a quotation from *King Lear*: "I'll teach you differences"'.

A perspicuous representation charts what Wittgenstein calls the 'grammar' that determines the uses and meanings of particular words. For Wittgenstein, the purpose of such a representation is to resolve or dissolve philosophical problems, which arise from conceptual confusion and misuse of words that are due to our entanglement in the variety of linguistic expressions. Such resolution or dissolution occurs through a conceptual clarification that disentangles and lays bare the use of particular words and the workings of language (PI:

§109). The account can make no reference to anything hidden or underlying, since the use and meaning of words cannot depend on something that is concealed to those who speak the language. The solution to philosophical problems therefore cannot involve explanation of any kind, but can only consist of description: 'Philosophy simply puts everything before us, and neither explains nor deduces anything. – Since everything lies open to view there is nothing to explain. For what is hidden, for example, is of no interest to us' (PI: §126).

It follows from this that a perspicuous representation does not involve the discovery of anything new, but consists in an arrangement or rearrangement of what competent speakers already know and do: 'The work of the philosopher consists in assembling reminders for a particular purpose' (PI: §127). Because the purpose varies in accordance with the problem involved, the arrangement that is required and achieved also differs. A perspicuous representation thus affords a surview of a particular segment of language, which depends on the purpose and the problem concerned. The description it involves is moreover not a uniform concept, but itself a family resemblance phenomenon, whose form depends on the words and issues involved (Hacker 2001b: 24). The perspicuous representation therefore provides *a* – not *the* – conceptual order of a particular portion of language through a description that is partial, both in the sense that it is incomplete, and in the sense that it is infused by a specific interest. To paraphrase Martin Holbraad and Morten Pedersen (2009: 381), the effect of such a representation 'is to provide, not a point of more general vantage, but rather one of further departure'.

Transposed to ethnography, the task is to describe the uses and meanings of particular words together with the activities they entail and the objects they involve. The relations that language-games involve mean that such description does not simply consist in the portrayal of a state of affairs. Instead, it involves the act of *unfolding* a language-game to lay out the uses of words, along with their attendant practices and things. The description must also chart the family resemblances between the different uses of the singular notions across the language-games in which they occur. In addition, it must sketch the additional words and concepts with which those of particular interest are used in combination. The account of *ikaa* therefore evokes and necessitates descriptions of the homestead (*kaa*), and the multiple uses and various language-games of *horu* that the activities that occur in and around it involve. It moreover requires accounts of the places, substances, conduits, beings and processes from, through, along and by means of which life force converts and conveys in different forms. A description of *ikaa* in other words involves an account of *kaa*, which extends into descriptions of *horu* and portrayals of the various notions that derive from *moo*. Methodologically speaking, this means that the description can trace relationships from anywhere, as the language-game can be unfurled from either the words, practices or objects it contains, or be folded out of any of the other language-games with which it enchains.

To provide a perspicuous representation, one must hence describe the multifarious uses of particular words or expressions, along with the activities they involve and the objects they engage. It proceeds through an account of the language-uses that surround specific activities and the objects they engage. It enables what Peter Hacker (2001b: 23) calls connective analysis, 'that is, a description of the conceptual connections and exclusions in the web of words'. Its emphasis on description affords an ethnographic openness, while the idea of taking something apart by joining it to something else, and combining something through taking it apart, resembles Marilyn Strathern's (1988, 1995, 2005) account of anthropology's relation. It recalls her elucidation of elicitation, detachment and decomposition as social processes, and affords a view of how vernacular conceptualizations combine and divide phenomena without presuming entities or relationships of a particular kind.

Since the perspicuous representation is a description that uses language to chart the grammar or use of words, there is an internal relationship and self-similarity between its means and ends (cf. Myhre 1998). Accordingly, it does not involve analysis in a conventional sense, where concepts are applied to a material that is different in scope or character. Instead, it consists in a moment and movement of unfolding and enfolding, where descriptions effectuate and multiply concepts as their result or end-point (Corsín Jímenez and Willerslev 2007; Myhre 2014, 2015). Despite the connotations of 'surview' and 'overview', the perspicuous representation locks into ordinary language on which it provides a peripheral perspective that traces relationships within and between language-games to describe conceptual structures from within or from the inside out (cf. Riles 2001). The description hence enables and entails a reverse or inverse move that confounds the distinction between the analytical and the empirical, and destabilizes the separation between anthropological and vernacular concepts (cf. Myhre 2013a). Vernacular concepts consequently become the subject of ethnography, which generates anthropological notions that this perspective places on the same footing (cf. Viveiros de Castro 2003, 2013). The approach allows the ethnographic to shape the anthropological, as vernacular and analytical concepts emerge together and constitute each other. The challenge, then, is not to provide a translation of a vernacular term, but to allow space where language-games may unfold so the concepts they involve can emerge and appear (cf. Strathern 1987a, 1988). Accordingly, I deploy established analytics, such as 'production', 'reproduction' and 'consumption', to approach the phenomena I consider, but these gradually give way to the notions of life force and dwelling, and eventually yield to *horu*, *ikaa* and *moo*. Wittgenstein's ideas of meaning as use, language-game, family resemblance and grammar thus constitute an 'infra-language' (Latour 2005: 30) where unfamiliar concepts may appear and receive a chance they otherwise do not get (Latour 2000: 368). His descriptive tools simply posit empty relations of similarity and difference, and are therefore 'thin' concepts that allow for 'thick' descriptions from which dwelling and *ikaa*, life force and *horu*, life and *moo* can emerge as concepts in their own right.

These considerations shed important light on the difference between my rendition of *ikaa* as dwelling and Tim Ingold's (2000) use of the same term. Inspired by Martin Heidegger ([1954] 1978), I adopted dwelling to grasp how *ikaa* summates a set of practices that occur in a particular place (*kaa*), where *horu* converts and conveys in different forms to constitute a specific mode of being or form of life (*moo*). Returning from fieldwork in 2001, I discovered that Ingold (2000) used the same Heidegger text and notion to advocate a 'dwelling perspective' that focuses on how humans generate material and immaterial forms through their practical engagement with their surroundings. Like *ikaa*, Ingold's concept affords a view of how persons, things and the world at large are crystallizations of activities that enfold and testify the unfolding relations between humans and non-humans. The two notions thus intersect as they consider how phenomena unfold as the outcome of practices and processes. But where Ingold's is a purely analytical concept that can be applied to any ethnography for the purpose of rendering the world in a particular way, my concept emerges from descriptions of the multiple uses of *ikaa*, which unfold the different language-games of which it forms part, including the activities and objects they concern and entail. 'Dwelling' is here then not a concept that is applied to an ethnographic material for analytical purposes, but the result and end-point of a description that reveals the effects of the vernacular notion of *ikaa*.

The Horizon of Language and Meaning

The account above shows how Wittgenstein's later philosophy emerged from an encounter with anthropology, and how it engages issues of ethnographic interest and import. It reveals a lateral conception of language and meaning, where words, practices and things combine in language-games that extend into and out of each other. It is this that grounds the most common interpretations of 'form of life', which in Oswald Hanfling's (1989: 162) view, 'is meant to convey the wholeness of the system, and also the fact that it includes action ("life") as well as passive observation or experience'. Similarly, Jerry Gill (1991: xii) argues that Wittgenstein 'saw this form of life as constituting a vast and ever-developing network of overlapping and criss-crossing "language-games", each tied in its own way to specific physical and social activity'. The idea of an interlocking web of games that enfold words, practices and objects conceptualizes language as something that exists and unfolds through time and space. Accordingly, Wittgenstein used a temporal and spatial simile to grasp the character of language: 'Our language can be seen as an ancient city: a maze of little streets and squares, of old and new houses with additions from various periods; and this surrounded by a multitude of new boroughs with straight regular streets and uniform houses' (PI: §18).

The conception of language and meaning as extensive phenomena is apt for a situation where cognate notions like *mooyi, mooy, omooyo* and *moo* occur throughout a geographical region. Such notions moreover speak to Wittgenstein's conception of language and meaning as convolutions of similarities and differences. Curiously, it is particularly apposite in light of how Bantu languages create and multiply verb-forms by adding and inserting prefixes, suffixes and infixes to stems or root-forms. Nouns – like *kaa* – moreover derive from verbs – like *ikaa* – to which they retain similarities, while registering difference. These grammatical features lend Wittgenstein's concepts of language-games and family resemblance even greater force, as they extend connections and overlaps between and across even further situations and contexts of use. Added to this are people's longstanding capacities for speaking and understanding multiple cognate languages, which they use to interact across ethnic, social and cultural divides. Thus, the Chagga-speakers from Rombo and the Kamba-speakers from Kenya used Swahili to communicate and coordinate the event in the plains, while they conversed among themselves and made their invocations in their respective languages. Such situations and capabilities extend similarities beyond the singular language, while they relocate difference in ways that do not coincide with the boundaries commonly recognized by anthropological analytics. Rather, they redistribute similarities and differences in space and time to constitute an extensive horizon within which concepts, practices and objects can appear as always already meaningful.

Today everyone is bilingual in Rombo, where Chagga is used for most everyday interaction, while the national language of Swahili is the medium of instruction in public primary education and the vehicle of cash-cropping and governance. Village and sub-village meetings together with those of the cooperative societies, the Catholic prayer groups (*jumuiya*) and the descent groups are thus all conducted in Swahili, which moreover replicate the same organizational form.[6] Swahili is also the language of liturgy in the Catholic Church, to which the vast majority of people in the district belong. In the past, Swahili was only the language of catechism, but the church then ran Swahili pre-schools that children attended as a preparation for primary school. While this suggests that the use of Swahili is intimately linked to colonial rule and postcolonial developments, John Iliffe (1979: 79) points out that its spread and significance dates back to the slave and ivory caravans, which rendered Swahili widespread in the east African hinterlands by the mid to late 1800s. Some parts of Kilimanjaro served as points of provision for these caravans, which camped at purpose-built sites on their way to and from the interior (Kersten 1869: 291; S.F. Moore 1986: 31). Accordingly, the missionary Charles New (1873: 377) claimed that on meeting the *mangi* of Old Moshi: 'I spoke in Kisuahili, which Mandara comprehends and speaks almost as well as if he had been bred at the coast, and many of the people also understand a good deal of this language'. Even earlier, the German missionary Johannes Rebmann, who arrived in western Kilimanjaro as the first known European in 1849, reported that, 'Next day, and again on the 8th of January I received visits from Muigno Wessiri, a Suahili, who has lived in Jagga for six years, and has been appointed by the king his medicine-man and sorcerer, personages identical in savage countries' (Krapf 1860: 251). Thirteen years later, the German explorer Baron Carl Claus von der Decken also met Munie Wesiri [*sic*], whom he claimed originated from coastal Pangani.[7] He had arrived in Machame as a caravan porter (Kersten 1869: 291), where he first gained influence for his abilities as a 'witch-master' (*Hexenmeister*), but later maintained a standing as an interpreter for coastal caravans arriving in the area.[8]

In addition to Swahili, many people in Rombo speak other often cognate languages that they acquired when living or working in other parts of Tanzania or the wider region. Such capabilities also have a long history in the area, which abuts that which John Sutton (1969: 12) describes as the most linguistically diverse part of Africa. Accordingly, the traveller Harry Johnston (1886: 210) described how both Swahili and Maasai were understood by nearly everyone in Taveta, in the plains below Rombo. Roughly 25 kilometres from where the Chagga-speakers of Rombo and the Kamba-speakers of Kenya gathered in 2008, Johnston (1886: 320) claimed that, 'You may sit here in the porch of your comfortable thatched house, which may be built in a few days from the materials at hand, and receive visits from representatives of most of the nations found in East Central Africa'. Listing and naming fifteen different groups that included people as far away as Buganda and Nyoro in present-day Uganda, Johnston (1886: 321) claimed that they 'all find their way to Taveita [*sic*] somehow, whether as slaves, traders, tramps, criminals, or refugees. You may hear about twenty African languages talked around you, and, by searching among the slave caravans, which stop here for repose, a list of hundreds of East African tongues might be composed'.

The multilingual situation was partly due to the caravans Johnston mentioned, but also to the fact that this area is located on the Bantu-Nilotic interface or borderland. It is evidenced by the now defunct age-set system that preoccupied some of the early ethnographers to Kilimanjaro (Dundas 1924: 209ff; Gutmann 1926: 321ff), but that primarily is described from and identified with Nilotic-speaking peoples (Gulliver 1963; Parkin 1990; Spencer 1988). The occurrence of age-sets among other Bantu-speakers along this interface (Kenyatta 1938; Ruel 1962) testifies to 'the sharing and transmission of symbolic elements across major linguistic and cultural boundaries, and the transformations and reversals that occur between neighbouring peoples of similar language and culture' (Southall 1972: 103). It is evinced by the plethora of Maasai words still used in Rombo, which manifests what David Parkin (1990: 195) calls a 'cross-fertilization of ideas transacted across constantly shifting cultural boundaries'. People's past and present multilingual capacities constitute an extensive semantic and conceptual horizon that does not coincide with linguistic, ethnic, social or cultural boundaries. Instead, it affords an openness that facilitates traffic in concepts, practices and persons, which the historical sources reveal.

An important factor for such traffic was the fact that Kilimanjaro had no iron, clay or salt, and therefore long relied on trade with surrounding areas for ingots, pots and the cooking soda (*mbala*) that is still in use in Rombo (Dundas 1924: 269ff; Johnston 1886: 440; Krapf 1860: 244; Marealle 1963: 67; S. F. Moore 1986: 26; New 1873: 348). Accordingly, the movement of persons and linguistic practices was accompanied by transfers of goods and objects over long distances. Thus, the caravans that brought persons like Munie Wesiri to Kilimanjaro also ferried goods like the cotton-cloth worn by the hundred-strong crowd of men and women who gathered shortly before von der Decken arrived in Machame (Kersten 1869: 290). Early reports of repeated requests for guns and gunpowder disclose that the people of Kilimanjaro already knew and desired goods of many kinds, in return for which they offered travellers ivory, slaves, food-stuffs and firewood. Indeed, the first travellers probably expanded people's knowledge of and aspirations for stuff, as they brought and gifted cutlery, scissors, needles and thread, tailored outfits, handkerchiefs and mirrors, as well as the usual beads and cloths (Kersten 1869: 292; Krapf 1860: 238). Some decades later, the one-time doctor of the German colonial station at Old Moshi reported how coastal and European clothes, such as the Arab-style *kanzu* and discarded *askari* and other uniforms, were increasingly common and popular (Widenmann 1899: 59).[9] Spears were no longer forged from pig-iron sourced from surrounding areas, but made from European iron-wire that was imported in rolls and used as a means of exchange, while Mauser rifle casings replaced animal horns as snuff containers (Widenmann 1899: 56–57, 67–68).

These sources describe a situation where persons, practices, objects and languages circulate in a wider region, where they attract attention and use for different purposes. The combined and concomitant transfers of words and things speak to Wittgenstein's notion of language-game, and reveal Kilimanjaro as an always already 'globalized' place (Piot 1999). Coastal porters, Arab traders and Europeans thus rubbed shoulders at *mangi* Mandara's homestead at Old Moshi, while a great number of people from other 'tribes' lived at the military and mission stations (Widenmann 1899: 48). The Chagga-speaking inhabitants came to these places to acquire matches that were known as 'Sweden', perhaps from the Greek trader who lived there by 1895, and bartered in the pewter rings he imported or the cloth and beads in which porters were paid (Widenmann 1899: 69–70). The German missionary Bruno Gutmann (1909a: 167) described how children were named *Ngiriki* or 'the Greek', following the visit of such a trader, which highlights how the people of Kilimanjaro actively solicited and entangled relations that extended far beyond the mountain.[10] It is underscored by John Iliffe's (1979: 100) account of Mandara despatching an emissary in 1889 to present the German Kaiser with an ivory tusk in the hope of receiving a canon in return. Instead, he was presented with a cloak and helmet from a production of *Lohengrin* at the Berlin Opera House by the commander Hermann von Wissmann.[11] Such movements extended in other directions too, as trade links between Zanzibar and India ensured that the rupee remained in circulation until the early 1900s, despite the introduction of an own currency by the German East Africa Company (Hasu 1999: 135). In Kilimanjaro, the rupee was perhaps bolstered by the Indian traders who had settled in Old Moshi and Marangu by 1898, where they offered goods of various kinds, including dining utensils and canned food from Europe, even comprising bottled beer from Germany (Hasu 1999: 203).

Rombo: A Relative Periphery

In terms of words and objects, these sources reveal how Kilimanjaro contained parts of Europe and the wider world long before the twentieth century. They concur with Sally Falk Moore's (1986) contention that the people of Kilimanjaro were entangled with wider, even global processes of transformation that predate yet imbricate with colonial rule. Nevertheless, the evidence shows that Rombo was on the fringes of these developments, at least in relation to parts of central and western Kilimanjaro. Thus, the early travellers like Rebmann and von der Decken skirted Rombo and even returned for later visits without setting foot there. It was not until 1871 that the first known European came to Rombo, when Charles New (1873: 448) arrived at Lake Chala at the southern edge of today's district. In 1883, Joseph Thomson (1885: 130ff) travelled through Rombo to Usseri in the north, and the next year Harry Johnston (1886: 287) followed, apparently after travelling through the forest above the inhabited areas. The accounts of their trips are scant, and together with Johnston's claim that the people of Rombo speak a completely different language from the rest of Kilimanjaro, they suggest that they stayed for a short time and engaged with people to a limited extent.

One reason the early travellers favoured central and western Kilimanjaro over Rombo was probably the fact that the latter had no provision points for the caravans and therefore was peripheral to the other areas. Accordingly, Widenmann (1899: 64) described Rombo as remote and lacking in traffic. However, the main reason was probably

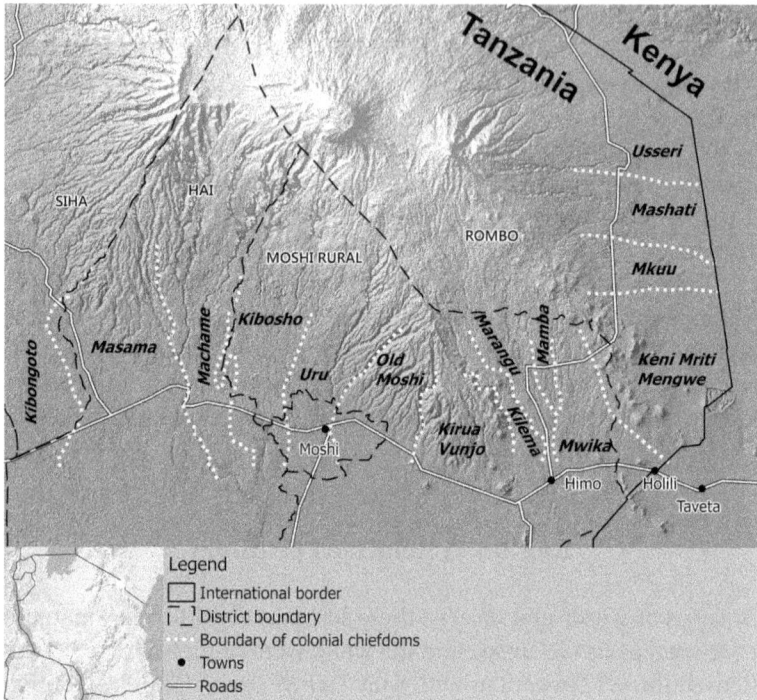

Map 0.1. Map of the districts and former chiefdoms of Kilimanjaro.

mangi Mandara or Rindi, who actively courted the early Europeans and schemed to ensure they stayed in Old Moshi for as long as possible. Indeed, this dynamic continued after the establishment of German East Africa and affected the German efforts to control the area. Thus, when Hermann von Wissmann's army arrived in Kilimanjaro in 1891, they became embroiled in the longstanding conflict between Mandara and *mangi* Sina of Kibosho (Iliffe 1979: 100). Both chiefs had obtained large amounts of firearms through Swahili traders, who procured them from earlier expeditions to Kilimanjaro upon their return to the coast and peddled them upcountry in exchange for ivory (cf. Widenmann 1899: 59). In addition, both chiefs employed soldiers or mercenaries from outside Kilimanjaro. Partly on Mandara's instigation, von Wissmann's army overran Kibosho, but when Mandara died later that year, *mangi* Marealle induced *Reichskommissar* Carl Peters to move his headquarters to Marangu. Subsequent schemes on Marealle's part further weakened Old Moshi's position, as Mandara's son was forced by the Germans in 1893 to give up his control of the surrounding areas and his people compelled to build a military station at the site of his fortress. It ensured that Marealle 'became effective paramount of eastern Kilimanjaro controlling 27 of the 44 Chagga chiefdoms' (Iliffe 1979: 101) and gained a powerful position as an important sub-chief maker (S.F. Moore 1986: 96). This proved the beginning of a powerful dynasty, as Marealle's London School of Economics and Cambridge-educated grandson, Thomas Marealle II, won an election for Paramount Chief or *Mangi Mkuu* of the Chagga people in 1951. Thomas Marealle, who only died in 2007, played a significant if restraining role in the decolonization of Tanganyika, as he accompanied Julius Nyerere to address the United Nations, where the latter demanded a date for Tanganyika's independence (Hunter 2009; Stahl 1969). There is little mention of Rombo in these historical accounts, but sources suggest it was under Marealle's authority. Thus, Iliffe (1979: 120) claims that Marealle's exploitation of Rombo became a source of conflict with European settlers, who wanted to use the area as a labour pool.

Christian missionaries also played a role in establishing the hegemony of central and western Kilimanjaro over Rombo. According to J.C. Winter (1979: 43), Mandara invited the first Church Missionary Society (CMS) missionaries to Kilimanjaro in 1885, as part of a plan to gain control over neighbouring chiefdoms. Once the CMS missionaries were settled in Old Moshi, however, Mandara prevented them both from doing meaningful work and from relocating to another area. After Marealle's ascendancy, the German authorities ordered the British missionaries to hand over their station to the Evangelical-Lutheran Mission of Leipzig. The first German missionaries arrived in 1893, but settled in Machame instead of Old Moshi and opened a second station on the border between Mamba and Marangu the following year. In 1891, the Catholic Holy Ghost Fathers established themselves at Kilema between Mamba and Old Moshi, and opened another station at Kibosho between Old Moshi and Machame two years later. The result was that central and western Kilimanjaro were divided between Lutheran and Catholic mission societies, which neighboured each other in alternating sections that ran up and down the mountainside. Sally Falk Moore (1986: 102) claims this arrangement was the colonial government's attempt to minimize competition between the different mission societies and Christian denominations. However, Iliffe (1979: 224) and Winter (1979: 45) maintain that competition remained strong between the Catholics and the Protestants, and that the *mangi*s exploited this to their advantage.

It was not until 1898 that the Holy Ghost Fathers established the first mission station in Rombo, at a location they called Fischerstadt.

The place was later renamed Mkuu and the district headquarters or *boma* became located in its vicinity. Unlike the other areas of the mountain, Rombo was not divided between different denominations, but came under sole Catholic influence. The earliest baptismal registries reveal that the initial progress was slow, but on the eve of its centenary in Kilimanjaro the Catholic Church reported phenomenal success: 18,857 out of a total population of 19,140 in Keni Parish were baptized Catholics (Anon. 1990). Of the remaining population, 280 were Protestants, while 45 were deemed 'traditional believers'.

Although the population remains overwhelmingly and loyally Catholic, several evangelical churches are active in the area. There is also a charismatic Catholic lay-movement that meets at several churches and appears to be tolerated by the clergy, as a bulwark against the evangelical congregations. However, in everyday parlance, the charismatic movement is often conflated with the evangelical churches, partly because they share a hard-line stance against activities like those that took place in the plains in 2008. The different attitudes adopted by different denominations in this regard at times play a part in conflicts between people.

In contrast to Moshi town and Machame in western Kilimanjaro, Islamic influence is virtually non-existent in Rombo. A mosque is located by the main road in the village neighbouring the one where I lived, but I have never seen anyone in or near it. Of the handful of people I knew who identified as Muslim, only one was a local convert while the rest were casual labourers or healers who originated from central or coastal Tanzania and wound up in Rombo, usually for a shorter period of time. There are probably more Muslims in the booming settlement and nascent urbanization that have sprung up around the district headquarters at Mkuu in the past decade.

The delayed missionization of Rombo was of a piece with its relatively late incorporation into the cash economy. The first coffee seedlings were allegedly brought to Kilema by the Catholic Church, which intended the crop to be a source of mission revenue (Marealle 1952: 63; S.F. Moore 1986: 103). According to Iliffe (1979: 154), local catechists began receiving seedlings from their missions in the 1890s, but the first native coffee entrepreneur was an adviser to Marealle, who established a sizeable plot in 1900, while Marealle and other *mangis* quickly followed suit. Winter (1979: 55) argues that Dr Emil Förster, a German colonialist with progressive ideals who settled in Marangu, was central to promoting coffee as a cash-crop among the local population, in contravention of colonial policy and sentiment. Meanwhile, S.F. Moore (1986: 119) emphasizes the role of one-time District Commissioner Major (later Sir) Charles Dundas, who encouraged the establishment of the first coffee cooperative. In any case, coffee arrived later in Rombo, as it was held that the dry climate made the area unsuitable for the crop. In 1922, the Agricultural Department reported the number of coffee trees in each of the administrative chiefdoms, which reveals that more than half of the coffee trees – 19,359 – were located in Marangu alone. By contrast, there were 263 trees at Mwika and 350 at Old Moshi, but only 45 trees in the whole of Rombo, all of which were located at Mashati (TNA AB/425).[12] These were only the coffee-bearing trees; the number of non-bearing trees was 10,185 for Marangu, 1,921 for Mwika, 1,185 for Old Moshi, and none in Rombo. The high figure for Marangu supports both Iliffe's claim that Marealle was central to coffee farming and Winter's contention that Förster was a catalyst. It shows how coffee was well established in certain parts with Marangu standing out, while hardly any was grown in Rombo. The great push appears to have occurred in 1923, when 300,000 seedlings were planted in Kilimanjaro to bring the total number of trees under 'native cultivation' close to half a million (TNA AB/77). It nevertheless seems that coffee became widespread in Rombo even later, as the area was reported to be a labour reserve for settlers in the 1920s.

A History of Anthropologists

The dominance of central and western Kilimanjaro was reiterated by the many anthropologists working in the area. One of the earliest and without doubt the most prolific ethnographer was Bruno Gutmann, a Leipzig missionary who served in Mamba, Machame and Old Moshi from 1902 until 1938. Like several of his colleagues, Gutmann published ethnographic accounts in both missionary and academic books and journals, in addition to pastoral and educational works. Gutmann is by far the best known of these missionary-ethnographers, partly due to the vast quantities of material he published.[13] In his intellectual biography, Winter (1979: 32ff) details how Gutmann was influenced by the scientific, philosophical and theological ideas of his day. He was especially taken by the psychology of Wilhelm Wundt, whose lectures Gutmann attended at Leipzig University before departing for Africa. In addition, he was influenced by Gustav Warneck's notion of *Volksmission*, on which the Leipzig mission policy was based. In Warneck's view, missionization should proceed through vernacular languages and local practices, in order to become a popular – *volkstümlich*

– church. Iliffe (1979: 218) argues that the ideas of the *Volksmission* 'attracted missionaries who, regardless of social origins, hoped to find in Africa the organic social unity which a rapidly secularizing Europe had lost'.

In line with this, Gutmann aimed to describe an organic sociality – *Gemeinschaft* – that in his view was constituted through the 'primordial ties' (*urtümliche Bindungen*) of descent, neighbourliness and age-grade fellowship. To document these relations in an unadulterated form, Gutmann concentrated his research on older members of the community, who recounted and reconstructed bygone practices from memory. Gutmann's last assistant, Ernst Jaeschke (1985: 45), claims that the three-volume work, *Die Stammeslehren* (1932), was dictated word for word by elders who came to Gutmann's house every morning for several years. Gutmann's house at Old Moshi, which has been converted to a church-run dispensary, still features the purpose-built niche where Gutmann would seat his informant, while he sat in the attic above recording the accounts, which floated up through an open ceiling. According to the priest who showed me the place, the arrangement enabled Gutmann to obtain information without his interlocutors' engagement being visible to the surrounding community. Gutmann's publications indeed often contain what appear to be verbatim dictations that are followed by his own distinct interpretations. While discounting Gutmann's pretension to present a precolonial past with little regard for the historical changes that were taking place around and because of him, one may still recognize that vernacular voices are discernible in his ethnographic descriptions, which make them unique historical sources (Hunter 2009: 154). Used with care and circumspection, they can be combined with fieldwork material and other sources for insights into historical transformations and the temporal depth of present processes.

Ethnographic material was also produced by Gutmann's colleague Johannes Raum, who worked in Machame, Moshi and Mamba from 1897 until his death in 1936. According to Winter (1979: 49), Raum and Gutmann were contemporaries who got on reasonably well, even if they competed for positions, influence and recognition both academically and professionally. Raum was influenced by the same ideas as Gutmann, but he seems a less creative thinker and his writings appear less overtly ideological. Raum's concerns were perhaps more practical, as he produced and published an early grammar and dictionary of the Chagga language, probably intended for future missionaries (Raum 1909). Johannes Raum's son, Otto Friedrich, obtained a scholarship from the Phelps Stokes Fund and a grant from the International African Institute (IAI) to train as an anthropologist under Bronislaw Malinowski. As an associate of the IAI at the LSE in the mid 1930s, Raum would have been a contemporary of Jack and Eileen Krige, Günter Wagner and Jomo Kenyatta, among others. He became especially close to another African academic with political interests, namely the ANC activist and later diplomat Z.K. Matthews. After obtaining his doctorate in 1938, Raum relocated to South Africa, where he first taught in a Lutheran teachers' training college in Natal. In 1949, he secured a post through Matthews at Fort Hare University, where he rose to become professor, first of education, and later of social anthropology (S.F. Moore 1996: xiii; Paul 2003: 198). Despite the fact that Raum was born and raised in Kilimanjaro – and returned from initial studies in Germany and England to serve from 1928 until 1932 at the teachers' training college his father founded on land provided by Marealle at Marangu – he based his doctoral dissertation and eventual monograph nearly entirely on Gutmann's writings (Raum [1940] 1996). His book was nevertheless influential and instrumental in making Gutmann's work more widely known, especially in the English-speaking world.

While Gutmann professed to portray a pristine past, he of course did not remain aloof of the events of colonization. Not only was he – as a missionary – an agent of colonialism, he also knew well the actors central to the introduction of coffee to Kilimanjaro. During his exploratory trip to Kilimanjaro in 1906–7, Emil Förster befriended Gutmann and implored him to visit his eldest daughter, Elisabeth, during his impending home leave with the prospect of marriage (Winter 1979: 54). Gutmann indulged Förster's wishes, and he and Elisabeth married in 1909. When Förster returned to Germany in 1908 to prepare for his settlement in Kilimanjaro, he brought with him Josefu or Joseph Merinyo, whom S.F. Moore (1986: 118ff) describes as a convert and student of Gutmann's, and Winter (1979: 55ff) refers to as Förster's servant. In Germany, Merinyo gained fluency in German, studied book-keeping, and was introduced to the principles of western agriculture and the peasants' cooperative movement. On his return, Merinyo started growing coffee on Förster's instigation, and later married Gutmann's housemaid.[14] Merinyo moreover became interpreter, clerk and informant for Charles Dundas, who compiled his own ethnographic account (Dundas 1924). In 1925, Dundas's successor Lt. Com. A.M. Clark enabled the first coffee cooperative, Kilimanjaro Native Planters' Association (KNPA), and made Merinyo its first president, while Nathaniel Mtui, another student of Gutmann's and informant for Dundas, became vice-president.[15] According to Klaus Fiedler

(1996: 129ff), Merinyo fell afoul of the Lutheran Church in 1930, due to a quarrel with Georg Fritze, a colleague and competitor of Gutmann's based in Mamba. The dispute concerned Fritze's imperious reaction to Merinyo's wife wearing European clothes when receiving communion, and occasioned a formal complaint by Merinyo to the Leipzig mission board. Raum dealt with the matter on behalf of the missionary council, but Merinyo was excommunicated on the basis of an anonymous accusation of adultery. Indicative of the competition between different denominations, Merinyo subsequently had his newborn child baptized by the Catholic Church, which was probably eager to poach a member of such high standing. Merinyo was reinstated in 1932, when Gutmann returned from home leave to intercede on his behalf with the missionary council (Fiedler 1996: 132). In the 1940s, Merinyo and another convert and teacher named Filipo Njau became pivotal for the Kilimanjaro Chagga Citizens Union (KCCU), which advocated for the establishment of the paramount chieftaincy to which Thomas Marealle was eventually elected. As Emma Hunter (2009) points out, this work was at least partly reliant on the existence and circulation of the works by Dundas and Gutmann, which provided an impetus for this particular political movement.

Gutmann clearly also knew Dundas, from whom he barely retrieved the manuscript for *Das Recht der Dschagga* (1926) before he was repatriated in 1920 as a consequence of the Versailles Treaty (Winter 1979: 62). In his memoirs, Dundas (1955) describes growing up as the child of an aristocrat in the British Consular Service in Hamburg and Oslo (then Christiania), where he attended both German and Norwegian schools. Dundas would therefore have been able to communicate with Gutmann in German, who in any case knew English from his missionary training in Leipzig. In his ethnography, Dundas mentions Gutmann's writings, but does not cite or quote any specific text. There is no other record of their interaction or communication, and Gutmann does not figure in Dundas's memoirs. It is nevertheless clear that Gutmann was central in the nexus of people and events that occasioned the introduction of coffee as a cash-crop, and was hence not far removed from the major catalyst for social change in Kilimanjaro – despite, or perhaps as a spur to, his interest in the idealized past.

If Gutmann's perspective and interests displaced historical concepts and hampered him from documenting social changes (Hassing 1979: 429), subsequent anthropologists have placed such matters at the forefront of their accounts, often in dialogue with Gutmann's work. It is most notable in the case of Sally Falk Moore, who engages Gutmann's (1926) magisterial treatise on 'Chagga law' for her processual anthropology.[16] A trained lawyer, Moore served at the Nuremberg Trials before she turned to anthropology, writing extensively on many aspects of life in Kilimanjaro, even if her reputation is chiefly as a legal anthropologist (Moore 2005a). Moore's work also comes out of central Kilimanjaro, where she did multiple bouts of short fieldwork in the neighbouring areas of Kilema, Marangu, Mamba and Mwika through the 1960s, 1970s, 1980s and 1990s. Similarly, subsequent works come out of central and western Kilimanjaro, and are based on fieldwork conducted in Machame, Kilema, Mamba, Marangu, Mwika and Moshi town (Hasu 1999; Pietilä 2007, Setel 1999; Stambach 2000). However, Moore (1986: xiv) ventured to visit the primary court in Keni-Mriti-Mengwe, and thus appears to have been the first anthropologist to set foot in Rombo. In another indication of how relations overlap and intersect in this area, Moore (2005b: 264) mentions staying at Kibo Hotel in Marangu during her fieldwork, which was founded by Emil Förster, and from whom it was confiscated as enemy property after the First World War (Winter 1979: 55ff).[17] At Kibo Hotel, Moore (2005b: 266) moreover hung out with Thomas Marealle's uncle, one-time colonial chief Petro Itosi Marealle, who showed her his correspondence with Malinowski that resulted from the latter's visit in 1934.[18] Her gratitude to Joseph Merinyo furthermore suggests a personal and direct link between her work and that of Gutmann, and a connection to the first converts and coffee operatives on the mountain (S.F. Moore 1986: xiv).

Moore's main conceptual contribution lies in the aforementioned time-oriented or processual anthropology, where she treats fieldwork as if it is current history. In this book, I follow Moore and combine fieldwork material with historical sources to plumb the depths and significance of particular occurrences. Like her, I also take as my starting point concrete events and cases, but my concern is not to situate these in an overarching historical process. Instead, I endeavour to explore and extract concepts, such as *ikaa*, *horu* and *moo*, from descriptions of the uses of language, and their imbrications with activities and objects. By charting the grammars of dwelling and life force, I thus aim to disclose the form life has in Rombo.

The book approaches this by way of the homestead – *kaa* – that derives its term from the notion and activity of dwelling – *ikaa*. For this purpose, chapter one considers historical changes and geographical variations pertaining to modes of production, settlement patterns and inheritance practices. It explores the significant yet overlooked roles that cattle, houses and women play in this regard, and investigates the changing structures and layouts of houses and homestead. The chapter also describes the productive activities that take place in and around the *kaa*, where an intensive form of horticulture imbricates humans, livestock and crops, and involves movements and transfers between the mountain and the plains. Finally, the chapter explores the ways in which these activities have come to encompass money both through cash-cropping and other forms of market exchange.

Chapter two departs from the fact that the homestead comes into existence upon the bride's relocation in marriage to consider the meaning and significance of the bridewealth prestations. It considers closely the invocation made in connection with the initial bridewealth prestation to show how this transaction and the relationship it involves affords the homestead as a place of dwelling, where *horu* transfers and transforms through production, reproduction and consumption. Attending to the mode of presentation, it considers how the notion of *ialika* or marrying involves a process of attachment and detachment that extends and suspends the being of the bride and groom between multiple homesteads. Finally, it explores how the bridewealth prestations gradually bring affines into contact and speech, and how language is another effect of *horu*, which in this case determines the transfers and relationships involved.

Chapter three considers sex and the reproduction that the bridewealth prestations enable. It investigates how persons through these activities convert and convey *horu* in different forms through different parts of the body for different effects. It moreover explores how these engagements constitute and bring into being different subject positions that engage and involve prominent features of the homestead. The chapter also explores how these engagements concern and entail the naming practices, and thus sheds further light on the concept of *ialika* as a state of extension. In addition, it describes a set of concepts that derive from the root-form *moo* to investigate how life also emerges as an effect of the transfers and transmutations of *horu*. On this basis, it expands on the relationship between language and life force to reveal how prohibitions concerning sex and reproduction channel *horu* in certain ways for particular effects. In this way, it is determined that dwelling concerns how production, reproduction and consumption nest as transformations of each other, and how *horu* is a life force that moves through them in different forms to afford beings of different kinds.

Chapter four uses a case of divination as a starting point for exploring the relationship between the dead and the living. The chapter describes historical changes and regional variation in burial practices, and investigates how these constitute processes of attachment and detachment to significant features and objects of the homestead that serve to gather the extensions gained through dwelling and life, and thus contract the person to emplace him or her in a specific place in the homestead. The chapter thus considers how burial too is an effect of the transfers and transformations of *horu*, and how the failure to bury a person may result in the dead being placed in a state of calling that affects the health and well-being of the living, and therefore requires particular interventions. Finally, the chapter considers how the ability to divine emanates from the relationship between the dead and the living, and the further light this sheds on the relationship between language and life force.

Chapter five, in turn, expands on this relationship by exploring cursing as a linguistic and material practice. It considers in detail one case to reveal how cursing involves and constitutes family resemblance notions that presuppose and operate through relationships of particular kinds. It moreover shows how cursing lends speech and language an ambiguous character, and how the curse has a capacity to replicate and move between houses and homestead like persons and prestations. These points are deepened by the consideration of cursing as a material practice, which engages for destructive purposes objects, substances and features that ordinarily channel *horu* in productive ways. In addition, the chapter describes a case of removing or washing a curse, and demonstrates how this involves that it is carefully removed from the homestead and its inhabitants, and then gathered and disposed of to ensure that its effects do not spread through the activities and relationships of dwelling and life. A comparison with the *ihora kaa* ceremony that cools or cleanses the homestead after burial deepens how these activities serve to reconstitute the transfers and transformations of *horu* and thus reorient the dwelling and life that they disrupted. Finally, it is shown how the ethnography entails that speech and language are *horu* in a further form, and thus not only results from and determines its transfers and transformations, but affects and effectuates them to actualize relations that may be either constructive or destructive.

Chapter six finally returns to consider the event that took place in the plains in 2008. It describes in detail the acts and statements that were made over the course of those two days, and explores how these relate to the notions, practices and material forms presented earlier in the book. Tracing the event from preparation to conclusion, the chapter describes how it concerned and involved the deployment of *horu* in certain forms to ensure its transfer elsewhere in other forms as presentations for the deceased that serve to emplace them and return a debt that the living owe for their dwelling and life. As they provide and channel powerful substances of different kinds, the living return life to the dead with the hope and aim of receiving rain that will afford fodder and foodstuffs, and thus secure and extend *ikaa* and *moo* into the future. The chapter considers how these transfers and transformations of life force engage the mountain and the plains, and hence a topography and orientation that feature throughout this book. It moreover shows how rain forms part of these movements and transmutations, and how water thus constitutes life force in yet another form. As the proceedings in the plains are succeeded by similar ones across the mountainside, the event unleashes a wave of life force that washes over the area to elicit and attract rain in its wake to afford dwelling and life. The chapter also considers how Christian notions and practices inflect the event and have affected the understanding of a precolonial concept of *ruwa*, which means the sun and has been interpreted as 'god', yet is better understood as an opening through which life force flows. Finally, it considers a set of notions that derive from *ihora* and that pertain to cooling, cleansing, curing and ceremoniality, to argue that *horu* concerns movements and interactions that afford beings in a calm and quiet manner that constitutes a state of plenty.

In this way, the book explores and extracts a welter of concepts, which include *ikaa* and *moo* that Peter used, as well as those that serve as the chapter headings. As it combines historical sources and contemporary fieldwork material, the book returns life to older descriptions and to anthropological issues, such as settlement patterns, modes of inheritance, bridewealth prestations, burial practices and, finally, activities to attract the rain.

Notes

1. Sally Falk Moore (1986: xiii) states clearly that she worked through Swahili and English. The same fact emerges obliquely from the way subsequent scholars mainly render Swahili rather than Chagga terms in their texts.
2. Curiously, neither H.L. Moore nor Sanders consider Ruel's work in their overviews and disquisitions on gender and fertility in eastern and southern Africa. Similarly, Geissler and Prince only consider Ruel's work on Kuria Christianity, yet leave untouched his ethnographic concerns with Kuria ideas similar to those that preoccupy them. These oversights are all the more curious in light of the fact that all these authors have con-

nections to Cambridge, where Ruel taught anthropology for most of his career.

3. Ruel does not account for the difference between *omohoro* and *obohoro*, which I assume involve the common Bantu-language practice of adding different prefixes to a common root-form, in accordance with different noun-classes.

4. I follow the convention in the commentary literature on Wittgenstein and cite his works by using an abbreviation of the title in question, followed by a page reference or paragraph number.

5. Wittgenstein borrows the dictum from Goethe's Faust, in opposition to the biblical 'in the beginning was the word'.

6. All these entities consist of an elected chairperson (*mwenyekiti*), a vice-chair (*mwenyekiti kaimu*), a secretary (*mkatibu*) and a treasurer (*mhazibu*), roles which moreover are commonly filled and performed by the same persons.

7. According to von der Decken, Munie Wesiri was known by the further sobriquet Nasiri.

8. All quotations from German sources are translated by the author.

9. At the time of writing, Widenmann was staff surgeon at the Kaiser Wilhelms-Akademie for military medicine.

10. Gutmann did not specify which part of Kilimanjaro his account concerned, but it was most likely Machame in western Kilimanjaro, from where most of his earliest writings drew their material (Winter 1979: 47).

11. Von Wissmann later became commissioner and governor of German East Africa.

12. Archival sources from the Tanzania National Archives are referenced by TNA followed by the accession number for the relevant files.

13. The *Festschrift* for Gutmann's ninetieth birthday includes a bibliography of more than five hundred items (Gutmann 1966).

14. Winter (1979: 56) claims that Merinyo married Gutmann's housemaid, while S.F. Moore (1986: 118) claims that he married a sister of *mangi* Salema of Old Moshi. It is of course possible that these are identical, although I doubt that a woman from a chiefly descent group would work as domestic help for a European missionary. The possibility that Merinyo had two wives is also unlikely, in light of the Protestant missionaries' opposition to polygamy. I have no solution to this discrepancy, but choose to rely on Winter's account.

15. According to S.F. Moore (1986: 119), KNPA counted 7,000 members by 1926. It was replaced by the Kilimanjaro Native Cooperative Union (KNCU) in 1932. KNCU was subsequently abolished as a result of the 1967 Arusha Declaration, but it re-formed in 1984 after economic liberalization. Once wielding a monopoly over the purchase, marketing, and sale of coffee, KNCU today competes with the multinational companies operating in the area.

16. Moore's citations make it appear that she only uses the rather poor trans-
    lation of this book that forms part of the Human Relations Area Files.
17. Moore (2005b: 265) incorrectly states that Förster married Gutmann's
    daughter, rather than the other way around.
18. One of Malinowski's letters to his wife reveals that he also visited Gut-
    mann in Kilimanjaro and even suggests he made a trip to Rombo (Wayne
    1995: 198).

Chapter One

KAA

HISTORICAL TRANSFORMATIONS
IN PRODUCTION AND HABITATION

A longstanding concern for the historically-oriented studies of Kilimanjaro is the consequences of colonization and cash-cropping for
demographic developments and land availability in the area. Sally
Falk Moore (1981: 232), for instance, argues that while 'there was no
general shortage of land in pre-colonial times', a population explosion
in the twentieth century – occasioned by decreased infant mortality
due to public health measures and mission-induced abandonment
of polygyny and birth-spacing practices – meant that 'virtually every
cultivable inch of Kilimanjaro is now occupied, and wherever possible
is under coffee and bananas' (Moore 1981: 236). Philip Setel (1999),
meanwhile, disputes Moore's claim regarding dramatic shifts due to
colonization, and instead argues that demographic pressure and land
shortage were felt already in precolonial times. Partly drawing on descriptions by the early travellers, Setel (1999: 44) pushes back the
timeline for these dynamics to claim that, 'by the turn of the [twenti-
eth] century, much of the land of the *kihamba* [banana garden] zone
appears to have been occupied'.

While there is no doubt that land is currently scarce in all of Kilimanjaro, these claims emphasize and generalize developments and
dynamics that obscure the historical and regional variation around
the mountain. More specifically, they cloud how demographic pressures affected different areas at different times, and they neglect how
this in turn had consequences for modes of production and habitation. Considering such variations provides a more nuanced picture,
and reveals details and dynamics overlooked by these authors that

serve as an entry point for the homestead (*kaa*) and the activity of dwelling (*ikaa*) from which it derives its name.

Considering Cattle

In a report from his visit to different areas of the mountain in 1931, Sanitary Superintendent B.T. Bailey claimed that western Kiliman-jaro was the most densely populated area of all (TNA 312). It housed one-fifth of the entire population and almost all of its land was under banana cultivation. This was in contrast to eastern Kilimanjaro, where he claimed that grass was plentiful. While Bailey provided no numbers, the District Commissioner accounted in detail for the dif-ferences in population density in a report from 1943 (TNA 63/11). He reported that Mamba had an approximate density of 700 people to the square mile and that this created severe land shortage. By con-trast, there were only 300 people to the square mile in neighbouring Mwika, while Kilema and Kirua-Vunjo had 400 and 250 people to the square mile, respectively. Usseri, on the other hand, he reported, 'is the only [area] in the district where large numbers of cattle are grazed on free range'. Its name indeed entails this fact, as Usseri in the Rombo dialect means 'fresh milk'. In combination, these two reports from 1931 and 1943 reveal significant variations in population density between different areas on the mountain. Furthermore, they suggest that the areas where researchers have tended to congregate were the most densely populated and the ones experiencing the most intense pressure on land. It would therefore seem that Moore's and Setel's arguments regarding the historical developments in Kilimanjaro are skewed both by, and in favour of, the characteristics of these areas.

While neither of these two sources makes specific claims or pro-vides statistics regarding the population density in Rombo, they fur-nish evidence that grazing land was more readily available there than elsewhere. They thus modify Moore's claim that all land in Kiliman-jaro was under cultivation and suggest that the mode of land use was different in Rombo than elsewhere. Other sources support this con-tention, and indicate that the extent and significance of cattle-keeping varied around the mountain. In line with Moore, Rudolf Lehmann (1941: 387) claimed regarding Marangu that, 'as the entire land is now divided up into *shambas* [farm plots], and the grazing places for the cattle are very scarce, the cattle are, for this and other reasons, dependent on stall-feeding'. He further mentioned the presence of tse-tse flies as a reason why cattle were stall-fed in Kilimanjaro. However,

Dundas (1924: 266–67) argued that eastern Kilimanjaro was free of tsetse flies and that 'normally sized stock is really only seen in Rombo country and Kibongoto, where the cattle are herded to a great extent'. Government reports support the claim that grazing varied around the mountain and recount how it was more common in eastern and western Kilimanjaro compared with the central areas (TNA 63/20).[1] For example, Kenyan Maasai were in 1929 granted permission to graze cattle in the forests of northern Kilimanjaro and on the plains between Usseri and Keni. The decision indicates that pastures were more plentiful in Rombo, even if repeated fighting broke out over grazing land between Chagga and Maasai in its wake.

Moore and Setel emphasize the role of population growth in causing land shortage, but the alienation of land for settler farms and mission compounds was probably more detrimental to grazing land. A report from 1931 on the political tendencies of the Chagga claimed that Kibosho and Marangu were worst hit in this regard, and held that the women of Marangu walked six miles to cut grass in the plains, because grazing land on the mountain had been alienated (TNA 19475). The same year, the Provincial Commissioner reported that canna was introduced as a stock-feed, in order to 'save the present waste of labour in grass cutting in the plains and carrying it up the mountain. Thousands of women are occupied in this wasteful manner' (TNA 11681).[2] In 1947, the District Commissioner estimated that a quarter of the total district land had been alienated, and efforts to repurchase land were announced after it became an issue of local agitation (TNA 28269). Yet two years later, even more land was alienated in western Kilimanjaro (TNA 63/A/20). To my knowledge, there were no settler farms in Rombo, which might explain the greater availability of grazing land – even though controversy arose over a large tract of land that was alienated for a mission compound at Mashati.[3]

Grazing was also more widespread in Rombo because the number of cattle there was greater. Indeed, there is evidence to suggest that cattle-holding in certain areas increased during the colonial era with a concomitant rise in the demand for grazing land. In 1923, the District Commissioner claimed that there were 150–160,000 heads of cattle in Moshi District (TNA AB/77). In 1925, he said that stall-feeding was becoming rarer and was increasingly confined to tsetse-infested areas, while ever more cattle were herded and kraaled on the plains in Rombo (TNA AB/86). During the 1920s, repeated epidemics of rinderpest, pleuro-pneumonia and east coast fever were reported from Rombo, 'as despite warnings Wachagga are continually bringing cattle over the mountain from the infected areas of Kenya Masai [sic] land' (TNA AB/23). Some cattle were probably imported for slaughter and sale, but it nevertheless seems that cattle-holdings increased in Rombo in this period.

The local variations in cattle-holding within Kilimanjaro became evident during the rinderpest vaccinations that were carried out in 1944. Illicit movement of Maasai stock introduced the disease to western Kilimanjaro, where all the cattle – 3,889 heads – were vaccinated. Meanwhile, import of cattle from Kenya caused another outbreak at Keni and Mkuu, where 24,331 cattle were vaccinated (TNA 63/12). There is no mention of vaccinations occurring as far north as Usseri, where another 3,000 cattle died from east coast fever in 1945 (TNA 63/13), and 17,000 cattle were dipped to prevent the same disease the following year (TNA 63/14). By 1938, the total number of cattle in Kilimanjaro had been reduced to 131,500 heads, of which 87,000 were said to be permanently stalled, while 44,000 were partly stalled and partly herded (TNA 26045). In addition, there were 119,000 goats and 66,000 sheep. Based on the vaccination numbers above, it seems likely that the majority of these animals were kept in Rombo. A slight decrease in cattle but a huge increase in goats was reported for Moshi District as a whole in 1954. In spite of this, it seems likely that cattle-holdings continued to increase in Rombo, where warnings of over-grazing were raised in the 1950s (TNA 63/21; 38/10/2).

A possible reason for the increase in the number of cattle in this period may have been the prevalent practice of livestock-lending – *ihara* – between different parts of the mountain. Both Gutmann (1926: 452) and Sally Falk Moore (1977: 23–24; 1978: 39; 1986: 70,100) describe how animals from Old Moshi and Vunjo were lent to people in other chiefdoms, and were even agisted as far as Rombo precisely because the pastures were better. Similarly, Dundas (1924: 68) asserted that Mamba people placed cattle with their 'Chimbii vassals', which most likely refers to present-day Shimbi, which neighbours Keni where I lived. Sally Falk Moore (1986: 101) maintains that livestock-lending 'diminished or virtually ended' in the early colonial period, but it remains an ongoing and important practice in present-day Rombo. Indeed, there is evidence that disproves Moore's claim even for central Kilimanjaro. For instance, in response to recurring livestock epidemics, restrictions were imposed on cattle movement in 1925, when the District Commissioner wrote:

> An attempt was made by the Veterinary Department to introduce a permit system for the movement of stock on Kilimanjaro between Chiefships. This is considered objectionable and unnecessary as it is a clean area. An owner say, in Marangu may have stock in Kibosho and two or

three other Chiefships and cattle enters so much into the life and customs of the tribe that any unnecessary restrictions of the kind outlined are to be deprecated. (TNA AB/86)

Cattle-lending is perhaps easily overlooked due to the secrecy surrounding *ihara* relationships and the fact that livestock most commonly are placed with unrelated persons, who often live at some distance from the owner.[4] Widespread cattle-lending was in any case practised at this point, and there is no reason to assume that it diminished, as reports on livestock movements only increased. In fact, intensified land pressure in central Kilimanjaro may have enhanced the importance of lending relationships with people in other areas, where pastures were available. Cattle numbers would then have appeared to diminish in central Kilimanjaro, while they rose in Rombo as animals circulated between different areas of the mountain.

In line with these historical sources, middle-aged and elderly persons describe a complex system of cattle-keeping that was intact until thirty or forty years ago. On their account, most people kept several heads of cattle at their homestead, which they pooled with their neighbours on a daily basis. The owners took turns in providing young boys to herd the animals on meadows between the homesteads on the mountain, and on vacant land above and below the populated areas. The cattle were gathered in a designated spot every morning and returned to their homesteads in the late afternoon, where they were milked, fed and kept indoors overnight. In addition to these animals, some people owned larger herds of cattle that were kept in the plains below the mountain, where they were herded by young men who lived in Maasai-style kraals or *bomas*. When a cow calved in the plains, she was sent with her calf to the owner's homestead on the mountain, where he and his family benefitted from her milk. At first, the cow and the calf were stall-fed on the mountain, but they eventually became included in the daily herding pool for as long as the cow produced milk. The animals were returned to the plains when the milk ceased, where they remained until another calf was born. This particular form of cattle-keeping meant that cows circulated between the mountain and the plains, in accordance with their reproduction. At the same time, *ihara* relationships meant that livestock circulated around the mountain, between homesteads of the different 'chiefdoms'. In addition, the practice meant that men circulated between the homesteads on the mountain and the kraals in the plains, depending on their age and reproductive relations. Starting as herd-boys on the mountain, they progressed to the plains as young men, where they remained until they married and returned to the mountain, where they raised children and tended cattle at their homesteads, until they eventually could establish their own *boma*s in the plains.

Elders who were in their sixties, seventies and eighties during my initial fieldwork had fond memories of their time in the plains, recounting perhaps tall tales of protecting the herds from marauding Maasai and wild animals. According to them, the system ended in the 1970s, when grazing land became scarce both in the plains and on the mountain, and hardly anyone had sufficient cattle to maintain a *boma* in the plains. Only one elder I knew kept cattle in the plains on the Kenyan side of the border, which he frequently went to inspect in his old Land Rover.[5] When he passed away, his two sons sold the remaining cattle and the car fell into disrepair. The old cattle track (*shia ya umbe*) that was used to ferry animals to and from the plains is now partly a footpath and partly a gravel road that descends towards a lower road that partly circles the mountain, and then extends into Kenya. Nevertheless, the memory of cattle circulating between the mountain and the plains is vivid enough that the term *shia ya umbe* remains in everyday use.

The claim that livestock-keeping and cattle-grazing were of greater importance in Rombo than elsewhere gains support from statements regarding the layout of homesteads and the activities conducted within them in the relatively recent past. Indeed, the statements indicate a mode of production that differs from the one described above by Moore and Setel, who emphasize banana farming and coffee cultivation. Considering a concrete case can bring out how this further modifies the picture provided by anthropologists of the historical developments in Kilimanjaro.

When Augustine passed away in 2006, his son Boniface reminisced about his childhood and youth in his father's homestead in the 1940s and 1950s. Standing in front of the plastered wattle-and-daub house that his father abandoned for Holili in the 1960s, Boniface pointed to the spot where his father's old grass-house once stood, adjacent to the present structure that now was surrounded by the extensive maize field he and his wife cultivated. Below, we could see the banana trees and coffee bushes that surround Boniface's own homestead, which he built on land provided by Augustine. Gesturing at the cleared and cultivated land around us, Boniface described how the area had been very different in his childhood. Only a restricted area was then devoted to banana cultivation, while the rest consisted of meadows and forest land, where cattle were grazed and fodder cut for small-stock, and firewood was gathered from the trees that he remembered sheltering baboons and colobus monkeys. He said the homesteads were then not

Figure 1.1. View of the upper areas of settlement on the mountain in Keni-Mengeni.

contiguous in the manner they are now, and the distance between their houses was accordingly even greater. Admitting that Augustine cared more about livestock than most – a factor that contributed to his eventual move to Holili where he grazed a large herd of cattle – Boniface nevertheless argued that livestock-keeping used to be of greater significance to the people of Keni than it is today. His claim is supported by other elders, who also describe how less land used to be under cultivation, while more was used for grazing.

There is hence evidence to suggest that there has been a historical development in Rombo from a situation where a complex form of livestock-keeping played a significant role to one where banana farming, livestock stall-feeding and coffee cultivation predominate. It seems likely that similar developments took place in other parts of Kilimanjaro, albeit at different points in time. Regardless, both historical sources and fieldwork material from Rombo qualify the developments and dynamics described from central and western Kilimanjaro, which have skewed scholarship in favour of specific dynamics and timelines.

Considering Houses

In tandem with these developments, there were historical changes pertaining to settlement patterns and inheritance practices. Early ethnographic sources show that Kilimanjaro was marked by what Max Gluckman (1950: 195) calls the 'house-property complex', where each wife of a polygynous marriage formed a separate unit with her children, whose allocated property the husband and father could not alienate.[6] Dundas (1924: 304) argued accordingly that 'each wife has her own hut, and the stock placed in her hut belongs to her family'. Gutmann (1907: 3) noted that the banana garden and other fields also belonged to the house, as he argued that 'each wife of a man has her own house, her own banana garden and fields as well as care for the livestock she is entrusted'. The one-time German District Commissioner Moritz Merker (1902: 4) furthermore suggested that each house was a separate unit with regards to production and consumption: 'Each wife has her own particular hut, where she lives with her children and maintains her own household'. The polygynous homestead thus contained and consisted of several houses, each of which was inhabited by one wife, her children and their livestock, and to which belonged a surrounding banana garden and any additional fields. Indeed, people today recount how the only houses were those of wives, among which all the livestock and land of the homestead were divided. The husband therefore had no house or property, but instead circulated between the houses of his wives, where he slept, took part in the work and was fed.[7]

Elders moreover describe how the groom's mother bestowed her house to her first-born son or 'child in front' (*mwana wa mbele*) upon his marriage, while she relocated with her remaining children to a new house behind or 'above' (*fondoho*) the existing one. She repeated this procedure for all but the second-born son, until her last-born son married, in whose house she remained to be looked after by him and his wife. The situation modifies Gluckman's (1950: 195) claim that the house-property complex entailed that a man inherited property from his mother. The practice in Rombo meant that a man was provided with a house and a banana garden by his mother while she was alive. In the case of a polygynous marriage, the practice in fact entailed that the bride was bestowed a fully functioning homestead by her husband's mother upon her marriage. Furthermore, its effect was a chain or line of homesteads occupied by brothers, which extended vertically up the mountainside. Elder brothers lived 'in front of' (*mbele*) or 'below' (*siinde*) their younger brothers in homesteads whose spatial extension across the mountainside actualized, incorporated and unfolded the temporal relationships of their establishment. Agnatic affiliation combined with polygyny occasioned more or less parallel chains, which created over time a patchwork of homesteads and a lattice of houses that were occupied by classificatory brothers, fathers and sons.

Current settlement patterns confirm statements that this practice changed fifty to sixty years ago, when more durable houses and permanent crops made people reluctant to give up their homesteads. While the African socialist policies of *ujamaa* and villagization had little impact in Kilimanjaro (Jennings 2008: 52), long-term Catholic influence combined with growing land scarcity to ensure that polygyny was practised in ever-fewer instances. Instead of mothers providing the wives of sons with complete homesteads, fathers began to give sons shares of land on which they had to build their own houses. The practice introduced a novel form of inequality, as sons began to inherit differentially, according to their position in the birth order. Currently, the first-born son (*mwana wa mbele*) is most commonly provided with a plot of cultivated land 'below the homestead' (*siinde ya kaa*), as was the case with Boniface who featured above. People say this is the best land, as the topsoil and manure is washed down from the homestead above. Furthermore, they also stress that this practice allows a father to keep his eldest son close for help and support. Meanwhile, the last-born son most often inherits the rest of the father's homestead, including its houses, where the parents remain to be cared for by him and his wife. The practice retains the effect of a spatial and temporal sequence of homesteads, where the child in front is located below or in front of the last-born son, who still cares for their parents. However, it is achieved at the expense of the first-born son, who now receives a share of cultivated land, rather than a complete homestead. Moreover, it turns the historical relations and locations of the homesteads around in significant ways, as the older homestead is occupied by the younger brother, and is located above the more recent homestead inhabited by the older brother.

In contrast to his brothers, the second-born son was allocated land by the *mangi*'s advisor or *mchili*. Most commonly, this was uncultivated land away from the natal homestead, where he and his wife were required to build their own house and plant a new banana garden. The positions of *mangi* and *mchili* were abolished after independence, along with the ability to allocate land. There is in any case no more land to allocate, so the sons between the first- and the last-born inherit only as far as the father is able to bestow. In 2000–2001, many said that if these sons have received secondary or higher education, they need not be given any land since their education provides them with a means of livelihood. If they received no education beyond primary school, however, it was necessary to provide land of some kind. If the father was able, he could buy land on the mountain from someone who was willing to sell, but most commonly he gave these sons whatever land he possessed or could access outside of his own homestead. Until quite recently, this often meant a plot higher up on the mountain that had been used to grow grass for fodder. More recently and most commonly, however, it means an uninhabited plot in the plains that has been used for seasonal crops. If the father does not possess such land, or the sons refuse to move to the plains, it is not uncommon that the parental homestead is divided between all the sons. Even then, there is bias in favour of the first- and the last-born sons, as the former receives more and better land, while the latter takes over the parents' house. All sons moreover receive a share of the father's plot in the plains, but the first- and the last-born sons tend also here to receive a disproportionate amount compared to their brothers.

Education has long played a central role in Kilimanjaro, where it closely entwined with missionization and coffee cash-cropping. Its early adoption and relative success meant that education, salaried employment and financial means offered an escape from the pressure on land. Taxes levied on coffee farmers boosted the treasury of the co-lonial Council of Chagga Chiefs, who used the funds to build schools, roads, dispensaries and courts. For the individual farmer, 'by far the most important cash investment the Chagga made ... was in paying school fees for their children' (S.F. Moore 1986: 129). The missions were the main providers of this education, as revealed by statistics from the 1952 annual report. At that point, there were 106 primary schools in the whole of Kilimanjaro, and of these the Holy Ghost Fa-thers ran 52, the Augustana Lutheran Mission ran 35, the Native Au-thority ran 18, while the Muslim Association ran one (TNA 63/21). In terms of student numbers, the Catholic and Lutheran mission schools educated nearly five times as many as the Native Authority and gov-ernment schools. The contrast was even starker earlier in the colonial period, as revealed by the District Commissioner's report for 1920, which states that no government school was yet established, while the missions ran an undisclosed number (TNA AB/3). By 1923, three government schools were in operation with a total of 110 students, while there were 9,737 students in mission schools (TNA AB/77). When the people of Kilimanjaro invested their coffee proceeds in their children's education, they thus gave their money to the missions that had been central in the introduction and promotion of this cash-crop. The link between coffee and education is still underscored, as people describe how they were provided with loans in the past from the coffee cooperative to pay school fees against collateral in the future harvest. The coffee cooperative that was established on the colonial authorities' instigation and staffed with early converts and mission students hence enabled people to pay school fees to the missions with the hope for future salaried employment that alleviated the pressure on land.

The expansion of secondary education in the 2000s has greatly increased the number of students with schooling beyond primary, but this has not translated into improved prospects for employment. Like many other parts of Tanzania, Rombo is full of Form Two and Form Four leavers in their mid to late teens who have returned home with few opportunities beyond farming. Not only do these young people add pressure on the land situation; their school fees have further impoverished their parents, at the same time as their partial education and unfulfilled prospects occasion disillusionment. There is always the possibility of migrating to Dar es Salaam, Arusha or other cities in the region, where many gain work from relatives or acquaintances who went ahead. Such migration has a long history in Rombo, where many elders tell of the times they spent working especially in Mombasa during their youth in the late colonial period. In towns today, people from outside Kilimanjaro tell stories of Chagga-speaking persons they know, who run small shops or bars they have set up with capital provided by their parents in lieu of land at home. Travelling through the region, one can easily spot the establishments run by Kilimanjaro natives from the names they bear, which sometimes even reveal the part of the mountain they call home.

The tourism trade that central and western Kilimanjaro have long benefitted from provides few opportunities for people in Rombo. Mountain climbing has occasioned large hotels in Machame and Marangu, where the gates to the national park are located and the main trails start. Meanwhile, there is only one restricted trail in Rombo, in an uninhabited area in the north called Rongai. Whereas many young men from central and western Kilimanjaro are employed in tourism in different capacities, I met only two men from Rombo who had worked as porters during my initial fieldwork. More have since followed in their footsteps, but their numbers remain negligible. People know of tourism from watching Land Rovers laden with tourists on their way to Rongai, which often sped past on late Sunday mornings when we emerged from the parish outstation by the main road in Keni. Until the road was paved in 2011–12, its poor state meant that a one-way trip from Keni to Moshi could take anything between two and six hours depending on the season. Unlike for central and western Kilimanjaro,

Moshi was therefore not within commuting distance, so those with jobs in town either had to move there permanently or commute on a weekly or monthly basis.

On this basis, one can conclude that the settlement pattern and inheritance practice that combine primo- and ultimogeniture, and that Moore (1981: 231) and Setel (1999: 253) present on the basis of Gutmann (1926) as a longstanding practice that dates back to pre-colonial times, are the effects of the introduction of cash-cropping and more durable houses. It is likely that these changes occurred earlier in central and western Kilimanjaro, where coffee cultivation caught on first and land became scarce earlier due to greater population densities. From Rombo, however, various sources and different kinds of evidence support statements that these changes happened relatively recently, which accords with the claim that the district constitutes a relative periphery.

Considering Women

Both the past and the present situation are partly yet insufficiently recognized in the scholarship of Kilimanjaro. Moore (1981: 231), for instance, argues with regards to precolonial Kilimanjaro that 'a polygynous man had to provide each wife with a separate hut and banana garden and, if possible, her own beasts'. Similarly, Setel (1999: 253) claims that, 'in polygynous marriages, each wife was meant to have her own *kihamba* to farm and reside on with her children'. However, neither appears familiar with the concept of the house-property complex, which is surprising in light of Moore's (2005a) personal familiarity with Gluckman and his work, and the prominence gender has played for this scholarship. In a comparative study, Thomas Håkansson (1989: 121) contrastingly points out how the complex makes women trustees and managers of the house-property, which in Regina Oboler's (1994: 342) view accords women a position of considerable power and influence. In line with this, the ethnography from Rombo reveals how women played a pivotal role, as houses and land passed from husband's mother to son's wife. Moore (1981: 231), by contrast, emphasizes the relationship between fathers and sons, as she argues that 'it was a paternal obligation to provide the firstborn son with a developed banana grove at the time of the son's marriage', while 'the father kept the youngest by his side, in his own *kihamba*, his banana garden'.[8] Accordingly, she misconstrues the dynamic of the settlement pattern to claim that 'there seems no doubt that efforts must have been made to keep intact the kinship integrity of the core lands occupied by a cluster of agnates'. In her view, the patchwork of homesteads occupied by agnates was the result of men's endeavour to maintain and preserve an original lineal kinship unity, when in fact it was the effect of a practice where women bestowed homesteads to their sons' brides upon their marriages. Moore shifts salience away from the relationship between women and onto the relationship between men, and is therefore unable to recognize how the settlement pattern is an effect of the relationship between women and houses, rather than a starting point for a relationship between men and land.

Similarly, Setel (1999: 33) emphasizes the relationship between fathers and sons to argue that 'ingratiating oneself to male patrikin was critical to gaining access to resources necessary to marry and to progress through the life course'. The reason was that fathers and agnates provided cattle and beer for bridewealth, and that 'fathers controlled access to land for first and last sons'. Furthermore, Setel (1999: 34) argues that 'the *kihamba* regime, it must also be noted, supported the political and economic interests of men over those of women, but did so within relations of carefully delineated interdependencies within marriage, among siblings, and between fathers and daughters'. Like Moore, Setel is misled by agnatic relationality and blinkered by presuppositions pertaining to kinship and social organization, which obscure the significant roles and relationships of women that the house-property complex entails. Contrastingly, men's dependence on their wives for a place to eat and sleep that my informants highlight indicates a very different situation.

The bias in favour of agnatic relationality and the presupposition of lineal significance is underscored by Moore's (1981: 227ff) claim that 'the localised patrilineages go on having considerable vitality in certain areas', and her conjecture that these once were corporate entities controlling land that clustered and combined to form a hierarchical political structure of districts and chiefdoms. By contrast, people in Rombo are organized in shallow agnatic descent groups that are designated by the Swahili term (*ukoo*), and that perform limited ceremonial tasks and divide peacefully when they become too large. It seems that scholars build uncritically on Gutmann's concern for descent relations and the corporate collective he designated with the German term *Sippe* to explore social life in terms of particular relationships that recognize specific kinds of entities and direct their attention towards certain kinds of efforts. As the house-property complex indicates, the ethnography from Rombo cuts across these dominant analytical figures to reveal other relationships and call forth other phenomena that provide a different dynamic and direction of social life in Kilimanjaro.

Shifting Houses

The change to more durable houses that accompanied and effected the changes in inheritance practices and settlement patterns also involved changes both in the kinds and numbers of houses within the homestead. Like the introduction of coffee cash-cropping and the opposition to polygyny, these changes to both the material structures and modes of habitation were the result of colonial and missionary efforts to intervene in life in Kilimanjaro. Again, these efforts took effect later in Rombo than elsewhere on the mountain, as the interventions seemingly met with greater resistance there compared with central and western Kilimanjaro. An examination of these changes provides an entry to the activity of dwelling (*ikaa*) from which the homestead (*kaa*) derives its name, as well as adjoining concepts that concern the relationships between persons and houses.

Current homesteads (*kaa*) in Rombo commonly consist of several houses (*mba*) that serve different roles and purposes. They include in most cases a residential house and a combined stable and cooking hut, as well as a latrine of some kind that is usually located at some distance. Nevertheless, some people, like my friend and collaborator Herman, only own a single house where humans and livestock largely occupy separate rooms.[9] The houses tend to be built with the doorway facing east; older people say it must face the direction of the sunrise, even though this is far from always the case.[10] Where it is the case, the geographical fortuity of Keni means that the doorway faces downhill with the plains stretching out below (*siinde*) it and Mount Kilimanjaro rising behind or above (*fondoho*).

Most residential houses are square wattle-and-daub structures, but rectangular houses built of cinderblocks are increasingly common. Like the house I stayed in, a concrete residential house usually contains one living room and a couple of bedrooms. These are furnished to a greater or lesser extent, and gradually accrue finishing details, such as plaster work, ceiling boards and perhaps electricity. Depending on its size, the house might have one or more doorways (*moongo*), but one in the front and another in the back are common. There is often a covered veranda with a concrete floor and railing in front of the main doorway, where guests, who are very rarely admitted into the house, are received and seated. The doorway and the veranda in front overlook the courtyard, which is called *sha* or *sha nduwe*, literally meaning 'outside' or 'big outside'.

A wattle-and-daub house, on the other hand, is usually a smaller structure that commonly consists of only one or two rooms. Some, however, are large and elaborate structures and the earliest ones, like Augustine's aforementioned house, were plastered and painted and are hard to distinguish from today's cinderblock structures. People's priority is to build rather than decorate, so wattle-and-daub houses tend to be sparsely furnished and electrified only in exceptional cases. They typically have only one doorway, which leads onto the main courtyard, where the roof might extend to create a small veranda for entertaining guests. In the back, nearly all houses have a small protruding roof under which drinking gourds, dried animal hides and other tools are stored. Guests are sometimes entertained here too, either during large events where different groups of people are seated separately, or for smaller occasions when only a select few are invited, whom the host may wish to conceal from others that enter the homestead.

The combined stable and cooking hut is nearly always a wattle-and-daub structure. It can be square, but more often is round with a conical roof that was in fashion some decades ago. While the residential house faces and dominates the *sha* courtyard, the stable and cooking hut is often to the side of the courtyard or the main house. It usually consists of one big room that is divided into two roughly equal sections, one for livestock and the other for the cooking space. If it is large, the house may have one doorway for each section. The livestock area is divided into separate pens for cattle and goats that are constructed out of wooden poles and planks with troughs from which the animals eat. The hearth (*riko*) is located directly inside the doorway, where three or four large hearthstones (*mashia*) are thrust into the ground between which the fire is lit and on top of which the cooking vessel rests. Women do most but not all of the cooking, sitting on low wooden stools around the hearth, where they are often accompanied in the evening by the children. The cooking area often also contains a rough and simple wooden table, where utensils and common ingredients, such as cooking oil and salt, are stored along with any leftovers. In many cases, there is also a bed (*uli*) along a wall of the cooking hut, where the oldest woman of the homestead sleeps. If she is the owner's mother, she is often accompanied at night by one or more of her grandchildren. Above the cooking area, there is an attic (*kali*) made out of planks or poles that form a rough and uneven floor, where firewood, old cooking pots and other miscellany are stored, and bananas are ripened for brewing beer. All houses without exception are currently roofed with corrugated iron sheets.

Previously, however, the house in Rombo was a tall conical structure thatched with grass that combined the living space for both humans and animals.[11] Such houses are virtually non-existent today, but they disappeared only recently; most people now in their forties grew up in such houses. In 2001, I tracked down one such house in Mashati that was being used as a stable. Elders describe how they constructed such houses by raising vertical wooden poles that were tied together at the top by means of withies called *mahafiyo*. Bundles of thin branches were then bound horizontally onto these poles with *mahafiyo* to create a grid framework onto which bundles of grass were 'sewn' by means of a long wooden 'needle' (*ngura*) and 'thread' made from *mahafiyo*. At the top of the house, where the poles and the thatch met, a cooking pot was placed, ostensibly to prevent the rain from entering the house. On the house I saw in Mashati, this pot had been replaced by a plastic carrier bag.

In contrast to many present-day houses, the grass-house had only one doorway (*moongo*). Immediately inside this was a small area called *uwango* that served for entertaining guests. Behind the *uwango*, there was a partition made from wooden planks that reached about two metres high, through which there was a doorway (though no actual door) that led into the main part of the house. The section of the par-

Figure 1.2. Grass-house nestled in the banana garden with an outdoor goat pen in the foreground.

tition to the left of the doorway was called *mangoni,* where tools and implements were stored by lodging them between the planks, while the area to the right of the doorway was called *ngoni.* To the left of the *mangoni* was the entrance to the *koombe* or pen where cows were kept at night. The *koombe* took up roughly one-third of the total area and ran along the entire left-hand side of the house. Its innermost area was sectioned off by a wickerwork wall called a *kishii,* which separated any bulls or calves from the cows. Facing the centre of the house was a crib (*kilii*) that ran along the innermost third of the *koombe* where the cattle could eat in the evening and during the night.

The hearth was located in the main section of the house, to the right of the partition's doorway. It was sheltered by a broad wooden plank called a *kisumbadini,* which formed the back of the *ngoni.* People describe how the senior woman of the household sat with her back against the *kisumbadini* while she cooked, and say that its purpose was to protect the hearth from the draft coming through the doorway. However, the location of the hearth in relation to the *kisumbadini,* the opening of the *mangoni* and the *moongo* doorway meant that it was impossible for anyone to see the hearth and what was cooking over it. The *kisumbadini* therefore protected the hearth both from the wind and from outside onlookers.

The bed (*uli*) was located to the right of the hearth. Depending on the size of the house and the number of inhabitants, there were one or more beds. The *uli* was slightly elevated above the ground and was made out of *isale* or dracaena sticks that were tied together. On top of this was a plaited mattress of dried banana bark (*mdawi*) that was covered with cured animal hides, where the inhabitants slept with their heads towards the centre of the house. Next to the bed, covering roughly half the area of the right-hand side of the house, was the goat pen (*msau*), which was also constructed from wooden poles. Its crib (*firamu*) consisted of two cleft sticks of roughly one metre in length that were thrust into the ground to form an elevated space, where bundles of leaves and grass tied together with strips of dried banana bark were placed. Such *firamus* are still found in today's stables and outdoor pens, where the goats graze during the day.

The centre of the house – between the *mangoni,* the cow pen, the bed and the *msau* – formed a relatively large and open unnamed space for the members of the household to sit in. There was an attic (*kali*) some three metres above the ground that covered the entire area of the house, even extending over the livestock pens. The attic was supported by pillars, some of which were the corner posts of the cow and goat pens, and accessed by means of a ladder that went up between the end of the *mangoni* partitioning and the entrance to the *koombe*. The floor of the house was unevenly cobbled with stones.[12]

One could surmise that the practice for people and livestock to share one house was a consequence of colonial poll taxation. Moore (1981: 230), for instance, mentions among the changes wrought by German colonial rule that the authorities 'imposed cash taxes, hut by hut'. Similarly, a 1947 government report states that a graduated tax scale was in effect, which meant that the amount paid depended on the number of huts in the homestead (TNA 28269). The absence of a 'Plural Wives Tax' meant that payment was only liable for one house, if the husband could place each wife, her children and their livestock under a single roof. Accordingly, the report stated that the majority paid tax for one hut only. In 1925, the annual report for Moshi District stated that a campaign was launched to persuade people to occupy separate houses from their livestock for public health reasons. Yet, rather than facing protest from the men – who were responsible for paying tax – the District Commissioner claimed that 'the elder generation and women are the stumbling-blocks to any reform in this direction' (TNA AB/86). Even if the settlement pattern was conducive to the poll tax regime in place at the time, it seems not to have been a response to colonial policy. Instead, the occupation of a single house by one woman, her children and their livestock appears to have been an entrenched practice. It accords with the house-property complex, which these sources thus confirm as the predominant mode of habitation.

Even if one cannot determine how far this practice dates back, it evidently persisted longer in Rombo than elsewhere in Kilimanjaro. Sanitary Superintendent Bailey thus reported in 1931 that up to 65 per cent of households in central Kilimanjaro provided separate houses for cattle and people, but only 10 per cent of households in Mkuu did the same (TNA 312). He claimed that the agents precipitating these changes were mission converts, who moreover provided separate houses for the husbands and elder sons. In line with the District Commissioner's claim above, the implication seems to be that women and unconverted elders were the obstacles to the desired development. In any case, Bailey hardly restrained his disgust at the conditions in which people lived:

> In the usual type of grass or banana bast hut, two thirds or even more of the floor space is covered by rough stalls for housing the cattle and goats, the remainder being used as a living space. Even where a separate dwelling for the male exists, the women cook food in their own filthy huts. The excreta from the cattle is removed daily, but the liquid

filth rapidly causes the ground to become 'sewage sick' and the filth oozes out through the walls.

He went on to describe what he considered the reasons for this arrangement:

> Failure to provide separate living accommodation for all seems to be due more to prejudice than to poverty. Many of the Wachagga owning large numbers of cattle, build huts to accommodate all of them in addition to huts for the storage of 'pombe' etc. and yet will not provide separate sleeping accommodation for themselves and families. Many aver that fear of theft of the cattle if left alone at night prevents them, but it seems that at heart the tribe actually prefer to live with the animals, for in numerous instances sick people have had their beds transferred to the cattle huts under the delusion that a quicker cure will result.

Finally, Bailey emphasized that the tendency to separate people and livestock was a recent development: 'The provision of dwellings apart from domestic animals, if only for males, however, is an encouraging beginning. During a visit to the area five years ago on anti-smallpox work, only a very small percentage of such were noted'.

In 1929, the Provincial Commissioner identified the vanguard of this process: 'It has been gratifying to notice that the more enlightened Chagga are beginning to abandon the old type Chagga hut, in which human beings, cattle, sheep, and goats live together, and are building four-walled houses. Some of the Chiefs have built good houses of European type and this example is followed on a small scale by their more intelligent people' (TNA 11681). It was in other words largely the same people who pioneered coffee farming who abandoned established settlement and habitation patterns. The Commissioner's optimism was not shared by Bailey, however, who professed two years later that 'only by constant propaganda will the prejudice of the very conservative Wachagga, in this direction, be overcome'. In this light, it seems that the living arrangements that were practised in Rombo until quite recently predated colonial policies, and that the change from round grass-houses to square wattle-and-daub or concrete abodes was linked to colonial public health campaigns, missionization, education and cash-cropping, which influenced other parts of Kilimanjaro at earlier stages and to greater extents.

A Green Place

Despite the changes that have occurred, people say that the space surrounding the house remains configured and named in the same way today as it did in the days of the grass-houses. Below or in front of the *sha nduwe* courtyard is the above-mentioned *siinde ya kaa* area, which literally means 'below the homestead'. This is where the members of the homestead are buried, usually near a tall and voluminous *isale* tree called *mbuho*.[13] The open area behind the house is called the *kaandeni* and is where the livestock are penned during the day. The *kaandeni* used to be enclosed by tall *isale* hedges, ostensibly to prevent people from looking in. These hedges are now mostly gone, but the livestock pens are still constructed so that people arriving at the homestead's courtyard are unable to see the animals.

Surrounding the courtyard, *siinde ya kaa* and *kaandeni* is the banana garden. Quotes above from Moore and Setel show how the banana garden is referred to in the literature as *kihamba* or *vihamba* in the plural. The term *kihamba* is actually used to enunciate claims to a specific plot, and hence pertains to the ownership discourse surrounding and concerning the garden. Meanwhile, the noun *mdenyi* is used to mean the banana garden as a physical phenomenon. *Mdenyi* is a locative construction that derives from the verb 'to cultivate' – *itchema* – which combines with the place adverbial suffix -*nyi*.[14] The noun therefore literally translates as 'cultivated place', which is used in opposition to the term *sakeu*, which can be rendered as 'bush' or 'wilderness' but is best translated as 'uncultivated place'.

The *mdenyi* is currently fenced in by various kinds of bushes and trees, which demarcate the boundary or *mrasa* between adjacent homesteads. People say that these markers consisted in the relatively recent past of *isale* hedges, which Dundas (1924: 258) confirms.[15] Some such hedges still exist, but the *isale* has been interspersed with or even replaced by other cultivars with leaves that can be used for fodder and branches that can serve as firewood.[16] As a result of such harvesting, tree trunks grow tall and straight until they are eventually cut down and used as building materials or sold for timber. Between these trees, various bushes that are also used for fodder grow to form thick, nearly impenetrable walls that together with the banana trees prevent people from seeing from one homestead to another. Sounds of activities carry between them, but it is virtually impossible to see from one *kaa* to another through the dense thicket of greenery. In fact, Rebmann described a similar scene from his first arrival at Kilema: 'Crossing the ditch on a very shaky bridge, consisting of a slim tree, we were again on pasture-land, where we could see the plantations of Kilema, but not the dwellings hidden in them' (Krapf 1860: 237). He described being received by Masaki, the 'King of Kilema', 'in a little hut, in the midst of a whole forest of bananas, and which completely shut out any view' (Krapf 1860: 238). His account underscores how the current settlement pattern is longstanding, and affords the claim that it has been intensified by population growth and density to render current homesteads contiguous: 'There are in Jagga no compact villages or towns, but only isolated inclosures [*sic*], separated from each other by open spaces extending about the eighth of a mile, and always covered with banana-trees. Each yard is occupied by a single family, in several huts, protected by hedgerows of growing bushes, which serves as a defence against wild beasts, more especially hyenas' (Krapf 1860: 244).

To an untrained eye, the banana garden looks like an unkempt jumble of plants and crops that fight for the sunlight dappling through the foliage. Banana trees of various kinds, shapes and sizes seem to grow in a haphazard fashion, interspersed with coffee bushes, large-leaved taro plants, yam creepers and the occasional bean- and maize-stalks. Except for coffee, these crops are mainly grown for subsistence and most predate colonial rule. Thus, Widenmann (1899: 72ff) and Gutmann (1913: 476) described how taro, sweet potatoes, yams and beans, as well as bananas, eleusine, maize and tobacco were grown in Old Moshi more than a century ago. New (1873: 370) too reported encountering 'Indian corn, pulse, wimbe (pannicum), etc.', where the latter most likely referred to eleusine or finger millet (*mmbeke*). Only taro figures extensively today, as it serves as an additional source of carbohydrates that is added to different banana-based dishes. Taro is also boiled with cooking soda (*mbala*) to produce a liquid that is fed to cows to increase their milk supply. Sweet potatoes and yams occur in most homesteads, but they are only roasted and consumed as occasional treats. Some people also grow a little tobacco for home consumption, either rolled up and smoked as cigarettes by men or ground as snuff that is used by both men and women.

The most significant crop of the *mdenyi* is the banana tree, whose different parts serve a multitude of purposes. The stem of the tree consists of layers of leaf-sheaths that are made of a porous yet fibrous material that contains an abundance of sap. The leaf of the tree emerges out of the centre of the stem in a rolled-up form and is known as *unanda* or *urongo*. Once it unfolds, the leaf is called *makosha* or *machawa*, but it only lasts in this state for a certain time before it withers and dries. The green leaves are therefore harvested by means of a *mwesho*, which is a long stick to which a curved machete is attached. The harvested leaves are either cut as fodder into the troughs for the cows and goats, or rolled up with branches from other trees and placed in the *firamu* for the goats. Under good conditions, a tree can apparently produce one leaf weekly, which totals sixty to seventy leaves in its lifetime (Ngeze 1994: 31). The stem of each leaf constitutes a sheath of bark that adds to the trunk of the tree, which hence consists of layers of overlapping semi-circular leaf-sheaths that can be stripped away to reveal no core to the tree.

Depending on its kind, the banana tree will at some point produce a flower stalk (*sabo*), instead of new leaves. Like the leaves, the stalk emerges from the centre of the tree, but it turns out and down towards the ground, instead of upwards. After emerging completely, the stalk opens to reveal the flowers that eventually turn into fruits. The resulting bunch that appears from the flower stalk is known as *iruu*, but this is a fractal and family resemblance concept that is variously used to mean the whole bunch, the singular fruit and the entire tree that carries a bunch, depending on the situation or the language-game involved.[17]

Each tree produces only one bunch of fruit and will eventually wither and die if left to its own devices. The mature bunch of unripe bananas is therefore harvested by slashing the trunk and cutting down the tree. Its remaining leaves are removed and cut for fodder and the trunk (*mbora*) is divided into sections and sliced finely with a machete for the same purpose. Most of the offshoots (*ndaka*) that appear at the foot of the tree are pruned and fed to the livestock in the same way, but only once they reach a height of one or two metres. The *mbora* is considered insufficient and suboptimal as fodder, but has nevertheless become the main source of fodder for the livestock. However, it is supplemented with other vegetative matter, such as the green *makosha* or *machawa* leaves. Grass (*mara*) is considered the best fodder, but this is in short supply due to the lack of pastures and available land to grow it. However, grass is cut by hand on the verges of pathways, and during my initial fieldwork it was harvested along with leaves by women and children in the forestland between the settled area and the national park, and carried back to the homestead in large bundles. Environmental degradation brought a ban on this practice in 2012, but women still bring grass and dried maize-stalks up from the plains. These they mainly feed to the cattle, while the goats eat leaves from the trees that serve as boundary markers. A small minority can afford to buy grass from the plains, which may be transported from as far afield as the Pare Mountains.

People claim it is only recently that they have come to rely on *mbora* for fodder, but both Gutmann (1913: 505) and Dundas (1924: 258) described how banana trees were fed to livestock. Thomson (1885: 130) reported that women in Rombo carried home grass they had gathered for their stall-fed livestock. Even if grazing and herding were more common in Rombo than elsewhere, and production in the past was marked by agro-pastoralism, stall-feeding was practised for small-stock and cattle that were kept in the homesteads. Both stall-feeding and the use of *mbora* as fodder thus have a long history in Rombo, as elsewhere on the mountain.

These practices entail an intensive and intrinsic relationship between banana farming and livestock-keeping that goes far beyond the issue of fodder. When a leaf is cut, the top of its leaf-sheath begins to dry and peel away from the stem of the tree. These dried pieces of bark (*mawilho*) are considered aesthetically displeasing and need to be removed from a well-kept banana garden. These *mawilho* are either cut off and left on the ground where they prevent weeds from growing and break down as compost manure, or they are placed in the livestock pens where they soak up urine and provide a dry place for the animals to sleep. Two or three times a week, these *mawilho* are swept up with the manure and placed at the foot of the banana trees in the *mdenyi*. Manure or *boru*, and especially that of cattle, is considered a prerequisite for the production of bananas, and one can easily tell a garden that has access to it from one that does not. Not only are its trees taller, bigger and more plentiful, but they produce bunches of greater size and improved quality. People may lament the labour-intensive nature of stall-feeding, but acknowledge manure as its chief benefit. It is also considered the borrower's main gain from the *ihara* relationship, even though he also enjoys the milk and receives some of its offspring, along with a share of its meat or the money when the animal is butchered or sold. Gutmann (1924a: 136; 1926: 426) also argued that manure was a precondition for the banana farming practised in Kilimanjaro. Similarly, a government report raised the importance of manure in 1938, claiming that enough of it was produced to keep constantly cultivated land in good fertility and that most land received manure (TNA 26045).

While bananas are today used only for human consumption, people say that they previously had a specific use in connection with gelded goats (*ndafu*) that men reared and fed inside the house. Rather than the fodder described above, the *ndafu* were fed *mbere* to increase the fat and taste of the goat. *Mbere* is made from *mnyengele* bananas and *kunde* beans that are boiled with soda and mashed into a semi-liquid consistency.[18] Dundas (1924: 267–68) described a similar practice, but with regards to other animals than goats: 'Bulls are kept in specially constructed huts where they are daily fed on quantities of bananas and never allowed out. They may be kept thus for as long as eight years with the sole object of fattening them, and are then slaughtered for a feast. A man may have ten such bulls ... Sheep are likewise fattened, the process lasting over some two years and more'. To illustrate how difficult life has become, people in Rombo point out that virtually no one rears *ndafu* anymore, and that *mbere* is now food for humans rather than livestock. Even if bananas are now only eaten by humans, peels and other by-products from their cooking are still fed to the livestock.

Animal Digestion, Human Arms

The result of the practices described above is a particular form of horticulture, where livestock are stall-fed leaves and stems of banana trees to provide manure, which is used to fertilize the garden. It appears to be an intensification of longstanding activities that seemingly has developed in response to demographic pressures and land shortage. Nevertheless, the result is an imbrication of activities that yield the bananas that form the staple food, along with milk, meat and an assortment of other foodstuffs and substances. Animal digestion plays a pivotal role in this regard, as it converts fodder into manure that is spread in the garden to grow crops that feed both livestock and people. Accordingly, Moore (1976: 363) argues that manuring meant that people connected excrements with fertility through 'technical experience'. However, she quickly adds that they cannot know the chemistry involved, so 'it was more likely something akin to what we would call a magical property that made manure a fertilizing substance'. Her argument misses the fact that salience here does not concern the property of any particular entity, but a process where both foods and fodder are brought into existence through mutually entailing activities. Indeed, Peter acknowledged these imbrications in his invocation in the plains, where he enunciated how neither humans nor livestock had anything to eat.

Along with animal digestion, the arm or hand (*koko*) plays a crucial role in these activities and the foodstuffs they yield.[19] For instance, people seek someone with a 'good arm' (*koko kesha*) to uproot excess offshoots (*ndaka*) and remove the stumps (*matonga*) of harvested banana trees. Such pruning ensures that the remaining trees grow and produce to their full potential without an abundance of offshoots to diminish their growth. It also adjusts the content of the garden, as superfluous *ndaka* are replanted to redistribute or augment certain kinds of bananas. Replanting is also delegated to someone with *koko kesha*, as this ensures that the offshoot 'seizes' or 'sticks' (*iira*) to grow and provide leaves, fruits and offshoots. Similarly, someone with *koko kesha* is tasked to lead a cow or goat to be covered, as the semen is then more likely to 'seize' or 'stick' (*iira*) and result in a calf or kid. *Koko kesha* hence secures the growth of the garden and its livestock pen, where arms harvest and slice fodder and sweep and spread manure. The arm thus turns leaves and stems into fodder, which animal diges-

Figure 1.3. Man uprooting excess banana trees.

tion converts to manure that the *koko* spreads to promote the provision of foodstuffs. The role of the arm is accentuated in conversation, where the act of slicing fodder is often neither named nor mentioned, but illustrated by a cutting motion with the arm, where the extended hand manifests the blade of a machete. The hand or arm is furthermore entailed by the notion of *ihara*, which is a causative verb-form deriving from *ihaa* that means 'to pick' or 'to gather', and is used to mean the act of harvesting coffee, fruits or wild berries. The concept of *ihara* thus enunciates how the relationship enables the borrower to pick or gather the everyday gains of manure and milk, as well as the longer-term benefits in the form of eventual offspring and a share of meat or money. In return for providing fodder by means of his arm, the borrower is hence able to harvest manure, milk, meat and money by means of his hand.

The fact that the borrower can receive money in return for cutting fodder indicates how cash forms part of these dynamics. People accordingly also delegate the pruning of coffee trees to someone with a good arm, as this ensures their growth and yield, which in turn is picked, pulped and prepared by hand. Such pruning and preparing are moreover subject to the sexual prohibitions that surround the handling of other plants and crops. In combination, this reveals that money has become integral to the same processes that govern food crops, which ensures that cash manifests and emerges from the arm and hand.

Figure 1.4. Man pulping coffee berries and women sorting coffee beans before they are to be washed and dried.

Farming in the Plains

While some maize and beans are grown in the banana gardens, these crops are mainly cultivated on uninhabited plots in the plains (*mway*), which are located as far as ten kilometres away from the homesteads. These fields are primarily tended by women, who hence circulate between the mountain and the plains in a similar way to how men did in the past. *Koko* features in this connection too, as the Chagga-speaking mountain-dwellers emphasize how they hoe their plots, in contrast to the Kamba-speakers of the plains, who plough their nearby fields by means of oxen. Beans of different kinds are sown in the plains in September and October, before the start of the short rains. Once these have flowered, their leaves are picked and used for food before the legumes are harvested in December and January. Eleusine meanwhile is sown in February and March, before the long rains, and harvested in June and July. Maize is mainly sown at the same time as the beans, although some may be added after the eleusine. While maize and beans can also be grown on the mountains, eleusine can only be farmed in the plains, where poor rains have ensured that hardly any has been harvested in the past decade. Eleusine is therefore imported from elsewhere in Tanzania and sold in local markets. Sunflowers and groundnuts have been recently introduced, and are also grown in the plains. Sunflowers are grown on a relatively large scale, and there are mechanized pressing machines in the villages for extracting their oil.

Figure 1.5. Young man and his elderly mother harvesting sunflowers and maize from a plot in the plains during the dry season.

Some sell the sunflower seeds – and even the extracted oil – but most people grow and press them for home consumption, which makes them less reliant on processed cooking oil that must be bought for cash. The refuse of the seeds is mixed with maize chaff and fed to the

Figure 1.6. Woman harvesting the leaves of flowering bean plants from the same plot in the plains after the rains.

livestock to increase their body weight and milk supply. Groundnuts are also grown as a cash-crop, but on a small scale since many have experienced failed harvests due to lack of rain, which has made people reluctant to buy the relatively expensive seeds. Pigeon peas and green gram are also grown for home consumption.

A century ago, Gutmann (1913: 477) remarked that maize was increasingly becoming the staple diet of the people of Old Moshi. However, Rombo occupies a rain shadow and is considerably drier than central and western Kilimanjaro, which makes maize harvests more vulnerable. Erratic rains throughout the early 2000s therefore ensured that by 2006 maize farming was increasingly abandoned in the plains and instead attempted on the mountain, where the few remaining grasslands were converted to fields. As a result of the rain shadow, all rivers in Rombo are seasonal and the famed furrows (*mifongo*) from central and western Kilimanjaro had little extension and use there (cf. Tagseth 2008: 469). Colonial sources accordingly report regular droughts and food shortages in Rombo, and record calls that were made for water supplies in the 1940s. The coffee board introduced the idea of a pipeline, and four of them began operating in 1947 (TNA 63/15). In the same period, maize land was turned into banana gardens and large tracts of new plots were opened in the plains (TNA 63/12), enabling the expansion of permanent settlement there. The development was partly the government's response to land shortages, but also a result of its encouragement to grow crops for the war effort from which the Chagga profited greatly. In 1950, plans were made to build fourteen dams in order to expand settlement in the lower areas of the mountain. However, it was held that 'Native Agriculture in Rombo and on the lower slopes of the mountain is not of high standard, and the tribe as a whole still have a lot to learn about anti soil erosion measures and land utilization' (TNA 63/A/20). Soil erosion was said to worsen in lower Rombo in 1952, when it was attributed to over-grazing, possibly due to the developments in cattle-holdings described above (TNA 38/10/2).

In 2000–2001, people experienced three grossly insufficient maize harvests and only a minuscule eleusine crop. In addition, the coffee price slumped, which extended through 2004 before it made a modest recovery.[20] In response, some people uprooted the coffee trees and started growing vegetables of various kinds, in a development that has since accelerated. However, the poor state of the road meant that access to larger markets was difficult and produce was likely to get damaged. In 2000–2001, bananas moreover had a limited market, with demand only for a few kinds used for foods. In season, people therefore sold small surpluses of maize or bananas locally, and to save transport costs women often carried the produce to the nearest large market at Mwika. When new stalls were built at Mwika, the surcharge levied to enter the market ensured that the banana trade relocated to Mamsera, just inside Rombo. This trade has since boomed, with all kinds of bananas in demand and vast quantities transported twice a week to Dar es Salaam and other cities. The trade is dominated by women, who buy bananas directly from farmers and hire lorries to transport them to Mamsera, where they are sold on. Farmers complain that the women acting as agents depress prices, which seasonal gluts in supply do not alleviate. Many women therefore still carry their bunches directly to the markets, where they sometimes end up underselling or even carrying them home for failing to find a buyer.

Weak coffee prices combined with increased needs and uses for money have thus created new markets for bananas and day labour, where people use their arms or their products to obtain money. Cash is increasingly used to obtain foodstuffs, such as the eleusine that fails in the plains or the meat and milk that those without livestock cannot access. These procured foodstuffs nevertheless combine with those grown in the homesteads and the plains, and hence form part of the same dynamics that involve particular body parts and take place in interaction between the mountain and the plains. It seems likely that this is enabled by people's long-term involvement in the monetary economy and entanglement in international commodity markets, as well as their engagement in production across different ecological zones. Nevertheless, the slump in coffee, the abundance of bananas and the absence of additional markets has led people to revert to subsistence farming and made them increasingly reliant on bananas for consumption. Accordingly, it seems that people have become increasingly impoverished during the time I have worked in the area. The trajectory sadly seems to be the extension and continuation of a long-term economic trend in the area, which entrenches Rombo's position as a relative periphery.

The current mode of banana farming and livestock stall-feeding that takes place within the confines of the homestead involves then an intensive form of horticulture that creates and involves an intense interdependence between humans, livestock and vegetation. The products of the banana garden combine through cooking and consumption with substances obtained from markets and crops grown in the plains, where women also gather fodder and firewood. The effect is a confluence and transformability of practices, persons and things that intertwine in multiple and complex ways. As I will reveal in the following chapters, it is these relationships and transformations that constitute the concept of *ikaa* or 'dwelling' from which the homestead – *kaa* – derives its name.

The products of these activities moreover feature as the central components of the bridewealth prestations that form part of the process of marrying – *ialika*. Furthermore, it is only upon marriage and the transfer of bridewealth that the homestead is acquired and comes into existence. Not only are the foodstuffs and substances that constitute the bridewealth the results of productive practices within the homestead; the bridewealth prestations and the marital relationship they afford bring the homestead into existence and thereby enable the activity of dwelling. The next chapter will therefore consider these transfers and activities, and the phenomena they bring into existence.

Notes

1. Moore (1977: 22) in fact confirms this.
2. Canna is a kind of flowering plant that serves several purposes, including the use of its leaves and stems as fodder.
3. My claim is supported by Kirilo Japhet and Earle Seaton's (1967) map of alienated land in the Northern Province in colonial times.
4. David Parkin (1991a: 62ff) describes a similar situation with regards to 'hiding the cattle' among the Kenyan Giriama to the east. The secrecy surrounding these practices may also account for the uncertainty pertaining to colonial cattle statistics.
5. The fact that the kraals of the people from Rombo could also be located on the Kenyan side of the border adds further uncertainty to the statistics provided by the colonial authorities, and could in fact mean that the number of cattle held by the people of Rombo was even greater than the sources suggest.
6. Gluckman's notion of the house-property complex was developed as a means of comparison to explore the differential divorce rates among the Zulu and Lozi of southern Africa. It is a sadly underexplored concept that in fact appears relevant for large areas of sub-Saharan Africa.
7. Some say men of means also retained a smaller grass-house called *veru*, where they kept their gelded *ndafu* goats and could on occasion sleep and eat.
8. In line with the situation I describe, Moore (1981: 231) recounts that 'middle sons were supposed to start new gardens for themselves in the bush'.
9. Herman is introduced more fully in chapter two.
10. A prescribed directionality for the house and an emphasis on the doorway facing towards or away from east is reported from different areas of

sub-Saharan Africa (Kuper 1982: 145; H.L. Moore 1986: 45). Several authors report that east is associated with life and west with death (Rigby 1968: 176; Sanders 1999: 53; 2008: 121; Wagner 1954: 33), while in Rombo significance rather accords to 'uphill' or 'above' (*fondoho*) and 'downhill' or 'below' (*siinde*).

11. Another kind of house of a lower and more round shape that was thatched with dried banana bark was common in western Kilimanjaro (Merker 1902: 7; Widenmann 1899: 60). Dundas (1924: 255) conjectured that the tall conical grass-house originated from Mkuu in Rombo, while Widenmann argued that houses were smaller in Rombo compared with Kibosho, Old Moshi and Marangu. Rebmann also described how people and livestock shared the same house (Krapf 1860: 244).

12. Widenmann (1899: 61) and Merker (1902: 9) largely describe the same layout of the house.

13. I consider burial practices and the role and significance of the *mbuho* in chapter four.

14. As later descriptions will underscore, the -*tch*- sound turns into a -*d*- when derivate forms and nouns are created from verb stems in Chagga.

15. Pietilä (2007: 18) indeed describes such hedges as a reality in her field site.

16. These are not the same, as the bare branches that are left after the leaves have been eaten are not used as firewood, but left to decompose in the banana garden.

17. The banana blossom (*nanua*) that remains as a purple drop-shape at the lower end of the stalk is used for various more or less ceremonial purposes, and allegedly plays a role in witchcraft activities.

18. *Mnyengele* bananas and *kunde* beans are, along with eleusine, the socially most significant crops, which will reappear in many different contexts throughout the book.

19. Like its Swahili cognate *mkono*, the Chagga *koko* means both the arm and the hand. For the sake of brevity, I have translated *koko* only as 'arm' here, even though some of the practices involve the hand to a greater extent.

20. BBC World Service reported that the coffee price had reached a sixty-year low. Statistics from the International Coffee Organization do not go that far back, but reveal a dramatic drop in 2001 that extended through 2004 (http://www.ico.org/new_historical.asp [accessed 13 January 2014]).

Chapter Two

IALIKA

MARRYING AS A MODE OF EXTENSION

The house-property complex described in the previous chapter entails that the homestead was in the past transferred from a woman to her son and his bride upon their marriage. Today, a man is usually provided a plot of land by his father, where he often builds a house before he marries. However, he does not move there until his bride relocates, when it is said that 'he has a hearth' (*nere riko*). Despite the last half-century's changes in settlement patterns, inheritance practices and modes of habitation, it is still upon marriage that the house and the homestead come into being. Bridewealth and marriage are therefore integral to the homestead (*kaa*) as a concept and entity, as well as to the notion and activity of dwelling (*ikaa*) from which it derives its name.

In contrast to many other places in Africa (see, for instance, Comaroff 1980; Kuper 1982), bridewealth in Rombo does not consist of livestock, but of foodstuffs and substances of different kinds. One could surmise that this is a consequence of population growth and incremental land shortage, and the ensuing depletion of herds and stock. However, Gutmann (1926: 126) described the opposite trend and a growing demand that prestations of beer and meat should be replaced by goats and cattle. The reason was that livestock could be retained by the inhabitants of the bride's natal homestead, whereas foodstuffs had to be shared with agnates.[1] Accordingly, both Dundas (1924: 228–42) and Gutmann (1926: 109–45) described protracted prestations that chiefly consisted of beer and meat, while goats and sheep were supplemental gifts. Gutmann (1926: 125) moreover claimed that the bridewealth prestations were even more numerous in the eastern parts of the mountain, where Rombo is located. If livestock ever played a role in bridewealth, it was therefore only for a brief period, and it was never the norm, as Moore (1981: 233) and Setel (1999: 33) seem to suggest.

In contemporary Rombo, bridewealth consists of an array of prestations of a variety of objects that stretch over several generations and are rarely, if ever, completed by anyone. Indeed, the purpose is not to complete these prestations, but to maintain a traffic that allows ample scope for negotiating their extent, content and timing. Similarly, Dundas (1924: 241) claimed: 'It is not decent to make demand for dowry payments with undue haste. In respectable families they may be left unclaimed during the lifetimes of the husband and wife to be recovered from their heirs. In Rombo it was formerly never the custom to claim anything until the woman was old and past bearing children, and under all circumstances nothing should be claimed until two or more children are born'. Dundas's description brings out the extended character of these prestations and highlights their link to reproduction. Yet his claim regarding Rombo contravenes the current consensus that a groom must present *some* bridewealth to his bride's relatives. In its absence, the claim to the children borne by a woman falls to her oldest brother, who assumes responsibility for their upbringing and provides his name as their middle name, instead of that of the father. Thus, in my adoptive family, Meki was born to an older sister, but his father – who was of a nearby homestead – provided no bridewealth. Oswald, the first-born son, therefore became responsible for Meki, who grew up with his mother's mother MaSway, even though his mother later married another man with whom she settled and had further children only some ten kilometres away. His mother frequently visited Meki, but the claim to and responsibility for him fell to her eldest brother.

Even more was at stake in the past, when it is claimed that a woman who became pregnant before or without the transfer of bridewealth was forced to reveal her lover's identity. The two were made to lie on top of each other as if making love, while a sharpened *isale* stick was driven through their lower backs to kill them both. The account may sound dubious, but Otto Raum ([1940] 1996: 69) described a similar practice, which he claimed was reported from four or five generations before his writing. Dundas (1924: 296), meanwhile, argued that this occurred when pregnancy resulted from sexual engagement between a young woman and an uncircumcised youth, which was considered 'the most heinous crime'. Today, premarital sex is common and even involves those who are not yet circumcised, while it is pregnancy without bridewealth that is frowned upon and lamented.

Going to Ask

The relationship between dwelling, bridewealth and marriage is substantiated by the prestation called 'going to ask' (*wande wesa*) or 'the milk to pour or place on the ground' (*marua ya iwikiya sumbay*) that my friend Herman made in September 2008. The prestation consists of one bucket of curdled milk and one bunch of bananas called *mlali*. These are shared among the bride's father's agnates, who bring the foodstuffs to their homesteads, where the bananas are boiled before the milk is added to make a dish called *kena*.

Wande wesa is widely considered the opening prestation, which should be made before the prospective spouses cohabit or reproduce. However, Herman and MaLasway had by 2008 already lived together for close to ten years and borne four children at the homestead Herman inherited from his late father, which he as the youngest son shared with his mother. Before living together, they courted for a long time, until MaLasway one evening refused to return to her parents' homestead. Instead, she remained with Herman and his mother, and began to take part in everyday life at their homestead. While many maintain that such actions and relationships are relatively recent developments, Gutmann (1926: 147) described the same phenomenon, which he termed 'bringing oneself to the husband'.

A few years after MaLasway moved in, she and Herman had a Catholic Church wedding. On that day, Herman brought a small amount of milk to her parents; he had told me they agreed that this sufficed as 'going to ask', and that he hoped to soon provide the next prestation, called 'the beer to tell' (*wari wa iamba*). During a visit to MaLasway's parents, however, Herman suddenly announced that he would present the milk and bananas after all. Her father Lasway was overjoyed to hear this, and the two men began to discuss and plan the details. They quickly agreed that Herman should not bring the actual foodstuffs. Instead, he should provide an equivalent sum of money, as he would harm (*imisha*) their children if he were to bring milk and bananas after they had reproduced. Lasway nevertheless promised to buy some milk since it would still be necessary to pour some on the ground, even if the prestation consisted of money and milk had been poured before the church wedding.

Two days later, Herman, MaLasway, my wife and I returned and were received by Lasway and his wife, MaShirima. While we sat on the courtyard, MaShirima washed a small gourd, which Lasway filled with milk he had procured from a neighbour. She then brought out a long-handled wooden ladle, often called a 'Chagga spoon' (*kilikiyo kya kishakka*), that was chipped and darkened from sustained use. Herman produced from his shirt pocket a sealed envelope, which he solemnly offered Lasway with both hands. However, Lasway refused it and told Herman to give it to his wife, who received the envelope with a grave expression before spiriting it away unopened. We all then entered one of the homestead's two small wattle-and-daub houses and squeezed into the small space just inside its doorway – *moongo*. Sitting on a low stool, MaShirima filled her spoon from the gourd and slowly poured the milk on the ground, next to a pillar behind the door, while addressing Lasway's deceased mother:[2]

> This milk, you female elder of the children (*msheku wa wana*), is that of placing by the *kisumbadini*, that which he brought that day, today he brought all of it, he brought this bucket and *mlali*, go cook *kena* and eat all of you ... give him power (*muiningie horu*); if he farms (*atcheme*), if he does something (*karunda kando*), let it enter his hands (*kaingiya maokoni*), you know it is indeed he who brings this ... if they arrive they shall bring again the beer for the male elders (*wameku*) ... congregate all of you (*mundesasa wose*), cook *kena*, congregate with your husband ... cook *kena*, today is the day of cooking *kena*, let us eat, *hai na hai*, receive this well, I request ... if they do something let it enter their hands, if they go to bed (*uli*) ... the place shall grow (*kufumbuke*), if they go to the cattle (*kwa umbe*) the place shall grow ... you know how to give them power and increase their ability so that he will come again ... and bring like he has brought ... give them power so that they shall go and he shall come again like he has, my mother ... congregate with the mother of your husband and the father of your husband and anyone else, congregate all of you ... it is indeed a child of ours that has brought this work here today ... your house shall give out smoke (*mba yaffo ubuke musu*) ... others shall come again like this ... let us grow here at the homestead (*dufumbuke kunu mrini*), let the place grow like this (*kufumbuke ado*) ... if another thing comes like this and another thing again ... and if god gives them the ability again (*mungu awekainingie se uwezo*) and if they come like this again ... you know how to toddle about (*umanya itongoria*) ... your homestead shall continue to have a fire burning (*mri waffo waswe motcho*), if you meet with illness, remove it (*kolya ni magonjwa haukefo*), you shall not have a fever again (*utawa se na homa*) ... you know to give them power, give us female elders power, you give them power.

MaShirima refilled her now empty spoon, while Lasway reminded her that she still had to address the married daughters of the homestead (*wana wa kaa*). MaShirima poured more milk to the left of the first, while addressing her husband's married sisters (*usi*). The skewing of generations in the Omaha kinship terminology means that these women address and are addressed by MaLasway as 'sisters' (*washiki*), even though the Swahili term *shangazi* is also gaining in prevalence:

This milk, you his [my husband's] married sisters (*usi akwa*), this milk ... your younger sister (*mwananu*) has brought it to her mother today ... you know how to share this milk ... her father's sisters (*shangazi*), receive this, if you share ... this milk ... you know your brother's daughter, today she brought this bucket ... I strongly request, she has already brought *mlali* ... receive her well, receive her well like you receive others (*mumambiliya usha shali mumambiliya wengi*) ... it is indeed she who brought this ... you know how to toddle about, do not bring fever here again (*mutahendefo kahoma ku*), you know to give her power, you know to give them power, and then another thing shall come again like this ... any other thing that comes here to the homestead shall go on the ground and be like this (*kengi kashe se ado na kengi kunu mṛini piu kuweenda siinde kuwe ado*), if it comes to this place it shall be like this ... all

Figure 2.1. Gathering inside the doorway to pour the milk on the ground.

your houses … you know how to toddle about, you know to give them power, you know to give them children, let us give them good health (*du-wainingie uzima*), if we work, let something enter our hands, they have already done so and have brought again to this homestead (*wamerunda shali wahende se kaa-kaa*) … I strongly request … cook *kena*, congregate all of you with your brothers and with everyone who comes, cook *kena*, and when they again bring beer for the male elders, things shall be like this again … you know how to toddle about, give them power so that when they get power again they come like this again (*muweiningia horu wakolye se horu washe se adi*) … let them bring some beer here … and let us just drink again with both his female and male intermediary (*mkara wakwe wa kifele na kisoro*).

When the address ended, MaShirima refilled the spoon and handed it to her first-born daughter MaLasway, on whose behalf the prestation was made, who drank its contents before she gave it back. MaShirima and Lasway discussed who should drink next, as the siblings who were born after MaLasway were not home. They decided that her two youngest siblings should drink, whom they called from the courtyard into the house, where they shared one spoonful. In contrast to other such occasions, the others who took part in the event were not invited to drink the milk. Instead, MaShirima placed the spoon upright with its head leaning against the wall and the tip of its handle on the ground between the two puddles of milk, next to the gourd contain-

Figure 2.2. The bride's mother pouring the milk, while the bride's father watches.

ing the milk. We then left the house and spent an hour chatting and drinking some banana beer that Herman and MaLasway had procured from a beer club we had passed on the way there.

At the start of her address, MaShirima said it was Herman who brought the milk and bananas, and requested that he in turn should be provided *horu*. As mentioned earlier, *horu* is a nebulous notion with which scholars of the area have struggled, just like researchers have with its cognates elsewhere in the region. Many of Gutmann's texts make mention of 'power' (*Kraft*) or 'life force' (*Lebenskraft*), but rarely provide the relevant vernacular term. However, Winter (1979: 141) relates that Gutmann struggled to conceptualize *oru* as 'life power', and that his assistant Ernst Jaeschke rendered it as 'health, well-being, success, and thriving'. Winter is dismissive of Gutmann's and Jaeschke's attempts to grasp and conceptualize this notion, but *horu* is used in line with both of them in present-day Rombo. There it is used to mean 'life force' or 'bodily power', which is constitutive of people's health, well-being and capacity. These phenomena are afforded in different ways, but most commonly through the consumption of foodstuffs and substances that contain *horu* to different extents and compound it through their combination and cooking. Milk is one substance that is high in *horu*, and may be added to other foodstuffs, like eleusine, meat, blood or bananas, to create various kinds of 'soft food' (*kelya kiholo*), including *kena* and *mbere* mentioned earlier. Through their consumption, these foods and substances increase the amount of blood (*samu*) and speed up its circulation, and raise the heat (*mrike*) of the body. They thereby capacitate the person, and render him or her active and vigorous, and thus capable of engaging in different kinds of activities.

MaShirima enunciated and anticipated the outcomes of this, as she first requested that Herman shall obtain results if he farms, but later included MaLasway and expanded the scope of the activities from which they should gain. After a general request that they shall obtain results regardless of what they do, MaShirima asked specifically that their homestead shall grow, if they go to bed and go to the cattle. In this way, she enunciated that both productive and reproductive relationships shall obtain between Herman and MaLasway as a result of this prestation. As she stated that the results of what they do shall enter their hands or arms (*maokoni*), she anticipated their engagement in banana farming, livestock stall-feeding, coffee cash-cropping and cultivation in the plains.[3] Accordingly, she alluded to *koombe* or the cattle pen, which in the old grass-house was located opposite the bed (*uli*) that she invoked to enunciate how sex and reproduction also should result from the prestation. As MaShirima mentioned or hinted at architectural features that previously were in close proximity, but that in current homesteads are often located in separate rooms if not different houses, she hence invoked a range of related practices that occur within the confines of the homestead.

MaShirima's statement thus concerned and enunciated the manner in which the prestation enables and effectuates the bride and groom's engagement in production and reproduction in the homestead they acquire and that comes into existence when she relocates. Moreover, it is then said of the groom that 'he has a hearth' (*nere riko*), which concerns and entails how the marital relationship also enables cooking and consumption. Through these activities, *horu* is combined, transformed and conveyed between persons to enable them to engage in productive activities, which bring forth further powerful substances and foodstuffs. Foremost among these are the banana farming and livestock stall-feeding that occur within the confines of the homestead, as well as the agricultural pursuits in the plains. Engagement in these activities also raises the heat (*mrike*) of the body, but in contrast to consumption it depletes the blood and diminishes the person's *horu*, which is converted and transferred to the crops and animals with which he or she works. This occurs by means of the arm or hand (*koko*), which turns leaves and stems into fodder that animal digestion converts to manure that the *koko* spreads to promote the provision of more fodder along with foodstuffs. These activities inosculate persons, livestock and crops, from which emerge the matter and substances that convey and contribute *horu* to persons and livestock. The resultant foodstuffs combine over the hearth, where the arm employs the long-handled ladle or spoon (*kilikiyo*) to prepare and serve foods that replace the *horu* people spend through production. As a result, the arm is a fulcrum that engages the world in multiple ways to channel life force in particular forms in certain directions to actualize beings of different kinds. Production and consumption thus intertwine through the concepts of *horu* and *koko*. As the next chapter will explore further, these concepts also encompass sex and reproduction, where *horu* converts and conveys in additional forms by means of other body parts. It is these imbricating activities through which *horu* is expended, transformed and transferred between humans, livestock and crops that constitute the concept of dwelling – *ikaa*.

Since the groom does not yet have a homestead, the milk and bananas that are presented are outcomes of banana farming and livestock stall-feeding in his father's homestead, as well as in the homesteads of their agnates, who are requested to contribute to such prestations. The prestation is thus the effect of particular productive relationships that body forth the *horu* of the groom and his agnates, from the arms and hands of whom the items originate and emerge. Furthermore, by presenting the milk and bananas, which are made into and consumed as *kena*, the groom acts upon relationships of consumption and nurture in the bride's father's homestead. The prestation channels the *horu* of these relationships in specific directions, as the milk is poured on the ground for the deceased and the remaining items are shared among the living, who MaShirima requested should all gather (*isasa*) to eat *kena*. The prestation thus deploys the effects of one set of preceding relationships within and beyond the groom's father's homestead to intervene in past and present relationships of another kind within and beyond the bride's father's homestead with the aim of affecting their future trajectories.

MaShirima's statement entails that it is upon the bride's relocation that the homestead becomes an entity and place of dwelling, which grows through its inhabitants' engagement in production, reproduction and consumption. Her claim that 'if they arrive they shall bring again' underscored how the incipient spouses are on their way to a place of dwelling that this prestation enables. The statement entails that the effects of dwelling from one homestead are deployed to intervene in dwelling in another one, in order to enable dwelling in a third. It moreover anticipated how Herman and MaLasway should return in the future with further prestations that result from their engagement in dwelling. Specifically, she requested that they shall return with beer, which is commonly the next prestation and was the one Herman initially hoped to make. Beer too is high in *horu*, and MaShirima assured her husband's mother that the prestations will ensure that her house has a burning hearth and will continue to give out smoke. MaShirima moreover requested of her husband's sisters that they who inhabit Lasway's homestead shall obtain results from their work, and grow as a result of this and of further prestations that others shall bring, presumably on behalf of MaLasway's younger sisters. Her statements thus entailed and enunciated that the bridewealth prestations not only constitute the marital homestead (*kaa*), but also ensure continued dwelling (*ikaa*) at the bride's parents' homestead. In this way, MaShirima articulated the recursive character of these proceedings, where prestations of *horu* enable practices and relationships through which life force converts and conveys to further dwelling. The same idea was captured and enunciated by MaShirima's request that Herman and MaLasway be provided *horu* to enable their homestead to grow, so they can return with further prestations.

The way in which the bridewealth prestations and marital relation-ship afford dwelling and the homestead is underscored by Dundas's (1924: 239–40) account of a ceremony that enabled the bride and the groom to share a house. The ceremony was called *mbaa*, which seems to be Dundas's rendition of the term for 'house' (*mba*), and took place after a protracted series of engagements and exchanges between the affines. The event involved the bride's utensils being brought to the marital house, where she was instructed in 'her household duties, especially in the matter of feeding her husband'. The following morn-ing, 'comes the father, bringing into the hut a cow, a female goat, a hoe and a slasher, which he gives to the couple, saying: "Receive this 'fat', as was given to me by my father". Finally he bestows his blessing on the young couple and allots them a portion of his banana grove'. In other words, the house with all its contents, as well as the banana gar-den and its requisite tools, were bestowed and acquired in this event and as part of the bridewealth prestations. The marital proceedings brought the homestead into existence as a place and entity of dwell-ing, where the bride and groom were enabled to engage in production, reproduction and consumption by means of the land, livestock and tools they received, along with the instructions they were imparted. In this way, they were enabled to engage in banana farming and live-stock stall-feeding, and capacitated to channel *horu* by means of their arms and gain results from their hands. Unfortunately, Dundas does not provide the vernacular term, but I suspect that 'fat' is either a mistranslation or poetic rendition of *horu* and an identification of life force with one of the forms it assumes and substances in which it ob-tains. If so, he would not be the first, as Johnston (1886: 525) trans-lated *uro* as 'semen', the significance of which will be considered in connection with sex and reproduction in the next chapter. If this is right, the vernacular statement Dundas rendered underscores how livestock and crops are *horu* in different forms that are transformed and transferred through their engagement in dwelling.

Since the groom already engages in production and consumption at his father's homestead, but depends on bridewealth to claim chil-dren that result from his sexual engagements, the onus is to enable reproduction. As such, the groom deploys the effects of productive relationships from one homestead, to act upon relationships of con-sumption in a second, to enable reproductive relationships in a third. It is the convergence of these activities through which *horu* trans-forms and transfers that constitutes the process of *ikaa*. The prestation thus summons dwelling and summates its different activities in a sin-gular event, yet simultaneously distinguishes these to enable one relationship to act upon another for the purpose of constituting a third. The event acts as a hinge that deploys a relationship between agnates to transform the relationship between a woman and her relatives into a relationship between spouses. It is the transformational character of *horu*, and the confluence of the practices that constitute dwelling, that make each relationship a metamorphosis of another (cf. Strathern 1988: 313). The presented life force is the effect of one relationship that transforms another relationship where *horu* circulates in other forms, into a further relationship where bodily power conveys in additional forms. In the process, a 'daughter' (*mwana wa kaa*) is transformed into a 'bride' (*mwali*), while a 'son' (*mwana wa homii*) becomes a 'husband' (*mii*) and eventually a 'man' (*msoro*). As the prestation enables their dwelling, its metamorphosis of their subject positions entails a transformation of their dispositions to act, which hence allow novel engagements with newfound effects.

The transformation was enunciated by MaShirima, as her address first pertained to Herman and MaLasway as singular persons, but later concerned a 'they' and a 'them', who are enabled to engage in dwelling. She thus enunciated how the prestation transformed Herman and MaLasway through a specific relationship, which enabled them to engage in specific productive, reproductive and consumptive activities with livestock, children and beer as their particular effects. These conceptual changes entwined with the pouring of the milk, in a performative recognition of how *horu* converts and conveys to transform relationships and enable activities, where life force transfers. It was precisely the transformational and processual character of these prestations that compelled Herman to make this prestation, rather than skipping it in favour of the next, as he initially planned. Doing so would have jeopardized the desired effect of turning MaLasway into his bride and a person of a specific kind. Because a reproductive relationship already obtained between them, he could moreover not present actual milk and bananas since this would divert *horu* from their homestead to affect their children. The character of their existing relationship instead required a modification of the prestation to achieve its desired effect without undue consequences.

Mkara: The Person Who Enables Dwelling and the Homestead

A consideration of the concept and position of *mkara* deepens how the bridewealth prestations bring the homestead into existence and create subjects who are enabled for dwelling. The *mkara* is the intermediary who makes the prestations on behalf of the groom and subsequently plays a central role for the couple, whose marital relationship he or she occasions. The *mkara* for instance serves as a mentor to the couple and acts as a mediator in case of conflict or strife between the spouses. As MaShirima's invocation reveals, there are in fact two *wakara*, one female (*mkara wa kifele*) and one male (*mkara wa kisoro*), who ordinarily are the groom's eldest sister and her husband. In connection with Herman's prestation, the question regarding *wakara* was less straightforward and occasioned some discussion between Herman and Lasway. The reason was that Herman's eldest sister is an evangelical Christian who disdains and wants no involvement in such matters. She is moreover widowed and could therefore not provide a *mkara wa kisoro*. Herman's eldest brother was ruled out as an unreliable drunk, and neither Herman nor Lasway had confidence in his wife. Eventually, it was decided that my wife and I should serve as Herman's intermediaries, and it was impressed upon us that this entailed an extended commitment since subsequent prestations could not take place without our participation.

Dundas (1924: 232) confirms the tasks of the intermediaries and that these are performed by the groom's sister and her husband. However, he claimed that the notion of *mkara* was restricted to eastern Kilimanjaro, while *mwisi* was the term used in the west. In any case, *mkara* is a noun that derives from the causative form of to dwell (*ikara*), so the notion literally means 'the person who enables or occasions dwelling'. Since the homestead also derives its term from *ikaa*, *mkara* also means 'the person who enables or occasions the homestead'. As the female *mkara* ordinarily is the groom's eldest married sister, while her husband acts as the male intermediary, it is these two who enable a man's marital relationship, as well as the homestead and the dwelling that it affords.[4] In relation to the polygynous house-property complex, this meant that the groom's sister and her husband played a facilitating role for the groom's mother's bestowal of her homestead to her son's wife upon their marriage. Despite Gutmann's emphasis on the agnatic *Sippe*, which has inflected subsequent understandings of kinship relationality, settlement patterns and inheritance practices, it was women and the multifarious relationships occasioned by marriage that were salient in connection with the house-property complex and the dwelling that occurs in the homestead. The enabling role the sister plays for her brother's marriage, homestead and ensuing dwelling gives sense to Lasway stressing that MaShirima should address and pour milk for his married sisters. Most likely, one of these sisters served as his female *mkara* who enabled their marital relationship and dwelling in the homestead where the milk was poured. This sister afforded the relationship and activities that resulted in the birth of MaLasway, whose marital relationship occasioned the milk to be poured. The milk was thus an effect of multiple relationships and activities that the sister made possible for Lasway and MaShirima, who in turn poured milk that results from these activities on the ground to ensure continued dwelling at their homestead.

A related concept is the verb *ikariya*, which is used in the sense 'to be brave' or 'to be strong or powerful'. In the latter sense, it is used interchangeably with, or as a synonym for, 'to have life force' (*ikeri na horu*).[5] For instance, if someone has exerted him- or herself, it is not uncommon that another person will respond by saying *wakariya*, which may be followed by the assertion *ure horu lhoy* ('you truly have life force'). *Ikariya* moreover is a causative-prepositional form of *ikaa*, so its literal meaning is 'to be enabled for dwelling'. People's emphasis that *ikariya* means to have *horu* thus underscores the connection between life force and dwelling. *Ikariya* is furthermore used to mean 'to be mature', but is in this sense mainly used about crops, for instance when people say *iruuli likariya* about a bunch of bananas that is mature.[6] In this way, *ikariya* accentuates how crops are *horu* in certain forms that enable and capacitate people for dwelling through their consumption. However, *ikariya* can also be used about a person who has gone through a developmental process and in this way matured. The connection between *mkara* and *ikariya* reveals how the intermediary facilitates one such process, where the bridewealth prestations serve to mature the marital couple as they enable them for dwelling. In line with this, the term also has an adjectival use *-ikari* that designates hardness, strength, solidity or stability.[7] In combination, these linguistic forms and usages that derive from *ikaa* entail and concern how a person who is enabled for dwelling is someone who is brimming with life force and is mature as the result of a process that has made him or her hard, strong, solid and stable.

Marriage as Detachment and Attachment

At the beginning of her address, MaShirima said it was Herman who made the prestation, but she later asserted that it was 'a child of ours that has brought this work here today'. Her claim entailed that it is the bride's presence in, and relationship to, her parents' homestead that attracts the groom and the prestation the *mkara* makes on his behalf. As such, her statement opens for consideration how these prestations take place between homesteads or houses, rather than between persons or groups. More specifically, her claim affords a view of how bridewealth and marriage are conceptualized as elicitations by one house or homestead from another, to which persons attach and detach as a result.

When the prospective spouses do not already cohabit, people say that the milk and bananas are brought to the bride's father's homestead by the groom's female *mkara* who carries them there on her head.[8] However, they say that she does not enter the bride's father's homestead in the usual way, by calling out *hodi* to make her presence known, but slips surreptitiously in without speaking to any of its inhabitants. Moreover, she does not hand the objects over to anyone, but leaves them by the hearth, which is located immediately inside the doorway of one of the houses.[9] In the old grass-house, the milk was left between the hearth and the bed, in the area called *mbaariko* that literally means 'inside or behind the hearth' and was where gourds were kept for curdling milk. The bananas, meanwhile, were placed on the other side of the hearth towards the *koombe* area. In the current homestead, where the living space is usually separated from the cooking and livestock areas, people stress that the objects should be left by the hearth, in the area that is still called *mbaariko*, in the building that houses the livestock and has an attic. At Lasway's homestead, we enacted aspects of this as we gathered inside the doorway, where MaShirima poured the milk, which she called 'that of placing by the *kisumbadini*' – the broad plank of wood inside the doorway of the grass-house, at the far side of which the *mbaariko* was located.

The manner in which the *mkara* sneaks in to leave the milk and bananas by the hearth entails that the prestation is made to the homestead or the house, rather than to one or more persons. Its term contains this fact, as *marua ya iwikiya sumbay* also means 'the milk to place on the ground', which concerns how it is left inside the house rather than given to someone. The silent and unseen manner of presentation makes the objects prevalent for this event and the relationships it entails and activates. The absence of the donor and the silence of the intermediary mean that the bride's family, at this stage, can only engage and relate to the items placed inside their house.

The objects remain by the hearth until the following day, when the milk reveals the character of the proposed relationship. If it rises to overflow from the bucket and spill on the ground, people say that 'the milk shows the pathway' (*marua yalhoria mko*). Such spilling is one sense of 'the milk to pour on the ground', and is the basis on which the bride's relatives accept the prestation. They then proceed to pour some on the ground, in a further sense of *marua ya iwikiya sumbay* that precedes the sharing of the foodstuffs among the bride's paternal relatives. In the grass-house, the milk was poured in the area called *kiraoni* that was located next to the hearth, on the side towards the *kisumbadini*. Similarly, Gutmann (1909c: 83) described how women poured a mixture of milk and eleusine flour at 'the hearth post', and Dundas (1924: 179) related that beer, milk and honey were poured close to the supports inside the house.[10] In the homestead where I lived, milk was poured at the foot of an attic post to the left-hand side just inside the doorway, which MaSway rested her back against when she cooked. At Lasway's homestead, meanwhile, MaShirima poured the milk at the foot of a wall-board stretching from ground to ceiling behind the door of their wattle-and-daub house. Both cases are approximations of the *kiraoni* that no longer exist in today's houses.

The *mkara*'s mode of presentation entails that one homestead or house extracts and attracts *horu* from another one, in a process where certain features of the house and the homestead play enabling roles. To make the prestation, the *mkara* leaves the groom's father's homestead and proceeds along the pathways (*shia* or *mko*) that criss-cross the mountainside. She enters the bride's father's homestead via the *mengele* pathway that ends in its *sha* courtyard, where she passes through the doorway or *moongo* to leave the objects by the hearth, before she departs the same way. Since the marital relationship is an effect of this prestation, the pathways and doorways are its preconditions. The doorways and pathways connect the homesteads, whose dense vegetation makes it impossible to see from one to the next, despite their contiguity. These architectural and spatial features open each homestead beyond its confines to allow the intermediary to enter and engage the house without interacting with its inhabitants. The doorways and pathways thus make the homesteads pervious phenomena with a capacity to elicit life force from each other with the aim of transforming their relationships of dwelling. The presented *horu* thus originates from the groom's father's homestead from where it is called forth on the basis of the bride's presence in, and relationship to, her father's homestead. The prestation is subsequently divided and distributed to other homesteads with the result that *horu* fans out from the bride's father's house along the pathways that traverse the mountainside to pass through additional doorways. It recalls Ruel's (1997: 120) account of how the doorway and gateway are passages for life (*omohoro*) that make houses and homesteads conduits for capacity, health and well-being. Indeed, in Rombo this extends beyond the homestead, as the cognate *horu* moves through the doorway and the surrounding landscape along and by means of its pathways.

The way in which the effects of certain relationships emerge through one doorway and enter another where they transform further relationships sheds new light on the house-property complex, and reveals how marriage is a process of detachment and attachment or displacement and emplacement. In line with Gluckman's notion, Dundas (1924: 305) described how property was inherited within the house, according to the relative seniority of sons, in a process where the doorway played a central role: 'Thus the hut, or "door" as the natives express it, is the determining factor in the distribution of inheritance'. His statement pertained to the previous polygynous pattern, where the homestead contained several houses that each were inhabited by one wife, her children and their livestock. However, Dundas (1924: 306) revealed that more than inheritance was at stake, when he claimed that: 'With the wife, or "door", go also the banana groves attaching to each hut and the women and children'. His claim entails that the door was more than a means by which property was distributed; it means that it was the door – rather than the wife – that owned the banana garden. Indeed, Dundas even stated that the women and children 'go with the door', which suggests that the wife and her offspring also belonged to the door, rather than that the door belonged to them.

The idea that people belong to the door recalls Claude Levi-Strauss's ([1984] 1987: 152) concept of 'house societies', where buildings are moral persons. Moreover, Levi-Strauss's ([1979] 1982: 173) claim that 'it is not individuals or families that act, it is houses' illuminates both Dundas's statement and the initial prestation. As argued above, it is the bride's presence in the house that attracts the prestation through the doorway, where the *mkara* places the presented objects in relation to the hearth, the bed, the livestock area and the attic. The milk and the bananas embody the *horu* of the groom and his agnates, who become attached to significant features of the bride's parents' homestead when the objects are left inside the house. In turn, this prestation affords the bride's eventual relocation to the marital homestead and hence her detachment from her natal homestead. The prestation that the bride's parents' house attracts thus enables the groom to attach himself and eventually detach and extract the bride from the same house through its doorway. Gutmann's (1926: 147) claim that elopement of the kind MaLasway performed was termed 'bringing oneself to the husband' suggests precisely that it is the bridewealth prestation that ordinarily transfers the bride to the groom. The idea of attachment and detachment is spelled out by Gutmann's

(1926: 217) account of how the bride's relocation could involve a mock robbery, where a feigned fight between the groom's agnates and her brothers resulted in parts of the house being destroyed.[11] The bride's attachment to the doorway meant that its elicitation of powerful foodstuffs allowed her detachment from it, but this involved or even required partial destruction of the house.

Currently, the bride relocates to the house that the groom built on land he received from his father, who most commonly divides this

Figure 2.3. The doorway of the grass-house.

from his own homestead. In the past, however, the groom's mother
bestowed her house to her son upon his marriage, while she relocated
to a new house with her remaining children. The effect of this practice was that the bride relocated to her husband's mother's house
from where the bridewealth presented on her behalf emerged. The
settlement pattern and inheritance practice thus actualized and highlighted how the prestations occur between houses or homesteads,
which attract powerful foodstuffs through their doorways due to the
presence and attachment of marriageable women, who in turn detach and relocate as effects of these prestations.

The process of detachment is further effectuated by the prestation
of 'the goat of the child's mother' (*mburu ya mae wa mwana*), which
the husband makes to his bride's mother sometime after she has borne
children at their marital homestead. The prestation is a *mooma* or a
female goat that has borne at least one kid, which is not slaughtered
but kept at the bride's parents' homestead, where it bears further kids.
The first of these is the claim of the bride on whose behalf the goat was
presented. She is at liberty to take the kid to her marital homestead,
but most commonly she leaves it with her parents, where her husband
may not access it.[12] Women say that this goat is a woman's security,
in case she is chased away by her husband. Alternatively, she may use
the kid or one of its eventual offspring for the reconciliation event that
is required if a physical fight where blood is drawn should occur between her and her husband.[13] Men meanwhile stress the importance
of presenting this goat as soon as possible after the bride relocates and
bears a child, since this makes it less attractive for her to return to her
parents' homestead in the case of a quarrel. The reason is that she may
no longer sleep in a bed in her parents' house once this goat has been
presented. Instead, she sleeps on a hide on the floor in the *mbaariko*
area, and thus manifests her gradual detachment from this house
and her attachment to another. Her transformation from daughter to
bride bars her from using one bed, while it enables her to occupy another.[14] However, her detachment from her natal homestead is neither
complete nor final, as she retains the claim to a kid from her mother's
goat, along with the opportunity to keep it at her parents' homestead.
She may also still sleep there, albeit on the ground.[15] In combination,
these considerations reveal how the process of marrying involves a
woman detaching from her natal homestead to attach to her marital
one, between which her existence consequently entangles.[16]

In the past, the bride detached from her mother's homestead and
relocated to her marital homestead, from which her husband's mother
simultaneously detached to establish another homestead, most com-

monly located above (*fondoho*) the one she bestowed on her son and his bride. When the mother repeated this process for subsequent sons, she became entangled with multiple marital homesteads, as well as her natal one. With advancing age, a woman thus became extended between a multiplicity of homesteads to which she detached and attached throughout her life and at various points in her reproductive career. In a similar way, her husband circulated between all of these homesteads and those of his other wives, where he also engaged in dwelling. Some results from this dwelling were moreover transferred as bridewealth to the natal homesteads of these wives to which he hence also attached and entangled. The existence of both men and women hence intertwined with multiple homesteads, whose numbers increased along with their age and successful dwelling. Men and women detached and attached to these homesteads in different ways and at different times, and in the process became extended across an expanded area. It is between these homesteads and across this area that the elders 'toddle about' (*itongoria*), in the way MaShirima enunciated in her address. The subject positions of male elder (*meku*) and female elder (*msheku*) hence involve a disposition to amble between multiple homesteads that traverse and connect across the mountainside through pathways and doorways. Persons still detach and attach to several homesteads, but these are fewer today than they were in the days of the house-property complex.

The way people progressively become suspended between multiple homesteads that extend over an area is central to the concept of *ialika,* which means 'to marry'. *Ialika* is the stative form of *iala*, which means 'to spread out', 'to extend' and 'to unfold'. *Iala* is for instance used for the act of spreading a hide on the ground or putting a sheet on a bed. 'To marry' then means 'to be in an extended state' or 'to be in a state of unfolding', which captures how people's existence becomes suspended between different homesteads through processes of detachment and attachment that extend across an expansive area.[17] The bridewealth prestations involve a set of actions integral to the processes of detachment and attachment, but their import is to enable a state or a disposition to act in certain ways that the stative verb-form entails (cf. Hanfling 2000: 69). 'Marrying' thus creates particular persons with dispositions to engage in certain activities with specific objects in distinct ways that combine to form the concept of dwelling. As such, the bridewealth prestations involve a process that enables people to dwell and matures them as persons of a specific kind, as entailed by the conceptual connections between *ikara* and *ikariya*. To be brave and powerful or forceful is to have a disposition to act in certain ways that extend or unfold the person through time and across space. The facilitating role of the *mkara* means that it is the groom's sister and her husband that enable the unfolding or extension of a man and his bride. The conceptual links between *mkara, ikaa* and *kaa* entail then that dwelling is a process of unfolding, which occurs in a place that extends across the land, as a woman relocates to establish new homesteads upon the marriages of her sons. The homestead is therefore not a place, but a set of locations that proliferate and expand through space and time, in accordance with people's successful engagement in dwelling. It is between these effects and manifestations of their unfolding or extensions that the elders toddle about (*itongoria*), as MaShirima enunciated in her address.

After relocation, the bride engages in dwelling in her marital homestead, which currently comes into existence as a new place and entity upon her marriage. In the past, however, she upheld and extended dwelling in her husband's mother's homestead, at the same time as the bridewealth prestations contributed to dwelling in her mother's homestead. Dundas claimed that the results of her engagement in dwelling – like her children, livestock and the banana garden – attached to the doorway of her house, which presumably grew as a result, in the way MaShirima stated. The fact that the effects of her dwelling attach to the doorway suggests that her engagement in dwelling also attaches her to the house. The claim gains support from the statement 'he or she gave birth on the pathway' (*neleatcha shia*), which is used about both men and women who conceive children out of wedlock. The frequently heard phrase not only enunciates how reproduction pertains to and concerns the homestead and the house; its use regarding married men and women who conceive children with someone other than their spouse articulates how bridewealth, reproduction and the house conjoin as phenomena and processes. The pathways enable the bridewealth prestations, but the house is the locus of reproduction, which attaches those involved to its doorway and emplaces them in the homestead.

The Left-Hand Side as the Side of Life

These considerations give sense to Gutmann's (1966: 50) claim that people distinguish and designate the person's right-hand side as paternal and the left-hand side as maternal, which conjoin to constitute the person. In his view, the connection between the left and maternal origin was evidenced in the saying that 'life comes from the left-hand side'—*moo ni ora lo kumoso fucheye* (Gutmann 1966: 50). I have never encountered such a saying, but his claim gains support from Dundas (1924: 129), who argued: 'The ancestry is further divided into two sets commonly called those of the right and those of the left. Those of the right hand are: father, brother, mother, sister and their ascendants. Those of the left are: mother's father, mother's brother, mother's nephew and their ascendants'. Similarly, Raum (1911: 177ff) claimed that the 'spirits' (*Geister*) were divided between those of the right-hand side and the left-hand side, which respectively were the paternal and maternal relatives from which a person descended. Accordingly, a person's maternal relatives are addressed as 'those of the left-hand side' (*wa kumoosoni*) in today's ancestral invocations in Rombo, where a man moreover owes his mother's brother a particular piece of meat that is cut from the left-hand side of every animal he butchers. Called *uvaha*, this share is one of only two pieces that are cut from one side of the butchered animal – the other being the *ngari*, which often includes the right foreleg as the claim of the classificatory agnates. While all other shares of meat span both sides of the animal, the *uvaha* and *ngari* manifest how one's paternal and maternal relatives are those of the right- and the left-hand side. These distinctions furthermore enjoy a wider regional distribution, as others also describe that maternal relatives or the female side are linked with the left or left-hand side (Beidelman 1961: 252; de Boeck 1994b: 462; Devisch 1988: 265; Needham 1960: 25; 1967: 429; Rigby 1966: 3).

Even if the idea that life comes from the left-hand side no longer appears as a statement, it does emerge from an explication of the notion of 'left' or 'left-hand side'. Given by Gutmann as *kumoso*, it is in Rombo termed *kumoosoni*, which deploys both the locative prefix *ku-* and suffix *-ni* to frame, contain and inflect the concept of *moo* that Peter used in his invocation to Horombo and that translates as 'life'. As mentioned before, such constructions are common in Bantu languages, where prefixes, infixes or suffixes expand or extend a root-form to create new yet related concepts and meaning. In this case, it makes *kumoosoni* a compound concept that literally renders the left-hand side as 'the place of life' or 'the place from which life emanates'.

The idea that maternal relatives are 'of the place of life' concerns the enabling role they play in reproduction. The ability to create new life namely resides in and is extracted from the bride's natal homestead, on the basis of prestations of foodstuffs high in *horu* that originate in the homestead of the groom's father and their agnates. In the past, when a mother relocated for each son's marriage, the effect was a line of agnatic homesteads extending up the mountainside. Affinal relationships consequently entered and extended from the side, along the pathways and through the doorways that still connect and open houses and homesteads beyond their confines. It persists today, as the first-born son or 'child in front' (*mwana wa mbele*) receives land 'below the homestead' (*siinde ya kaa*) of the father's homestead, where his youngest brother will remain. As affinal relationships enter and emerge as life force in various forms that move along pathways and through doorways, they constitute and articulate on a horizontal plane of lines and openings. This contrasts with the agnatic relationships, where houses and homesteads emerge and exist vertically in terms of 'below' (*siinde*) or 'in front' (*mbele*) and 'above' (*fondoho*) or 'behind' (*mma*).

It is significant that the 'right' or 'right-hand side' is *kulo* in present-day Rombo, and related as *kuljo* or *kulyo* by Gutmann (1926: 275) and Walther (1900: 40). The Chagga counterpart to *kumoosoni* thus appears a cognate of the Swahili *kulia* that construes 'right' as 'for eating', and that a leading dictionary links etymologically to the prevalent practice of eating with the right hand or 'the hand for eating' (*mkono wa kulia*) (Johnson 1939; see also Rigby 1966: 3). 'To eat' is *ilya* in Rombo, where *ku-* is not an infinitive marker like in Swahili, but a locative prefix that renders 'right' or 'right-hand' as 'the place for eating'. *Kulo* as the counterpart to *kumoosoni* hence concerns how bridewealth prestations in the form of powerful foodstuffs and substances transfer from 'the place for eating' to 'the place of life'. As these foodstuffs move counter to a marriageable woman, the wife-takers enable the wife-givers to eat, and thus extend dwelling and life at their homestead, while the wife-givers enable the wife-takers to reproduce, and thus afford dwelling and life at the marital homestead. In combination, the conceptual pair concerns and enunciates how affinal relationships exist and articulate on a horizontal plane, where women and foodstuffs move counter to each other along pathways and through the doorways of houses and homesteads. *Kumoosoni* and *kulo* thus do not concern paternal and maternal descent as Gutmann argued, but the places between which women and powerful foodstuffs transfer and circulate. They moreover do not pertain to 'sets' of persons who trace lineal descent as Dundas claimed, but locations in a topography where *horu* moves to enable and extend dwelling and life. Raum (1911: 177, 181) indeed touched on place and location when he argued that 'spirits of the right-hand side one designates those *from where* the person originates, namely *from where* one's father and grandfather come', while 'spirits of the left-hand side one designates those *from where* the mother descends'. Like his contemporaries, Raum nevertheless failed to escape the idea of descent and to see that the issue concerns how affinity articulates as horizontal relationships, where *horu* transfers between homesteads to enable reproduction that manifests as vertical lines of agnatic homesteads.

Mri and *Mṛi*: Extensions and Entanglements in One Place

The transfers that occur between homesteads are predicated on the fact that houses and landscapes belong to a topology through which *horu* moves in different forms to attach and detach as beings of different kinds. Regarding persons, livestock and crops, this is indicated by the different meanings of the term *mri* that is used to mean both the veins of persons or animals, and the roots of trees and crops. The fibrous tendril-like roots that extend from the corm of the banana tree in fact resemble the veins that bulge along the arms and legs of people, and curl along the udders and bellies of cows and goats. The link between veins and roots is moreover underscored, as the abundant sap of the banana tree is known as water or *mringa*, but on occasion is also called its blood – *samu*. Indeed, *mri* appears to be the root of the concept of *mrike*, which thus renders the idea of bodily heat as being in a state of circulation.[18] The uses of *mri* to mean both veins and roots deepen the sense of how production conveys and converts *horu*, as they entail that engagement in the intertwined practices of banana farming and livestock stall-feeding links the veins of the homestead's human inhabitants with the roots of crops and the veins of livestock, along and through which life force transfers in different forms. Through their engagement in these practices, persons hence expend and channel *horu* by means of their arms to inosculate their veins with the roots of crops and trees. These extend to involve the livestock, as the *koko* cuts leaves and stems as fodder and spreads manure to ensure growth of fodder and crops that in turn provide powerful foodstuffs and substances that convey *horu* to persons. Humans, livestock and crops thus interlink through their *mri*, which extend both into and out of the ground to attach them to the homestead. Engagement in dwelling hence extends and entangles *mri*, which convey and transmute *horu* to emplace persons, livestock, crops and foodstuffs. The idea is supported by the term *mṛi*, which means 'town' or 'city' like its Swahili cognate *mji*, but is primarily used to mean the homestead, as both Peter and MaShirima used it in their addresses. The resemblance and conceptual connection between *mṛi* and *mri* suggests that the homestead is a circuitry of vein-roots that transfer and transform *horu* to attach persons, animals and crops both to the homestead and to each other, through their engagement in dwelling.

The uses of *mri* and *mṛi* moreover mean that when the husband's mother in the past relocated to an adjacent homestead with her remaining children for the sake of her first-born son and his bride, she extended the reach of her veins and expanded the area through which her *horu* moved. When she repeated this for subsequent sons, she became with increasing age extended between multiple homesteads (*mṛi*) between and through which her veins (*mri*) extended and her *horu* conveyed. Her husband, meanwhile, extended his veins even further through his involvement in dwelling in the proliferating homesteads occupied by his other wives and their children, and his ongoing bridewealth prestations on their behalf. Through life, both men and women extended the area in which their veins were sunk and through which their *horu* transferred. This lends further sense to the notion of *ialika* and the way in which people are in an extended state or a state of unfolding through processes of detachment and attachment that expand the area through which their veins extend and their *horu* transfers. As the banana tree attaches in one place through the extension of its tendril-like roots, so persons adhere and emplace through the extension of their veins over a large area of several homesteads. It is important to grasp that the claim is more than an analogy, as the concept of *mri* entails that these roots and veins interlock, while the notion of *horu* involves that persons and crops are life force in different forms that the root-veins transform and transmute. Accordingly, Gutmann (1924a: 129) argued that the banana tree literally attaches persons to the ground and therefore is venerated as the protector and connector between generations.[19]

The idea of the house as a permeable entity to which persons and things attach and detach through their engagements in dwelling is finally supported by the terminology for kinship and marriage, where 'daughter' literally means 'child of the homestead' (*mwana wa kaa*), and people talk about marital relationships in terms of which house a woman comes out of (*ifuma*) and which she goes into (*iingia*). There is no Chagga noun for 'marriage', only a vocabulary concerning how persons extend as women move out of and into houses counter to prestations of powerful foodstuffs. Gutmann's (1926: 77) translation of *mka* as 'wife', along with Dundas's (1924: 233) and Winter's (1977: 37ff) renditions of *mamka* as 'mother' and 'wife's mother', reveal how these kinship terms and subject positions derive from the notion of 'homestead' – *kaa*. Gutmann (1926: 174) argued that *mka* meant 'the woman attached to a place', which derived from the ramified stem-form *kala* or *kara* that he claimed meant 'remaining or staying behind'.[20] Neither *kala* nor *kara* is a stem, but causative verb-forms derived from *ikaa*. Nevertheless, the point remains that *mka* can be glossed as 'person of the homestead', while *mamka* can be rendered as 'mother of the homestead' or 'mother of the person of the homestead'.[21] Both terms indicate how the married woman attaches to and is emplaced in the homestead through her engagement in dwelling. Meanwhile, the conflicting translations of *mamka* grasp both how the mother detached to bestow her homestead to her son and his wife, and thus became the mother of their homestead, as well as how the wife's mother enables the homestead through her daughter's marriage.

As the feature of the house to which persons and things attach, and the opening through which they detach, the doorway plays an enabling role in these processes and relationships. The house is therefore not a passive container, but an active presence that attracts and extracts persons and things through its doorway. MaShirima enunciated its subjecthood with the locative prefix *ku-* in her request that the homestead should grow – *kufumbuke*. Gutmann (1926: 85) corroborates that the form *ku* means 'defined by location', which he moreover claimed was the root for the terms for 'bridewealth', *ngosa* and *wuko*. In Rombo, *ngosa* does not mean bridewealth in general, but concerns one particular prestation that finalizes the transfers. Gutmann's claim nevertheless entails and supports that bridewealth involves actions and processes of detachment and attachment, where persons become in a state of extension or unfolding with dispositions to act in certain ways. It follows that subject positions are constituted through attachments to and detachments from houses, which render persons defined by the doorway they belong to and the homestead in which they are emplaced.[22] As Dundas pointed out, persons are therefore not in possession of houses, but are beings who are determined by the houses between which they extend and to which they attach.

Bridewealth as a Process of Determination

Elders say that sometime after the initial prestation, the groom should send a leg of meat from a head of cattle to the bride's father, who shares the meat with his agnates. The prestation is called 'the leg that speaks or tells' (*kitchende kiamba*) and is described as the event that brings the *mkara* into direct contact with the bride's parents for the first time and that reveals the groom's identity. The prestation is also a means for reclaiming the bucket in which 'the milk to place or pour on the ground' was sent, which the bride's parents only return in exchange for another prestation. People claim that this stems from earlier times, when milk was presented in more precious gourds and cooking pots, rather than in today's plastic buckets. Regardless, these accounts hint at a central dynamic to the bridewealth prestations, namely the way in which the extractions and attractions of powerful foodstuffs between houses and homesteads gradually bring persons into contact and dialogue, where language is used to determine the situation and the relationships involved. As 'the leg that speaks or tells' suggests, it opens for consideration the ways in which language is an effect of the transfers of *horu,* which involves a double dynamic that enables people to manipulate life force in different forms to produce statements of certain kinds, as well as use language to conjure *horu* in particular forms.

The dynamic emerges clearly from the prestation called 'the beer to speak or tell' (*wari wa iamba*) or 'the beer to ask them if they love each other' (*wari wa uwewesa wakundana*). Many describe this as the prestation that follows 'the milk to pour or place on the ground', which accords with MaShirima's request that Herman and MaLasway should return with beer in the future. *Wari wa iamba* was moreover the prestation Herman initially hoped and intended to make, on the assumption that the milk he presented on the day of their church wedding sufficed as 'going to ask'. Others, however, argue that 'the beer to speak or tell' is a recent introduction that is necessitated by an increase in men's abduction of brides, and women's escalating tendencies to do like MaLasway and move in with their boyfriends without telling their parents. The purpose, they profess, is to inform the woman's parents of her whereabouts and of the couple's intentions to marry. There is no evidence to support this being a recent introduction, but on the occasions I took part in this prestation, the bride and the groom did already live together and they arrived jointly at her natal homestead. On the other hand, Gutmann's (1926: 106) description of a prestation called 'the beer of the mutual questioning', along with older references to bride capture, suggest that this may have a greater longevity than people acknowledge.

One day in 2001, Boniface invited me to take part in a *wari wa iamba* prestation that was to take place on behalf of one his daughters.[23] When I arrived at his homestead in the afternoon of the day in question, it became clear that he had invited most – if not all – of his agnates and their wives, along with other neighbours, friends and in-laws. Boniface had moreover ensured that we were in place before the groom and the bride arrived from Arusha, where they lived and had salaried employment. Awaiting their arrival, we took our seats on wooden benches in the manner common during large social events, where the men are placed along the perimeter of the *sha* courtyard and the women seated in the *kaandeni* area behind the house.

After some time, the bride and groom arrived in a hired mini-bus, accompanied by twenty-odd followers, who in addition to the groom's parents mainly consisted of his agnates. However, the group neither entered Boniface's homestead nor did they make their presence known by calling *hodi*. Instead, they stood silently at the opening of the *mengele* pathway that leads into Boniface's homestead. When their presence was noticed, Boniface and some of his elder agnates went to receive them, while some younger agnates relieved the guests of the three barrels of beer they had brought. The barrels were carried to the *sha* courtyard, where Boniface led his guests, who shook hands with and were greeted by his agnates, opposite whom they were given prominent seats. The bride and groom joined his parents and agnates, and an anticipatory silence fell on the crowd once everyone was seated. Boniface then rose and welcomed everyone before he explained why we were gathered at his homestead. While he spoke, Boniface's agnates sat quietly and appeared ignorant of the occasion, but nodded in recognition and muttered in agreement as he spoke. At the end of his speech, Boniface asked the groom's father to present the couple, who were called to rise and face the gathering, standing between their fathers. Boniface first asked his daughter if she loved the groom and wished to marry him. When she answered affirmatively, the groom's father asked his son if he loved the bride and wished to marry her. When he too gave his affirmation, the groom was instructed to give his right hand to the bride.

Next, the groom's father picked up a drinking gourd (*shori*) from a pile on the ground and drew beer from one of the barrels they had brought. He took a sip from the gourd and presented the *shori* to Boniface, who also tasted the beer. The groom's father then drew and tasted a second gourd, which he presented to Boniface's wife, who also took a sip. The groom's father sat down before Boniface rose and drew two gourds, which he served first to the groom's father and then to the groom's mother. Once Boniface sat down, the groom and the bride simultaneously presented their respective parents-in-law with one additional gourd, so that both his and her parents had received two gourds each. In each case, the gourds were handed over and received in the same manner, with the person presenting the gourd tasting the beer before giving it to the recipient, who in turn took a taste from the *shori* even if it was placed on the ground to be consumed later. When both the bride's and the groom's parents had received two gourds each, one of the groom's brothers presented the bride and the groom with one *shori* each. He was then helped by two others from their entourage in serving one gourd to every person in the crowd, ensuring that the bride's father's agnates were served before those of the groom's father. When everyone had been served beer, the formalities were over and the participants drank and chatted in no distinction to any other social event. Boniface, his wife and some of his elder agnates entertained and got to know the groom's parents and his elders. Although they had never met before, they now engaged in the free and easy manner that characterizes the emphasized and valorized relationship between *watoi* – persons whose children have married. A cordial atmosphere quickly developed, but the groom and his followers only took part in the beer from the first barrel. Once this was empty, they shook hands with Boniface and his agnates to bid their goodbyes, and left them to share the remaining two barrels with their friends, affines and neighbours.

Both the terms for this prestation and the way it is conducted reveal how this is the occasion when the groom and his agnates are brought into direct contact and verbal exchange with the bride's father and his agnates. At its inception, the groom and his party stand silently at the beginning of the *mengele,* until they are noticed and welcomed into the homestead, where the bride's father's agnates appear ignorant both of their identity and the reason for their arrival. It is only when the guests are greeted that the silence is broken, and only when the bride's father recounts why they are gathered and the groom's father presents the couple that the character of the event is spelled out. At this point, the prospective affines only address and talk to each other, while dialogue is introduced when the bride and the groom are asked whether they love each other and intend to marry. The distinction between monologue and dialogue is entailed by the terms for this prestation, where the short form – the beer to speak or tell – concerns direct address, while its long form – the beer to ask if they love each other – involves an exchange of words. It is hence through this prestation that the silence surrounding and pertaining to the initial prestation is broken, and the groom and his agnates are made known to and brought into dialogue with the bride's father and his agnates. In this way, the initial prestation of powerful substances gives way to their verbal addresses to each other, which in turn yields to an exchange of words that is followed by mutual prestations and joint consumption of beer by persons who address each other as *watoi* and engage in the free and easy interaction characteristic of this relationship. It was acted out by Herman, as he silently presented the envelope of cash with his hand, first to Lasway and then to MaShirima, who received it in the same way before she spoke and poured the milk. In both cases, the process reveals how marital and affinal relationships gradually emerge through prestations of life force that transform relationships to enable persons to act in novel ways with specific effects.

These proceedings entail that the transfers of powerful foodstuffs that began with the initial prestation of milk and bananas eventually summon the groom and his agnates to the bride's father's homestead. In this way, the prospective affines are brought together and made known to each other with the result of mutual exchanges of beer and dialogue. The arrival of the wife-takers and their interaction with their prospective affines are hence effects of the transfers of *horu* between homesteads that were set in motion by the initial prestation. Their verbal statements and dialogic exchanges are further effects of these prestations that moreover seek to determine the character of the proceedings and relationship that the transfers enable and constitute. Thus, by providing beer, the groom and his agnates were able to enter Boniface's homestead, where they were received and greeted by his agnates. After an announcement regarding the reason for gathering, the questioning of the bride and the groom determined the character of the relationship between them, which the prestations of *horu* enabled and occasioned. Both the meeting of the prospective affines and the statements made during the event were hence effects of the transfers of *horu* between homesteads that were set in motion by the initial prestation. The beer to tell formed part of these transfers along with the movement of the groom and his agnates, while the statements sought to determine the character of these flows and the relationships they entail. The point is underscored by another term for this prestation, which literally translates as 'the beer that comes to tell' (*wari washa iamba*), highlighting how these transfers of powerful substances afford the verbal exchanges that the event involves.

Gutmann (1924a: 144) touched on this when he described how malted eleusine flour was added to banana wort, while it was stated that the beer should heal the tongue of the elder who drank it and that he should speak healthily as a result. Indeed, Gutmann suggests that the primary effect of beer is as a creator or amplifier of speech.[24] Ruel's (1997: 14) account of self-praise brings out a similar point, as he relates how an inebriated elder would rise at a beer party and make a series of jumps before declaring his merits in terms of bravery, reproductive prowess and ownership of cattle. Such praise could in turn be challenged, as another elder would rise to declare his claim to fame. The account suggests that speech emerges as a result of the beer, and that the praise concerns the effect of the person's life force in the form of children and cattle. As this was challenged, it moreover means that beer yields talk that in turn occasions more words, which arrange persons and determine their relationships to each other in terms of status.

In the case of the bridewealth beer, both the substance involved and its mode of prestation contribute to determine the relationship as one of a particular kind. Since beer is the only foodstuff that is presented in a prepared form, it contains more *horu* than other prestations. Not only is beer made from powerful substances, like *mnyengele* or *mhoyo* bananas and eleusine, but these ingredients are transformed through ripening and malting, where their life force is enhanced before it is multiplied by their cooking and combination.[25] Compared with the initial prestation, this beer therefore contains or embodies more *horu*, which the groom and his agnates bring to the bride's father's homestead to act upon and intervene in their dwelling. As the groom's father serves the bride's parents, and the groom's agnates provide for those of the bride's father, they use their arms to channel *horu* in certain directions to act upon and transform relationships of nurture and consumption both in and beyond the bride's father's homestead. The bride's father reciprocates to the groom's parents, in a way that suggests relational mutuality, but the mode of presentation entails that the transfer of *horu* emerges from and is directed by the wife-takers to the wife-givers. The prestation therefore not only connects the people involved, but also differentiates them as people who either provide or receive *horu*. In this way, the substance involved and its mode of presentation separates them as givers and receivers, based on an existing connection established through the initial prestation of *horu*. In this way, the event distinguishes those involved through an intervention in dwelling that channels *horu* in a specific direction to constitute the specific *watoi* relationship.

It is in this respect that the oblivion displayed by the bride's father's agnates gains significance. Like me, they knew they had been invited to a specific kind of event, but they did not know the particular relationship and the circumstances it concerned. We knew we would attend a *wari wa iamba* event, but we did not know which persons it concerned or the past initiation and prospective development of their relationship. Sitting in Boniface's courtyard, we anticipated the arrival of someone, but did not know who they would be or from where they would come. Our behaviour was therefore not what Meyer Fortes (1962: 3) calls 'mimicry of ceremony', where people wilfully deny an existing relationship in order to create another. It was in fact not an affectation or dissimulation, but a genuine oblivion and lack of knowledge regarding a specific relationship between particular persons that a transfer of *horu* had occasioned and that this event would determine through statements and further prestations.

The claim gains support and significance by the fact that the same ignorance and oblivion occur on the occasions when this prestation takes place between people who live nearby and know each other well. Like elsewhere in Africa (Fortes 1962; Sommerfelt 2016), it is not uncommon in Rombo that marital relationships occur between people who relate in this manner. Indeed, marriages often occur between children of people who address each other as 'neighbour' or *mamrasa*. The notion derives from the term for the boundary – *mrasa* – between homesteads and literally means 'person of the boundary'. The settlement pattern and inheritance practices ensure that neighbouring homesteads tend to be occupied by agnates, but the term *mamrasa* is used to address and mean the inhabitants of homesteads over a larger area than those adjacent to one's own. The term concerns a highly valued relationship of closeness and cooperation that extends geographically to entail that neighbourliness intertwines with agnatic and affinal relationships. The result is that the *wari wa iamba* prestation is often made by people who know each other well and already connect in a multiplicity of ways. However, when their agnates, affines, neighbours and *watoi* are summoned for such an event, they do not know which relationship it concerns, who the persons involved are, or the surrounding circumstances. The groom's and bride's agnates therefore engage as virtual strangers because they do not yet know in which capacity they interact on this occasion. By behaving in this way, they explore and determine the character of the relationship that the transfers of *horu* have constituted and set in motion to summon them to this particular place. They expect and anticipate that its character will be revealed, but only if they maintain an open and patient attitude, and await the arrival of those concerned and for the beer involved to bring them into speech and dialogue. In this way, the material transfers occasion and entwine with the verbal statements, which determine the relationship that is transformed to afford new dispositions.

The dynamic recalls another aspect of the initial prestation, where the overflowing milk shows the character of the incipient relationship, and occasions a verbal address and a provision of *horu* to the deceased. Similarly, Gutmann (1926: 81) described a situation where the groom's mother requests that the eleusine she malts for a bride-wealth prestation of beer should germinate prolifically for a good pro-spective daughter-in-law, but fail for a bad one. She moreover inspects the appearance and quality of the froth that the malt forms on the fermented beer for clues regarding the character of her son's future bride. According to Gutmann, these invocations conjured the powers or forces (*Kräfte*) of the groom's mother's world for hints regarding the fortunes or misfortunes that the prospective daughter-in-law would bring to the homestead. On this occasion, words were used to summon and occasion transformations of powerful substances and foodstuffs to show the auspiciousness of a particular relationship, which the prestations of *horu* enable and entail. It resembles and recalls Peter's injunction that Horombo should 'just look' at how the people were finished, which Peter made Horombo see by means of his words and the beer he poured. In present-day Rombo, it is most common that the transformation of a powerful substance occasions words, for instance when the bridewealth milk overflows to show the pathway and afford an address like MaShirima's, or when statements and dialogue occur between the living during *wari wa iamba*. Arguably, these cases involve obverse dynamics or processes distributed along a gradient, where transfers of *horu* through certain relationships elicit language, or lan-guage conjures transformations of life force that facilitate and deter-mine the character of certain relationships. It is crucial to note that these statements are not 'about' relationships, but rather effectuate or are effectuated by transfers of *horu* that specify these movements and the relationships they afford and involve. The statements are therefore not informative of something that is of a different status and charac-ter, but formative of the transfers and transformations of *horu* and the relationships they concern (Myhre 2012, 2013b).

In conclusion, one can say that these dynamics are far removed from the anthropological conception of bridewealth and marriage, where rights in women are transferred between men in exchange for material objects (Kuper 1982; Levi-Strauss 1969; Strathern 1984a, 1984b). By contrast, they involve transfers of life force that gradu-ally bring persons together to elicit statements and forms of action that determine the relationships and social situations that they en-able and involve. Widenmann (1899: 47) was hence correct when he claimed that 'marriage has an essentially profane, material char-acter', although probably not for the reasons he meant. These events do not involve persons using material objects to foster relationships, but concern transfers of *horu* between homesteads that connect and separate persons, who detach and attach to houses as their effects, and undergo transformations that enable them to act in novel ways with newfound effects. It makes houses conduits for life force through which persons and things move in accordance with their engagement in dwelling. In the past, this entailed that persons extended dwelling in established homesteads, while currently they bring new homesteads into existence as entities and places of dwelling. The fact nevertheless remains that persons are in a state of extension or unfolding through their involvement in dwelling, where subject positions and dispositions are defined and enabled by the houses to which they belong and the doorways to which they attach.

These descriptions imply that social engagements and relationships involve both connection and separation to proportion distances between persons, houses, livestock and crops. The next chapter will explore this further by considering claims and actions pertaining to sex and reproduction. These considerations will expand on how persons convert and convey *horu* in different forms by means of different parts of the body, and will regard several of the vernacular concepts considered in this chapter. It will thus pursue further the ways in which language and *horu* intertwine and affect one another to constitute life – *moo* – in this particular part of the world.

Notes

1. The desire for livestock instead of foodstuffs might have been an effect of land shortage, as prestations particularly of cattle to be stall-fed would allow the bride's parents to benefit from manure and milk over an extended period of time.
2. The addresses are only edited for repetitious expressions, whose excisions are marked with ellipses.
3. *Maokoni* is a further locative construction that combines the plural form of *koko* with the adverbial suffix, which here is pronounced closer to *-ni* than *-nyi*.
4. As I argue elsewhere, the cattle-linking described in connection with bridewealth and marriage in southern Africa involves the same dynamic and relationship (Myhre 2012). It hence appears to be a phenomenon with wider prevalence in Africa, which assumes different forms in various settings.
5. People render *ikariya* in Swahili as *kuwa hodari* or *kuwa na nguvu*. Later chapters will show how the Swahili concept of *nguvu* often appears in the form of *ngufu* as a vernacularized synonym and replacement for *horu*.

6. The phrase then replaces and serves as a synonym for *iruuli lakua,* which also means 'this banana or banana bunch is mature'.

7. People render this in Swahili as *imara.*

8. I have not participated in this mode of prestation, but rely on accounts made by multiple informants from various contexts over many years.

9. Some people claim that the intermediary avoids being seen entering, leaving or conducting her errand in the bride's father's homestead. However, most dispute this and say that the *mkara* re-enters the homestead in the usual way and engages with its members after she has left the objects inside the house.

10. The hearth post was one of two supports for the round house that was common in western Kilimanjaro.

11. Dundas (1924: 238, 240) similarly described how the bride is forcibly removed from the house.

12. Similarly, Dundas (1924: 233) describes how a prestation of two pots of beer, a sheep and a goat called 'goat for the child's mother and for the hoe' was presented to the bride's parents by the *mkara* to announce the groom's intention to claim his bride, while Gutmann (1926: 126) described how the bride's mother was presented with a butchered goat called 'the goat to take the child from its mother'.

13. Such incidences are unfortunately not rare in some homesteads, where they require repeated 'cooling' by means of blood and chyme. These current-day events resemble Dundas's (1924: 155–56) description of a woman biting or striking a man as one of a range of 'sins' that require 'purification' by means of various objects and substances, which include the blood and chyme of various animals.

14. In her statement above, MaShirima enunciated the significance of the bed for the relationship between the bride and the groom, which the bridewealth prestation enables.

15. Similarly, Gutmann (1926: 60) described how a woman was not allowed to sleep in a bed in her brother's homestead, but instead slept on a hide on the ground. In the context of the house-property complex, where a son received his homestead from his mother, the prohibition concerned the woman's natal homestead, in the same way as in present-day Rombo.

16. Accordingly, Gutmann (1909b: 138) described how ceremonial events took place for a woman with children at both her marital and natal homestead.

17. Gutmann (1926: 173) argues that *yalika* is the intransitive form of the verb *yala,* which he claims means 'to be presented' (*dargeboten sein*). He moreover claims that it has the same meaning as *yara,* which is to lend and place livestock in the care of others. While I agree that *ialika* is an intransitive form, it is a stative form of a different verb, namely to be extended or spread out, which is distinct from *ihara.* When asked, people stress that it would be an insult to use these two notions with a suggestion that they are linked.

18. This is underscored by the fact that bodily heat (*mrike*) is distinguished from the word *muu*, which is used to mean the heat of the climate or weather.

19. In turn, this gives new sense to Monica Wilson's Nyakyusa ethnography of how certain trees are planted to secure the 'power of growth' and emplace the chief, while banana trees serve the same purpose for the commoners (Ruel 1997: 67, 74).

20. Gutmann's claim that *kara* is a ramified (*sprossenreich*) notion echoes Wittgenstein's idea that certain concepts are ramified.

21. As I will describe in connection with naming practices, the prefix *ma-* can be added to yield a compound term, meaning 'mother of-'. Neither of these terms is in use in Rombo, where the term for 'wife' is *mfele*, which also is used to mean 'woman'. I will consider the use and significance of this term in chapter three.

22. To paraphrase Karp (1978: 11), 'doorway' is a concept that is used in a situational and relative manner to talk about social relations, and a physical phenomenon that enables different modes of behaviour.

23. Boniface was briefly introduced in chapter one.

24. The second and third effects are respectively as a reminder of the sense of deference and as a paralyser of speech.

25. I describe the preparation of beer more closely elsewhere (Myhre 2007a; 2007b, 2015).

Chapter Three

HORU

CHANNELLING BODIES AND SHIFTING SUBJECTS IN AN ENGAGING WORLD

One day in 2001, Herman and MaSway were cutting grass for fodder in a small meadow that borders a seasonal riverbed below Atali's and Oswald's homesteads. They had left the grass to grow tall and dry, so it was perfect fodder and a good supplement to the cattle's staple diet of banana trees. Herman and MaSway did not cut all the grass at once, but harvested what they needed for a day and left the rest for later. Using small sickles (*ishami*), they sheared the grass to work their way across the meadow, when suddenly they encountered a patch of flattened grass that had not been visible. There was a wallet lying on the patch, which Herman opened to find a membership card for the local branch of the ruling Chama Cha Mapinduzi (CCM) party. The card identified the owner of the wallet as a man named Alois, who lived in a nearby homestead. In the privacy of the *sha* courtyard, Herman and MaSway laughed and said that Alois has used this secluded place to commit adultery after dark, and that his wallet must have fallen out in the process. After all, it was well known that Alois was a philanderer, they held.[1] Suddenly serious, MaSway said they should place a thorny creeper on the patch to prevent the lovers from returning and repeating their act. Herman agreed, but added that at least their tryst had not occurred in the banana garden. That would have necessitated tossing the *mahande* since sexual activity in the *mdenyi* would sap the *horu* of its crops and plants.[2]

This vignette reiterates the point made in the previous chapter that sex and reproduction pertain to the house and should be confined to marital relationships. It furthermore reveals that sex and reproduction form part of the transfers and transformations of *horu* that occur through dwelling (*ikaa*). This chapter will therefore consider sex and reproduction more closely to further describe the concepts of *ikaa* and *horu*, as well as explore the notion of *moo* with which they entwine. The account will reveal how persons convert and convey life force in different forms through different parts of the body for different effects. It will show how engagement in these activities constitutes and brings into being different subject positions, and demonstrate how these engage and involve prominent features of the homestead. Exploring how these also concern and entail naming practices, the chapter will shed further light on the concept of *ialika* as a state of extension, where persons, houses, livestock and crops unfold and enfold in space and time. By describing a set of concepts that derive from or inflect the root-form *moo*, the chapter investigates how life emerges and is an effect of specific conversions and conveyances of *horu*. In addition, the account will expand on the relationship between language and life force to reveal how prohibitions concerning sex and reproduction channel *horu* in certain ways for particular effects. On this basis, it will emerge that dwelling concerns how production, reproduction and consumption nest as transformations of each other and how *horu* moves through them in different forms to afford the becoming and constitute the being of persons, houses, livestock and crops.

Sex and Reproduction

As argued in the previous chapter, men and women may engage in premarital sex, but a man's claim to the children borne by a woman depends on the transfer of bridewealth of some kind. Both sex and reproduction are conceptualized and discussed in terms of *horu*, where bodily fluids of different kinds are transformed and transferred between persons. These transfers and transmutations occur by means of different body parts and affect men and women in different ways that in turn have ramifications for their involvement in other kinds of practices.

Like in production and consumption, sex generates and increases the heat (*mrike*) of the bodies of those involved. The heat that is generated during sex originates from the enhanced circulation of the blood (*samu*) of men, which is transferred to women in the form of semen. To engage in sex, men therefore require a diet of powerful foodstuffs, where meat and beer are held to be particularly important. Since these foodstuffs increase the amount of blood and make it circulate faster, they enhance men's sexual abilities and increase their desire. People therefore recount how men return home drunk to demand sexual favours from their wives. Elderly men moreover used to blame the spread of HIV/AIDS on younger men and their propensity to drink, which created a surfeit of *horu* that compelled them to commit adultery and engage with prostitutes.

Men's circulation of blood and expenditure of semen in turn raise the heat, increase the blood and boost the *horu* of women.[3] While men surrender and transfer *horu*, heat and blood in sex, women gain the same qualities and substances, which they in turn lose through menstruation and the loss of blood in childbirth. In line with such current claims, Moore (1976: 365) reports that menstrual blood is 'the fountain of life', and Gutmann (1926: 11) held that a young wife is venerated as a 'giver of life' (*Lebensspenderin*).[4] Otto Raum ([1940] 1996: 77) meanwhile argued that the Chagga 'hold that the embryo results from the union of the semen with the menstrual blood, which, after impregnation, is diverted into the uterus to be used in the gradual completion of the foetus'. His claim gains support from Gutmann's (1926: 115) account of how the thick and sticky character of a woman's first menstrual blood indicated her ability to conceive quickly and easily. It is underscored by his description of how the groom's mother sent the loin-band containing the remnants of the bride's first menstruation after relocation in marriage to her natal homestead, where the bride's mother rubbed butter onto it and said: 'May your fat be in love with that of your husband. May it not turn to water. If your fat cannot combine with that of your husband, then I will die ... My child, bear children like I did, without harm and bad omens. Your blood shall be thick like mine' (Gutmann 1926: 115–16). Her statement concerns how blood is central to a woman's ability to conceive and enunciates how conception results from her 'fat' conjoining that of her husband. As with the earlier quote from Dundas in chapter two, it seems that 'fat' is a mistranslation of *horu* and an identification of life force with one of its forms.[5]

Both current and historical statements thus entail that the child results from the combination of *horu* in the form of different bodily substances that originate from a man and a woman. The child is hence a composition of the parents' life force, which it bodies forth in a particular form. Accordingly, the child's delivery depletes its mother's *horu*, along with the attendant blood loss. Women are therefore confined after childbirth and swaddled in clothes to regain heat. The length of confinement depends on one's wealth and ability, but in most cases the parturient woman remains inside the house for three months.

During this time, the woman stays in bed with her baby and is provided various kinds of 'soft food' (*kelya kiholo*) that convey life force to replenish the blood and increase the heat she lost in childbirth. The foods contribute to her capacity, health and well-being, yet also increase her lactation, which in turn conveys *horu* to the child in the form of breastmilk. Gutmann (1926: 10) accordingly argued that breastmilk is a 'fountain of life' (*Lebensbrunnen*), and Moore (1976: 365) holds that 'milk is the very source of a baby's life'. Both echo current claims that emphasize and expand on the transformational character of *horu*, as people stress how powerful foods increase blood and afford breastmilk, which contributes to the child's heat, blood and life force, and thus allow its growth.

These considerations show how sex and reproduction consist in conversions and conveyances of *horu* in the form of different bodily substances. They moreover show how these transfers and transmutations engage various parts of the body that channel and convert the different forms *horu* assumes. Gutmann (1926: 659) recognized this, as he argued that reproductive organs are conceptualized as 'dispatchers of power' (*Kraftentsender*) or 'transmitters of force' (*Kraft-träger*), where the penis and the breasts are the most efficacious. Moore (1976: 365) too touches on this, as she claims that semen is male milk that combines with female blood to form a child, whose birth occasions breastmilk.[6] She argues that this is proof of dual symbolic classification, but the connection persists in conceptual form in Rombo, where the term *mawele* is used to mean both a woman's breasts and a man's testicles. The different usages of this singular term do not concern social categories that classify and order natural substances, but enunciate how semen and breastmilk are mutual transformations that manifest *horu* in different forms.

However, the conversions and conveyances of life force involve additional body parts that differ from those one might expect and surface in surprising places. More specifically, they appear in the statements and practices that surround the butchering of animals, when each share of meat is the claim of particular people who stand in a specific relation to the person responsible for the event (Myhre 2013b). On such occasions, a man provides his father with a section of the beast's breast called the *ikamba* because his father lay on his chest when he was conceived. Similarly, the man gives his wife's mother the *moongo* section from the animal's back because she lay on her back (*moongo*), first to conceive and later to give birth to his wife. The claims entail and enunciate that the reproductive transfers and transformations of *horu* occur by means of the man's chest and the woman's back, which are employed to create the child and bring it into the world. People accentuate this when they recount the tale rendered in chapter two of how a man and woman were punished in the past if they became pregnant before the transfer of bridewealth. As she rested on her back and he lay on his chest, they were killed as though they were making love, manifesting the body parts employed in their transgression. Since the punishment only occurred when sex resulted in pregnancy, it underscores the role of the chest and the back in reproduction, and accentuates that the child is an effect of relations where parents transform and transfer *horu* in different forms through various body parts. Consequently, the child is born with both a chest and a back, which its parents employed to bring it into existence. In this way, the child personifies and embodies the relations that effectuate its existence and compose its being.

However, the woman's use of her back extends beyond conception and childbirth to also involve nurture and care. A further reason why a man owes his wife's mother the *moongo* meat is namely that she carried her daughter on her back (*moongo*) when she was an infant. Gutmann (1926: 311) touched on this, describing how one term used for infants is 'the swung ones' (*die Geschwungenen*). While he claimed that this concerns a playful practice of lifting the child and swinging it over the shoulder, in my view it may also regard how mothers carry infants on their backs, where they swing along with her activities. Even large toddlers sleep slung this way, while their mothers go about their day. In this connection, it is also significant that women spend their confinement in bed, where they rest on their backs with their babies on the breast. The practice means that the back also features when the onus is on the woman's recovery from birth and nurture of her child. It furthermore entails that additional body parts besides breasts are involved in the care for and feeding of the child, and that the back is central for transfers of *horu* to and from women in different forms.

Providing Soft Foods

During confinement, close watch is kept on who enters the house where a woman and her baby rest. Whenever I was invited into such a house, I was invariably asked, 'do you have a bad thing?' (*ure kindo kiwiishwa*) and queried whether I was a *mwahay*. While the former is a euphemism for witchcraft, the latter is a person who unwittingly startles to harm something beautiful (*usha*) he or she encounters. Usually, this assumes the form of a newborn child, germinating crops or a house that is under construction. Babies therefore have charcoal rubbed on their foreheads or sewn into fabric tied around their wrists, which distracts the *mwahay* and prevents harm from being inflicted. For the same purpose, banana blossoms (*nanua*) are propped on sticks in planted fields and in front of half-finished houses, so the *mwahay* sees these before the emergent crops or buildings. The significance here is that the notion of *moongo* is used to mean both the doorway of the house and the back or backbone of persons and animals. The usages entail that the doorway is closely guarded regarding what and who passes through it, in order to secure the mother's use of her back in caring for her child. The movement of persons and things through one *moongo* is controlled to ensure the transfers of nurture by means of another *moongo*.

The practice reveals that the transfers and transformations of *horu* not only involve parts of the human body, but engage the world and most notably features of the house and homestead. The point is broadened by the soft foods that the confined women keep in thermos flasks or wooden bowls beside their beds. These foods include the eleusine porridge *mswa* that is boiled with milk and topped with *msika* butter, and *mtori* that consists of boiled and mashed *mhoyo* bananas diluted with broth and pieces of boiled meat.[7] *Mhoyo* bananas can also replace the kind called *mlali* to make *kena*, which features as a confinement food in addition to being made from the milk and bananas of the initial bridewealth prestation. *Mtori* is in fact a cognate of Maasai *motori*, which similarly is a soup that makes people strong, and which replaces blood and increases the milk supply of nursing women (Århem 1990: 205). The conceptual and substantial connections of these two foods testify to Rombo's location on the Bantu-Nilotic interface and the longstanding interactions between the mountain and the plains.

Elders reminisce how parturient women in the past were served a dish called *mlaso*, which consists of blood that is let from a bull and mixed with milk and *msika* butter. They describe *mlaso* as a most powerful food, and regret and complain that it is not available due to the reduction of livestock and the paucity of herding. Stall-fed cattle lack the requisite *horu* for blood-letting and no-one risks killing a bull to make *mlaso*. Blood from slaughtered animals is mixed with broth to make another powerful food called *kisusio*, but such blood is not used to make *mlaso*, which derives its term from the verb 'to let blood' – *ilasa*.[8] It is precisely because *mlaso* is made with blood from a living animal that it contains and conveys more *horu* and provides more heat than that from a butchered animal. Such current claims are deepened by Gutmann (1924a: 126), who described how the arrow used for blood-letting was sprinkled with 'cooling water' (*Entsühnungswasser*) and furnished with a skin-ring, while an invocation was made for its 'power of fortune' (*Glückskraft*) for the cow, the child and the parturient woman. The notion of *Glückskraft* indicates the concept of *horu*, which gains support from Gutmann's claim that the skin-ring encompasses the life of plant, animal and human. In combination, these notions and activities reiterate and underscore how life force not only transfers and transforms through human bodily substances, but also conveys and converts between persons, livestock and crops.

Consisting of eleusine, milk, meat, bananas, butter and blood, the confinement foods contain ingredients that have served these purposes for a long time. Thus, while Gutmann described how blood was let for parturient women, Dundas (1924: 200) recounted other ingredients: 'The woman must be well cared for and liberally supplied by her husband as well as by her own family with meat, milk, fat, blood and what else is held to be nourishing'. While supply of these foods rested primarily with the husband, the responsibility extended beyond the marital homestead: 'To provide these supplies is the absolute duty of a husband and an obligation on the parents-in-law. Tardiness on the part of the former invariably results in desertion by the wife, while lack of attention on the part of her family is a definite indication of ill-will. Only the wealthy are able to supply all that is required out of their own stock, the less opulent have to beg and purchase supplies elsewhere, and by consequence the husband is kept constantly on the move, seeking the needful nourishment here, there and everywhere' (Dundas 1924: 200). Feeding a confined woman is still a collaborative effort to some extent, but it involves fewer relationships than Dundas claimed. Raum (1911: 182) even argued that a man could lend his daughter's husband a cow with which to feed his daughter, if the latter was poor and lacked livestock. The bride's relatives currently contribute little to her upkeep. Instead, it is the husband's responsibility, even though he requests bananas and to some extent milk from agnates, friends and neighbours. Elders argue that the reliance on others was more pronounced in the past, when the less-yielding *zebu* was the only cattle available. Accordingly, Gutmann (1926: 143–44) argued that it was the *Sippe*'s responsibility to care for the confined woman and that her 'life-power' (*Lebenskraft*) diminished when this mutual reliance terminated.

Regardless of who provides these foods, they result from the productive practices at the homestead, where the arm or *koko* harvests and slices fodder, and sweeps and spreads manure in the form of horticulture where livestock stall-feeding and banana farming yield bananas, milk, meat, blood and butter. The latter in particular implies the arm, as the term *msika* derives from the verb *isika* which means the act of shaking a gourd to churn milk into butter. These foodstuffs combine with eleusine grown in the plains or bought at the market, where the money used also results from the arm in cash-cropping or day labour. All the substances combine over the hearth, where the ladle (*kilikiyo*) is used to prepare and serve the foods. The comestibles are therefore effects of multiple relationships, where the arm converts and conveys *horu* to replenish the life force expended through production and reproduction by means of different body parts. It moreover underscores how the arm engages the world in multiple ways to channel life force in particular directions. When the husband provides such foods to his confined wife, it moreover means that his arm adjoins her mouth to help fill the breasts that feed their child. The arm deploys the effects of production for consumptive purposes occasioned by reproductive engagements, and thus directs the activity of dwelling (*ikaa*) from which the homestead (*kaa*) derives its name. As the arm pivots production, consumption and reproduction, it forms part of an array of world-relations, where persons, livestock and crops conjoin in a purposive network that both affords and results from the transfers and transformations of *horu*. Its result is an engaging world, where everything is *horu* in a particular form that may transmute into something else, depending on the anatomical feature employed to channel it in certain ways.

Confinement entails that both parents make extended and extensive reproductive contributions to the child, which broaden the range of body parts involved in reproduction. The last point is brought out and extended by Raum's ([1940] 1996: 105) account of how children in the past not only were nursed, but also fed by means of other body parts: 'Mother's milk was and still is considered insufficient. From the second day the child has food spat into its mouth. This is done frequently during the day, and two or three times in the night. Milk and butter are specifically used for fattening the infant. They are often added to unripe *mshare* bananas and soda (which is found in the plains and used as salt). The baby also gets its share of the *mlaso* meal'. Such practices no longer occur, except when a certain root is chewed and the juice spat into the mouth of a newborn child to induce diarrhoea and remove a black substance called *shang'a* from its stomach. However, Raum's account is corroborated by Bailey the sanitary inspector, who singled out Rombo as a particular concern in this regard: 'An objectionable and dangerous practice observed especially on the Eastern side, is the mastication of food by the parent prior to its conveyance (from mouth to mouth) to the child' (TNA 312). Neither Raum nor Bailey specified who spat such foodstuffs into the child, but it is clear at least from the former account that they involved the foodstuffs that result from the arm in the horticulture of the homestead. As the foods in this case do not go via the mother's breasts, such spitting expands the range of people and body parts involved in the transfer of *horu* to the child, and enlarge the relationships that compose the child. Accordingly, the child not only has a chest and a back, but also a mouth and arms of the left- and the right-hand side that embody and manifest the broader productive and consumptive relationships that constitute its existence and well-being.

Shifting Subjects

The way in which the father provides foods so the mother may nurse entails a distinction between feeding and growing that allows him to grow the child by way of feeding her (cf. Strathern 1988: 238). In Kilimanjaro, these practices have further effects for the persons involved, which manifest in the terminologies concerning subject positions.

Gutmann (1926: 310ff) claimed that an infant was called *matuma* for the first five to six months of its life, until the first tooth arrived and the child was named. Due to its small size, the infant was also called *mkoku*, which people described as *moitšuṛya nden* or 'something that fills the womb'. Gutmann claimed that *matšovila* or 'swung ones' was used interchangeably with *matuma*, but mainly by the nursemaids who swung the children over their shoulders. The fact that the term was used by the nursemaids must mean that *matšovila* only featured once the mother emerged from confinement and began carrying the child on her back. The succession of *matšovila* from *moitšuṛya nden* means that the child emerged from its mother's womb and shifted onto her back during confinement. Today, this is captured by the use of *moongo* to mean both a person's back and the doorway of the house from which mother and child emerge from confinement. The different uses of the singular term enunciate how the infant emerges from one *moongo* to be carried on another *moongo*.

The infant's movement from its mother's womb to her back suggests that it is nursing that shifts the child, and that it is the mother's use of her breasts that moves the child from one part of her body to another. It gains support from Gutmann's (1926: 312) account of the midwife's return to 'rub the tooth' (*isinga heho*), which finalized her work of bringing the child into the world. After applying certain leaves to the child's gums, the midwife rubbed these on the mother's breasts, while saying: 'May your womb conceive'. The act and statement manifest that it is the breasts that shift and release the child from the womb, so the mother may conceive again. However, conception will re-engage her back in sex and childbirth, so the result is that one part of her body affords the use of another for reproductive purposes. The recursive character of these processes was enunciated by the midwife, who said that she received the child's tooth, just like her mother had received the tooth of the child's father, and she would return to do the same again, presumably for another child yet to be born.

Gutmann (1926: 316) claimed that it was only once a toddler could run that it was fully released from the womb and called a 'child' (*mwana*). His claim means that the child is gradually separated from its mother to become a being that moves of its own accord. The argument above means that this separation occurs by means of the mother's breasts, but these are at least partly filled by her husband, who provides the foods that replenish her *horu*. The father's arms are hence instrumental in bringing forth the child and shifting it in relation to its mother's body. The capacity to move extends the emergence of mother and child from confinement, which continued when she brought the child to announce its first tooth to the grandparents (Gutmann 1926: 312). The gradual movement and separation of the child in relation to the mother hence concurred with its emergence from the house and its ambulation in relation to other homesteads.

While the child becomes a being that is able to move, it simultaneously becomes one that can consume foods of certain kinds. Thus, when the midwife arrived to rub the tooth, she was greeted with a bowl of soft food made from milk (*Milchbrei*) that was called the 'child's meal' (Gutmann 1926: 312). The way the midwife was presented with the bowl with a request that she receive the child's tooth suggests that it was the food itself that brought forth the tooth. If this is true, it means that soft food was presented to afford the tooth, which in turn enabled the child to eat more solid foods. The arrival of the tooth shifts the child from breastmilk to other foods, which in turn separates it further from its mother. Raum ([1940] 1996: 124) realized this, when he described 'the nutritional devolution of the original symbiosis between mother and embryo to the quasi-parasitic stage of infancy, and the ultimate independence of the two metabolic systems'. However, Raum overlooked how this separation renders acute the arm that provides these foods, and how the capacity to eat extends the movement of the child by means of its parents' body parts. Arguably, this was enunciated by the nursemaid when she announced the arrival of the child's first tooth. While holding the child, she took up position underneath the roof of the eleusine granary and called out, 'the house has gained a prop' (Gutmann 1926: 311–12). The birth of a child and its attainment of an ability to eat necessitate foods, so it extends dwelling (*ikaa*) and adds to the house of the homestead (*kaa*), where the arm deploys the effects of production for consumptive purposes that are occasioned by reproductive engagements. Like the initial bridewealth prestation, the tooth's emergence thus summons and summates dwelling, as the nursemaid locates the child in relation to the granary to recognize its newfound capacity to eat more solid foods, like the eleusine porridge *mswa*.

Relationship terminology reveals that these processes not only move the child, but also shift the other subjects involved. When a woman in Rombo relocates to her marital homestead, she is addressed as 'bride' (*mwali*) or 'bride of child' (*mwaliamwana*). The usage continues until the bride is confined, when she is known as *mfee* instead. Gutmann (1926: 170; 1924a: 134) accordingly translated *mfee* as 'parturient woman' (*Gebärerin*) and *wufee* as 'parturient care or provision' (*Wochenpflege*). Both nouns derive from the verb *ifee*, which Raum (1909: 148) rendered as 'to give birth' (*gebären*) and Walther (1900: 41) translated as 'to beget' (*zeugen*). Only *mfee* is used in today's Rombo, but the other terms deepen how the confined woman is someone who has conceived a child and given birth, and therefore receives particular care. Gutmann (1924a: 134) described how a banana was roasted over the first fire that was lit in the house after the birth, and the following statement was made while the soot was scraped from the banana so that it covered the hearthstones: 'This is your *wufee*! It comes from the banana that the forefather (*Ahn*) planted for protection and help for the home. You both are the ones who help us to see and provide for the child'. The statement reveals how the parturient provision stems from the banana trees of the garden, and hence emerges from the arms of the homestead's inhabitants.

The *mfee*'s use of her back lends credence to Raum's ([1940] 1996: 125) claim that *moongo* meant 'nursing mother' and was used as a praise-name for a woman who had borne six or more children and whose eldest son 'is able to prove his might and mettle'. Meaning a person who repeatedly and intensively uses her back for reproductive purposes, the usage moreover accords with Gutmann's (1926: 170) rendition of *mongo* as 'sucked one' (*Gesogene*). However, Raum ([1940] 1996: 125–26) referred to an essay by Filipo Njau and argued that, 'when a woman becomes the guardian and tutor of her grandchildren, she is greeted as *makitshutshu*, the exhausted one, intimating that her breasts have been sucked to depletion by her children and grandchildren'. *Makitshutshu* resembles the term for 'female elder' (*msheku*) in Rombo, where *moongo* means the back that *mwali* uses for sex and childbirth and *mfee* rests on while nursing, as well as the doorway through which the husband brings soft foods to replenish her *horu*. Its multiple meanings reiterate a recursion, where *horu* transfers and transforms through anatomical and architectural features in the reproductive and consumptive practices that are integral to dwelling (*ikaa*).

However, Gutmann and Raum receive support, as people in Rombo claim that young people retain more of the breastmilk they were fed. The young therefore have more heat (*mrike*) than elders and suffer less from the cold and drizzle that descend between June and August. Conversely, they say that those who have reproduced have less heat and suffer more than those who have not yet borne children. In this way, they enunciate how age and reproduction deplete *horu* and exhaust bodily substances.[9] In light of the discussion in the previous chapter, this occurs as the person extends the reach of his or her veins and proliferates their connections with *mri* of other beings through production and reproduction. *Horu* is therefore finite and diminishes with age, as people expend blood, semen and breastmilk that are only partly remedied by the consumption of powerful foods. Accordingly, the man who marries an elderly woman's youngest daughter presents the *msheku* with a woollen blanket, which replaces the heat she expended through reproduction and that he removes from the homestead when her daughter relocates.

People nevertheless say that an ample supply of soft foods can cause a woman to lactate, even if she has not delivered a child. They claim that foster mothers relied on this to nurse the children of women who died in labour, but Raum ([1940] 1996: 104) argued that this task was assumed by the child's father's mother: 'if the mother dies in childbed, the husband's mother, as a rule, takes over the maternal duties. The substitution is both physiological and sociological. The baby is put to its grandmother's breast, and in return she receives the special diet of the confinement period, during which she is freed from heavy work. Occasionally an old woman uses charms and medicines to make the flow of milk return, but this "late lactation" cannot be equivalent to real suckling'. Such practices no longer occur in Rombo, as people say they both lack the food and worry about illness, witchcraft and other bad things.[10] Raum's claim concerning the inadequacy of such lactation nevertheless corroborates how *horu* is finite and diminishes with age through production and reproduction.

Moongo: Extension and Transformation through Doorways and Backbones

The use of *moongo* to mean both the doorway of the house and the back or backbone of a person or animal enunciates how life force enters and emerges from persons and houses, and moves through beings of different kinds. It is especially brought out by the aforementioned share of meat called *moongo* that a husband owes his bride's parents whenever he slaughters. The *moongo* is carved from the animal's lower back to include three ribs from both sides of the animal, inside of which the kidneys remain attached. It also includes the lower section of the belly, so that the *moongo* emerges as a large, circular piece of meat. The *moongo* is shared by the wife's parents and is sent to their homestead, if they do not take part in the event. Its justification emphasizes the bride's mother and her use of her back in conceiving, birthing or caring for her daughter, but the account above reveals how these activities also involve the bride's father's chest and arms. The justification hence concerns different yet related activities, where the bride's parents receive, transform and expend *horu* in the form of different bodily substances to enable existence of the woman on whose behalf the *moongo* is presented.

Meat is moreover a powerful substance, so the *moongo* is a further prestation of *horu* to the wife's parents that follows and supplements the initial milk and bananas, and the subsequent *wari wa iamba* beer. Its basis in specific activities entails that the *moongo* prestation is a 'replacement' (Weiner 1980) that compensates for the *horu*, heat and blood that the wife's parents expended in conceiving, birthing and caring for their daughter. It is hence with the wife's parents and their reproductive efforts in mind that the daughter's husband carves out and presents the *moongo*. The *horu* expended by the parents is moreover constitutive of their daughter's capacity, health and well-being, which she deploys in dwelling at the marital homestead, where she employs her back in conceiving, birthing and caring for her children. The *moongo* meat is therefore simultaneously a compensation for the *horu* expended by the wife's parents by means of their backs, and a replacement for the back and *horu* that the groom detached from their house.

However, these prestations are not simply made by the groom in exchange for the bride's bodily substances, including her back (Hunter 1936: 192; Strathern 1987b: 290). Rather, they entail the stronger claim that she *acquires* a back through these prestations. After all, it is the bridewealth prestations that afford her legitimate engagement in reproduction, which deploys her back at her marital homestead. The transformation of her subject position from 'daughter' to 'bride' hence also effectuates bodily transformations that bestow or afford dispositions to act in novel ways, where *horu* transfers in additional forms. As such, these prestations mature (*ikariya*) the person and enable her to dwell (*ikara*), and make her unfold or be in a state of extension (*ialika*).

These claims gain support from the connection between bones and blood that was enunciated by the bride's mother when she inspected the remnants of her daughter's first menstruation after relocation to her marital homestead. According to Gutmann (1926: 115), the bride's mother anointed the remnants with butter, while saying: 'Loin-band of my daughter, you have returned to me the milk of the child, with which she greeted her husband's homestead! She is now prepared for her marriage. Let the bones of my child mature and be pliant like the Mbolea snake. Let them mature and neither dry up nor turn into water. They shall mature like mine, which matured and habituated to my husband, so that I bore him children. May this also occur to you, my child, N.N.'.[11] The statement underscores the transformational character of bodily substances, as it enunciates that the bride's menstrual blood is a conversion of the breastmilk supplied by her mother, which in turn was a transformation of her blood. It expands on this as the statement enunciates that bones too are a conversion of these substances, and that bones mature through marriage where they transform back into bodily fluids in reproduction. The idea was deepened by Gutmann's (1926: 114) account of how the mother's brother could be suspected of interrupting his sister's daughter's menstruation, if he was dissatisfied with his share of the bridewealth presented on her behalf. The mother's brother would then be approached with a prestation of beer and requested to release his anger, to which he responded by saying: 'May your bone no longer be dry, but may it trickle'. In combination, the claims underscore that blood transfers as an effect of the bridewealth prestations, yet also entail that bones, blood and breastmilk are mutual transformations.[12] Such transformations contrast with reports from elsewhere that the mother contributes the blood or flesh to a child and the father provides its bones, yet accords with the idea that the child is a composition of life force that the parents supply in different forms.[13] Gutmann (1926: 114) furthermore revealed that the flow of menstrual blood pertains to the homestead, as he reported that the bride's first menstruation in her husband's mother's house was called 'the greeting of the homestead' (*idikirya kan*). Combined with my material, Gutmann's account reveals that the prestations of powerful foodstuffs provide the bride with a backbone, which constitutes *horu* in one form that she deploys in reproductive activities, where life force transmutes and transfers in the further forms of semen, blood and breastmilk. It underscores how the bridewealth prestations involve conversions and conveyances of *horu* that effectuate bodily transformations or 'affections' that afford novel capacities for acting and being acted upon (Patton 2000: 78). The indebtedness of the bride to her mother's back is rendered by the *moongo* prestation, which follows her relocation and reproductive engagement by means of her own back. The *moongo* meat registers the transformational relationship in its form, while the *horu* it contains extends dwelling in the bride's parents' homestead. Foodstuffs high in *horu* are thus not only trafficked for women and their bodily substances, but deployed to affect bodily transformations and capabilities that are conceptualized and actualized as life force in different forms.

The fact that the homestead comes into existence upon the wife's relocation entails that it too is dependent upon the wife's parents. People may say that a man then has a hearth (*nere riko*), but a doorway is simultaneously obtained. Moreover, it is through this doorway that the *moongo* meat emerges that he presents to his wife's parents. Before a goat is butchered, it is held just inside, in or in front of the doorway, where an invocation is uttered while eleusine grains are rubbed onto certain parts of its body. A head of cattle, meanwhile, is kept in either the indoor or the outdoor pen (*koombe*), where curdled milk is tossed onto it by means of *isale* leaves while an invocation is made. Both kinds of animal are usually killed and butchered in the courtyard, while they face the *moongo* of the house, inside of which they were kept and stall-fed.[14] The *moongo* meat hence emerges out of the *moongo* of the house as a manifestation and rendition of its debt to the claimant's use of her *moongo* in bringing her daughter into existence, whose marital relationship enabled the house. Extracting the *moongo* meat from the *moongo* of the house hence recognizes its debt on a person's *moongo* and the *horu* expended through it, which the meat replaces.

Arms and hands (*maoko*) feature centrally in butchering too, as one person firmly holds the animal while another person rubs eleusine into its fur or tosses milk onto it. It is even more pronounced in the case of goats, which are most commonly suffocated by a person applying his bare hands around its muzzle until it dies. Once the animal is skinned and parted, the shares of meat are solemnly presented with two hands to their rightful claimants, who receive them in the same manner. Just as arms and hands stall-feed the animal and carry and present the bridewealth prestations through the doorway, so the *maoko* carve the *moongo* meat and extract it from the *moongo* of the house.

The emergence or attraction of milk, bananas and beer out of one doorway and into another hence affords the detachment and emergence of a woman, which currently brings a third doorway into existence from which the *moongo* meat is extracted and emerges. The bridewealth prestations thus involve not only the elicitation of foodstuffs and women through different houses, but also the elicitation of one doorway from a backbone. Like the bride, the marital house that comes into being on her relocation owes its existence to the bride's mother's back, with the result that its doorway also comes into being through her *moongo*. The acquisition of the doorway coincides with the bride's acquisition of her back, which emerges through the doorway of her parents' house to enter into that of the marital house. This was recognized and underscored in the past, when the bride's relocation involved her being carried on the male *mkara*'s back to the groom's mother homestead. Once placed inside the house, the bride was not allowed to leave, and hence pass through the doorway, for the following month. Instead, she was fed powerful foods that were sent by the bride's mother and from all the homesteads that had received meat from an earlier prestation (Gutmann 1926: 113). The way she was carried suggests that the bride did not yet possess a backbone, which instead was grown by means of the foodstuffs that arrived through the doorway of the groom's mother's homestead. The different meanings of *moongo* hence entail and conceptualize how backbones emerge from backbones through doorways, while doorways emerge out of doorways by way of backbones. Doorways and backbones simultaneously come into being as effects of the movements of *horu*, whose transfers and transformations detach and attach persons to houses, and make houses the extrusions of backbones. Thus, as the bride emerges from her parents' house, she acquires a back and enables a doorway to which she and her children attach as a result of her dwelling. The effect is that one house everts *horu* through its doorway in the form of a bride, who uses her back to evert and convert life force, which enables and grows the marital homestead. Persons and houses are thus conversions or inversions of each other that emerge through doorways and backbones.

This dynamic was more pronounced in the past, when the bride's acquisition of her back coincided with the groom's mother's acquisition of a new doorway that was located behind (*mma*) or above (*fondoho*) the house she bestowed on her son and his wife. The doorway of the new house faced the back of the old house from which the former budded as an effect of the marital relationship. One house thus yielded another, which unfolded around the doorway that thereby came into existence, as it gradually developed into a homestead (*kaa*) and a cultivated place (*mdenyi*). As the bride was turned in through the doorway of the existing house to acquire a back, so the new house was turned out from its doorway, in through which the groom's mother and her back were turned. The bride was thus folded into an existing house through her marital relationship, while the new house was folded out from the groom's mother's back that brought her son into existence. The bridewealth prestations thus appear as forms of detachment and elicitations (Strathern 1988), where persons and things move into and out of homesteads, but they are best considered processes of transformation, where persons and houses turn into and out of each other through their respective *moongo*. These transformations moreover occur through the processes that suspend persons between multiple houses and homesteads. The result is that the state of extension or unfolding that the concept of *ialika* entails is achieved or effectuated through the backs of persons and the doorways of houses. Persons extend through their movement and suspension between different homesteads that are occasioned through people's engagements with doorways and backbones.

The transformational dynamic between persons and houses is reinforced by the fact that the *moongo* prestation is made by a house to certain persons, while the initial prestation was made by a person to a house. Where the first prestation was made by the groom's *mkara* and occasioned by the bride's presence in her parents' house, the *moongo* prestation is made by her marital homestead and occasioned by her mother's reproductive use of her back. The detachment of the bride from one homestead, and her attachment to another, thus transforms her from being the cause of one prestation to the agent of another (Strathern 1988). These prestations succeed each other in time, but they concern preceding relationships that moreover are of different kinds. Where the initial prestation intervenes in the relationship of nurture and consumption in the bride's parents' homestead, the subsequent *moongo* prestation compensates for her parents' antecedent reproduction. The prestations thus activate relationships that unfold in different temporal directions to recursively reiterate and extend them into the future by means of the *horu* they contain. In this process, houses and persons alternately extract *horu* from each other to unfold their enfolded relationships and extend dwelling through various *moongo*.

The multiple meanings of *moongo* allow for a reconsideration of the ceremonies for bringing newborn children out of the house that once were common in the region (Beidelman 1997: 92; Schapera 1940: 237; Wagner 1949: 307). In one account that stems from his tenure at Machame in western Kilimanjaro, Gutmann (1909a: 165–66) described how the birth of a child was marked with streaks of ochre on the doorpost of the confined mother's house. Cow's milk was then sprayed in the child's face and some was given 'to open its gullet' before the child was put to the breast for the first time. Three months later, the child was brought out of the house by a 'magician' (*Zauberer*) who placed it onto the roof protruding over the doorway.[15] There, he spat on it four times and tied a string of beads around its wrist before he held it aloft in front of those gathered in the courtyard (Gutmann 1909a: 169). The next day, the mother came out of the house, anointed in butter and decorated with chains, bells and strings of beads. She made visits both to her husband's and her own parents, as well as their relations, where she received butter and gave eleusine grains in return.

In another account that most likely stems from his subsequent tenure at Old Moshi in central Kilimanjaro, Gutmann (1926: 217ff) described a more elaborate ceremony that was conducted after the birth of a woman's first child. The ceremony removed the restrictions on her interactions with her husband's father and took place a week or so after the birth of the child, when its umbilical cord had fallen off. Beer was then prepared and the child was shown to the father's father and his eldest brother. When the men entered the confined woman's house, she gave the child to her husband's mother who assisted her, and served beer in the same way as the *wari wa iamba* was shared at Boniface's homestead. On receiving the beer, the husband's father said: 'Grow at this homestead, young mother'. Gutmann does not provide the vernacular terms, but it most likely featured the concept of *ifumbuka* that MaShirima when she requested that they should grow at the homestead (*dufumbuke*) and that the place should grow (*kufumbuke*).[16] The husband's father then anointed his son's wife with butter, which he applied by means of an *isale* leaf that he pulled out of the homestead's boundary hedgerow – *mrasa*. The paternal grandparent of the same gender as the child then lifted it towards the ceiling before chewing a roasted banana and transferring the pulp to the mouth of the child, while saying: 'Today I seize my grandchild. I now enter elderhood with my wife. Henceforth, we will remain at home to care for the child and spit food into him. But you, young mother, will go to the fields with your husband and bring us food out of your hand. Today, I have begun to spit food into him. He is my grandchild' (Gutmann 1926: 220).

The proceedings that occurred the following day reveal how these dynamics concern conversions and conveyances of *horu*. According to Gutmann (1926: 221), the father's father then gathered and told his agnates: 'I have received a child here on our land. Now I am thinking of anointing its mother with fat', to which they responded: 'Allow us too to lick the fat of the child'. The men slaughtered two goats and used their juiciest and fattest pieces for a meal to strengthen the newly delivered mother. When the meat was presented to the *mfee*, the husband's father told his son's wife: 'Receive, my young mother, this fat that I give you, so that you regain power [*Kraft*] to farm. We will meanwhile be the guardians of the child'. Together with his statement above, this entails that the groom's father replenishes the *horu* of his son's wife following her birth of a child that transformed him and his wife into elders. The *horu* they present and provide enables her use of her *koko* to produce and bring them food, which they will spit into the child, as they henceforth remain at the homestead.

These statements reveal how the birth of the child not only transforms its mother from bride (*mwali*) to confined woman (*mfee*), but also turns the father's parents into male and female elders. Termed respectively *meku* and *msheku*, these elders no longer farm, but instead receive food from the *maoko* of their son and his wife, which they expectorate into their grandchild. As these elders stop farming, they cease to transform and transfer *horu* by means of their arms and instead begin to do so by means of their mouths. As they shift subject positions, they shift *horu* in other forms by means of other body parts. In this regard, it is significant that the *ikamba* section that the male elder claims when his son butchers includes a piece of the animal's digestive tract. The *ikamba* thus manifests both how the elder lay on his chest to conceive his son, and how he spits food into the mouth of his son's son. The meat registers both his past and present use of different body parts for transferring *horu* in different forms. Since the claim rests on the son's reproduction, it turns on the bridewealth prestation that turned the claimant's child (*mwana wa homii*) into a husband (*mii*), who can impregnate a bride (*mwali*). Meanwhile, her birth of the infant (*matuma*) makes her an *mfee* for the *mii* to care for, and transforms his parents into elders for whom they jointly provide. Each notion and position is a transient mode of being that becomes as an effect of a relational matrix, where persons transform and transfer life force in different forms by means of different body parts. Their mutual transformations mean that persons move through this matrix, as a result of the conversions and conveyances of *horu*. Persons turn into and out of each other as effects of the transfers and transformations of bodily substances, and thus emerge as shifting subjects in a double sense, who transfer *horu* by means of different body parts to move the positions of self and others.

Coming-out ceremonies of the kind Gutmann described are no longer performed. The main reason is perhaps that women now give birth at the government health-station or district hospital, and not in the homestead. Nevertheless, their sense and significance are discernible from the meanings of *moongo* described above. In the past, the newborn child entered the house through one *moongo* (the mother's back) which differed from the *moongo* (the doorway) through which others entered the house. The child's arrival inside the house was therefore marked on the outside, on the doorpost next to the opening that the child was later brought out of and placed on top of by the *mwaanga*. The child was thus attached to the house and its doorway, while the milk and the roasted banana it was fed emplaced it in relation to the livestock, the banana garden and the hearth. Their mixture with spittle connected them to the father's parents, whose expectorations inserted the child into the transfers of *horu* that the foodstuffs involve. In this way, the child was attached to significant features and persons to make it a child of *this* house and *these* people. The dynamic of emplacement and attachment was underscored by Gutmann's (1928: 439) account of how the father's father warmed a leaf from the *ndishi* banana tree on the hearthstone, while saying: 'I acknowledge growth at the homestead, growth like the bees. I acknowledge the enchainer [*der Verbinder*], who enchained the descent group land [*Sippengrund*]. May he thrive like the *Lale*-bush, may he thrive like the taro, may he thrive like the *ndishi* banana, may he last like this creator'. He then placed the warmed leaf on the child's back and said: 'I receive you here in the world. You have been in the montane forest, where the elephants are, in a place where no one saw you. Thrive, grow tall like the *ndishi* banana, reach an age like your grandfather and apical ancestor. Enchain, like they enchained'.[17] The concept of *horu* does not feature, but Gutmann's description of how the newborn child both emerged from and was inserted into a process of growth that imbricates persons, crops and homesteads recalls the transfers and transformations of life force that occur through dwelling.

The emplacement and attachment of the child are today achieved by other means, once the mother and child emerge from confinement. The stump of the child's umbilical cord, which the mother keeps after it falls off, is then thrown in the indoor goat pen (*msau*). It remains there for a few days before it is swept up with the manure and placed at the foot of a *mnyengele* banana tree that leans uphill (*fondoho*) or towards the mountain. When the bunch from the tree matures, its bananas are ripened in the cooking hut attic and made into beer for the homestead's agnates, friends and neighbours. Like the acts that Gutmann described, this too serves to attach the child to significant elements of the homestead, such as the livestock pen, banana garden, attic and hearth, as well as to its inhabitants and their relations, who consume the beer. In fact, the child is emplaced in relation to many of the same features of the natal homestead that his or her father attached himself to in the mother's father's homestead by means of the initial bridewealth prestation. Like that prestation, this too is an intervention in the relationship of nurture and consumption that inserts the child into the transfers and transformations of *horu* that bodied forth the beer through the relationships of production.

In a related way, Gutmann (1928: 440) claimed that the mother was implored to care especially for the banana trees that produced the leaf that was warmed and placed on her child's back. In particular, she was to ensure that these trees received manure first and had space to expand in relation to other trees. He furthermore said that the carrier cushions on which the pot of bridewealth beer rested inside the bride's mother's house were made from the leaves of an *ndishi* and a *mlali* tree under which the groom's umbilical cord was buried after birth (Gutmann 1926: 102). The groom thus bodies forth the tree to which he attached as a child, which in turn bodies forth the beer he presents as bridewealth. Dundas (1924: 199) meanwhile described how the umbilical stump was kept in a gourd with eleusine grains, until the child was taken out of the house. The cord of a boy was then placed on the roots of a yam, while that of a girl was placed by an *ndishi* banana tree. He claimed that, 'thenceforth these plants are known as the "root" of the child, and their fruit may not be used by anyone but the senior woman who officiated'. The term *mri* is not used to mean the umbilical in Rombo, but Dundas's account suggests that the stump of the cord that conveys *horu* from mother to child is made to connect to the roots of crops and veins of animals, along and through which *horu* circulates in different forms. The vernacular statements Gutmann rendered reveal that the aim of this is to ensure the growth of persons and crops at the homestead where the child is born and attached. They echo MaShirima's pronouncement that the homestead and its inhabitants shall grow and that this occurs through transfers and transformations of *horu* that enable children and livestock to multiply. Disposing of the umbilical cord emplaces and attaches the child by connecting or inserting its *mri* into the circuitry of *horu* that constitutes the homestead (*mṛi*). It contributes to the separation of the child from its mother, which eventually enables a male youth to attach himself to another homestead by means of bridewealth and a female youth to detach in marriage. The tangled mass of vein-roots is thus central to the state of extension and disposition for unfolding that the concept of *ialika* entails and contains. The birth of a child prolongs, enchains and enhances beings of different kinds, as he or she eventually occasions a new homestead between which his or her parents will toddle. This extension or unfolding is initiated by the disposal of the umbilical, which connects the child to other *mri* that allows *horu* to move in different forms through parts of the child and the house, as well as the crops and livestock that belong to the homestead.

Naming and Necessity

When the *mfee* emerges from confinement, she reverts to be addressed as *mwali* and *mwaliamwana*, until she has borne two or more children. She is then known as *mfele*, which is used to mean both 'wife' and 'woman'. *Mfele* derives from the intensive form of *ifee* to mean someone who intensively births and cares for children, and is thoroughly nurtured with soft foods. As such, *mfele* is someone who intensively channels *horu* in different forms by means of different body parts in sex, parturition and nursing. These processes bring the infant into existence and move it to become a child (*mwana*), which simultaneously shifts and establishes the mother as 'wife' and 'woman'. Like the child, the *mfele* thus emerges from the *moongo*, when she comes out of the house with her second-born child. The concept and position of *mfele* hence also becomes as an effect of sustained engagement in transfers and transformations of *horu* that occur by means of different anatomical and architectural features. The gender category and position is therefore a gradually emergent mode of being that becomes as an effect of particular relations.

However, the intensive verb-form is also a double prepositional construction, so *mfele* is a person who gives birth both to and for someone else. The construction pertains to the naming practices, which expand on how persons extend or unfold through reproduction. These practices have both a historical longevity and a wider geographical extension, yet remain underexplored arguably due to an anthropological preoccupation with kinship terminology.[18] However, personal naming is of great social significance (Parkin 1989; Ruel 1997: 252), which in Rombo imbricates with the settlement patterns and inheritance practices to actualize a specific spatial and temporal field and movement.

Each person in Rombo has three names that consist of a personal name, a father's name (which is the father's personal name) and a descent group name, which are bestowed according to the person's place in the birth order. The first-born son receives 'the name of the homestead' (*rina la kaa*), which is the personal name of his father's father. Meanwhile, the second-born son is given 'the name of the pathway' (*rina la shia*), which is the personal name of his mother's father. Both receive the same father's name, but only the first-born son receives the father's descent group name, while the second-born son receives his mother's father's descent group name. Male children who are born after the second-born son may get any personal name, but they all receive the same father's name and the father's descent group name. Certain directions and restrictions may be placed on their naming by deceased relatives on either the father's or the mother's side, but these make themselves known later, when they require the person to change his name or take an additional one.[19]

In a similar way, the first-born daughter is given her father's mother's personal name, which is 'the name of the homestead', while the second-born daughter receives 'the name of the pathway', which is her mother's mother's personal name. Subsequent daughters receive any name, but may also be compelled to change these by a deceased relative. Personal naming of female children is thus a mirror image of that of male children, but significant differences obtain with regard to their father's name and descent group name. Like their male siblings, all female children receive their father's personal name, but this is changed to the personal name of their husbands upon marriage (I return to the significance of this below). The first- and second-born daughters receive respectively the descent group names of their father and their mother's father, and subsequent daughters all receive their father's descent group name. However, a woman's descent group name differs from that of a man in that it is prefixed with *Ma-*, which means 'mother of'. For instance, my adoptive mother was the third-born daughter of a man with the descent group name of Sway, so her descent group name is MaSway. The usage gains sense and significance from the fact that the second-born son of every woman is named after her father and her second-born daughter is named after her mother. The practice entails that she gives birth to and becomes the mother of her own father and mother.

The effect of the naming practice is that a marital couple reproduce their own parents, whose names are carried and extended by their children's children. It is this that accounts for the double-prepositional verb-form, which enunciates how people reproduce those who gave birth to them, and thus simultaneously give birth *to* children and give birth *for* someone else. Indeed, people claim that the first- and second-born children not only are named after their grandparents, but that they *are* them. This identification across alternate generations is underscored by the fact that children are addressed by the same relational terms that are used for and by those they are named after. A woman thus addresses her daughter's second-born son as 'my husband' (*miiakwa*), while her husband addresses the child as his 'age-mate' (*ndau*). Conversely, a man addresses his daughter's second-born daughter as 'my wife' (*mfelewakwa*), while his wife addresses her as 'co-wife' (*mweri*). Children who are named after one pair of grandparents are moreover referred to as 'husband' and 'wife', while they are talked of as *watoi* – people whose children have married – in relation to their siblings, who are named after the other pair of grandparents. On top of this, grandchildren have a freer than usual relationship to the grandparents they are named after and even assume their position in ceremonial settings, especially after their namesakes are dead. When MaSway poured milk for the dead on the ground inside her cooking hut, she therefore called on Atali's first-born son Richard, who replaced her deceased husband Ngufumari, whose baptismal name the boy carries. In contrast to the 'sweet relationships' between namesakes in alternate generations (von Clemm 1962: 131), people claim that men in the past deferred to their first-born sons, whom they addressed as 'father' (*ndie*), but this is something I have only seen and heard in jest.

Nevertheless, these practices give sense to the agnatic descent group that is currently termed by the Swahili word *ukoo*, but according to Gutmann (1926: 2) in the past derived its term from 'childbearing'. The term *utchari* is now defunct and archaic, but appears to be a noun derived from the causative form of the verb *iatcha*, which is currently used for both men and women reproducing. As a man may call on his agnates for contributions to his bridewealth prestations and the foods for his confined wife and children, and his children in turn reiterate his parents and reproduce himself and his wife, the practice entails that agnates occasion or cause childbirth– *iatchira*. *Utchari* then concerns the people who afford and contribute to each other's reproduction of themselves and one another.

Many parents pester their children to continue reproducing until they get grandchildren who carry their names. In 2008, Herman and

MaLasway for instance told me that they did not intend to have more children beyond the three sons and one daughter they had, due to the problems and expenses they experienced feeding and schooling them. However, MaShirima consistently complained that she had not received her grandchild, so on my return in 2011 I found that Herman and MaLasway had borne two more children in rapid succession since MaShirima would not let it rest. The last-born child was a girl, who accordingly received her mother's mother's name to finally make MaShirima content. MaShirima's persistence gains support and significance from the vernacular statement by the bride's mother above that she will die if her daughter's 'fat' does not combine with that of her husband to conceive children. A daughter's failure to reproduce means there is no child to carry her name, which hence will die.

People describe how these naming practices were complicated by missionization and christening. As the church demanded that saintly names should replace vernacular ones, the result was that children were not named after their grandparent. In response, the elders took the names of their identical grandchildren as their Christian names, when they converted and were christened. The effect was that grandparents were named after their grandchildren, rather than the other way around. Their choice of names could on occasion moreover be used to bolster certain other claims. Thus, when a now middle-aged friend failed his Standard Seven exam in the late 1960s, it was believed he forfeited his opportunity for secondary education. However, his resourceful father arranged for him to assume the place of another boy, who had passed his exam but whose father could not afford the fees. However, the arrangement required that the first boy assumed the name of the one he replaced. In fact, he not only received his entire secondary and tertiary education in that name, but still conducts his professional life under it in town. To preserve his personal name, he adopted the assumed name as his father's name, so when his father was christened in the early 1970s he chose this as his Christian name to bolster his son's assumed identity. While the elder has since passed away, all of his sons' first-born sons carry this name as their personal name. The mendacious move to ensure his son's continued education hence extends in the form of names more than forty years later.

In a similar way, a person may name a child after a particular person to create a relationship and establish an obligation. Thus, when the wife of an older classificatory brother of mine bore a son in 2001, he named him Christian after me and argued that I had a particular responsibility for the child. In the words of the vernacular statement provided by Gutmann above, he used my name for his child as an attempt to enchain me and ensure growth at his homestead. Gutmann's report of how children were named *Ngiriki* after the Greek trader arguably refers to similar attempts at ensnaring this person and enabling claims to his goods. As such, it means that people deploy their conceptual resources to engage foreigners in their language-games for particular gain.

However, parents' claims to their children's children are not restricted to their naming, but are exercised in more concrete ways. In the first few years of a couple's marriage, there is an absence of children to perform certain tasks, such as fetching water, collecting fodder and firewood, tending babies and assisting cooking. The couple solves this by either borrowing one of their younger siblings or borrowing an older sibling's children. Thus, a younger sister of MaLasway and a son of an older brother of Herman's lived and worked in their homestead in 2000–2001, as their two children were too small to help, but had returned to their parents' homestead on my later arrival, when the two children were able to work.

A similar problem recurs when all or most of a couple's children are married, and perhaps only the youngest son remains.[20] Until he marries and his children can help, the homestead suffers a lack of labour, which the elders address by claiming one or several of their grandchildren to come and live with them. No child can deny a parent's request for a grandchild, but negotiations take place regarding who shall provide which child. However, most homesteads go through a phase where children are numerous and the prospect of sending some away to be fed and schooled by others is welcome. Claiming and lending thus redistribute children between homesteads to ensure labour for the childless and relief from the pressure of provision for those with many children.

Parents may claim grandchildren from both their male and female children, and can be provided with any child regardless of his or her place in the birth order. However, there is a clear tendency for a son to send his first-born son or daughter to live with his parents, and for a daughter to send her second-born son or daughter to her parents. Elders thus tend to claim grandchildren who are themselves or who replace a deceased spouse – a fact they often stress and emphasize through the use of relationship terms. In contrast to a young childless couple, the grandparents do not eventually obtain their own children, so the claimed grandchildren often spend their entire childhood and adolescence with their grandparents, whose claims thus extend into and shape their lives.[21] If no grandchild is available or able to stay, the grandparents may request a child from someone else. Thus, when a daughter of Oswald's who had long lived with MaSway was brought back to Dar es Salaam, MaSway borrowed the daughter of a remotely related agnate to help her cook and clean. The girl's father suffered a drinking problem, so her mother was grateful that she stayed with MaSway, whose relatively prosperous son could provide a stable environment. Meanwhile, the father used his daughter's presence as a pretext to visit and request drinks and money when Oswald came from Dar es Salaam.

The identification of children with the grandparents for whom they are named was even stronger in the past, when the mother bestowed her homestead upon her son and his wife, and relocated to another with her remaining children. As described earlier, the settlement pattern entailed that the 'child in front' (*mwana wa mbele*) was emplaced below (*siinde*) or in front (*mbele*) of his siblings, who received homesteads in sequential order behind (*mma*) or above (*fondoho*) each other. Its effect was moreover that the first-born son received the homestead that his father had received from his father upon his marriage. In this way, the first-born son inherited the homestead that his father's father once inhabited, whose name he also carries. The first-born son thus not only assumed the relational position of his father's father, but occupied his geographical location. To paraphrase Raum's claim regarding foster mothers, the one substituted for the other both physiologically and sociologically. The first-born son thus 'replaced' his father's father (Weiner 1980), whose being he reiterated in a different body and at a different time. The effect and sense of replacement and reiteration was exacerbated by a preferential marriage practice, which people call 'returning the old woman to the homestead' (*naura msheku na kaa*) and describe as a man taking a wife from the same homestead where his father's father married.[22] I know of very few such marriages, but it is valorized and considered to involve little risk, as it replicates a relationship between homesteads where the inhabitants know each other. If a first-born son performed such a marriage in the past, it meant that he reiterated his father's father's geographical and relational position, and replicated his marital relationship, and thus would replace his father's father to the greatest possible extent.

Replacement also subtends the naming of second-born children, as people claim they must 'return' (*iuya*) or be given back to the mother's natal homestead.[23] The naming of the second-born children arises from the debt a woman owes her parents for her existence and a man owes his wife's parents for taking her as his wife from their homestead. Some even argue that the second-born son belongs to the mother's father's descent group and should inherit land from his mother's brother. It is often argued that the second-born son receives land away from their natal homestead because he does not belong to their father's descent group in the same way his brothers do. In line with this, Michael von Clemm (1962: 330) claimed that even-numbered sons occasionally inherited land from their mother's father in western Kilimanjaro, but that this depended on the latter's goodwill. I know of only one case where this happened in Rombo, and the events and contestations that ensued are considered in chapter five (see also Myhre 2009). In all other cases, the second-born son remains a member of his father's descent group, and no attempt is made to disenfranchise or dismiss them on the basis of their place in the order of birth.

Nevertheless, Gutmann (1926: 111) recounted the bride's father's instruction when she relocated in marriage: 'you will bear children, one of whom will be able to nurse the grandparents in your parental home when the sons have died. One of your children will protect the homestead of the mother's brother if there is no owner left'. The statement suggests that the bride's son who will be named after her father has a claim and potential to take over her natal homestead, if her father and brother should fail to provide an heir. Accordingly, the second-born son today maintains a closer connection to the mother's parents' homestead than his brothers do. He and his second-born sister, for instance, are not required to make the *kisango* prestation that enables persons to enter their mother's natal homestead via the *mengele* pathway. The *kisango* consists of the *uvaha* share of meat, which is the mother's brother's claim when an animal is butchered.[24] It accords with the fact that the prestation is usually made by adults, at a time when the mother's natal homestead is inhabited by her brother. Herman, for instance, only made this prestation in 2006, when he was in his mid-thirties. Before this, his frequent visits to his mother's brother's homestead were made via an auxiliary pathway that passes through the banana garden. A woman's second-born son and daughter are moreover not required to call *hodi* and make their presence known when they arrive at their mother's natal homestead. Unlike everyone else, they do not behave as guests in relation to the homestead and its inhabitants, but act in a way that manifests their attachment to the homestead by virtue of their names.

The second-born children who bear the names of the pathway thus return along the *shia* that the *mkara* traversed to make the bridewealth prestations. Their attachment to their mother's natal homestead and their link with affinal relationality is enunciated by their conceptual connection to the topographical feature that facilitated the bridewealth prestations, and is manifested by their ability to enter and leave their mother's natal homestead via the *mengele*. The effect of these conceptions and capabilities is that the second-born children form part of the transfers between affines. Their return to their mother's natal homestead constitutes another prestation and replacement of *horu* that further suspends the marital couple between multiple homesteads. The latter's state of extension that was effectuated by the bridewealth prestations thus unfolds through their reproduction, as their ensuing children are named after the inhabitants of another homestead to which they are returned. These children thus suspend between several homesteads, as their names entail a state of extension that unfolds further when they marry. In turn, this enables them to claim their daughter's children, whose names of the pathway are effects of their state of extension to which their daughter's marital relationship contributed. The result is that every person is in a state of extension or unfolding, whose reach depends on their age and engagement in the transfers and transformations of *horu* that occur through dwelling.

It is this unfolding state of extension that gives sense and direction to the change that occurs in a woman's patronym when she marries. The fact that a woman carries her father's name when the initial prestation is made and changes it to that of her husband when she relocates could suggest that it concerns a transfer of rights between the two men. The change does indicate that the father gives away a part of himself, and that the husband's claim to his wife is stamped on her name. However, the change does not signal a transfer of rights, but entails that a part of the father is detached from his homestead when his daughter relocates and his *horu* transfers to her marital homestead. Her change of his name for that of her husband concerns the transformation of her subject position from someone's daughter to another person's bride, which is effectuated by her detachment from one homestead and her attachment to another. Alongside her transformation from *mwana wa kaa* to *mwaliamwana* goes a change in her middle name that reveals a shift in the relational definition of her being. However, the subject transformation is not complete, as evidenced by the fact that Lasway still addressed his married sisters as 'children of the homestead' (*wana wa kaa*) when MaShirima poured milk on the ground. In addition, the fact that the bride's second-born children are named after her parents means that they retain a claim to her reproductive powers, which replaces the *horu* extracted from their homestead. Instead of signalling a transfer of rights in a woman, the changing of her name concerns her gradual detachment from her natal homestead and her growing attachment to her marital homestead, as an effect of the transfers of *horu* this involves. Her changed name thus enunciates her state of extension or unfolding (*ialika*) that concomitates her increasing separation from her father and his homestead, and her growing connection with her husband and their marital homestead.

The reach and state of a person's extension registers in the forms of claims he or she is able to make. Children with the names of the homestead are most closely attached to their natal homestead, and may hardly make claims on anyone or anything outside it until they make the *kisango* prestation. Children with the names of the pathway by contrast may freely enter the mother's natal homestead and engage its inhabitants to which they return and partly attach. Their father attached to this homestead through the bridewealth prestations that enabled him to detach their mother, who then attached to the marital homestead through her dwelling. Her relocation and attachment extended her parents, who thereby were enabled to claim two children with the names of the pathway from her marital homestead. Together with *moongo*, the notion of *rina la shia* underscores how a person's extension goes along pathways and through doorways that lead into and out of the homesteads. These engagements involve and occasion transfers and transformations of powerful foodstuffs and bodily substances that employ both architectural features and parts of the anatomy to enable claims to persons who bear certain names. As the state of unfolding that *ialika* involves takes place by means of pathways, doorways and backbones, it enunciates and underscores how *horu* transfers and transforms through houses and persons who thereby suspend between homesteads.

It follows from this that naming practices and terminological equivalences are neither a form of 'quasi'-reincarnation (Ruel 1997: 252) to ensure that deceased relatives are remembered, nor a child-exchange between alternate generations (Allen 2000: 70), where a man gives away his daughter for the future return of a child. Rather, these practices form an integral part of the transfers and transformations of life force that take place through dwelling, which extend or unfold persons over time and across space as they detach and attach to homesteads. The names of persons are effects of the extensions of persons and the movements of *horu* that occur along pathways and through doorways that connect homesteads across their boundaries. As grandparents claim certain children on the basis of their engagement in dwelling, so the names of these children are debts their parents owe to the preceding generation for their reproductive efforts. Names are thus also effects of dwelling that are transferred between homesteads and along pathways, parallel to the prestations of *horu*. It expands and deepens the point made in the previous chapter concerning how addresses and dialogic exchanges are enabled and emerge from prestations of *horu*.

Extending through Time and Space

The mode of extension that *ialika* entails and effectuates is simultaneously topographical and temporal. As described earlier, in the past the first-born son received his mother's homestead, while she relocated to another one with her remaining children. This practice meant that the first-born son extended dwelling in an existing homestead, which his father received from his father upon marriage. Meanwhile, his mother established a new homestead, which she bestowed on the third-born son, when he married. By repeating this process for each son until the last-born one married, the parents gradually extended between an increasing number of homesteads that occupied an ever-expanding area, as they turned more land into banana gardens that they bequeathed to their sons. Each new homestead was in turn handed down to the succeeding generation, which extended its existence in time. The effect was a replacement of generations in one place, but this combined with a movement through space, as each homestead hived off iterations to create a sequence of houses that extended up the mountainside. New generations thus extended the roots and veins (*mri*) of persons, livestock and crops ever-deeper into the ground of existing homesteads, and simultaneously spread their root-veins laterally to encompass new land.

The combination of replacement and movement pertains also to the second-born son, who was provided land away from the natal homestead. Like *mwana wa mbele* and *rina la kaa*, so the notion of *rina la shia* involves both a generational and geographical position that presuppose both past and future generations. Yet unlike *mwana wa mbele*, *rina la kaa* and *rina la shia* do not presuppose other locations below and above. Instead, they entail places to the left and the right that relate laterally through pathways and doorways. In combination, these notions create two simultaneous and interlocking spatial and temporal figures. The first involves a replacement of alternate generations that trail off into the past and the future, and the second involves homesteads that attract powerful substances along pathways and through doorways to enable new homesteads that divide off as self-similar iterations that extend through space.

The same spatial and temporal figures recur in the form of banana cultivation, which simultaneously spreads and entrenches across the mountainside. Bananas reproduce through parthenogenesis, where the root or corm of the tree produces offshoots that grow up beside its stem. When they emerge, these shoots are called *wana wa ndaka* or the 'children of the banana tree', which for one plant can number as many as ten (Ngeze 1994: 28). As mentioned in chapter one, most are uprooted as they otherwise deplete the *horu* and diminish the stem and bunch of the parent plant. Commonly only one child grows to maturity, usually the one that emerges below (*siinde*) or in front of (*mbele*) the existing tree. This one is known as *imwana imbele*, which resembles and reiterates the name and location of the first-born son, who is emplaced below or in front of the parents. As mentioned, the pruning of offshoots is delegated to someone with a good hand, who considers with care and circumspection the location of trees in relation to each other to anticipate and plan for the growth of food and fodder in the future. Gutmann (1928: 440) touched on this, as he described the instruction that the woman who tends the tree that provided the leaf that warmed her child's back shall ensure its 'scope for life' (*Lebenspielraum*).

In some cases, depending on the location and relation of the tree to others in the vicinity, two offshoots are left in place. These are usually on opposite sides of the existing tree, so that the second offshoot is located above (*fondoho*) or behind (*mma*) the parent, on the opposite side of *imwana imbele*. The second offshoot will be the start of a new line of trees and is known as *mamka wa ndaka*, which employs the term that Winter (1977: 37ff) renders as both 'mother' and 'wife's mother'. If located below and above an existing tree, the *imwana imbele* and *mamka wa ndaka* occupy the positions of the first-born child in relation to the mother, and thus relate in the way homesteads did in the past. But if they are located on either side of the existing tree, the two offshoots occupy positions of the left and the right, and thus relate like affinal homesteads. As the *mamka wa ndaka* occasions a new row of trees, it relates to these as the wife's mother that enables a line of homesteads. Both practices entail and ensure that banana trees relate topographically to become located in lines extending up and down the mountainside, just like the homesteads of agnates and succeeding generations that also maintain lateral relations to their affines.

When a bunch is harvested, the stump (*itonga*) of the tree is left to stand 10–20 centimetres above the ground. The stump protects its *imwana imbele*, which it provides with water and prevents from blowing over, as this grows up to produce fruit. The growing tree gives out offshoots long before its bunch appears, so the result is that three generations are discernible at any given time. These consist of the stump, the tree and the offshoot, which grow in a straight line and are nourished through the same *mri* that extend from the stump at one end, across the tree in the middle, to its child at the other end. Such trees that share an origin are called *kisumu kimu*, which literally means 'one corm' or 'one stem'. In Swahili, they are known as 'one descent group' (*ukoo mmoja*), which reiterates the link to human reproduction that the notion of *imwana imbele* involves, and that Gutmann (1928: 440) indicated when he used the term *Sippenbanane* to mean such a cluster of related trees.

The stump of the old tree is uprooted by means of an iron shovel called a *shumbwa*, once the tree of the middle generation is cut down and its bunch is harvested. However, the dense and heavy pieces of the corm are not removed from the garden, but turned upside down and placed around the stem of the remaining tree, which usually is its 'grandchild'. As the stump is composted, people say it provides *horu* for the grandchild to grow tall and produce plentiful fruit. Just as the father's father in the past enabled the first-born son of his son to dwell by providing him a name, a homestead and a wife, so the stump provides life force in the form of compost manure for its offspring's offspring. Each 'one' enables another 'one', so that persons and banana trees, like houses and subject-positions, emerge and exist as multiples of one. It surpasses analogy, as persons, houses and banana trees equally involve generational and topographical transfers and transformations of *horu* through *mri* and *moongo* that enable the emergence of new entities of the same kind. In each case, one generation gives birth to and nourishes the next, yet contributes to the third, which reiterates its own being. As each generation gives birth to the one that provided it with life, it becomes burdened with its past at the same time as it is pregnant with its future. The current generation is therefore in a continual process of emergence or becoming that constitutes the 'now' as an ever-present forthcoming, which brings with it a past and contains a future.[25] In Ingold's (2000: 196) words, it offers 'a particular vista of past and future; but it is a vista that is available from this moment and no other. As such, it *constitutes* my present, conferring upon it a unique character. Thus the present is not *marked off* from a past that it has replaced or a future that will, in turn, replace it; it rather gathers the past and future into itself, like refractions in a crystal ball'.

The same temporality is implied by the naming system, where the personal name of the first-born son is both that of his father's father and that of his future son's son, while his middle name is both that of his father and that of his eventual first-born son. Each person thus carries with him or her both his or her past and future, in the form of names that implicate both preceding and succeeding generations. The naming system, settlement practices and inheritance patterns hence reproduce a common temporality that reiterates in banana farming. At the same time, the naming system implicates the bridewealth prestations and affinal relations, which not only anticipate children as their outcome, but return some of them on the basis of debts accrued through reproduction. Accordingly, MaShirima's address shifted perspectives between past dwelling and future life, and revealed the present as part of and emergent from movements of *horu* that give motion to events and ensure their extension through time and across space. By her statements, the prestation was laden with history at the same time as it came to contain its own future to constitute dwelling as an ever-present forthcoming.

There is a multiplicative and expansionary potential to these practices and processes that puts the area's population growth and land shortage in a new light. Since every son names his first-born son and daughter after his father and mother, and every daughter names her second-born son and daughter after her father and mother, a man and a woman are provided with one reiteration for every child they bear. As the case of Herman and MaLasway shows, every couple ideally and hopefully reproduce their parents, which means that each person is reiterated by both his sons and daughters. Since a man moreover calls on his eldest sister to serve as his female *mkara*, she not only reproduces her parents but also enables her brother to reproduce them. As her husband acts as her brother's male *mkara*, he not only reproduces his wife's parents as well as his own; he also facilitates his wife's brother's reproduction of their parents. The impetus of the naming system may be to reproduce the person who gave life to you, but its effect is that every person receives multiple reiterations. Moreover, since each son was previously provided with a house and homestead on marriage, an increased number of sons placed a greater area under cultivation. The result of the naming system thus appears to be a multiplication of persons for every generation that together with the settlement pattern and inheritance practices occasioned a proliferation of homesteads across the mountainside. The population growth and land shortage that preoccupy the scholars of the region are hence the result of the expansionary potential and multiplicative logic of spatial and temporal movements that occasion ever-more persons, houses, livestock and gardens. The logic and movement were perhaps rendered more efficient by improved public health and the opportunities created by the market economy, but they are engendered by vernacular conceptual resources and capabilities.

Life and Its Inflection

The ethnography above shows how the person is composed of *horu*, which is transformed and transferred through production, reproduction and consumption. Accordingly, the person emerges as an effect of multiple relations that encompass a multitude of beings. Gutmann (1926: 9) touched on this when he claimed that the right earlobe of a child belongs to its father and the left belongs to its mother's brother, and that they therefore are tasked with piercing one ear each. His claim gains sense from how 'left' (*kumooso*) and 'right' (*kulo*) are locative constructions that derive from the noun *moo* and the verb *ilya*, which respectively mean 'life' and 'to eat'. As shown in the previous chapter, these notions pertain to the bridewealth prestations, where women and foodstuffs enter and emerge through doorways and along pathways to enable reproduction and create life. In this context, the notions pertain to the way a woman grows and feeds her child by means of the blood in her womb and milk in her breasts, while the father contributes to the child's growth by way of feeding its mother. As the mother provides *horu* and affords life directly, so the maternal side is that 'of life', while the paternal side is that 'of eating' since the father provides life force in the form of foods for her to eat.

The woman's ability to convey life is accentuated when she gives birth and the emphasis is placed on her back, whose term – *moongo* – also derives from *moo*. Her *moongo* moreover features in sex and conception, where the chest and penis of the man convert *horu* in the form of blood and convey it as semen, which she receives by means of her back and vagina. The role of the back in this regard gives further sense to Gutmann's (1966: 63) claim that the conjunction of left and right is a symbol of copulation that brings out how the person is a conjoined being. The emphasis on the woman's *moongo* for sex, conception, childbirth and care entails that the paternal and maternal contributions to the child conjoin through this part of her anatomy. As Raum suggested, it is in her womb (*ndeu*) that her *horu* and that of the man combine to form new life, but this is released into the world by means of her *moongo*. These processes conjoin the left- and the right-hand side of the child, so these connect through and extend from his or her own back. Gutmann's claim can therefore be modified to mean not only that the combination of left and right is a symbol of copulation that makes up the person, but that they concern material transfers and transformations that occur through or by means of the mother's back. As the left and right conjoin through activities where the *moongo* plays a prominent role, it follows that they extrude from the person's own back.

However, *moongo* is also the doorway through which the bride-wealth prestations arrive, and from which the bride departs to gain the back she employs in sex, conception, birthing and childcare. One of these prestations is the *moongo* meat of butchered animals that emerges from the doorway of the bride's marital homestead to replace the *horu* her parents expended and her husband removed through the doorway of their homestead. The notion of *moongo* thus derives or un-folds from *moo* to capture how powerful substances transfer through doorways to detach a bride, who deploys her back in reproduction, where life force converts and conveys as bodily fluids that are compen-sated by shares of meat from animals' backs that emerge from other doorways. The meanings of *moongo* thus concern how doorways and backbones are openings and lines through and along which *horu* transfers and transforms between places and persons to afford life. Its derivation or inflection of *moo* means that *moongo* can be rendered as 'conduit of life', whose uses and meanings concern and facilitate transfers and transformations of *horu* through persons, houses and livestock.

The last point is underscored by the chyme of the animal that butchering brings out, and whose term – *mooshe* – also derives from *moo*. Its link to life recalls Ruel's (1997: 98) claim that 'Kuria spoke of chyme as the "life" or "wellbeing", *obohoro*, of the animal, and com-pared it to *ubukima* as the staple, grain-derived food of themselves'. In Ruel's (1997: 101–2) view, the salience of chyme stems from the fact that life depends on the ingestion of natural resources from 'outside' and their assimilation to the domain of social life at 'home'. By con-trast, *mooshe* concerns the role of bovine digestion as a site and pro-cess for the horticultural activities of the homestead, where the leaves and stems of banana trees are harvested and sliced as fodder, which provides manure that secures the growth of further food and fodder. Chyme does not here concern appropriation and assimilation of nat-ural resources for social purposes, but transfers and transformations of *horu* within and around the homestead. This was brought out as Gutmann (1909b: 133) argued that the capacity or power (*Wirkungs-kraft*) of fodder was potentiated (*potenziert*) in the chyme, and Moore (1976: 363) held that 'manure had peaceful, cooling, fertility-causing, life-bringing in it'.[26]

As an intermediate form between fodder and manure, chyme forms a pivot or hinge on which the transformational process that is the growth of the banana garden turns. *Mooshe* therefore derives from *moo* to capture chyme as a 'substance of life' that converts and conveys *horu* between vegetative, animal and human being.[27] Accordingly, Gutmann (1924a: 124) claimed that people sensed a 'unity of life' (*Lebenseinheit*) with livestock and crops. He moreover conjectured that the 'primordial human' (*Urmensch*) experienced this in terms of the 'cultic bonds and forces' that arose from the 'enjoyment and exchange of life-sap, spit, milk, and blood' (Gutmann 1924a: 145), which Raum (1907: 292) similarly deemed 'vital substances' or 'life-carriers' (*Träger des Lebens*).[28] Gutmann (1926: 425) revealed how this even encompassed the barter and trade of the market, where persons exchange the results of different activities as part of a 'uniform and equitable life circle' (*einheitlichen und gleichbedingten Lebenskreises*). These claims gain sense from how persons transform and transfer *horu* in the form of different bodily substances through productive and reproductive endeavours that grow crops, raise livestock and foster children.

In accordance with the centrality of chyme, intestines can show (*ilhoria*) the state and character of dwelling and life in the homestead where the butchering occurs or the animal has been kept.[29] This is done by removing the intestines and placing them on top of the large stomach (*haya*), where the 'courtyard' (*sha* or *washa*) and two 'arms' (*maoko*) are carefully inspected in the form of the spiral loop and the cecum and jejunum.[30] White dots on the courtyard show rain, children or kids and calves at the homestead, while fatty threadlike growths show ropes for tying livestock in the house. If the two hands are evenly filled with chyme, people see (*ilholhya*) that the inhabitants will obtain results from their pursuits. In combination, these claims imbricate and underscore MaShirima's request that Herman and MaLasway should obtain results from their productive and reproductive engagements. Conversely, discolouration shows illness on the part of the inhabitants, while unevenly filled, limp or even empty hands make people see that problems are in store. It is chyme's role as a hinge in the horticultural activities that affords the ability to reveal past, present and future effects of people's engagement in the productive practices and reproductive relationships that constitute dwelling and enable life in the homestead.

The concern for digestion entails that the *moongo* share is a conversion and extroversion of *mooshe*, whose *horu* is everted and conveyed, when the animal is carved and claimed by the bride's parents. In fact, the entire animal body is a transmutation of *mooshe* that is divided and distributed on the basis of different relationships through which life force is transformed and transferred. As already mentioned, the claims to and justifications for some of these shares concern the conception, birthing and care of children. Others, meanwhile, regard the acts of cutting fodder and sweeping manure, where chyme is transformed and transferred to grow crops and raise animals, and thus afford further food and fodder (Myhre 2013b: 117). Thus, a share of the liver is called 'to gather grass or leaves' (*imanyamadu*) and given to the person who cut fodder for the animal, and the third stomach (*itasura*) is presented to the one who swept the manure and placed it in the banana garden. Similarly, the *uanga* or caul is given to the eldest woman of the homestead to show her how well she cared for the animal. It is namely fodder that builds the *uanga*, which surrounds the intestines and converts to milk or semen that transfers through reproduction and lactation. When an animal is butchered, the caul's appearance is therefore eagerly anticipated, as its size and heft reveal and manifest the health and *horu* of the animal. Conversely, a small or thin *uanga* is attributed to poor fodder or the animal's age and reproduction that have diminished its *horu*.

Animals of both genders are butchered in the same way, but a female animal must first have borne offspring, like the goat that the Kamba-speakers brought to the plains in 2008. Such an animal is called *mooma*, which is another compound concept, where *moo* combines with the suffix -*ma*- which means 'mother' or 'mother of', and ordinarily features as a prefix in women's agnatic descent group names. The account above shows how this pertains to the naming practice and the way in which a woman gives birth to children who reproduce her parents, and who return (*iuya*) and retain a closer connection to her natal homestead. When added to the descent group name, the notion of -*ma*- enunciates the reiteration, where a woman gives birth to those who gave birth to her. Tacked onto *moo*, it renders *mooma* as 'mother of life' or 'life-mother', which articulates both how the female goat has borne at least one kid, and how the animal is a site for the process where chyme transforms and transfers *horu* between vegetative, animal and human beings.

Similarly, the notion of *moombe* that Peter used to address Horombo when he poured beer on the ground in the plains combines *moo* with the term *mbe* which is used synonymously with *meku* to mean 'male elder'. My translation of *moombe* as 'great one' is based on people's Swahili translation of the term as *mkubwa*. However, it is best rendered as 'life-father' or 'life-elder', which enunciates how Peter and the members of his descent group owe their existence and hence life to Horombo. However, the term also formed part of his request for food and fodder that would enable their continuation of dwelling (*ikaa*), which they had enjoyed for so long. As he requested that people should receive something to eat, and pointed out how the livestock had no fodder and the banana trees were finished, Peter conjured the imbrications between banana farming and livestock stall-feeding on which humans, livestock and crops depend. As I will show in chapter six, he in fact invoked bovine digestion and chyme when he tossed milk on the bull-calf and requested that Horombo should give them some manure (*kaboru*) and something to eat.[31] He thus ordered his request to enunciate how foodstuffs emerge as transformations of chyme, while he tossed and poured *horu* in the form of milk and beer to return the life they owe Horombo with the hope and anticipation that they will receive *horu* in other forms that will enable them to extend dwelling and life. In line with this, Gutmann (1926: 667) argued that *moo* relates to the term for the hearth-fire (*modo*), and that it means a 'vitalizing glow' or 'inner fire', which accords with the 'glowing fire in the house'. Something similar is at play in Rombo, but there the hearth-fire (*motcho*) transforms powerful substances into soft foods (*kelya kiholo*) that replenish people's *horu* and raise the heat (*mrike*) of their bodies.

In combination, *kumooso, moongo, mooshe, mooma, moombe* and *motcho* concern places, conduits, substances, beings and processes from, through, along and by means of which *horu* converts and conveys. They enunciate how life (*moo*) is an effect of transfers and transformations of life force that take place between persons, houses, livestock and crops through dwelling or *ikaa* that occurs in and around the homestead – *kaa*. Each of these notions moreover involves different body parts that convert and convey *horu* in different forms and engage the world in different ways. They thus concern a vectorial person that transfers and directs *horu* in different forms through different anatomical features for different effects. The arm hence expends *horu* in the form of blood, as it cuts fodder to create chyme (*mooshe*) and sweep manure, and thus yield powerful foodstuffs. In turn, these may be presented as bridewealth through the doorway (*moongo*) of a homestead of the left-hand side (*kumoosoni*), which not only affords an additional homestead and doorway, but also enables reproduction where the back (*moongo*), chest and genitals convert and convey *horu* as blood and semen. In addition, powerful foodstuffs are transformed over the hearth-fire (*motcho*), where the arm employs a ladle to convert and convey soft foods that replenish the *horu* expended in production and reproduction, and fill the breasts that nurse children or load the mouths that chew and spit foodstuffs into them. In each case, *horu* assumes a particular form depending on the body part or architectural feature through which it converts and conveys. Furthermore, the forms that emanate from the different body parts are deployed by other features for further transfers and transformations of *horu*. Each notion thus gathers particular body parts and material beings in a specific language-game, yet yields entities that are engaged by further notions in additional language-games, where *horu* converts and conveys by means of other bodily components. As *horu* transmutes and transfers to facilitate further conversions and conveyances, these notions concern processes where the means and ends are self-similar and intrinsic to each other (cf. Myhre 1998). Accordingly, they share a common core in the concept of *moo*, which enunciates how the purpose of these transfers and transformations is life and its living.

Life and Language

The vectorial person that converts and conveys *horu* in different forms through different anatomical features for different effects recalls Daivi Rodima-Taylor's (2016: 91) account from among the Kuria, where 'personhood seems predicated on facilitating an assemblage of transitory connections and relations through directing material and relationship flows'. Her claim pertains to the notion of *omooyo* that is used for the gullet and windpipe through which food, air and water pass to facilitate *obohoro* or life, health and well-being (Rodima-Taylor 2016: 80; Ruel 1997: 121). However, the *omooyo* connects to and interacts with other openings, like the corral gateway of the homestead and the doorway of its house. Ruel (1997: 123) therefore points out that 'the *omooyo* is simply one of the passages or connections upon which all life depends, in this case the life of persons'. As cognates of *moo* and *horu*, *omooyo* and *obohoro* hence equally concern how life is an effect of material transfers and transformations that occur through parts of persons, houses and the environment.

Ruel (1997: 116, 119) moreover argues that *omooyo* also concerns speech and communication, which pass along the same passageway. Similarly, Gutmann's (1926: 314) account of how the child's name was revealed once its first tooth had emerged shows that language entwines with the transfers and transformations of *horu*. The nursemaid was then secretly informed of the name and was the first to use it, as she gave the child to its mother and encouraged her to nurse it. On hearing the name, the mother feigned surprise and asked when the child had received it, before she welcomed the infant and asked when it had found its fortune (*Glück*) on the way. In reply, the nursemaid turned to the child and said: 'Tell her: yes, sucked one [*Gesogene*], I had to wait long for it!' The mother then repeated her joy and said: 'As I told him: welcome, and may he bring fortune to us and his grandfather!' The interaction suggests that the name slowly emerges from the child itself, which the mother then engages in a form of conversation where the nursemaid ventriloquizes on its behalf. The content of the conversation supports and gains sense from the ethnography above, as it too entails that the child gradually emerges to be welcomed by its mother. The use of the term 'sucked one' reiterates how the child's emergence is facilitated by the mother's breasts, while her hope that the child shall bring fortune to its parents and grandfather concerns the naming practice, whereby it reiterates its grandfather and eventually reproduces its parents.[32] In combination, this means that the name is gradually made known as the effects of nursing, and that the ability to speak slowly emerges along with the tooth that enables the child to eat more solid foods. Names and speech thus entwine *horu* and convey along the same openings and passages.[33]

These dynamics gain further support from Gutmann's (1926: 315) account of how the name of the child was announced to the oldest man and woman of the agnatic descent group (*Sippe*). For this festive occasion, the two elders were invited to the homestead, where the mother sat with her child directly in front of the doorway. Her husband sat by her side and their parents sat on either side of them. The mother and father seized the child's arm and placed its hand in that of the male elder, while the nursemaid repeated its name before the mother said: 'Behold, my husband's father, this is your grandchild'. Gently seizing its hand, the elder greeted the child by name and said: 'My grandchild, it was your grandfather who mentioned your name. May you grow like the *mrie*-tree'. The mother replied on the child's behalf by saying: 'Welcome, my grandfather, who begot me'. The account reveals how the child emerges from the doorway of the house to receive a name from a grandparent, who the child reproduces. The proceedings moreover involved powerful foodstuffs, as the elder afterwards requested beer that he received and drank before the others. Like the arrival of the child's tooth, the emergence of its name also released and was accompanied by powerful foodstuff in the form of beer. Once everyone had enjoyed the beer, the party took its leave by saying: 'The spider's silk knots itself, the name of the grandfather has returned to our land. We shall not become extinct'. The worry about extinction echoes Peter's lament in the plains that they were finished, and articulates how the concern is to extend life and enable its living. Meanwhile, the spider's silk knotting itself concerns something that doubles back on itself to actuate a form and realize a phenomenon. It enunciates how the birth of a child is a reiteration of a grandparent, and the way in which *horu* folds back on itself in a particular way to manifest a specific being.

It is the imbrication of language and life force, which the vectorial person directs and transfers through particular openings and passages, that accounts for the event with which this chapter opened. Sex of the kind that Alois and his lover enjoyed was of concern for MaSway and Herman, as it involved transfers and transformations of *horu* in other forms and by other means than those that pertain to the banana garden. In this case, they did not use their arms to convert and convey *horu* in the form of blood for the purpose of yielding food and fodder. Instead, Alois engaged his chest and penis to transform his blood into semen that he transferred to his lover, who received it by means of her back and vagina. She moreover carried the *horu* away either in the form of an increase of her blood or as a foetus that combined from his semen and her blood. In either case, the *horu* was not redeployed in another form to enable further transfers and transformations in relation to this homestead. Instead, it amounted to a removal of life force that according to Herman would be extracted from plants and crops of the banana garden. In light of the notion of *mri*, this suggests that they imbricated their veins with the roots of plants and crops when they engaged their body parts in the banana garden, and that this served to convert and channel *horu* away from the latter.

In accordance with this, sexual prohibitions obtain with respect to practices and relationships that pertain to production and consumption. For instance, the person who uproots banana stumps (*ikaba matonga*) must not have sex the same day, lest the trees that they nurture lose their *horu* and fail to produce fruits and further offshoots. Meanwhile, the person who replants the excess *ndaka* must refrain from sex otherwise it will lose its power and fail to seize or stick (*iira*) in its new location. Similarly, the person who leads an animal to be covered must also abstain, lest the semen fails to seize or stick (*iira*) and result in conception. Sexual prohibitions actually pertain to seeds and slips of all kinds, including those sold for cash or grown in the plains. Women therefore refrain from sex after sowing maize, eleusine, beans, groundnuts and the like in the plains, and men abstain after pruning the coffee bushes in the *mdenyi*. The latter is done twice a year, most commonly by an expert with 'good hands', who does so for a fee. As for the person uprooting stumps and replanting offshoots, it requires careful deliberation and delegation to someone who can be relied on not to have sex and thus sap the crops of their *horu*.

Similar prohibitions apply to practices pertaining to cooking and consumption. In particular, they apply to the different stages of brewing, where engagement in sex on a given day may prevent the bananas from ripening in the attic or the eleusine from sprouting to make malt, and the beer from 'turning around' (*iunduka*) to ferment and gain the right consistency. At each stage, engagement in sex diminishes the *horu* of the substance that is handled to jeopardize the outcome of the process. Like for the prohibitions above, these concern the potential for sex to sap the *horu* of the foodstuffs that people engage by diverting it through other body parts and to other beings. Gutmann (1926: 659) grasped how sex involves such transfers, when he described the penis and breasts as 'dispatchers of power' (*Kraftentsender*) or 'transmitters of force' (*Kraftträger*). Unfortunately, he did not provide the vernacular terms for these body parts, but the current uses of *mawele* to mean both a man's testicles and a woman's breasts enunciate how semen and breastmilk are mutual transformations that manifest *horu* in different forms. Its uses underscore how the sexual prohibitions ensure that the conversions and conveyances of life force are channelled through specific body parts in particular activities to ensure desired outcomes.

Like the notions that derive from *moo*, the uses of the term *mawele* entail and engage different body parts and material beings, and thus form part of language-games that involve and contain a plethora of world-relations. In fact, these interlocking concepts concern processes that constitute the world and all it contains, as they pertain to how persons, houses, livestock and crops come into being as the effects of body parts and architectural features that channel *horu* in particular ways. Like the Lunda notion of *mooy*, they thus concern and reveal how *horu* is a relational force that exists between, acts upon and refracts through beings of different kinds. However, *horu* does not exist in itself, but assumes a particular form on the basis of the lines and openings through and along which it conveys and converts. *Horu* is therefore a phenomenon that effectuates beings of different kinds. It is reminiscent of Günter Wagner's (1949: 161) claim regarding the Lurogoli and Luvugusu terms *ekilili* and *sisinini* that can be rendered as 'shadow', but in fact mean a physical energy or an actuating force that occasions every bodily function. Gutmann (1935: 8) was on the track of this too, when he argued that 'all the ingredients of community life grow out of undivided protoplasm.

But without the stimulus to activity they wither away'. His claim suggests that *horu* is a uniform life force that brings phenomena into being when it is directed through particular relations: 'The family, however, itself requires for the sustenance of its own life direct and uninterrupted access to the stream of life which flows through the tribal society so long as the social strata which are its channels are preserved' (Gutmann 1935: 3). *Horu* is therefore not some*thing*, but concerns a movement or interaction that affords beings of different kinds, depending on its direction and magnitude. *Horu* is therefore a life *force* that effectuates everything that is, depending on the places, conduits, substances, beings and processes from, through, along and by means of which it converts and conveys. Together with the notions that derive from *moo*, *horu* thus enunciates how life is an effect of material transfers and transformations, and the manners in which persons, houses, livestock, crops, and foodstuffs come into being and exist within and of life (cf. Deleuze 2006).

As the sexual prohibitions channel *horu* in specific directions, they actualize beings of particular kinds, which emerge as transformations of life force. Indeed, the sexual prohibitions are themselves transformational, as they articulate and manifest how persons, houses, livestock, crops and foodstuffs contain each other as alternative states of being (cf. Strathern 1999: 304). In this way, they enunciate how production, reproduction and consumption nest as transformations of each other, and how *horu* moves through them in different forms. It is this set of nesting activities through which *horu* transfers and transmutes that constitutes dwelling – *ikaa* – and animates life – *moo* – in Kilimanjaro.

According to Raum (1909: 105), the verb 'to be' – *ikeri* – derives from *ikaa*, which thus enunciates how dwelling effectuates that which is, and, by extension, how this is by virtue of *horu*. However, the oft-heard phrase that 'the blood of a person walks or moves around' (*samu ya mdu itchambuka*) reveals how *horu* and its movements must not be confused with human agency. The phrase is used with regard to the circulation of blood within the body, but also occurs in connection with other related phrases, like 'the blood of a person does not get lost' (*samu ya mdu ilechekiyaku*) and 'the blood of a person returns to the homestead' (*samu ya mdu iuya kaa*). The former is used when someone has suffered a violent or accidental death to mean that the blood of the victim will seek out and avenge the person responsible. The second statement is used regarding cases where a child who was 'born on the pathway' finds its way to the homestead of its father, usually after suffering problems of some kind. Once the child has been received, it may enter the homestead and engage its inhabitants without calling *hodi* or behaving as a guest. The child thus attaches to the homestead by virtue of its blood, which is acknowledged as the factor that compelled its arrival. It is hence the blood that brings the person to the homestead (*mṛi*) where his or her veins (*mri*) connect to others through the *horu* that afforded and constituted his or her being. As *horu* in one form, the blood extends beyond the person and possesses a perambulatory and agentive capacity in a spatial and temporal field or topography.[34] As veins emplace the person in this field and compel him or her to act as an effect of the life force that moves through them in the form of blood, the notions of *samu, mri* and *horu* delimit human agency, volition and intention.

As *horu* cascades through production, reproduction and consumption, it provides a corrective to the 'alimentary model' advocated by Grace Harris (1962) and the 'procreative paradigm' propounded by Eugenia Herbert (1993).[35] The imbrication of activities that dwelling entails involves neither the deployment of one activity as a model for another one, nor the construction of analogies between different practices. Instead, it concerns the manner in which different activities contain or entail each other as transformations through which *horu* transfers and transmutes. Meanwhile, the ethnography shows that the concept and position of *mfele* comes into being as an effect of sustained and intensive engagement in such transfers and transformations. Similarly, the groom or husband (*mii*) becomes a man (*msoro*) as a result of success in production and reproduction, and acts of bravery (*ikariya*). Gender categories are thus gradually emergent modes of being that become as the effects of particular relations, where the uniform and ungendered *horu* converts and conveys by means of different anatomical features. In contrast to the accounts by Sanders (2008) as well as Geissler and Prince (2010), it is not a matter of a complementarity of genders, but an issue of the complementarity of body parts that conjoin to convert and convey life force in different forms, and thus bring genders into being.

Perhaps unsurprisingly, these concepts and activities do not only concern and articulate becoming and being through processes of generation, composition and transformation, but also entail and enunciate obverse dynamics concerning death, decay and decomposition. These are the topics of the next chapter, which will explore further concepts and activities that derive from or relate to the ones considered thus far for the purpose of illuminating the relationship between the dead and the living.

Notes

1. Herman later told me he knew that Alois's lover was the wife of one of MaSway's classificatory sons, which might explain why he refrained from revealing this to her at the time.

2. *Mahande* is when a mixture of animal blood and chyme is flung onto persons or objects by means of a whisk made from plants to 'cool' (*ihol-holhya*) and 'remove' (*ifumwa*) 'bad things' (*mawiishwa*). I describe these concepts, activities and substances more closely in subsequent chapters, including an ambiguity regarding the meaning of *mahande* (see note 21 in chapter five).

3. Conceptual connections between semen and blood are common in sub-Saharan Africa, especially in Bantu languages. Ashton (1952: 26) says that *mali* means both blood and semen among Sotho, while Ingstad (1989: 252) reports that the Setswana cognate *madi* has the same meaning. Green (1999a: 57) describes a similar situation from Pogoro, but does not supply vernacular terms. De Boeck (1994a: 271) describes how sex and the loss of semen diminishes a man's blood, which must be compensated with food. Outside the Bantu context, Piot (1999: 186) claims that a singular term is used for both blood and semen among Kabre of Togo, while Hutchinson (2000: 58) states that milk, semen and sweat are blood among Nuer, even if they do not equate blood with physical strength. In Rombo, however, semen and blood are *horu* in different forms that may be converted from one into the other.

4. Moore (1976: 365) cited Gutmann as the basis for her claim, but the page reference she provided does not support her claim. It is conceivable that she meant the claim by Gutmann I quote here, as *Lebensspenderin* is rendered as 'fountain of life' in the English translation of the Human Relations Area File, on which Moore relied for her article. By contrast, I have chosen to translate this notion more accurately as 'giver of life'.

5. As mentioned in chapter two, Johnston (1886: 525) made a similar mistake, when he translated *uro* as 'semen'.

6. Here too Moore cited Gutmann as the basis for her claim, but again the page reference provided does not appear to support her claim.

7. Such porridge is fed to children most mornings until their teens to ensure their growth. If people are able, they supplement the eleusine with groundnut flour or dried lake sardines (*dagaa*), which provide additional *horu*.

8. According to Gutmann (1926: 449), the person who lets blood is called *molasa*, where *mo-* is a prefix of the human noun-class.

9. Similarly, Green (1999b: 263) describes how aging is conceptualized as a process of drying out by the Pogoro of southern Tanzania.

10. In contravention of Raum, Dundas (1924: 201) reported that a woman never allowed another woman to breastfeed her child, as this would be fatal for the child.

11. This statement is immediately followed by the one rendered above about how her fat shall conjoin with that of her husband and not turn into water.

12. Gutmann does not say so, but I would add that blood and bones substantiate *horu* in different forms. It is entailed by current vernacular statements concerning how an animal's engagement in reproduction progressively makes its meat stick to the bones. It also features in the prevalent practice of incising the torso of infants to remove dirty blood that remains from its *in utero* existence, which otherwise occasions a condition called *kifira* that makes the child struggle to breathe. Removing the blood hardens the ribs (*ngari*) of the child to afford its growth and prepare it for work.

13. Jacobson-Widding (1990: 61), Kuper (1982: 19), Lan (1985: 91–98) and Snyder (1999: 230) describe how a person's flesh and blood are provided by the mother and the maternal side, while the bones originate from the father or the paternal side. Hasu (1999: 286) claims that similar ideas prevail in Mwika, but this is not the case in nearby Keni.

14. Smallstock are on occasion butchered in the banana garden below the homestead (*siinde ya kaa*), where the animals are placed so that their heads face uphill and above (*fondoho*), and thus most commonly the doorway of the house.

15. The German term 'Zauberer' is probably Gutmann's translation of the notion *mwaanga*, which is used to mean healers and diviners of different kinds.

16. *Dufumbuke* and *kufumbuke* are imperatives of the direct and locative forms of the verb 'to grow' - *ifumbuka*. The basis for my conjecture that this verb is at play here is Gutmann's inclusion of the term *ifumbucha* in another context, which I describe in the conclusion.

17. Gutmann does not provide any vernacular terms, but it seems likely that the notion he translated as 'the enchainer' or 'the connector' (*der Verbinder*) was *monikiwalo*, which I will return to consider in the next chapter. *Ndishi* is a short variety of the *mhoyo* bananas that feature in the initial prestation.

18. Gutmann (1909b: 86), Dundas (1924: 145) and von Clemm (1962: 157) described naming practices similar to those of Rombo, but did not explore their full significance. Otherwise, identical naming practices are reported from among Kikuyu, Sukuma-Nyamwezi and Kuria, while the use of reciprocal kinship terms between grandchildren and grandparents is described from among Marakwet and Zulu (Brandström 1990: 167; Gluckman 1950: 175; Kenyatta 1938: 15–16; H.L. Moore 1986: 57; Ruel 1997). Heald (1999: 173) recounts how Gisu children are named after a recently deceased person from the grandparental generation, while Parkin (1989: 86) claims that Giriama boys are often named after their grandparents. In the case of Kilimanjaro, the significance of these naming practices is arguably missed due to some confusion and inconsistent ethnographic recording. For instance, Gutmann (1926: 32) claimed at one point that it was the third-born son who was named after the mother's father and referred to as 'wife's father' by the daughter's

husband. Conversely, he stressed the identity between the father's father and his son's first-born son (Gutmann 1926: 59). Elsewhere, he stated that the second-born son was named after the mother's father, and the first-born son and daughter named after the father's parents (Gutmann 1909a: 167; 1909b: 86).

19. I will describe such matters more closely in the next chapter.

20. I say perhaps because the youngest son might be absent, working in Moshi, Arusha or Dar es Salaam. Under such circumstances, these dynamics become even more important.

21. Von Clemm (1962: 159) corroborates that grandparents tend to claim those grandchildren who bear their names. In contrast to the situation in Rombo, however, he contended that the children were returned to their natal homesteads when they started school.

22. In contrast, Gutmann (1926: 73) mentioned that it was preferred to take a wife from the descent group one's own mother came from, which he referred to as 'returning the mother to the homestead'.

23. *Iuya* is the root of the causative verb form *iura*, which occurs in the phrase 'returning the old woman to the homestead' (*naura msheku na kaa*).

24. I describe this prestation elsewhere (Myhre 2013b: 119).

25. Similarly, Comaroff and Comaroff (1997: 381) claim that the precolonial person involved a state of becoming rather than being, and de Boeck (1994b: 457) describes a notion of 'becoming a person', which takes place through a process of 'growing' interrelations with others.

26. Similarly, Moore (1976: 366) argued with regards to the offering of chyme to the ancestors that, 'I was told that the reason for offering stomach contents was that a beast's stomach is the very essence of its life...'.

27. Unlike for the Kuria, this does not involve articulated judgements or statements, but a concept that unfolds from the root-form of 'life' or *moo*.

28. Elsewhere, Gutmann (1913: 496) claims that 'primitive animism' attempts to connect as closely as possible the 'powers that secure life' to human relatedness.

29. Such haruspication has a long history and was described by Dundas (1924: 138), Gutmann (1909b: 150) and Widenmann (1899: 34) from Kilimanjaro, and mentioned by New (1873: 329) from Taita.

30. Gutmann (1926: 98) similarly described that a part of the intestines was called 'the land of the homestead' (*kiwandza*).

31. *Ka-* is a diminutive prefix.

32. Gutmann's account concerns a male child that appears to be the first-born.

33. It is underscored by the fact that the intestines of the animal may also show that 'there is a mouth' (*kure dumbu*), which manifests gossip and slander on the part of the homestead's inhabitants or their relations.

34. Similarly, Comaroff (1985: 128) describes from precolonial Tswana how 'personhood was not confined in space and time to a corporal cocoon: it permeated the world through its material and spiritual extensions'.

35. Broch-Due (1990, 1993) also emphasizes an 'alimentary idiom' as central to Turkana life and thought.

Chapter Four

IDAMIRA

BURIAL AS EMPLACEMENT AND DISPLACEMENT

In early August 2001, Herman and I went to visit a middle-aged diviner (*mwaanga*) named MaKawishe, who lives and works not far from the district headquarters at Mkuu. Unlike most other diviners, MaKawishe also works as a healer, and I knew that Herman had visited her on multiple occasions, both as a client and as a facilitator for others to whom he had recommended her services.[1] Herman, MaLasway and I had in fact taken their then-youngest daughter to be treated by MaKawishe just a few weeks before.[2] To save transport costs, Herman and I set off on foot along the pathways that wend their way around the mountain. En route, I asked him if there was a particular reason he wanted to go back so soon, but he replied that he had no specific complaint and that he only wanted to be 'tested' or 'measured' (*ibimwa*). The ensuing session reveals what most *waanga* do to divine (*ilafya*) and provides an entry for considering the relationship between the dead and the living, and the way in which this is an effect of the burial practices, which is central to the diviners' concerns.

A Case of Divination

When we arrived at MaKawishe's homestead, there were three people waiting in the courtyard. At first, they behaved as if they were unrelated, but when we engaged them in conversation they turned out to be two brothers, who were accompanied by the wife of one of them. MaKawishe was nowhere to be seen, but after a while she emerged from the homestead's main house. She carried a large wooden ladle of the kind MaShirima used to pour the bridewealth milk on the ground, but MaKawishe's *kilikiyo* differed by having several skin-rings (*fishong'u*) twirled around its handle.[3] It also lacked the dark patina that most ladles have which results from their use in cooking and serving food. MaKawishe greeted us and chatted briefly before she went to the enclosure where she receives her clients. The enclosure is located at the lower end of the *sha* courtyard and consists of a frame-work of poles that is hung with dried banana bark. She soon called the group of three to come and see her. The woman walked straight to the enclosure, while the two brothers went to fetch *isale* leaves from one of the dracaena bushes that line the courtyard and dot MaKawishe's banana garden. Herman and I had talked to them in Chagga, but they did not master the dialect and now we could hear MaKawishe talk to them in Swahili. I pointed this out to Herman, who guessed that they had come from Marangu to the south or from Usseri or Tarakea farther north.

When the three persons emerged nearly an hour later, MaKawishe called for us to come. Herman went to fetch *isale,* while I went straight to the enclosure, where MaKawishe sat on a low stool of the kind women use while cooking. She sat so that she faced west or above (*fondoho*), and the spoon was placed on the ground between her feet so that its handle pointed east or below (*siinde*). The result was that the bowl of the spoon opened towards MaKawishe. The bowl was filled with water (*mringa*) and there were thirty to forty eleusine grains ly-ing at its bottom. There was a bench beside MaKawishe for us to sit on, so that we all faced the same way. It contrasted with the place of most other diviners, where the client most commonly sits opposite the diviner, and thus faces both her and the spoon.

When Herman joined us, he carried four *isale* leaves, which he handed to MaKawishe. She wiped the dew and dirt from them on her *kanga,* while making small-talk. However, she fell silent as she fanned the leaves out in her hand and began inspecting their lower ends, which are white from lack of sunlight. She shuffled the leaves to exam-ine each one closely, occasionally dropping one or two on the ground, before picking them up for renewed scrutiny. Simultaneously, she be-gan to make noises and emit air through her mouth, which sounded like belches or hiccups. As each one emerged, she straightened her torso, as if a wave passed through her body when the noise rose from her belly.

When MaKawishe eventually began to speak, she asked Herman how many sons his father had and where in the birth order he is lo-cated. Herman replied that they are five brothers, and that he was the last-born. She then declared that Herman has two homesteads – one on the mountain and one in the plains. Herman confirmed this, even though he only has a house on the mountain and his plot in the plains consists only of farmland. Using vague hand gestures, MaKawishe described the geography of Herman's place in the plains, indicating its position in relation to a seasonal riverbed, a nearby pathway and a small forest. At relevant points, Herman confirmed what she said, but only by uttering a monosyllabic *eeh*. Combining a possessive construction and a causative verb-form, she asked if they have made the 'owner of the place' (*monikiwalo*) 'stay' or 'sit' (*idamira*) at the homestead.[4] Herman responded that they have, but that it was a long time ago. MaKawishe retorted that Herman must bring the *monikiwalo* to his homestead (*umhende kunu kaa kwaffo*). To do so, Herman should fetch a stone from a small forest near a riverbed in the plains and bring it to his homestead on the mountain, where a goat must be slaughtered. In addition, Herman needed 'to buy the name' (*iola rina*) of the *monikiwalo*. She pointed out that Herman has suffered cold shivers recently and that these are due to the *monikiwalo*'s name causing him problems (*ilauka*).

MaKawishe stopped inspecting the leaves and turned her attention to the spoon on the ground. Using one leaf at the time, she passed its white end through the water, making the eleusine grains whirl up. She paid close attention to their movements and the configurations they formed when they came to rest in the spoon. She also made cutting motions with the leaves that divided the grains in two groups, one on either side of the bowl's centre. While doing so, she remained silent, only emitting her belch-like noises, until she suddenly asked Herman if he had presented the *kisango* to his mother's brother. He denied this, which she was incredulous to hear, considering his age. However, she did not pursue the matter further, but instead asked if Herman's father is still alive. When Herman said that his father is dead, she asked where he was buried. On hearing that he was buried at the homestead on the mountain, she asked if 'he has been taken out from the rocks' (*afumwa mawenyi*). When Herman confirmed this, MaKawishe instructed him to obtain a whole male goat (*horo*) that he shall give to (*iningia*) his father so that he can 'congregate or gather with the male elders' (*isasa na wameku*). In addition, he needed to slaughter a *mooma* goat, so his father can congregate with the female elders (*washeku*). Herman then needed to get hold of another *horo*, which he shall give to his father, so that he can give it to his father, who shall give it to the 'owner of the homestead' (*monikaa*), who is the 'owner of your name' (*monirina laffo*).[5] Herman needed to fashion and wear a skin-ring (*kishong'u*) from the hide of this last goat. In addition, he had to toss soil on the ground (*ikombia kyala*) for his mother's father, who shall send it to Herman's mother's brother (*wafije*). Herman later needed to bring his *wafije* a 'thing of blood' (*kindo kya samu*), while the mother's brother in return should pour beer on the ground on his behalf.[6]

MaKawishe had nothing more to say at this point, but asked if Herman would like to enquire about anything in particular. In a soft voice, Herman asked if there was something wrong with the house where he keeps his livestock since he does not get kids and calves anymore. At that point, Herman only kept sheep, but he had told me many times how he used to successfully rear both cows and goats. Suddenly, however, they had started dying for no apparent reason. He therefore turned to sheep, which are hardier animals. MaKawishe returned to the leaves and grains, and replied that his house is built on a 'place that is not good' (*uwasha usha ku*). She explained that there are human bones where it was built, and that this causes problems (*ilauka*) for his livestock. She consulted the *isale* again and enquired about the position of the stable in relation to the house where Herman and his family live, and said that he will eventually have to build a new stable below (*siinde*) the present house. MaKawishe turned to me and explained that when a homestead is divided and re-divided over generations, it is impossible for grandchildren and great-grandchildren to know where the old graves were located. They therefore end up constructing houses on top of graves, which makes the livestock suffer when they are housed there. It is usually fine if it is a house for people, but sometimes they are not able to live there either. They are then woken at night and physically beaten to find themselves outside the house in the morning.

MaKawishe returned to scrutinize the *isale*, but this time she addressed the homestead of MaLasway's parents at Shimbi. She described its layout too, stating the number of its houses, and specifying how they are positioned in relation to each other and how they are located vis-á-vis a nearby pathway. She said that a father's sister (*shangazi*) of Herman's wife had died and was buried before she married and had children. The *shangazi* is now causing problems (*ilauka*) for MaLasway and their children, asking 'why do you have a husband and family when I do not?'. Herman therefore needed to tell Lasway to bring this woman home, in order that she will not bring their children problems. Like the *monikiwalo* of Herman's homestead, the woman was located below the homestead (*siinde ya kaa*) from where she needed to be brought home.

At this point, the session petered out in small-talk, but before we left MaKawishe reminded Herman of his tasks. He nodded solemnly in

response to each instruction before he thanked her and gave her a fee
of TZS 300.[7] On our walk back, Herman talked excitedly about how
well MaKawishe divines and he reminded himself of all the things he
had to do. While MaKawishe's statements and activities conformed
to those I observed from other diviners, the session diverged in the
magnitude of problems she identified. Nearly all of the problems that
the deceased may occasion occurred in this one case, which therefore
is highly suited for unravelling the relationship between the living and
the dead. As such, it provides an opportunity to consider how generation and transformation entail and imbricate death and decay, as well
as a basis for exploring the ability to divine and heal that MaKawishe
demonstrated.

Death and Emplacement

Several of MaKawishe's utterances concerned how a deceased person
is causing problems for a living relative because he or she is somehow
displaced or dislocated. It was involved in her claim that *monikiwalo*
must 'be made to stay or sit' (*idamira*) at Herman's homestead, and
in her verdict that MaLasway's father's sister needed to be brought
to Lasway's homestead. It was also at play in MaKawishe's enquiry
whether Herman's father was still 'in the rocks' (*mawenyi*). These
claims and queries gain their significance from the burial practices,
and the relationships they entail and effectuate between the dead and
the living. In turn, these pertain to the state of extension or unfolding
(*ialika*) that occurs through dwelling and that emplaces persons at the
homestead. Indeed, the concept of *idamira* itself entails and enunciates how attachment and emplacement are crucial concerns for the
burial practices.

Today, people are buried in the homestead where they dwell. The
graves of men, women and children are usually located next to each
other, most commonly at the *siinde ya kaa* area below the house and
the courtyard. Nearly everyone is provided with a Catholic funeral
Mass, which one of the parish priests reads in the *sha* courtyard.[8] At
the end of the Mass, the casket is interred by young men, who dug the
grave that same morning and hastily fill it using shovels and spades.
The attendants participate in this work, as they each toss a certain
number of handfuls of soil on the coffin.[9] Graves are oriented so that
the head of the deceased is uphill or above (*fondoho*) and is directed towards the courtyard, the doorway and the interior of the house, while
the feet are downhill or below (*siinde*) and are directed towards the

homestead's boundary (*mrasa*) and the plains below. Once the grave is filled, its outline is traced with rocks to raise a wall, inside of which soil is heaped to create a raised rectangle that can stand several feet above the ground. The godparent of the same gender as the deceased – or the person who currently dwells in his or her homestead – plants a cross at the head of the grave, which bears the person's name, along with the date of birth (if known) and that of death. Subject positions in certain relations to the deceased are called out, so that these persons come forth in a particular order to place flowers on the grave. It starts with the mother's brother (*wafije*) or the person occupying his homestead, and ends with the grandchildren or great-grandchildren the deceased may have. In my early periods of fieldwork, people placed a flowering creeper on the grave that they gathered in the homestead or along pathways and riverbeds. Those who can afford it have since begun supplementing this with plastic flowers decorated with tinsel or foil of either aluminium or plastic. When the burial is over, the result remains a defined mound that is covered with flowering creepers and an assortment of fading fake flowers. Over time, the mound collapses and its soil washes away to leave a low oblong of moss-covered rocks and packed dirt that is overgrown with various plants. As the grave is thus slowly erased, it requires increasing efforts to be discerned over the decades. To prevent this process, affluent people build concrete tombs that differ in size and elaboration, but that all aim to endure in a way that the other graves do not.[10]

Figure 4.1. A new grave decorated with flowers.

The current burial practice is the latest manifestation in a process of change that has occurred over the past century. Those in their seventies and eighties describe how people previously were buried inside the grass-houses, where the men were interred in the *kishingiro* area to the right of the doorway and women were buried in the *ushiini* area on the side where the beds were located. They describe how a shallow hole was dug in the ground, where the body was placed in a sitting position with its legs folded up to the chest and the head sticking up above the earthen floor. The body was covered with manure (*boru*) that was swept from the livestock pens on the day of the burial, and a cooking pot with the 'mouth' broken off was placed over the head. A large hearth-fire was maintained for the subsequent month to drive away or camouflage the smell of the decaying body.

These accounts gain corroboration from historical sources, which moreover reveal regional differences that form variations on a theme. From Marangu, Lehmann (1941: 390) described how a man was buried opposite the doorway, while a woman was buried on the left-hand side of the hut. Dundas (1924: 182ff) also claimed that his account stemmed from Marangu, but described how both men and women were buried underneath the place where the milk was stored. In Rombo, this would have been the *mbaariko* area that features in the bridewealth prestations and detachment of the bride from her parents' house. Dundas described how the body was placed in the cattle-stall for all to see while the grave was dug, before it was wrapped in animal hides or *ndishi* leaves and interred with its face towards the mountain. Before the grave was filled, those present tossed chyme on the body, while they said: 'We send you with meat and milk and fat which is derived of cattle. Go in peace' (Dundas 1924: 184). Dundas (1924: 190) claimed that the fire was not extinguished inside the house for the following year and a half, while Gutmann (1909b: 135) described how the fire was kept burning only for four days.[11] Raum's (1911: 183–84) account is a translated manuscript compiled by a convert teacher named Yohane Msando from Old Moshi, which mirrors Lehmann as it describes how a man was buried underneath the doorway, near the main post of the house, while a woman was buried at the back of the house, opposite the doorway from where she faced the plains.[12] While these accounts appear irreconcilable, their differences need not be resolved, but can rather be considered related practices that concern the emplacement or attachment of the deceased in relation to features and orientations of the homestead that gain their significance from dwelling and life, and that the concept of *idamira* concerns and enunciates.

The age of those who claim to have seen their grandparents buried inside the house suggests that this form of burial was practised in Rombo, at least by some, until the 1950s. However, in 1931 the sanitary inspector Bailey reported:

> It was apparently the Tribal custom until a few years ago, to bury the dead actually under the floor of the dwellings, and after a certain period to exhume the remains for re-burial in the banana grove in the vicinity. This custom however seems to been dropped [sic], for not a single instance was met with, and the A.D.S.I's state that this is so. The present custom is burial in the banana grove of the deceased some distance from the dwelling. The depth of the grave is usually at least a [sic] five feet deep, and often more. The graves are not marked and rapidly become lost to view in the undergrowth. The mission settlements are of course provided with properly laid out cemeteries for the converts (TNA 312).

The contradictory character of current claims and historical sources makes it difficult to determine when burial inside the house ended. However, it seems possible that it continued longer in Rombo, especially in light of the fact that exhumation persisted longer there than elsewhere in Kilimanjaro.

As Bailey pointed out, the body was exhumed after some years, when the bones were placed at the foot of a tall *isale* tree called *mbuho* that remains located in the *siinde ya kaa* area of all current homesteads. When people today describe how the exhumation was performed, they employ language and notions that stem from agricultural production and food preparation. Thus, some say the soil from the grave was winnowed in the same way as threshed eleusine, as the dirt was tossed in a large *mboriko* bowl until only the bones remained. Others claim that the bones were gathered on a dried cowhide and sifted like *kunde* beans to ensure that all of them were removed from the grave and gathered by the *mbuho*.[13] Some even claim that persons who stood in particular relationships to the deceased carried specific parts of the body to the *mbuho*, and that these corresponded to the shares they claimed from animals butchered at the homestead. Most people deny this, but they do emphasize that the body was not passed through the doorway of the house, either for burial or exhumation. Instead, it was brought through an opening that was made by removing a section of the wall, but replaced and repaired after the burial. Dundas (1924: 191) confirmed this: 'The grave is not opened in the hut, but access to the body is gained by digging down from outside the hut'.

Such exhumations continued in Rombo long after indoor burials ended. The last case I know of from Keni was Ngufumari's eldest brother, who was exhumed from his garden in the 1990s. His eldest son, who now occupies the homestead, showed me where the grave had been located, along with the purpose-built 'vault' where he keeps the skulls of those who dwelled there before him. Claims by people to have participated in exhumations elsewhere in Rombo even more recently were confirmed in 2008, when Boniface was invited to disinter his father's mother's brother at Mashati farther north. Boniface declined the invitation, but sent his classificatory son who described the event in terms that largely confirmed accounts from Keni.

These days, people perform a different kind of exhumation that does not involve the actual unearthing of bones. Instead, it consists in the removal of one or more stones from the grave of the person concerned. Known as *ifuma mawenyi*, it was this MaKawishe meant when she enquired whether Herman's father had been taken out of the rocks. The event takes place years, if not decades, after a person has died. It consists of two parts that often take place on consecutive days, but that may be separated by greater lengths of time. The first part, called *irukwa*, only involves a few people from the homestead, who remove one or more stones and some soil from the person's grave. In May 2001, I took part in this on behalf of the mother of an elderly man called Basil. Basil was assisted by an unrelated elder called Prosper, whom I knew well and who was renowned for his knowledge of such matters. In addition to us, the event only involved Basil's eldest son and his wife. Prosper instructed Basil to fetch four *isale* leaves from the homestead's *mbuho*, which he placed on top of each other in a star-like formation on the ground above his mother's grave. On these leaves, Basil placed four small stones and four handfuls of soil that he took from the head, foot and both sides of the grave right at the point where it rose out of the ground. Prosper then folded the leaves so they formed a parcel, which he tied shut with a strip of dried banana bark (*mdawi*) from a *mnyengele* tree. He placed the parcel by the foot of such a tree close to the *mbuho*, and covered it with dried leaves and branches.

Prosper and I returned the next day for the second part of the event, which is called *iumba* – 'to conjoin'. Two of Basil's sons brought a male *horo* and a female *mooma* goat from their homesteads, which they tied inside the cooking hut that Basil's mother once occupied. The animals were made to face uphill, as Basil stroked the *mooma*'s back and uttered a brief invocation, requesting his mother to sit (*itchamia*) with her co-wives (*waeri*), children and grandchildren. Both animals were then led out and tied to separate banana trees located between the grave and the *mbuho*. A cooking pot full of beer, which was decorated

Figure 4.2. Male elder using *isale* leaves to enfold soil removed from the grave in an *irukwa* ceremony.

with four strips of *mnyengele mdawi*, was placed on the right-hand side of the *mbuho*. A gourd of curdled milk was placed on the left-hand side of the *mbuho*, while the parcel we made the previous day was placed in front of it. The parcel was opened so the soil and rocks were resting on top of the *isale*. Basil took four pinches of the soil and placed them at the foot of the *mbuho*, while saying: 'Today we remove you from the rocks and conjoin you' (*lunu dukufuma mawenyi, dukuumba*).[14] He then used a drinking gourd to draw a small amount of beer four times from the cooking pot before he drank it. These acts were repeated by Basil's four sons in order of seniority and then by their wives, before they were performed by the mother's brother (*wafije*) and brother (*msasha*) of the deceased. Subsequently, they were followed by the members of the agnatic descent group and the homestead's affines, and care was taken to ensure that the married daughters of the homestead (*wana wa kaa*) did the same. In this way, the people who enabled her existence and effectuated her extension at this particular homestead removed her from the rocks and conjoined her at its *mbuho*.

While these acts continued, first the *mooma* and then the *horo* were suffocated and butchered beside her grave. Shares of meat were prepared and presented to the deceased's mother's brother, brother, and her married daughters, and boiled in a large *sufuria* or aluminium pot on an improvised hearth beside the grave. Basil shared half of the remaining meat between himself and his sons, while some was given to two agnates and another male elder, who helped with the butchering. The latter sent their meat to their respective homesteads, while the rest was placed in the *sufuria* for general consumption. When the meat was cooked, the parcels were re-presented to their claimants, who ate them in separate groups. The men of the homestead and their agnates ate half of the general meat by the graveside, while the rest was sent to their wives inside the cooking hut.

When the meat was finished, the recipients wrapped the bones in banana leaves and returned them to the grave, where they placed them on the ground. The homestead's agnates carefully ensured that no bones were left out, and explained that their return was an acknowledgement by those who had received the meat that the person in question is dead and that their responsibilities for her are over. We had moreover finished the beer, so Basil overturned the cooking pot at the foot of the *mbuho*. Watching how the lees ran downhill, Basil said in Swahili to his younger brother: 'yes, show the way' (*ndiyo onyeshe njia*). Basil then poured curdled milk at the foot of the *mbuho* and mumbled an invocation, before he and his brother stepped on the gourd he had used so it broke. Finally, Basil placed the four stones from the grave at the foot of the *mbuho* and added the bones of the goats, while he said in Swahili: 'she now has received her home' (*amepata nyumbani kwake sasa*). The event was over, so we gathered the cooking pot, drinking gourds and benches we sat on, and walked back to the courtyard, while taking care to ensure that nothing was left behind, as we were instructed not to look back at the *mbuho*, to which no-one would be allowed to return until the following day.[15]

MaKawishe's question whether Herman's father had been removed from the stones gained sense and impetus from the changing practices of burial, exhumation and reburial. Both early ethnographic sources and current statements entail that the burial of people inside the house involved careful and deliberate emplacement of the deceased in relation to certain areas, features and objects of the homestead. In burial, the body was literally made to sit (*idamira*) in a specific location and face in a particular direction, where he or she became attached to the places in the house where sleeping, livestock-keeping and cooking occurred. Through this emplacement, the deceased was attached and gained a relationship to architectural features, such as the doorway, the hearth, the livestock pens and the bed. The deceased thereby connected to objects and substances, such as cooking pots, gourds, milk and manure, that still feature prominently in dwelling and life. He or she of course already related to these phenomena through dwelling and life in the homestead, but became attached to them in a new way when he or she was buried in a particular proximity to and distance from them. As death and interment arrested the deceased's ability to move around the homestead and along pathways, he or she gained an immobile or static relationship to these phenomena. While the deceased became emplaced to gain a different relationship to the homestead, its living inhabitants continued to engage these features and objects, with the result that dwelling and life revolved around the dead.

When the body was exhumed and removed from the house, it became detached from these features and elements. However, this entangled the deceased in other activities that involved *mboriko* bowls and cowhides, as the bones were sifted and gathered in the courtyard to be placed by the *mbuho*. The bowls and hides feature in drying crops and preparing foods, while the courtyard is where large parts of dwelling and life occur. Also, these artefacts and features had been engaged by the deceased in life, but were in exhumation re-engaged to emplace him or her in a novel way and at a new location in the homestead. Burial, exhumation and reburial were hence extensions and continuations of dwelling and life, where the dead was detached from and attached to objects, substances and features to emplace him or her in the homestead in a new way. Its culmination was the conjoining (*iumba*) of the bones at the *mbuho*, where they remain visible in some homesteads.

MaKawishe's use of the concept *idamira* – 'to cause (someone) to sit' or 'to make (someone) stay' – enunciated how these practices involve concomitant processes of attachment or emplacement, and detachment and displacement. *Idamira* is the causative form of the verb 'to sit' (*itchamia*), which was quite literal in the past, when the body was made to sit in the grave. However, *idamira* also means to enable someone to stay or remain in one place, which is entailed by the use of *iumba* to mean the act of placing the bones by the *mbuho*. *Idamira* hence entails both making the body sit in the grave and making the bones stay at the *mbuho*, where the person conjoins with the other deceased. These concepts and activities imbricate and resonate with the bridewealth prestations, where powerful foodstuffs serve to attach the groom and his agnates to some of the same features of the bride's father's homestead. Affines come to relate as they attach their *horu* in certain forms to specific aspects of their homesteads, where the *mkara* or 'the person who enables dwelling and the homestead' plays a crucial role. In this regard, it is significant that the Chagga concepts of *itchamia* and *ikaa* are conjoined in the Swahili cognate *kukaa*, which means both 'to live in one place' and 'to sit'. Their cognate character enunciates the conceptual, practical and material connections that the process of making someone stay or sit through burial, exhumation and reburial has to dwelling. Interment and disinterment thus engage and extend the emplacement and attachment of a person in the homestead that occurred through *ikaa*. Concomitantly, they entail a progressive detachment and displacement of him or her in relation to the same phenomena, on the basis of the relationships fostered through dwelling and life. As in life, the dead move through space over time to partake in dwelling in novel ways.

Ferrying the Dead

These considerations gain depth by two further ceremonies that are currently performed shortly after someone's burial. The ceremonies are called 'to bring the person from the mother's brother' (*mhende kwa wafije*) and 'congregation' or 'gathering' (*msaso*). They are distinct events that should be performed on separate days, but often are conducted on the same day in a certain order. The first event is said to occur because the deceased fled and sought refuge at the mother's brother's homestead upon his or her death and therefore must be brought back home, where the second event enables or makes the person gather or congregate with its other deceased.

In June 2001, the two events were performed on behalf of Oswald's wife, Valeria, who had suddenly passed away in Dar es Salaam the previous December. A few days after her death, Valeria's body was brought back to Rombo and buried next to Ngufumari at the *siinde ya kaa* of Oswald's homestead. The following June, Oswald returned to conduct these events, which he had agreed with the inhabitants of Valeria's mother's brother's homestead. While we waited for them to arrive, a classificatory father took Oswald aside for certain preparations. First, they entered MaSway's cooking hut, where the elder poured beer on the ground and requested that the deceased should sit together and drink this fluid.[16] Next, they went to the stable, where the classificatory father rubbed eleusine grains onto the shoulder and lower back of a *mooma* goat, while addressing the deceased. Finally, he fed the remaining grains to the goat.

After hours of waiting, I suddenly noticed two men and one woman standing silently at the end of the *mengele* leading into the homestead. I alerted Oswald to their arrival and he went to receive them. The guests did not speak, but entered the homestead and walked straight to the cooking hut, where the wives of two of Oswald's brothers –

Valeria's classificatory co-wives (*waeri*) – received them. Inside the cooking hut, the woman placed a small stone she had brought from the *wafije*'s homestead. As soon as it was placed in the cooking hut, the guests exited to greet and socialize with those present. They explained that the woman who brought the stone was not allowed to talk or look back after she had picked up the stone, lest Valeria returned to their homestead. She was therefore accompanied by two men, who walked in front of and behind her to greet and talk to anyone they met. The *waeri* welcomed the three back into the cooking hut, where they were served gourds of beer and given a place to sit. When the beer was finished, the two men went with Oswald into the stable, where they seized the *mooma* goat by its ear and said: 'today we have brought you, dwell at your homestead, may you all congregate with the grandfathers and female elders' (*lunu dukuwahende, ukae kunu kaa kwaffo, mdesasa wose na wasahoye na washeku*). They then returned to the cooking hut, where they received another gourd of beer, which they finished before saying goodbye and returning to their homestead.

Members of the neighbourhood prayer group (*jumuiya*) then came and decorated the courtyard for a Mass that Oswald had requested from the parish. An altar was improvised on the small veranda of MaSway's house, which was located so that the priest faced the courtyard and the graves below, while the congregation faced him and the doorway above. The Mass was mainly attended by the *jumuiya* and the agnatic descent group, and ended with the priest blessing and combining water and salt to make holy water (*maji baraka*). The priest led the members of the homestead in a procession to *siinde ya kaa*, where we encircled Valeria's grave and said the Lord's Prayer and Hail Mary, while the priest tossed holy water on it. He then handed the vessel over so that first Oswald and then his eldest son could do the same.

The priest apologized for having to leave for a Mass somewhere else, while young men carried a barrel of beer out of the cooking hut and placed it in the courtyard. The *mooma* and a *horo* were brought out of the stable and held in the courtyard so they faced the doorway and uphill, and a point was made that the *mooma* had to be on the left-hand side (*kumoosoni*) of the *horo*. The men of the descent group gathered in a semi-circle and said grace in Swahili before the two animals were suffocated, bled, skinned and butchered in rapid succession. On this occasion, a parcel of meat was made for the *wafije* from both the *mooma* and the *horo* since the animals concerned two separate events. When the *wafije* returned, they were welcomed as if they had not been there earlier that day, and were shown a secluded place to sit in the *kaandeni* area. They were provided with beer to accompany the meat and a member of the agnatic descent group was tasked with serving them. Other relatives and neighbours arrived throughout the day and were seated in different locations depending on their relationships to the homestead.

When *msaso* is performed on the same day as *mhende*, the mother's brother and his entourage often only walk as far as the end of the *mengele*. They then turn around and re-enter the homestead, but this time they call out *hodi* to make their arrival and presence known. Like on the occasion for Valeria, they are received by the homestead's inhabitants as if they are long-lost guests. In many homesteads, they then moreover butcher three goats, where one is for *mhende* and the other two are for *msaso*. The former is then of the same gender as the deceased and only concerns him or her, while the other two are of separate genders and concern his or her conjunction with the male and female deceased of the homestead. Accordingly, the former is butchered near the grave, like we did for the *irukwa* above, while the other two are butchered in the courtyard. MaSway actually worried that the event was wrongly performed for Valeria, as she asked me repeatedly how many animals were butchered at a subsequent ceremony in another homestead. Many people also stress that the stone the *wafije* bring must be deposited on or underneath a bed, ideally inside the cooking hut, where a plank of wood on the ground may serve as a substitute if no bed is present. At another event, the stone was similarly first placed on a bed inside the residential house before the deceased's classificatory husband led the *wafije* to the grave where the stone was placed and soil put over it, as if to bury it.

The links between these events and *idamira* became clear when Herman brought a deceased relative to his homestead in December 2006. His act followed another divination session at MaKawishe's, which was precipitated by a persistent headache and ringing in the ear that Herman suffered after he tripped and fell on the path. This time, MaKawishe said there was a deceased person, whose name they do not know (*mrina*), who was lost outside (*sha*) and wanted Herman to bring (*ihende*) him back to his homestead (*kunu kaa kwaffo*), where he should make him sit or stay (*idamira*). She said Herman should do so by taking a stone from beside a nearby pathway and bringing it to his homestead, where he should place it until he obtains some beer to pour on the ground. Later, he should get hold of a whole male goat (*mburu horo*), which he should butcher to make the person sit or stay (*umdamira*).

MaKawishe used the term *mrina* to designate the lost or displaced relative, but Herman later emphasized that the person in question was the *monikiwalo*, whom he referred to as *mrina monikiwalo*. He added that the area where he needed to fetch the stone had previously been occupied by their agnates, but that Herman's father and father's father had failed to maintain it when these people moved away. The land therefore passed onto others, but it made sense that he had unknown relatives in the ground on land that is occupied by others. One of these deceased relatives now wanted to be brought home, and the only way he could make this known was by causing problems (*ilauka*) for the living, which he had done by making Herman trip on the path. Herman substantiated this by relating how a man and a woman from two of these neighbouring homesteads, close to where the stone should be fetched, fell ill some years ago, but recovered once they requested and received names of past relatives from Herman's homestead. He also added that MaKawishe and two other diviners had told him about this person before.

Early the following evening, Herman, my wife and I left the beer club we were in and went to fetch the stone. It was not yet dark, so we stopped by Herman's homestead to retrieve a piece of cloth in which to wrap the stone. We walked down a pathway from his *kaa* and crossed a seasonal riverbed before we climbed a narrow *shia* between homesteads on the other side. Herman first searched for a stone on one side of the path towards the boundary of a homestead, but failed to find a suitable specimen. I offered to light a torch to help him see, but Herman refused. We instead walked a bit further, where Herman searched on the other side of the *shia*, close to the *mrasa* of another homestead. There he found an acceptable stone, which he wrapped in the cloth while mumbling a statement, of which I only heard: 'today we are bringing you to the homestead' (*lunu dukuhende na kaa*). Herman placed the stone in his pocket and we set off back down the hill with me in front and my wife at the rear. Herman had warned that he could not speak once he had the stone, but started talking about how happy he was to have found it on that side of the path towards the homestead where he knew his agnates had lived. When I hesitated to reply, Herman explained that we could talk among ourselves, but that he was not allowed to speak to anyone we met along the way. As we crossed the riverbed and walked back uphill, we glimpsed a couple coming down towards us. Herman said I had to greet them and he would remain silent, which he did in spite of his otherwise fastidious politeness.

When we reached Herman's homestead, he placed the stone at the foot of a *mnyengele* tree that was located by the side of the *mengele* pathway, close to where it opens onto the courtyard. He again muttered a short statement, of which I caught: 'today we have brought you to the homestead, protect your homestead' (*lunu duwakuhende na kaa, uringe mṛi waffo*). It differed from the previous statement only in its use of the past tense, which articulated how *mrina monikiwalo* now had been brought to the homestead. It moreover acknowledged the homestead as belonging to this person, who was requested to protect it. Herman placed some pieces of an uprooted and overturned banana stump (*itonga*) over the stone to ensure that his children would not remove it.

The following afternoon, Herman bought some beer from a nearby club that he ascertained was made from *mnyengele* bananas. He sent his eldest children off to fetch water to ensure that they were out of the way, while he and I entered their cooking hut. We sat down on low stools right inside the doorway, while MaLasway and my wife watched from its opening. Herman poured three small sips into a gourd, which he drank before he added three more sips and began pouring the beer on the ground. He poured the beer at the foot of a blackened pole behind the doorway that was right beside the bed where his mother slept with two of his children. Herman pointed out that the pole supports the cooking hut attic and thus serves as a substitute for the *kisumbadini* of the grass-house. While pouring the beer, he said:

> I request strongly (*hai na hai*), you male elder, elder Alfred gather (*ndesasa*) with elder Tengio, this person I have brought (*ngilehende*), welcome him at the homestead (*kunu kaa*), in the homestead (*kunu mṛini*) ... he found that he was lost, now that I know, I have brought him (*luwaha ngilemanya ngilemhende*), may he sit at the homestead (*atchamie kunu mṛini*) ... I shall find again another little thing that will make him sit (*ngitafuta se kandoka kemdamira*) ... gather all of you, sit together, he has found a homestead (*mundesasa mose mutchamie nakolya mṛini*) ... sit all of you ... welcome him, he has found a homestead (*nakolya kaa*), may he not bring problems again, if it was he who brought these problems ... may he cool (*ahorere*) and be well, you *mangi* ... may the final prestation be in the form of a head of cattle.

Herman then added three more sips into the gourd, which he poured next to the first round of beer, while saying:

> And this here, I request you strongly, take it (*muire*) ... bring it to Shimbi to the mother's brother ... may they sit (*watchamie*) ... may they drink ... this is a small thing I obtained (*ni kandoka ngakolya*) ... may they all sit ... and if it is this person who claims a name, he shall get his name, may they not break the bones, may they cool (*wohorere*) and be well...

Herman then poured three more sips into the gourd, which he added to the same place where the first round of beer was poured:

And this, I request you strongly, you elder, when you have arrived (there) and returned (here) (*ukashikauya*), come and sit with your father Tengio … sit together and drink, this is your share for taking (*kiirya*), you have been used as a messenger … sit together here and drink, gather all of you (*mosase mose piu*) … sit together all of you … with the youth and anyone else we do not know, go and give to the women, when they are given milk … they shall cook *kena* for me, you give them, you elder, this is the thing I request you … sit and drink calmly, do not bring problems to your homestead … this is the thing I request you, you elder.

Herman poured three final sips, which he drank before he leaned the gourd upright against the wall. He referred to this last beer as *macha*, which means 'spit' or 'spittle', but in this context is better rendered as 'backwash'. Its use in conjunction with his address entails that Herman finished the beer by means of which the deceased were requested to gather, so that they would sit together and drink to welcome the person he had brought, once he realized this person was lost. His statement enunciated that the beer was something he obtained, and he affirmed that when he gets something else he will use it to make the person sit. However, the statement also entailed that he owed the beer to his deceased agnates and mother's brothers, and that it thus involved a debt that replaced the *horu* expended by the deceased. In return, Herman hoped to receive life force in further forms that he could provide them in turn. As the beer was shared among the deceased, it mixed with their spittle, which Herman ingested. His acts and language hence entailed that *horu* in different forms transfer in several directions, as beer is poured from Herman's hand to return *horu* he had received, before spittle flowed along the gullets of the deceased to form the backwash Herman consumed with the hope that *horu* should emerge in other forms in the future. By pouring beer, he thus aimed to set off a cascade of *horu* where powerful substances of different kinds transfer and transform to unfurl dwelling and extend life at the homestead.

Nearly three weeks later, Herman obtained a *horo* goat for making the *mrina monikiwalo* sit. To do so, we first retrieved the stone from the *mnyengele* tree and broke a discarded cooking pot to obtain a shard. We brought these items to the banana garden, just above (*fondoho*) the courtyard, where Herman's eldest brother and closest neighbour Nico dug a small hole in the ground. He placed the stone in the hole and covered it with the pot shard before replacing the soil. He then buried three other stones in a triangle around the first one, while he said:

This thing has been wanted for a long time, I request you, today I am placing here the *mrina wa monikiwalo,* may he sit here, it is indeed he

who has brought problems here at the homestead, I request you elders
and grandfathers, help him, it is here I am placing him today, I have
made you stay (*ngakudamira*), sit here in your homestead (*utchamie kunu
mṛini kwaffo*), protect this homestead, this thing has been wanted for a
long time, it is indeed this thing I request you and may god help me, so
today we are making him stay (*dumdamira*), no child shall come and
take anything from here, it is indeed this thing we request you, as of today we have given you your homestead, we are making you stay, *mangi*,
we request you dwell quietly (*dukuterewa ukaeho sii*).

Herman and Nico pointed out how the three stones formed the
configuration of the hearthstones (*mashia*) and that they are placed
as if the *monikiwalo* has received a hearth (*riko*) and that the pot shard
is as if he is provided food. In Swahili, Herman pointed out that this
is to ensure that the person calms down in that place (*ili atulie pale*),
which echoed Nico's request that he shall dwell quietly. As Herman
said when he poured the beer and Nico now reiterated, the *monikiwalo*
thus received a homestead. The claim that he was provided a hearth
and food, alongside the beer he received earlier, entails that he was
emplaced and enabled to dwell. As he thus had a hearth (*nere riko*), we
served as *wakara* for the *mrina monikiwalo* to enable his dwelling at a
specific homestead.

Once this was done, we entered the cooking hut, where Nico tied a
length of dried banana bark around the neck of a penned goat. Herman seized hold of this and received some unthreshed eleusine from
MaLasway. We led the animal to the open space just inside the doorway and made it face uphill (*fondoho*) before Nico uttered an invocation. While doing so, he rubbed the eleusine on the animal's head,
neck and shoulders, before he continued on its breast, along its back
and onto its rump. He seemed in doubt about what to do and say,
but received pointers from Herman so the result was a statement that
echoed the one above. The main difference was that Nico addressed
deceased persons of specific subject positions while he rubbed eleusine
onto the parts of the animal that their living classificatory relatives
receive when it is butchered. Nico moreover reiterated how the event
served to emplace the *mrina monikiwalo*, saying that this person discovered that he was lost on the pathway (*mkoni*), but that today we
took or seized him (*dumira*) and made him stay at his homestead (*dumdamira kunu kaa kwakwe*). He again requested the deceased to sit together and eat, and cool the homestead (*mohorere mṛi*).[17]

We then brought the goat to the banana garden, where we butchered it beside the buried stones. From each share it was carved into,
Herman and Nico cut small pieces of meat that they put aside and
roasted separately. This meat is called *ndaswa*, which derives from the

verb *ichasa* that means to place foodstuffs on the ground for the deceased. A noun made from a passive construction, it is best rendered as 'that which is offered or presented'. When the *ndaswa* was roasted, Nico placed seven large *isale* leaves on top of the goat's chyme, which rested on green banana leaves in the garden. Three of the *isale* leaves were for the dead men, while four were for the deceased women. Nico cut small pieces of the *ndaswa* and placed three pieces of meat on each of the leaves for the men and four pieces on each of the leaves for the women. We hurriedly ate the rest of it, but set aside four pieces that we wrapped in dried *mnyengele* bark and later presented to Nico's wife. Usually, this meat is presented to the women seated inside the cooking hut, in return for the embers the men requested to light the improvised hearth in the banana garden. In this way, the men make a prestation of *horu* that increases the heat (*mrike*) of the women's bodies to compensate for and replace the fire (*motcho*) they removed from the cooking hut.[18]

Nico then made the following invocation over the *ndaswa* meat:

> I request you god (*mungu*) my father, you god father, I request you, this person is *mrina wa monikiwalo*, he discovered that he was lost in the wilderness (*sakeu*), we have brought him, we have made him sit today, you *mangi*, this homestead is his, this is indeed the thing we have placed here, may he sit (*atchamie*), may he dwell here, this is his homestead (*akaeho ni kaa kwakwe*) ... may he stop the problems at this homestead, may he not bother a child, may he not bother a grandchild ... we did not know anything, we encountered this thing from the old days, today we request you strongly, sit here, may he sit, gather all of you with the female elders and the grandchildren and the youth, sit and eat this thing I have given you, I request this thing shall be well, may we be together, thank you very much, may he sit and the thing be well, you *mangi*.

Nico largely reiterated the previous addresses, but this time used the past tense. The shift in temporal markers enunciated a chain of events, where the things they earlier said they would do and were doing now were being finalized. He moreover used *sakeu* to denote where the *mrina monikiwalo* was lost, which is the opposite of *mdenyi* and means an uncultivated and uninhabited place. The stone was in fact retrieved from a cultivated and inhabited area, but it was outside the boundary (*mrasa*) of a homestead, so *mrina monikiwalo* was in limbo or between places. In combination with the earlier claim that he had been lost on the pathway (*mkoni*), it suggests that he was dislocated and displaced.

Nico also wrapped some morsels of raw meat in a small *isale* leaf, which he placed by the foot of a *mnyengele* tree, close to where we buried the stones. He uttered an invocation over this meat too, where he for the first time addressed *monikiwalo* directly and recognized that he had founded the homestead, to which their father merely came later:

> You male elder *monikiwalo*, I request you, sit here, protect your homestead, this homestead was indeed begun by you a long time ago, my father came here, therefore I request you, sit with everyone, protect your homestead, leave the problems, neither child nor grandchild shall be bothered, you know to protect your homestead, I request you strongly, *monikiwalo* I request you, protect, I request, I go and I fetch and recognition (*tambulisho*) has already come to show that person (*imlhora mdu shu*) that I have today presented with his homestead ... they request, may he sit, may he cool (*naholholhye*), may he leave people so they can seek, if they receive again they will give you, *mangi*.

The statement acknowledged that if the *monikiwalo* sits and cools, he will allow people to seek and obtain, so that they will be able to provide him a return in the future. As they shall receive and provide, the statement points to the use of arms, hands and other body parts in *ikaa* and *moo*. It moreover reveals how dwelling and life in the present are effects of the relationship to *monikiwalo* to whom they are indebted and whom they rely on for their extension into the future.

Our final act was to plant an *isale* sapling at the head of the three stones that surrounded and enclosed the stone we brought to the homestead. Herman pointed to other *isale* trees growing in the vicinity and recounted how they had been planted for other deceased relatives. This included the *monikiwalo* he had brought from the plains in 2001, as a result of MaKawishe's divination above. When we packed soil around the sapling, Herman said: 'dwell here in your homestead, *monikiwalo*', to which Nico added: 'dwell here in your homestead, we are leaving, we request that we may dwell in peace'. In this way, the imperative form fused with the act of planting to effectuate *monikiwalo*'s emplacement and dwelling at the homestead.

Gathering Extensions, Contracting Persons

The Swahili term *mfano* is equally used to mean the stone that Herman fetched along the pathway, the stone the mother's brother brings from his homestead, and the stone that is removed from the grave in the *irukwa* ceremony. The most common meaning of the term *mfano* is 'example', but it also means 'substitute', 'likeness', 'resemblance' and 'emblem' (Johnson 1939: 89). These meanings may suggest a form of representation, where the stone serves as an image or a symbol that stands for the deceased. However, the noun *mfano* derives from the verb *kufaa,* which means 'to be of use' or 'to suffice', and thus renders *mfano* as 'something that is of use'. Rather than a symbolic represen-tation of the deceased, the stone is a material entity that suffices or is of use for bringing the deceased back from the mother's brother's homestead or the wilderness and for removing the person from the grave and emplacing him or her by the *mbuho.* Its non-representa-tional character was at stake in Herman's refusal to use a torch for finding a stone and in his satisfaction regarding where he found one. Both instances entail that the stone that is to be removed allows itself to be found at the place where it is located. It is therefore not a matter of finding and using a stone as an arbitrary symbol for a person, but of detecting a particular stone for the purpose of bringing home a specific being.

As mentioned above, people say the deceased must be brought from the mother's brother's homestead because he or she fled there upon his or her death. However, the practice entails that the *wafije* brings the attachment that the deceased has to his homestead. The attach-ment consists either in the *kisango* prestation that the deceased made to the *wafije* or the name that he or she received from the mother's brother's homestead, which are both effects of the extension that the deceased's mother's marriage involved. A stone is especially useful or suitable for conveying a person's attachment between homesteads since it forms part of the ground and soil that is engaged through dwelling. By bringing the attachment from the mother's brother's *kaa,* some of the extensions that the deceased has are contracted and gath-ered at the homestead where the stone is deposited. The attachment and extension is first deposited inside the house before it is placed on the grave and eventually located by the *mbuho.* The burial, exhuma-tion and reburial practices hence not only consist in connecting the deceased to certain features and elements of the homestead that are central in dwelling, but also involve contracting extensions and cut-ting connections to other homesteads. In this way, the dead person is drawn together to be gathered (*isasa*) and conjoined (*iumba*) at the *mbuho.*[19]

The invocations that are uttered over the animals and made when beer and milk are poured on the ground support this understanding. As those rendered above reveal, such invocations are formulaic and resemble each other, regardless of the circumstances in which they are made. Like the address MaShirima made when she poured the bridewealth milk on the ground, they nearly always involve requests that the homestead's ancestors shall congregate or gather – *isasa* – to consume the foodstuffs they are presented. Indeed, the *msaso* event takes its name from this verb, which recurs in such requests. For instance, on one occasion when beer was poured on the ground in Oswald's homestead, the following address was made:

> You, elder Ngufumari, I request (*ngiterewa*) you, you (plural) sit and eat this thing, give me *horu*, sit together (*motchamia*) all of you. Congregate (*mundesasa*) with your father and with *monikiwalo*, sit here. And you, elder Kahumba, take this beer and send it to the place of your mother's brother, they shall sit together all of them. It is your grandchild who asks that you give him life force. When you have finished, come back and drink this, this is your share (*kiirya*). If a bad thing (*kindo kiwiishwa*) comes, you shall stop it, together with those of the left-hand side (*wa kumoosoni*).

The person who uttered these words was Oswald's and Atali's middle brother, who requested their father to receive the beer he poured on the ground, and asked him to sit and drink with his father and *monikiwalo*. His aim was thus to bring together his deceased father, grandfather and the 'owner of the homestead', and enable them to sit (*itchamia*) in one place. The request hence entails and enunciates that the act of pouring the powerful substance on the ground is an instance of *idamira*, which recurred during MaKawishe's divination. The address links *itchamia* and *isasa*, which in everyday use means 'to combine' or 'to bring something together'. MaKawishe used this notion too, when she instructed Herman to slaughter two goats in order for his father to gather or congregate with the male and female ancestors. These goats would be part of Herman's father's exhumation or removal from the rocks, and the process of emplacement it involves. The use of the same notions in this address and the one by MaShirima in chapter two suggests that even commonplace offerings, like pouring milk or beer on the ground, form part of processes that enable or occasion the deceased to sit or stay (*idamira*) at the homestead, where they consequently congregate (*isasa*) and conjoin (*iumba*). The dead is hence further emplaced every time a powerful substance is poured or placed on the ground by the living. Accordingly, Herman literally said that the thing he will obtain and provide shall make the deceased stay (*kandoka kemdamira*). Similarly, the vernacular statement rendered by Dundas (1924: 184) above enunciates that the person is buried by means of powerful substances, like meat, milk and fat, while the act of tossing chyme recognizes how these emerge from *mooshe* and result from dwelling. It is underscored by the fact that milk and beer are poured on the ground inside the house, where the deceased were buried in the past, while the *ndaswa* meat is placed with beer and milk on the ground by the *mbuho* where they gather and conjoin after exhumation. The locations where the dead are provided powerful substances coincide with the places where they were first interred and subsequently conjoined, and where the deceased gather and become increasingly emplaced.

Through burial, exhumation and reburial, the extensions that the person unfolds through dwelling and life are gradually contracted and gathered in one place. Like the New Ireland *malangan*, the *mbuho* thus becomes a repository of the life force of the deceased, where his or her efficacy is accumulated from the various places to which it dispersed (Gell 1998: 225ff). In the past, the gathering of the deceased's *horu* was literal and physical, as life force in the form of bones were dug up and collected by the *mbuho*. Currently, however, it takes the form of a stone that bodies forth the person's extensions and attachments to another place. When the *malangan* is destroyed, an image is released to lodge in the minds of the participants, who carry it with them to redeploy and extend the capacity of the deceased. The *mbuho* does not involve an image, but *irukwa* releases the name, which is redeployed to reiterate and extend the deceased. As *irukwa* is a stative form of the verb *iruwa* or 'to open or be open', it means that exhumation places the deceased in a state of openness. *Irukwa* is moreover the end-point of a process that begins years if not decades before, at the ceremony to cool or cleanse the homestead (*ihora kaa*) that takes place three or four days after the death of a man or a woman. On this day, an item of the deceased's clothing is folded up and tied with dried *mnyengele* banana bark and placed in the cooking hut attic of the homestead. When the large *matanga* ceremony is performed ten to fifteen years later, the parcel is retrieved and the garment unfolded and shaken out, while imperative statements are made imploring the deceased to be released or to be in a state of openness (*harauka*). Its culmination in the *irukwa* ceremony gains support from Dundas's (1924: 191) report that the deceased was 'released' upon exhumation. He claimed that the release pertained to the deceased's ability to avenge his or her living enemies, but in my view it concerns the person's name, which is set free to be used by others in succeeding generations. Names thus issue and disperse through time and space as the effects of exhumation (*irukwa*) to append to relatives, who reiterate the deceased and extend and attach to the homesteads that belonged to him or her. The ability of grandparents to elicit grandchildren to carry their names is thus enabled by the emplacement of preceding generations by the *mbuho*, which allows names to circulate as effects of *horu* that moves and extends persons between homesteads. Names thus transfer from the deceased, who are in a state of openness due to exhumation, which

gathers and emplaces them in a particular place as the result of dwelling and life.

Like the *malangan*, the *mbuho* gathers a past to project a future that
emerges from the *horu* it contains. It is entailed by Dundas's (1924:
192) claim that 'such a place is called *Mbuo nyi*, meaning "the root
of the clan". Here are planted lines of Dracæna, each one proceeding from three stones around every skull that has been placed there'.
Admittedly, I have never heard *mbuho* used in connection with the
notion of *mri* or root, but the account of how three stones were placed
around each skull coincides with the arrangement provided for *mrina
monikiwalo* at Herman's homestead. Moreover, the claim that *isale*
grows ever-wider and higher from the bones of the deceased suggests
that the present and the future extends from the *mbuho*, and that the
homestead and the banana garden folds out of or from the *horu* that
the *mbuho* gathers and contains. Unlike the *malangan*, the *mbuho* is not
a temporary repository of power, but a permanent store of life force
that the living replenish through their prestations of foodstuffs and
substances. It accords with Gutmann's (1935: 8) claim that the 'undivided protoplasm' 'withers away without the stimulus of activity'.
However, the prestations that replenish the *mbuho* result from dwelling and thus body forth *horu* that is deployed to channel the life force
that it contains. Life (*moo*) thus emanates from judicious engagements
with *horu*, which issue from the *mbuho* to permeate dwelling (*ikaa*) in
the homestead (*kaa*). Even Rebmann was on the track of this, when he
described how he 'heard that the people of Jagga, too, pray to the souls
of the dead, which they call Warumu; but instead of rice and palm-
wine, like the Wanika, they place milk on the graves. This custom,
diffused far and wide in Eastern Africa, proves a strong yearning after
life in a future state' (Krapf 1860: 241). The act of placing powerful
substances on the ground by the *mbuho* anticipates a future as a reiteration of the past, which conjoin to constitute a present.

Death and Displacement

These considerations entail that a failure to take Herman's father out
of the rocks would have involved a misplacement or displacement that
would have blocked or diverted the *horu* that emanates from the *mbuho*
as the effect of exhumation. Accordingly, MaKawishe's assertion that
Herman needed to bring the *monikiwalo* to his homestead (*umhende
kunu kaa kwaffo*) and make him stay or sit (*idamira*) entailed that he
had been buried outside of the homestead, and thus was misplaced or

displaced. *Monikiwalo* or 'the owner of the place' was the person who first cleared the land. He is therefore also known as 'breaker of the bush' (*mbara kisaka*), who turned an uncultivated and uninhabited place (*sakeu*) into a cultivated place (*mdenyi*) of dwelling (*ikaa*). People emphasize that *monikiwalo* lived in the distant past and is not related to those who currently occupy the homestead. As they came later to find the cultivated place, they do not and cannot know the name of this person, whom they instead call *monikiwalo*.

The way that Herman brought a stone and we slaughtered a goat to make *mrina monikiwalo* stay relates to the practices performed when a person dies away from home. Like in the case of Valeria, provisions are nearly always made to bring the body of someone who dies away from home back to Rombo for burial. Such efforts require and occasion contributions from agnates, affines, friends and neighbours. They are common occurrences that represent a significant expense, due to the number of people who live and work away. In 2006, Oswald told me how people from Keni and the surrounds who live in Dar es Salaam had arranged a mutual burial society. Each household paid a set contribution to take part, which released a large sum of money and practical assistance to transport a deceased person and organize a burial back in Rombo.

However, if a person is buried away from home, he or she must 'be made to return to the homestead' (*iura kaa*), lest problems will ensue. To do this, at least two people travel to where the person was buried and remove a stone from the grave. They bring this back and place it by the homestead's *mbuho*, where a goat is slaughtered to make the person stay or sit. If no goat is available, the stone is placed at the foot of a *mnyengele* banana tree in the homestead, like we did both for *mrina monikiwalo* and during *irukwa*.[20] In anticipation of its emplacement by the *mbuho*, the stone is hence preliminarily attached to the *mnyengele* tree. Its connection to *mhende kwa wafije* and Herman's retrieval of *mrina monikiwalo* is underscored by the fact that the person who carries the stone must neither speak nor look back, until the stone reaches the homestead. Like Herman and the mother's brother, the one carrying the stone is therefore accompanied by another person who does the talking. I have never seen a stone brought back from far away, but heard frequent claims that the practice stems from the past, when people were killed in war and not buried properly. The survivors then retrieved a stone from the battlefield, which they buried at the homestead. Gutmann (1909b: 137) similarly described how those who fell in battle were left in the bush without a burial, and that a stone was retrieved from the area's boundary that faces the direction in which he or she departed. Gutmann (1909b: 137) moreover described how a stone was placed in the banana garden and a goat slaughtered on behalf of a childless person, who had not been buried properly and therefore caused illnesses or other problems for the living. Gutmann did not mention the notion of *idamira*, but his account concerns a process of emplacement by means of a stone and a prestation of *horu* that resemble today's practices.

The notion of *iura* that is used for the act of bringing back the wrongfully buried person is the same that Peter used when he returned life to Horombo and which is used when a man takes a wife from the same homestead where his father's father married – *naura msheku na kaa*. It is a causative form of the verb *iuya* (to return), which moreover is used to justify how the second-born children are named after their mother's parents. These conceptual uses reveal that the burial practices relate to marital relations and reproduction that form part of dwelling and life. In turn, this sheds light on MaKawishe's instruction 'to bring home' MaLasway's father's sister, who was also buried away from the homestead.

MaKawishe told Herman that MaLasway's *shangazi* brought problems because she died unmarried and childless, while her brother's daughter has both. The issue remained the last of Herman's priorities, but he related how a stone should be taken from the father's sister's grave. Instead of burying the stone, however, they would provide it with a husband.[21] To do so, the stone would be brought to Lasway's homestead and placed on the bed inside the cooking hut. After a short while, the stone would be removed from the house and brought to the homestead of an eligible man, where it would be placed inside the cooking hut. The man would then be pronounced her husband with the words: 'Now you have been married, do not bring us problems again'. Like in *mhende kwa wafije* and for *mrina monikiwalo*, a stone is also in this case removed to gather and detach the person from one place. In this form, she is conveyed to her father's house from which she comes out (*ifuma*), in order to enter (*iingia*) another house. In this way, she is married (*ialikwa*) to a person of this house, where she attaches or is made to stay or sit (*idamira*).[22]

As the practice resembles and reiterates those above, it reveals how a person's death before marriage and reproduction constitutes a further form of displacement. It is indeed even possible that MaLasway's *shangazi* was not given an ordinary burial, but rather was interred outside the homestead and thus literally displaced. The early ethnographers claimed that only married people with children were buried inside the homestead, while those who were not were dealt with in different yet related ways. Lehmann (1941: 390), for instance, claimed that dead children were simply left in the banana garden, while Raum (1911: 184) argued that the same fate befell the childless. At one point, Gutmann (1909c: 92) described how the bodies of unmarried people – and especially children – were left under old trees in the forest, but elsewhere he argued that it pertained to childless women in particular (Gutmann 1909b: 140). Similarly, Dundas (1924: 181) reported:

> According to old custom the only corpses which might be buried were those of married people who had offspring. Thus it was absolutely unlawful to bury sterile men and women, as also unmarried persons and children. A sterile woman or man was carried into the bush and deposited there with all his or her belongings, excepting of course livestock, for clothing or utensils of a dead person may only be used by that person's child. Youth and girls were laid in the banana grove under the shade of the Dracæna hedges, and wrapped in banana leaves with face towards Kibo. It is curious to note that the corpses of such persons were washed, while bodies which are to be buried are not so treated. Small children's bodies are plastered with cow dung and mud and placed likewise in the banana groves. Such bodies are eaten by hyænas and jackals, and may be dragged away, but the parents will always look for the skulls and place them among the Dracæna stems, where they remain indefinitely.

Dundas's account suggests a hierarchy of practices, where the sterile and barren received the harshest treatment, and were banished from the homestead. Current statements corroborate this, as some say the childless were thrown in the bush or down a river valley, while others claim they were buried in the forest above the homesteads. Accordingly, they point out that the forest at Mamsera is called 'the forest of the barren' (*ngudu ya waumba*). The same term is used for a large tree that is surrounded by tall and thick *isale* trees in the settled area of Shimbi. The tree is left to grow because barren women and childless men were thrown or buried at its foot in the past. The place resembles the groves of unfarmed land below the *mbuho*, where Gutmann (1909b: 141; 1909c: 92) claimed the bodies of the childless were thrown. Echoing the name from Mamsera, these were known as 'bush for throwing away people' (*ngasi yĕkumba vandu*). Resembling in appearance the tree at Shimbi, they were moreover marked by thick *isale* stands that sprouted from the stems used to carry the bodies, which had been wrapped in dried banana leaves. The tree at Shimbi differs greatly from the cultivated character of other trees, whose branches are harvested for fodder and firewood.[23] Some still bury childless women towards the boundary (*mrasa*) of the homestead, and thus away from the *mbuho* and at a greater distance from the house and its courtyard.[24] Nevertheless, all children and most of the childless are given the same burial as everyone else. However, children are subject to a shorter period of mourning, which moreover ends with a simplified ceremony 'to sweep the footprints' (*ihaya nduwa*), rather than the elaborate event 'to cool or cleanse the homestead' (*ihora kaa*). MaKawishe's claim that MaShirima's *shangazi* was located below the homestead could thus mean that she was buried outside or at its boundary. If so, she was deliberately displaced in death because she was not attached to a marital homestead, where she should have been gathered and emplaced through burial and exhumation.

Burial's contingency on marital relations and reproduction brings out its relationship to dwelling, and the process of attachment and emplacement that this facilitates and involves. As I have shown, bridewealth and marriage enable reproduction and bring into existence the homestead to which its inhabitants attach through dwelling. In turn, this affords their burial within the confines of the homestead and eventual emplacement at its *mbuho*. Not marrying means not obtaining a homestead in which to be buried, and thus relegates you to the bush, the riverbed or the boundary of your parents' homestead. Not reproducing, meanwhile, entails no grandchild to carry your name, which instead is withdrawn from the turning of generations and the temporality of dwelling. Accordingly, Gutmann (1909b: 140) described how the childless woman was thrown in the bush with all her belongings – including her cooking pot and ladle – in a place where no one was allowed to cultivate crops. Her body was moreover not brought out of the doorway of the house, but removed through a hole in the wall that was made for the occasion. Not using one *moongo* (her backbone) meant that she did not attach to another *moongo* (the doorway), out of which she therefore could not come. By contrast, a childless man was brought through the doorway, even though he was also thrown in the bush. He attached to the doorway through the back of his mother from whom he would have received the house in the past. Meanwhile, the childless woman and her means for converting and conveying *horu* were banished from the homestead and its dwelling. On this basis, it seems likely that the displacement of MaLasway's *shangazi* was not a mistake or an oversight, but a careful and considered dislocation that was due to her state of non-extension.

However, a displaced person can make a living relative ill (*ilauka*) to ensure that he or she takes his or her name. The name will then be passed on to this person's children and thus be extended into the future. The notion of *ilauka*, which recurred in MaKawishe's statements, is the stative form of the verb 'to call' (*ilaha*). It enunciates that the deceased is in a 'state of calling', which occasions problems for the living who hence are in a 'state of being called' (*ilaukiwa*). These terms concern how such illnesses and problems are claims that the deceased make on the living to ensure that the latter extend the former by assuming his or her name. In this way, the deceased ensures that the name is reinserted into dwelling and life, and will be used by future generations as it is released when the person being called is eventually emplaced by the *mbuho*. It was this MaKawishe meant when she instructed Herman 'to buy the name' (*iola rina*) of the *monikiwalo*. Such a procedure requires that a goat is slaughtered and a pronouncement made that you assume a particular name. A skin-ring (*kishong'u*) must be made from the animal's hide and worn by the buyer for a certain number of days. If the identity is unknown, the deceased person is simply referred to as *mrina* or 'the person of the name', which will then also be used for the living. The adoption by Herman of *mrina monikiwalo* shows that the deceased may compel the living to act on the basis of relationships that extend beyond reproduction. It is emphasized that the current inhabitants of a homestead do not descend from the *monikiwalo*, so it is the relationships forged through dwelling in the same place that enable him to call the living. It is hence the transfers and transformations of *horu* that occur through dwelling that enable the deceased to call and claim the living through further relationships than those of reproduction.

The act of buying a name can also simply involve beer or another powerful substance being poured on the ground. This emerged when Herman and I returned to MaKawishe in 2008 to enquire about his second-born son, who was shouting in his sleep and waking up at night. Stirring and inspecting the eleusine, MaKawishe determined that the issue was an older brother of Lasway, who had died unmarried and childless, and was buried at what was now his brother's homestead. Now this person wanted to be provided a wife and for Herman's son to carry his name as the name of the pathway. Herman needed to inform Lasway about this fact, but also to pour beer on the ground for his wife's father's brother and pronounce that his son would carry this man's name. Ten days later, Herman acquired some beer, which we poured on the ground at the foot of the pillar inside his house, while he addressed his father:

> This beer, you male elder Alfred, go and take it and seek your older brother, you shall congregate (*mundesasa*) with your elder named Nyenga-Nyenga, go and congregate, take (*mundeira*) this beer, climb to the homestead of those whose child married your child (*watoi*), go and

tell them that there is someone there who now is remembered, and this elder, if it is this elder who wants his name, let him not bring trouble to this child again, brother of the homestead, you cool it (*wohorere*), if it is his name, he will get it, please sit (*techamieni*) and drink calmly, do not leave a single person out, sit and drink all of you, congregate with those whose child married your child, prevent any bad thing (*kindo ki-wiishwa*), do not leave this child so he gets problems again, sit and drink calmly, do not break your homestead (*mṛi wenu*), do so that everything is good, sit calmly, you elder.

Herman refilled the gourd and poured more beer, while adding:

And this here, when you return (*mukauya*), you elder, when you return, sit (plural) and drink this beer, you elder, sit and drink this beer silently in this place, this is your homestead (*mṛi wenu*), you are here, do not leave a bad thing here at your (plural) homestead (*kunu kaa kwenu*), you elder, sit calmly and drink, sit with your wives, give them and drink together, tell them 'this thing we were given', sit and drink calmly.

Herman's address accentuates how beer is poured on the ground to gather the deceased in one place and enable them to share and consume the foodstuff. It moreover reveals how this effectuates and ensures the emplacement of the deceased at the homestead, where it secures and extends dwelling by preventing bad things from occurring. Most significantly, the statement enunciates that beer may be poured on the ground to enable names to be resumed and used by the living. It thus entails that names emerge and emanate as effects of prestations of *horu* in different forms. Beer, meat and milk are hence deployed to transform the subject position of persons who risk oblivion because they died without children and therefore will have no grandchildren to carry their names. However, a powerful substance poured on the ground enables a living person to assume the name and project it into the future. Similarly, the case of Herman's *monikiwalo* and MaLasway's *shangazi* reveal how *horu* in the form of livestock may be used to relocate and emplace deceased persons. Their subject positions are transformed, as they are provided with a house and homestead from which their life force may issue forth into the future. These cases moreover imbricate with *mhende* and *msaso*, where extensions are contracted and persons gathered to be emplaced in the homestead. In different yet related ways, *horu* is hence deployed to reinsert and embed persons in dwelling and life.

Herman's address furthermore reveals how he provided beer for his father with a request that he should find his older brother. They should then bring this beer to their elder before proceeding to present it to Herman's affines. As his statement concerns how beer is presented to one person so that he may present it to others, it concerns the same mode of service and consumption that occurs during beer parties.[25] On such occasions, guests sit and wait for beer to be served, which begins when the owner of the homestead draws a gourd of beer that he presents to a trusted person, often a younger brother or son. Standing in front of this person, the host drinks ostentatiously from the gourd before handing it over with a request that the recipient shall serve the others. The person who receives the gourd also tastes the beer, but immediately hands the gourd to someone else for safekeeping. He then stands up and draws a gourd that he offers to the host in the same manner that he was served. He then serves the others and endeavours to do so in order of seniority and significance to the event. If it is a small occasion, he tastes each gourd before handing it over, but this is not done at a larger party, where several people take part in serving the beer.

Herman's statement hence entails and enunciates that the act of pouring beer on the ground is a presentation of beer of the same kind as the living make during social events. The point is underscored by the notion of *itchambika*, which is used to mean the host's presentation to the person he delegates the task of serving the beer. *Itchambika* is a cognate of the Swahili term *kutambika*, which means 'to make offering to propitiate the spirits of the dead and ask them not to trouble the living' (Johnson 1939: 449). In both cases, one person presents beer to another, and requests him or her to serve others so that they may sit together and share the brew.[26] It is corroborated by Gutmann (1926: 93), who reported that a leg of meat that formed part of one bridewealth prestation was called *odambiko* or 'the presentation' (*Überreichung*). It gains support from the use of the term *kiirya* in the invocation at Oswald's homestead to mean the share of the deceased person who was addressed. The noun *kiirya* derives from the verb *iira*, which means 'to seize, take, hold, carry, stick, or support'. Herman used this term in his request that his father and the father's brother should take the beer he poured and bring it to Shimbi, in return for *kiirya*. *Kiirya* is the share that is set aside during a party for those who carry the barrels of beer out of the house and place them in the courtyard, and that they share with the person who serves the guests. *Kiirya* literally means 'a thing for taking or seizing', which regards how this is for the taking of those who take the beer out of the house and serve it. By extension, it is a claim made on the basis of their exertion and expenditure of *horu*, which the beer replaces.

The similarities between pouring beer on the ground for the dead and serving it to the living shed additional light on the language used in the addresses made to the deceased. The person who poured the beer on the ground in Oswald's homestead began his statement by requesting (*iterewa*) his father to receive the beer and sit and drink with his fellow deceased. Although *iterewa* is used to mean the act of praying as religious worship, its primary use and meaning is 'to ask someone for something'.[27] Its use in this sense has a long history that arguably precedes the arrival of Christianity. Thus, Raum (1907: 272) claimed: 'Among the Chagga, requests for protection and mercy are usually accompanied by a gift of a head of cattle or something similar, so that the person the requests are directed to is convinced about their sincerity, and will not be able to overlook them. *Itereva na kindo*, to request someone with a thing, they say' (cf. Raum 1911: 166). Similarly, Thomson (1885: 70) described how *mangi* Mandara sent a messenger with a cow and a goat, 'asking' him to come and visit. The phrase *iterewa mdu na kindo* is still in use to mean the act of giving someone something with a request for something else in return. Combining a request, a presentation and a prestation, the notion provides an instance of what Wittgenstein calls a language-game. As in the addresses above, such requests proceed through an existing relationship and involve a petition that the addressed person shall bring the object and the request to someone else, to whom he or she has a closer connection. Thus, if I want something from someone I do not know well, I do not address the person directly, but provide a gift and voice a request to someone close to me who knows the person in question. The intermediary then delivers the object and passes on the request to enchain the recipient and hopefully elicit the desired response. A similar feat occurs in the bridewealth prestation by the *mkara*, while the requests above reveal that it also occurs when substances and foodstuffs are provided for the deceased. Oswald's brother thus requested first his father and then his grandfather to bring him *horu*, before he asked them to protect him from a 'bad thing' (*kindo kiwiishwa*). As Parkin (2000: 140) points out with regard to its Swahili synonym *kuomba*, *iterewa* does not concern a transcendent deity, but a mode of acting upon the world, which in this case involves one person reaching out to another through a relationship to enable and ensure a desired effect.[28]

Oswald's brother requested *horu* in return for the beer, which itself is a powerful substance. It reveals how the provisions of foodstuffs and substances to the deceased are further prestations of life force that imbricate with the transfers and transformations of *horu* that occur in the bridewealth prestations. It is underscored by Gutmann's (1926: 97) account of the statement made over a bridewealth prestation of meat that the bride shall find a 'permanent seat' (*Dauersitz*) and 'root firmly' (*festwurzeln*) when she is brought to the homestead.[29] Gutmann's language indicates that the notions of *idamira, mri* and *mṛi* are at play, and that the prestation emplaces the bride at her marital homestead and enables her veins to imbricate the roots, where *horu* conveys and converts to permeate dwelling and animate life. Over time, she and her husband thus become increasingly rooted, as revealed by the statement made when a man was shown and spat food into his son's son (Gutmann 1926: 220). Stating that he and his wife would henceforth remain at the homestead, the man implied that elderhood made them stay or sit, as they would stop circulating between the mountain and the plains, and presumably instead only toddle about among the homesteads between which they are extended. Although the notion surfaces especially in connection with burial, *idamira* hence extends through life and beyond death to include the provisions of powerful foodstuffs and substances to the deceased. The way in which these provisions concerns transfers and transformations of life force is underscored by the fact that the participants may not engage in sex after such provisions, as this will divert their *horu*. The conception of the ancestral offerings as prestations of *horu* that form part of the transfers and transformations of life force recasts the relationship between the dead and the living as a mode of sociality or a shared form of life. Like the relationships between and within homesteads (*kaa*), the one between the dead and the living centres on provisions and conversions of *horu* that permeate dwelling (*ikaa*) and constitute life (*moo*). Accordingly, the living and the dead occupy an existential continuum, which is enunciated by the fact that the term for the ancestors – *warimu* – belongs to the Chagga noun class that is strictly restricted to human beings. It provides an instance of Igor Kopytoff's (1971) 'eldership complex', but surpasses his largely linguistic argument to concern and consider the material and practical forms that imbricate the uses of language. It is facilitated by the notion of language-game, which affords ethnographic explorations of the relationship between the living and the dead.[30]

Warimu derives from a root-form -*rim*- that subtends the notion of *mrimwa* that is used for the act of slaughtering livestock or pouring beer and milk on the ground. People render *mrimwa* in Swahili as *mila* or 'custom', but it is better considered a prestation of life force that is made by means of particular objects and in relation to specific features of the homestead (*mṛi* or *kaa*). The act serves to emplace (*idamira*) the deceased (*warimu*) and ensure that life force emanates in other forms through the veins and roots (*mri*) of persons, animals and crops to extend dwelling (*ikaa*) and afford life (*moo*) in a particular place. Such acts are misrepresented when considered as ancestral offerings to propitiate or atone spirits that are subject to cultic worship. Instead, they are provisions of life force for the deceased that replace the *horu* they expended to enable the existence of those who now engage the features and objects that are intrinsic to the conversions and conveyances of life force. Failing to do so places the dead in a state of calling that rests on and activates the debt that the living owe to the dead. The asymmetrical relationship between them stems from the fact that the living owe their names, homesteads, spouses and children to the dead, who in turn extract names, houses, spouses, children and prestations of life force from those who otherwise jeopardize dwelling and life.

Divination and Dwelling

The subjunctive mood Herman used when he poured beer on the ground on behalf of his son for his father and father's brothers reveals how *mrimwa* is another attempt to determine the transfers and transformations of *horu* in which people entangle. By pouring a powerful substance on the ground and making a conditional statement, Herman sought to determine whether his son's problems stemmed from a particular deceased relative and whether the reason was that this person's name no longer circulated among the living. As Herman manipulated beer, he experimented with names and language to probe the existence and character of a particular relationship in which his son possibly took part. The relationship exceeded their knowledge and use of language, but concerned a particular name that had not been projected into the future by the living. They were obliged to do so, on the basis of their connection to the homestead where the deceased was supposed to have received a house in which to dwell and be emplaced. Similarly, Nico's insistence that they knew nothing of the *mrina monikiwalo*, but had encountered a problem from the old days, entailed that the activities they performed were effects of processes that they attempted to determine. Accordingly, Herman's emphasis that he brought this person when he came to know about him entailed that the beer he poured was an effect of having been made to know. Meanwhile, his inclusion of anyone else they do not know of entailed an admission and recognition that there are further phenomena that exceed their knowledge and await determination. In this way, he tried to anticipate and pre-empt the disruptions and dislocations of dwelling that these will involve, as he owned up to the limits of his knowledge.

The combined use of powerful substances and language to probe and determine the transfers and transformations of *horu* rests on their entwinement as they move along the gullet and windpipe. It moreover imbricates with divination as a mode of knowledge that involves claims to see a truth on the basis of an ability that is shown in dreams by one's deceased relatives (Myhre 2006). The claims entail a set of related notions, where 'to see' (*ilholhya*) is an intensive verb-form that affords both the concept of 'truth' (*lhoy*) and the causative-passive construction that construes 'to dream' (*ilhoswa*) as 'to be made to see', 'to be shown' or 'to be instructed'. Both the capacity to divine and the ability to heal are designated by the abstract noun *uaanga* that features in the term for both healer and diviner (*mwaanga*). Both forms are presaged by an illness or malady that eventually proves that the person in question is in a state of being called (*ilaukiwa*) by a particular deceased relative. In 2006, MaKawishe and a fellow diviner described for Herman and me the problems they had suffered and the array of remedies they had sought as a result. Eventually, they were diagnosed by a diviner as being called (*ilaukiwa*) to divine. In both cases, the person who called was a female relative of the grandparental generation, whose names they carry. The ability to divine and heal is hence also transferred between alternate generations, along with names and homesteads. However, they differ in that *uaanga* is nearly invariably acquired in middle age, when the person who bestows it has passed away. Unlike names, which are often transferred between living grandparents and newborn grandchildren, divination and healing are conferred from a deceased person to his or her living reiteration.

Both MaKawishe and her colleague described how they recovered once they slaughtered a goat at their namesake's former homestead and brought a stone from her grave to their marital homestead, where another goat was slaughtered to make her sit or stay.[31] MaKawishe moreover stressed that she uses the spoon that her deceased namesake employed for divination, and highlighted how the skin-rings (*fishong'u*) twirled around its handle are from the goats she slaughters to dream or be shown by this person. The skin-rings are thus traces of the prestations of *horu* she makes to her deceased namesake from whom the ability to see the truth emanates. These rings manifest her relationship to this particular relative and testify to her legitimacy as a diviner. Similarly, the skin-rings people wear on specific occasions, and the bones from the goat they place at the *mbuho* during *irukwa*, show particular relationships between the dead and the living. In addition, they manifest successful dwelling at the homestead, which

the living aim to extend into the future through prestations that replace the *horu* the deceased expended in enabling their dwelling and
life. Thus, Nico claimed that the meat he wrapped and placed by the
mnyengele tree was a recognition (*tambulisho*) that showed (*imlhora*)
mrina monikiwalo that he had been provided a homestead. His use of
words entails that 'showing' extends beyond the specialized practice
of divination through its imbrication with the transfers and transformations of *horu*.

Herman enunciated that the ability to see or be shown a truth entwines with the transfers and transformations that occur within and
between homesteads, when he pulled out *isale* leaves for MaKawishe's
use in 2008. Holding the leaves firmly, he uttered the following words
before he yanked them out from a dracaena tree below MaKawishe's
courtyard:

> Please show me the pathways of my homestead (*tengilhorie shiasi fo kaa
> kwakwa*), I beckon, you elder, you elder Alfred and you Tengio, please
> show me how things are at my homestead, if something comes, you
> show me, I beckon you, and you of the left-hand side (*we wa kumoosoni*),
> I beckon you, show me my homestead.

Herman's request was again directed first at his father, then at his
father's father, and finally at his mother's brother. However, the request was not for them to show anything regarding particular persons, but rather to show the state and character of his homestead. He
moreover petitioned that they should show him the pathways, along
which *horu* conveys to constitute the affinal and reproductive relationships that enable the homestead and afford the extended state of its
inhabitants. His request, in other words, was for the dead to show the
avenues along which *horu* moves to extend and unfold the living, who
thereby become emplaced in a particular homestead.[32] The subject
of divination is hence the homestead and the pathways in which it
entangles, through and along which *horu* transfers and transforms in
dwelling to constitute human, animal and vegetative life.

Accordingly, the objects engaged in divination gain their significance and salience from the roles they play in dwelling. Thus, eleusine
grains that are high in *horu* suspend in water (*mringa*) in the bowl of a
spoon or ladle (*kilikiyo*) that is otherwise used to prepare and serve soft
foods for human consumption.[33] The ladle hence ordinarily converts
and conveys *horu*, which eleusine and water manifest and contain,
to contribute and constitute the health, capacity and well-being that
afford engagement in dwelling. In divination, the spoon establishes a
zone of indiscernibility (Deleuze and Guattari 1994), where *horu* in

one form suspends in another form inside a ladle that converts and conveys life force. When the *isale* leaves roil the water and whirl the grains, established forms dissolve into their animating forces, which are isomorphic with the movements and transformations of *horu* in dwelling and life. These objects and practices thus show the state and character of homesteads and their inhabitants because they partake in and project from that which they concern. The *isale* leaves gain their poignancy from the *mbuho* and from the boundaries (*mrasa*) that shape the transfers of *horu* between homesteads to constitute particular relationships. As boundaries (*mrasa*), the *isale* are spatial limits or separations around or across which neighbours (*wamamrasa*) gather and connect. As *mbuho*, the *isale* is a temporal limit inside the homestead around which the living and the dead gather to connect across their separation in time. Indeed, as *isale* sprouts from the *mbuho*, the spatial boundaries of the homestead extend out of this temporal limit from which *horu* and life emanate. The homestead thus folds out of or from the *mbuho*, whose outer and spatial limits are of the same kind as its internal and temporal ones. The *isale* enfolds these relationships, which affords its leaves the capacity to reveal in their growth the truth (*lhoy*) of dwelling and life, which the diviner sees or is shown. Rather than persons, it is therefore dwelling and the place in which it occurs that are the subjects of divination.

The way the divinatory objects partake in and are isomorphic with dwelling and life entails that they do not symbolize the transfers of *horu* and the relationships they involve. Franz Steiner (1954: 367) realized the particular character of these objects, when he argued in an essay on Gutmann that:

> The survey of Chagga truth concepts would not be complete without a mention of certain signals or signs – I hesitate to call them symbols, as they seem to me part of the language and in no way more symbolic than other parts of speech behaviour, though resisting verbal conceptualization both in Chagga and in our languages. I refer to certain ejaculations and to the use of the Dracaena leaf.

Steiner's claim that the dracaena and the ejaculations are part of language anticipated Wittgenstein's notion of language-game, where words, actions and objects interweave. His conclusion extends to the other divinatory objects, which do not even signal or signpost, but rather engage and entail each other in processes where *horu* in different forms fold into and out of each other. Through indiscernment, these forms of *horu* dissolve and resolve configurations and formations. They thus contain and entail each other, just like the language-game of divination contains and entails these objects and concepts. Steiner's reference to ejaculations indicates how the diviner's statements fold out of these objects and their combination and engagement.[34] Thus, the burp-like emissions MaKawishe expelled at the beginning of her sessions eventually entwined with her words and utterances to create a mode of speech where statements and verdicts became articulate to eject through her gullet and mouth. Her pronouncements thus projected from beyond her volition and cognition as effects of her manipulations of the divinatory objects. It was therefore less a matter of her conducting divination than of divination conducting itself through her.[35] Herman's responses lent the event a dialogic quality of questions and answers, but his comments went beyond Parkin's (1991b: 178) account of clients helping diviners along with 'words of encouragement and agreement throughout the divination'. Instead, his responses channelled and affected MaKawishe's engagement with the divinatory objects, which occasioned further claims and statements. As MaKawishe manipulated powerful things to unfold statements and verdicts, Herman used words to affect her engagements that folded his statements back into the transfers and transformations of *horu*. They thus both deployed words and objects in a mutual exploration of the transfers and transformations of *horu* that entangle yet transcend their mode of being to permeate dwelling and animate life. Divination is thus a further context where *horu* and language entwine and interact to channel and affect each other with the aim of exploring, effectuating and extending dwelling and life. In this way, dwelling projects a point of view on itself and the transfers and transformations it involves, which divination manipulates and emerges from. The objects and utterances used in divination are consequently neither symbols nor signs or indexes, but *horu* in different forms that contain and unfold from each other to constitute divination as a language-game or a slice of human activity.

As the transfers and transformations of *horu* surpass human agency and intentionality, they also exceed language and conceptualization. They therefore occasion attempts at their own determination, which are restricted to employ language and manipulate *horu* in different forms. Divination is one way of determining these relationships, but their partiality lends them a contingent and provisional character that eventually is subject to eruption and dissolution. The way in which words and language emerge as the effects of *horu*, and are used to channel and affect dwelling and life, go beyond the situations and contexts considered so far. They will therefore be explored further in the next chapter, which concerns the practice and activity of cursing, where speech, objects and practices imbricate in further language-games with potentially detrimental effects and consequences for dwelling and life.

Notes

1. There is no terminological distinction between a diviner and a healer, who are equally termed *mwaanga* in the singular and *waanga* in the plural.
2. The case is described elsewhere (Myhre 2009).
3. Such skin-rings feature in many ceremonial contexts and settings in Kilimanjaro. *Fishong'u* is the plural form of *kishong'u,* which also features in this chapter.
4. *Moni-* is the possessive prefix in Chagga, which is a cognate of and equivalent to the Swahili *mwenye-*. *Idamira* meanwhile is the causative form of the verb 'to sit' (*itchamia*), and another instance where the *-ch-* sound converts to *-d-* or *-t-* in a derivate form.
5. The terms *monyi kanyi* and *mon-kan* were reported by Dundas (1924: 145) and Gutmann (1926: 33) to mean the present occupier of the homestead and not the person who created it. *Monikaa* and *monikiwalo* are very occasionally used with this meaning in Rombo, but they are nearly always used to mean an unknown person in the past who broke the ground and established the homestead. In line with this, Gutmann (1913: 480) also described that the present occupier must give 'the master of the homestead' (*menikihamba*) an offering of beer before farming commences. Similarly, Raum (1911: 191) claimed that the one-time occupier of your homestead wants an offering of your produce. Unfortunately, he did not provide the vernacular term for the person in question, but it seems likely this is *monikiwalo.* Both claims entail that current dwelling is indebted to that of the past, and concern how this involves transfers and transformations of powerful substances.
6. After the session ended, Herman explained that tossing soil on the ground is an act that can substitute temporarily for an offering of some kind. He also explained that MaKawishe meant the *kisango* prestation by the phrase 'a thing of blood'.
7. The exchange rate at the time was roughly TZS 650 to 1 USD. The fee was hence a little under 50 US cents.
8. Those who are not given Catholic funerals receive Pentecostal or other evangelical funerals. These are also conducted at the deceased's homestead, where the body is buried in the same way. Occasionally, no parish priest is able to read the Mass, in which case one of the lay church stewards reads a shortened version, where no Communion is given.
9. The participants toss three handfuls of soil if the deceased is a man and four if it is a woman. This is in line with a recurring gendered number

practice that has wider prevalence and significance along the Bantu-Nilotic interface that Rombo occupies (Southall 1972).

10. Some of these tombs are tiled, while others are fitted with strip-lights.

11. Thomson (1885: 60) described similar practices from Taveta.

12. Not much is known about Yohane Msando, but according to Raum (1911: 160) he was a Christian Chagga teacher. It is therefore likely that he was one of the first persons baptized by the missionaries from the Leipzig Lutheran Mission Company, who celebrated their first baptisms in 1898 (Winter 1979: 45).

13. These descriptions are not contradictory, but concern activities that may occur in sequential order.

14. If the deceased is a man, each person removes three pinches of soil from the grave, while four pinches are removed for a woman, as part of the aforementioned gendered number practice.

15. There are variations in how this is performed. Some plant three or four *isale* shootings by the *mbuho* to create a house for the stone, while others wrap it in the caul (*uanga*) of the goat. Some taste the milk before pouring it on the ground, while others leave it in an *mboriko* bowl at the *mbuho*. Only men conduct the proceedings around the grave and the *mbuho*; women arrive only to place the soil by the *mbuho* and taste the beer, before they return to the homestead to drink their own share of beer inside the cooking hut.

16. He poured the beer at the foot of a pillar behind the door, which supported the attic and was close to the *mbaariko* area of the cooking hut. As mentioned in chapter two, Dundas (1924: 179) claimed that offerings of beer, milk and honey were poured into holes dug by the side of the supports inside the hut. Gutmann (1909c: 83) argued that offerings of beer to the male ancestors were made at 'the spear pillar', while milk was poured for the female ancestors by 'the hearth pillar' of the round house made from banana bark that was common in central and western Kilimanjaro. Msando also described how beer, honey, eleusine and milk were offered to the deceased, but he did not describe where and how it was done (Raum 1911: 175).

17. I will return to consider the concept and activity of cooling in chapter six.

18. MaLasway was not allowed to share in this meat since she is not circumcised. The men usually walk in a single file back to the courtyard without speaking or looking back, in order to present this meat after eating their share in the banana garden.

19. The use of these stones is hence not to embody and bring to mind a deity, as Gutmann (1928: 424) speculated, but rather is bound up with the extensions of persons that occur through dwelling and life.

20. If *mhende kwa wafije* and *msaso* are performed on different days, that stone is also stored by the foot of an *mnyengele* tree.

21. Relatedly, Dundas (1924: 194) argued that younger siblings could only be married after the 'pretence of giving in marriage' had been performed for an elder sibling who died before marriage.

22. Such a posthumous marriage is also performed on behalf of men, but then involves building a miniature house in the father's homestead. The end of a banana blossom (*unanda*) is placed inside the house with the words: 'Now you have received your homestead, do not cause us problems again'. A younger brother's wife subsequently gives birth to a child in the deceased person's name. These practices underscore arguments from earlier chapters regarding how homesteads are acquired or come into existence upon marriage, which for men involves the receipt of a house to which women are brought as brides.

23. The tree at Shimbi resembles rather certain trees known as *fiungu* (*kiungu*, sing.), which I describe in chapter six.

24. Gutmann (1926: 61) reported that a married woman who returns to her brother's homestead is buried in this manner.

25. A more complicated form of this occurred during 'the beer to tell' at Boniface's homestead described in chapter two.

26. This is also evident from the above address made when beer was poured in the homestead in which I lived, where the father was requested to receive the beer and bring it first to his father and then to the *monikiwalo* and the mother's brother.

27. In a religious context, for instance, the phrase *iterewa mungu* (to pray to god) is used.

28. See also Ruel (2000:82-83) for a different yet related account of the various relationships entailed by 'prayer' and 'invocation' among the Kuria of Kenya.

29. Other statements made in connection with the same prestation were mentioned in chapter three.

30. Kopytoff's argument has been criticized (Brain 1973; McCall 1995; Mendonsa 1976), although it is corroborated by linguistic evidence from other Bantu languages, where the term for the dead also belongs to the human noun class (Ashton 1943: 22; Beidelman 1963: 72; Hobley 1922: 27; Ingstad 1989: 249; Jacobson-Widding 1990: 50; Lan 1985: 31). Brandström (1990: 174–75) captures the situation, when he argues: 'The living and the dead ... form one community ... [where] ... the humans are involved in a *sharing* with the ancestors ... the relationship between the living and the dead is one of reciprocity, characterized by gifts and countergifts'.

31. Male healers often stress that they both inhabit the homestead and possess the name of the ancestor from whom they gained their abilities. They describe how their situation improved once they butchered a goat for this person at his former homestead and thus became able to perform this work. For men, the occupation of the social and geographical position of the particular ancestor hence coincides with the ability to perform this person's work, while for women it involves bringing the deceased person in question to their homesteads.

32. The same idea was at play in the *iumba* ceremony above, when the dregs of beer was said to show the way.

33. Later chapters will show how water too has a central role in life and dwelling.
34. It is possible that Steiner refers to certain kinds of expectoration, like the ones that were described and chapter three and others that will be considered in chapter six.
35. MaKawishe underscored this in 2008, when her verdict that Herman's mother was called to assume the divining abilities of a deceased relative entailed that it is the name that possesses the ability and performs the task of divination.

Chapter Five

IABISA

CURSING AS A LINGUISTIC
AND MATERIAL PRACTICE

When William was buried just after New Year's Day 2001, the court-yard of his homestead was thronged with people. This is common when any elder dies, but since William belonged to the former chiefly descent group that traces its origins to Horombo, the event attracted even more people than usual. As a son of the last reigning *mangi* Tengia, who had thirty-seven wives and eighty sons, William had more classificatory relatives than most. People perhaps also came be-cause of William's longstanding and well-known conflict with his wife and children, which was partly due to their conversion from Cathol-icism to Seventh-Day Adventism, but was exacerbated by William's wish to leave his homestead to his daughter's son, rather than his youngest son.[1] As if to underscore the anomalous character of the event, neither of the two parish priests could attend, so a shortened Mass would be read by a lay steward (*mzimamizi*) from the village out-station. The burial was moreover not organized by the descent group and the neighbourhood prayer group (*jumuiya*), but by William's wife and children who relied on help from their evangelical church even though it would be a Catholic ceremony.

At the end of the burial, the secretary (*mkatibu*) of the descent group rose and read in Swahili the short history of the deceased's life (*historia mfupi ya maisha ya marehemu*). As usual, the account listed the year and place of William's birth, as well as the time and location of his christening, his marriage and his death. It related the number of children he had, and what he had done for a living. The account also included a section regarding his long illness and recounted how

William was treated at the local government health-station, the Catholic dispensary of a neighbouring parish, Huruma District Hospital and Mount Meru District Hospital in Arusha. Perhaps because a priest was expected to be there, it left out William's visits to various *waanga*. Those present eagerly awaited any announcement regarding *ihora kaa* or the ceremony to cool or cleanse the homestead, which allows its bereaved inhabitants to resume the banana farming, livestock stall-feeding and cooking that agnates and neighbours conduct on their behalf in the days after the burial. *Ihora kaa* hence affords a resumption of dwelling, which the death and burial disrupted.[2] The event almost always occurs three days after a man's burial and four days after that of a woman, but its date and a blanket invitation are always announced at the end of the funeral.[3] Before his death, William had let people know that he wanted *ihora kaa* to be conducted on his behalf and that he had specifically kept a head of cattle and a goat to be butchered for this event. However, the religious convictions of his wife and children, together with the state and character of their relationship to William, made many people uncertain whether the event would take place. Finally, the secretary of the descent group declared that William had wished for *ihora kaa*, but that his wife and children refused to conduct it due to their religion (*dini*). He said the descent group had decided to comply with their wishes, and would therefore only participate in the burial. A din of voices rose before one man shouted: '*Ihora kaa* shall be held anyway'. It was by now clear that William's family would not provide the beer that those attending a burial sip before they depart the homestead, so everyone filed out via the *mengele*. However, you are exposed to bringing the 'bad things' (*mawiishwa*) of the death with you if you neither eat nor drink before leaving a funeral, so people tore off and chewed pieces of leaves from the banana trees on their way out.

As we queued out of the courtyard, one of William's classificatory sons shouted that William's wife and children had already butchered the animals he had raised for his *ihora kaa*. To prove this, a young neighbour ran into the combined cooking hut and stable, and emerged holding aloft the cow's severed head. The crowd cheered as the two men ran out along the *mengele*, hollering and holding the head up by its ears. It emerged that William's wife and children not only had butchered the animals, but had not divided the carcasses so shares of meat could be presented to the rightful recipients. Instead, they had prepared a large *sufuria* of *machalari* that they now invited people to share.[4] Rather than providing different shares of meat for different people on the basis of their relationships to William, they offered an undifferentiated meal that everyone was welcome to eat. The effect was an erasure of the relationships that composed William's being, in which few wanted to take part.

A large group of people that included several members of William's descent group congregated on the pathway outside the homestead. As they discussed what had taken place, many agreed that William's wife and children had made a big mistake by going against his instructions. One person pointed out that William had kept the two animals, so they were his to dispose of. Another added that the wife and children had stolen from William, and several said 'they had slaughtered at night like thieves'. William's daughter's teenage son Andrew, to whom he had left his homestead, came out and joined the crowd. Despite their excitement, people did not seem to hold animosity towards him. In defence of what had happened, Andrew told us how they had found evidence of what William had done to curse – *iabisa* – his wife and children. Many nodded in recognition of what appeared to be common knowledge, at least among those of his descent group. Some replied that William was justified in cursing them, considering what they had done to him. Not only had William's youngest son not visited him for over four years, but his other sons had smashed his figure of the Virgin Mary that had been blessed at a nearby parish church. Andrew listened patiently, but added that he was unperturbed by William's curses – they would have no effect since the intended targets were born-again Christians.

William's funeral remained the topic of conversation in the beer club that evening. It was endlessly repeated how his wife and children had made a big mistake, and many wondered why they could not just perform the *mrimwa*. The Arabic-derived Swahili term *dini* recurred, as some argued that 'religion only brings problems'. Others, meanwhile, blamed differences in denomination for sowing discord among people. Most swore to remain Catholic and never join the evangelical churches. Despite the Catholic clergy's consistent and constant opposition to *mrimwa*, many included this in the 'Catholic way' (*kikatoliki*). They perceived little distinction and opposition between the two, and were explicit that remaining Catholic was the only way to ensure that *mrimwa* are performed. Echoing statements from earlier that day, people claimed that problems would ensue for William's family, as a result of a curse – *fyao* – incurred by not following his instructions.

Rumours swirled the following week. A sister's son (*mhua*) of William's, who is a neighbour (*mamrasa*) of MaSway's homestead, told us that whoever stays at William's homestead will eventually move away. It will be a 'bad place' (*handu hawiishwa*) that cannot be used for anything, except perhaps as a plot for a school. Like many others, he stressed that we could just wait and see since the problems would soon strike. A classificatory brother of William's named Albert told me that William's eldest son had approached him the day after the burial. He had asked if Albert would share in the meat, if they were to butcher a goat on William's behalf. Albert had replied that the issue was up to William's mother's brother (*wafije*), who is most significant for a person's burial. Another classificatory brother argued that William's son had been compelled by the curse or *fyao* that the mother's brother made when he left the burial. Angry at what had occurred, William's *wafije* had stated that he would never return to this homestead, unless a hyena digs up his bones and brings them there. It was a powerful curse that had scared and prompted his children to seek forgiveness (*samehe*) from the descent group. In turn, the descent group responded by telling them to replace the animals they had butchered and perform the *mrimwa* William wanted. The descent group also accused William's children of not burying him where he had uprooted coffee trees to make room for his grave. A stone should therefore be taken from the grave and placed where William had wanted to be buried.

Cursing as a Linguistic Practice

The notion of *fyao* was used above to mean both the curse that William's wife and children called on themselves by going against his instructions, and the curse that his mother's brother made before he left the burial. *Fyao* is accordingly a family resemblance notion that is used to mean a diversity of related phenomena. However, people say that *fyao* can only be made by a parent over a child, a husband over a wife, a grandparent over a grandchild, or a mother's brother over a sister's son. The *fyao*, in other words, presupposes and operates through relationships of reproduction that the curser and the accursed either engage in or depend upon.[5] Similarly, Susan Reynolds Whyte (1997: 158) argues that 'cursing implies connectedness, and the power of the curse lies in the relationship between the curser and the cursed', and Devisch (1991: 127) claims that a curse spreads along 'existential interdependencies'. In Rombo, these relationships and interdependencies involve an asymmetry, which is what enables the curser to harm the accursed.[6] It is hence impossible for a child to curse its parent or for a man to curse his brother. Accordingly, Gutmann (1908: 302) argued that a curse presupposes a descent relationship, and that it was most severe when it was uttered by a father or a mother, whereas

Raum (1911: 188) claimed that a curse made by a sister was the most terrible kind. While Gutmann's claim unduly restricts the relationships through which a curse may work, Raum's statement pertains to the role a sister plays as a man's *mkara,* who enables his marital and reproductive relationship, and affords his homestead and dwelling.

The *fyao* moreover centres on and involves speech and language, either as an intentionally harmful statement or as an effect of deliberately contravening or disregarding someone's request or instruction. While the curse presupposes a relationship, it does not require that anyone is present or hears that it is uttered. It moreover need not assume a particular form to take effect. Thus, the curse made by William's mother's brother seemed at the moment no different to me than other utterances, such as factual statements or threats. Undoubtedly, this was due to my imperfect grasp of linguistic nuances. However, there is an air of ambiguity and ambivalence that surrounds the various uses of language for different purposes. It is especially acute with regards to cursing, which is underscored when people say that *fyao* can be a simple statement of the kind: 'Your children shall treat you like you treated me'. As a statement, *fyao* thus simply specifies an effect that shall ensue on the basis of an existing relationship. The curse is indeed made known by its effect, which seizes (*iira*) the accursed and assumes a form that depends on the wrong the curser suffered and what he or she stated in the curse. Illness is a common result, especially in the form of persistent problems that pertain to swelling of the legs and an inability to walk, and emaciation or swelling of the torso.[7] Unless a specific incident is known or suspected to have precipitated a curse, it is only once the health-station, hospital and healers have been consulted that *fyao* is considered, which nevertheless requires determination by a diviner.

A curse will have no effect if the person making it was not wronged in some way. Instead, the curse will in that case return to harm the curser. Cursing hence implies and involves an element of justice or fairness, which prevents a person from harming a dependent out of spite or simply because they entangle in a particular relationship. The curse can be removed if it does seize, but this requires that the victim requests forgiveness (*iterewa samehe*) from the curser. If this is accepted, the curser simply enunciates his or her forgiveness, and the two involved share beer or meat. It was this William's children sought when they suggested butchering a goat and sharing the meat with the descent group. It is important to note that the notion of *iterewa* features in the removal of curses, as it does in the offerings to the dead. Here, however, *iterewa* combines with the Arabic-derived Swahili notion of *samehe*, which suggests that a Christian discourse of forgiveness impacts the grammar of cursing. Its resemblance to the offerings is nevertheless underscored by the fact that both involve verbal articulation that combines with a powerful substance. As they conjoin words, actions and things, they constitute different language-games, which involve and redirect relationships where *horu* and language convey and entwine.

Many claim that a curse does not seize its victim until the curser dies or unless the victim requests forgiveness before this happens. People therefore fear that a dead or dying person has left a curse, which will be impossible or very difficult to remove. Similarly, Dundas (1924: 170) described a 'dying curse' called *mviyago* that a person uttered on their deathbed to avenge a wrong committed by someone more powerful. *Mviyago* is a dialectical variation of *fyao*, just like the notion of *mvia-ho* that Gutmann (1926: 61, 74) translated as 'death curse' and 'curse of the dead'. According to Dundas (1924: 170), the curse could assume the following form:

> I die in misery and poverty and hunger because of you. If it was just for you to do so, I go to the spirits, to my grandfathers, that they may take me to Ruwa himself to put my case before him. If I am defeated before Ruwa, if you did this to me in justice, I shall not come again to demand aught of you. But if I win my cause before Ruwa, if it is seen that I have been truly oppressed, then I shall return to you with demand. First I will slay your first-born, then I shall slay your other children, and lastly your wife and you yourself shall die.

While I shall return to the notion of *ruwa* in the next chapter, the pertinent issue here is how the curse is marked by a subjunctive mood that specifies different 'if so' relationships. By means of the curse, the curser thus grapples with the world and attempts to determine the character of specific relationships and the reality of particular deeds. Like the notion of language-game, the curse hence involves particular world-relations. Meanwhile, the use of the subjunctive mood occurred in the earlier addresses Herman made to his deceased father, and the 'beer to tell' was characterized as a mode of determination in chapter two. Their imbrications reveal how the curse is not simply a destructive phenomenon, but forms part of wider relationships between language, life force and the world they constitute.

Dundas (1924: 170ff) claimed that the *mviyago* could be removed by a particular 'class of medicine men'. However, it is currently maintained that such a curse will affect the accursed until his or her death. It is in fact claimed that the curse will repeat itself to haunt future generations. This was implied by the example above, which stated that the accursed shall be treated by his or her children in the same way he or she mistreated the curser. As a result, the accursed will eventually curse his or her offspring, who in turn will suffer and curse their own children. The curse thus replicates and reiterates in the same way as persons, houses, livestock and banana trees, as it turns the accursed into a curser who bestows the same misery he or she experienced. It is underscored by the naming practices, which entail that the accursed simultaneously curses both his children and his parents. One can therefore say that the curse not only conveys along relations of reproduction, but that it reproduces itself by means of persons and their relations. Dundas revealed this, as the curse he rendered stated that the curse shall slay the children in their order of birth, before affecting the accursed and his wife. In William's case, the curse could only take effect after his death, as it arose from instructions concerning his burial. It hence could not be removed and was therefore considered particularly severe.

These considerations show that the curse has an ability to replicate and move between houses and homesteads, in a manner reminiscent of persons and prestations. They moreover show that the curse resembles other kinds of statements, as it operates through and emanates from particular relationships, whose state and character it reveals through its effects. The curse is hence an affective phenomenon that partakes in the processes of emplacement and displacement that occur through dwelling and life. This is brought out by further kinds of curses, which do not operate by words alone, but also involve material objects. A consideration of this will furthermore deepen the understanding of cursing as a language-game that imbricates words, practices and objects in certain ways.

Cursing as a Material Practice

The curses that Andrew said they found evidence for at William's homestead were different from *fyao*. These curses do not presuppose a relationship and may even be made without the curser's knowledge of the accursed's identity. Such curses are resorted to by someone who claims to have been bewitched, but are more commonly used by victims of theft.[8] In addition to verbal statements, these curses engage specific objects that play central roles in the transfers and transformations of *horu* that occur through dwelling and life. Indeed, it is their significance for such relationships and the transformation of subject positions they involve that affords them a capacity to affect.

Andrew claimed that William had cursed his wife by pouring milk on the ground by the *kisumbadini* inside the cooking hut.[9] As I have shown, the *kisumbadini* or its equivalent is where the *mkara* deposits the initial bridewealth prestation, and where milk and beer are poured on the ground for the deceased. It is hence the place to which the groom attaches to his bride's father's homestead, and the place from which she eventually detaches in marriage. Conversely, she attaches to the *kisumbadini* of her marital homestead, as she leans against this architectural feature when she cooks. As beer and milk moreover serve to emplace the deceased, the *kisumbadini* plays a role in this regard too. Accordingly, it was impressed on me that there must be at least two people present when beer and milk are poured on the ground for the deceased inside the house. The reason is to ensure that the person pouring the liquid does not request that the deceased shall harm a person from the agnatic descent group. Requests are normally made for *horu*, but can hence also be made to harm someone else.[10] Moreover, milk is usually poured on the ground by women, which William inverted for the purpose of cursing his wife. He hence engaged and manipulated foodstuffs and features that ordinarily channel *horu* in productive ways to divert or redirect it for destructive purposes. As constructive and destructive purposes and processes intertwine, the material elements that feature in the bridewealth prestations and offerings for the dead are lent an ambivalent and ambiguous character (cf. Geissler and Prince 2010: 7).

Andrew also claimed that William had cut down a banana tree at night and scooped up sap from its stump. He had brought this to another part of the garden, where he poured it into a hole in the ground while he uttered a curse over his children. Using the Swahili term *kizazi*, Andrew argued that the act meant that William disowned his offspring and wanted to start a new 'generation'. William had also uttered a curse over a banana tree in his garden, whose fruit he left hanging until it rotted and fell to the ground. According to Andrew, the intention was that one of William's children or grandchildren was supposed to die each time a banana hit the ground, but their religion had literally 'saved' (*kuokoka*) them. While Andrew did not specify how he knew about these activities, those listening to him nodded in recognition, knowing how dwelling imbricates banana farming and reproduction.

Finally, Andrew claimed to have found a hoe underneath William's bed that he had used to curse both his wife and children. The hoe lacked a handle, but was suspended from a string and had a piece of skin from a hyrax or *mbelele* attached to it.[11] Andrew argued that

William had held the hoe by the string and hit it with another piece of metal, while uttering a curse of the form: 'So-and-so, you will die and I will bury you with this hoe'. Such a curse is called *seso*, which derives from the verb *isesa* that people render in Swahili as 'to hit the hoe' (*kupiga jembe*). The Chagga cognate *iembe* is mainly used for a short three-pronged hoe that is chiefly employed for sowing beans in the plains. However, people claim it can also be used for cursing, if it is hit with a cattle-bell (*maanga*) of the kind bulls wore when cattle were herded in the plains.[12]

Seso is often conflated with another curse that is called 'to hit the cooking pot' (*ikaba nungu*). But where *seso* can be uttered by anyone with access to two pieces of metal, the *nungu* curse can only be made by certain people who possess particular objects and abilities. Similarly, Gutmann (1909b: 170; 1926: 621) argued that the *nungu* curse involved special cursing objects that the *mangi* possessed, and that were termed *nungu jesesa* or *nungu yekaba*. The first notion involves a conceptual link between hitting the hoe and hitting the cooking pot. One can therefore surmise that these rest on and involve a singular concept that has become diversified. It gains support from Walther's (1900: 41) claim that *isesa* means 'to curse' in general. In present-day Rombo, *isesa* is only used for one kind of cursing, while *iabisa* means to curse in general. As such, it includes and encompasses *isesa* as a particular kind. The adoption of *iabisa* and the narrowing of *isesa* are possibly due to the influence of the Swahili cognate *kuapiza*, which means 'to swear at or curse' (Johnson 1939: 18). In any case, *nungu* curses can today only be uttered by certain *waanga*, who have inherited the means and the ability to do so. These are moreover often said to be Kamba-speaking people from Kenya, which resonates with Gutmann's (1926: 621) claim that the cursing objects originated in Kahe or Taveta. The idea that *nungu* has its origin outside of Kilimanjaro remains strong, and forms part of the movements and transfers between the mountain and the plains. Nevertheless, the two *waanga* I met who claimed to be able 'to hit the cooking pot' were both from Rombo.

Despite its name, the *nungu* curse does not involve an actual cooking pot, but largely employs the same objects as the *seso*. A healer named Ludovic, who claimed to perform such curses, described how he uses the head of a small *iembe*, a cattle-bell and a doughnut-shaped stone of volcanic rock for this purpose. The rock resembles the carrying cushions (*ndalo*) that women make from the leaves or bark of banana stems, and place on their heads when they transport banana bunches or other heavy objects. Dundas (1924: 192) provides a picture of an identical stone, which he referred to as 'nungu' and a 'cursing stone'. Dundas claimed the stone was 'unearthed from the ruins of Horombo's Fort', which means that it most likely originated from Keni. Gutmann (1926: 658) also mentioned cursing by means of rocks with holes in them, but he considered this to be a subordinate and derivative form. On Gutmann's (1926: 620) account, the main objects involved in *nungu* were two figurines of male and female appearance, which Ludovic also claimed to use. Like Gutmann (1926: 630), Ludovic said the figurines are so powerful that they cannot be stored at the homestead, but must be kept in the plains away from human habitation.[13]

In contrast to Gutmann's (1926: 622) claim that the *nungu* is uttered at the marketplace, Ludovic said it takes place at the homestead of his client, who pays him a fee for the effort. It occurs just after nightfall, when he performs his acts naked. If the victim is a man, he only hits the cattle-bell and repeats the curse for three consecutive days. If the victim is a woman, he hits the *iembe* and repeats the curse for four consecutive days. The curse therefore does not involve a combination of complementary genders, but turns on gendered differences that date back to when men herded cattle in the plains and women cultivated plots, like they do today. It is moreover noteworthy that where William's curses involved substances and features pertaining to the house and homestead, the *nungu* engages objects that are or were employed in the plains. *Seso, nungu* and the other curses thus entail partial connections between concepts, practices and objects that summate and extend from dwelling and life, which in turn afford their current conflation in everyday speech.

Julius's Curse

In contrast to *fyao, seso* and *nungu* cannot be forgiven by the curser, but must be removed by a *mwaanga* who is also able to perform such curses. I first met Ludovic in late 2000, when he came to remove a *seso* curse or 'clean the cooking pot' (*isambiya nungu*) at a homestead in Keni. The curse had been made by Julius, an elderly widower who lived close to Ngufumari's homestead and was addressed by us as 'neighbour' – *mamrasa*. Julius was born in 1914 and was among the first in the area to be educated beyond very basic primary education, as demonstrated by his framed school teacher's certificate from 1938 that had pride of place on his living room wall. Always dapper and well dressed, Julius was convinced of his intellectual superiority, which many perceived as arrogance and stubborn obstinacy. I came to know Julius in a beer club close to his homestead, where he often nursed a soft drink in the late afternoon. He told me how his first job was teaching at a mission school in Nairobi, and how he returned to Rombo after four years to become district teacher supervisor. Later, he worked in Arusha, until he retired in 1978. He had owned several cars in his time, and the wreck of his last Volkswagen Beetle remained in his courtyard, as a trace of the relative affluence and social standing he once enjoyed. Despite his travels and employment elsewhere, Julius had married a woman from a nearby homestead. Both were strict Catholics, who refused to perform or participate in *mrimwa* of any kind. Nevertheless, Julius was known for his propensity for cursing.

In November 2000, the first-born son of Julius died at his home in Arusha. His body was brought back and buried at Julius's homestead, where the descent group was in attendance but offered no practical or financial assistance. Despite Julius's opposition to *mrimwa*, his other sons performed *ihora kaa* on their brother's behalf. This time the descent group members neither took part nor claimed the shares of meat to which they were entitled. In this way, the descent group denied its relationship to the homestead and its inhabitants, even though many of its members were Julius's immediate neighbours. The reason was that many regarded the death as being due to a curse uttered by Julius, even though their views varied with regards to when, why and how it had happened. Some claimed Julius had made the curse two years earlier, as a result of people owing him money. They said Julius had posted a note in a central area of the village, where he listed the names of his debtors and the amounts they owed. It also contained a warning that he would curse those who did not pay within ten days; the only person who failed to do so was his first-born son. According to Herman, several people had seen Julius uttering the curse. He had allegedly walked around the garden in the early morning, wearing a black *kanzu*-like outfit and hitting a hoe, while requesting (*iterewa*) that the person who stole from him should die.[14] When his eldest son subsequently fell ill, many people had begged Julius to remove the curse, but he refused and the result was that his son's body swelled up until he died.

Two of Julius's classificatory brothers meanwhile claimed that the curse was uttered in the mid 1980s, in connection with a dispute over land between Julius and his sons. At that time, his first-born son prepared to marry, so Julius divided off a plot of land for him below his homestead. Before his son had built a house, however, Julius took the land back and sold it to an unrelated man, who established a homestead for his second wife. As recompense, Julius gave his son land above his homestead, but for unknown reasons he took this land back too before his son could build. The role houses play in the constitution of subject positions means that Julius barred his son's transformation from a son (*mwana wa homii*) to a husband (*mii*) and eventual man (*msoro*), when he denied him land for a house where he and his bride could dwell and attach with their future children. A dispute resulted, in which Julius's younger sons took their older brother's side. It prompted Julius to write a letter to the descent group, declaring that he would curse his children. In response, the descent group called a meeting to hear the case, but they failed to reach a resolution. The descent group did voice its displeasure with Julius's plans, but he replied that he wanted nothing more to do with them. When his son fell ill in 2000, the descent group had urged Julius to remove the curse, but he refused. Instead, he invited a priest to read Mass at his homestead and toss holy water on his houses.

A month or so after his son's death, Julius's first-born daughter fell and broke her arm. A minor accident, yet many attributed it too to the curse, and said it had moved on to seize her. Julius's daughter was a member of the charismatic Catholic movement and just as opposed to *mrimwa* as her father. However, rumours spread that she had begged Julius after her accident to remove the curse. Just before Christmas 2000, his youngest son informed me that a healer would come from another village 'to wash the cooking pot' at Julius's homestead, and he invited me to join them.

When the day arrived, I went to the homestead of Julius's second-born son, who lives in Moshi but lends his house to his younger brother. The homestead is located below that of Julius and neighbours the land Julius took back and sold to the unrelated man for his second wife. Three of Julius's sons were present, along with the wife and daughter of the son who died. Another son and the daughter who broke her arm were absent, but they had sent items of clothing that would take their place in the proceedings. The men impressed on me that they were only doing this because of pressure from the descent group and emphasized that they as Catholics saw no reason for what was about to take place. After a little while, four elders from the descent group arrived. Once they had shaken hands and greeted everyone, the elders sat down and betrayed no indication that they knew what was going on. But when Ludovic the *mwaanga* strolled in not long after, they immediately asked if he really would 'clean the cooking pot' (*isambiya nungu*). One elder stressed that 'we do not want the curse to come back and destroy our children', while Ludovic calmly replied that a curse is indeed a bad thing, saying: 'It destroys the children and the children's children'.

When the elders were satisfied with Ludovic's answers, the third-born son of Julius went into the combined cooking hut and stable, and came out with a whole male goat (*horo*). Followed by his wife and their two small children, trailed by his two brothers, the deceased brother's wife and child and Ludovic, he led the goat along a path that passed through the banana garden and ended at Julius's homestead. The elders worried that Julius would refuse to have the curse removed if everyone appeared simultaneously. They and I therefore waited a little before we walked around to enter Julius's homestead via the *mengele* pathway. Acting as if we knew nothing of what was going on, we were received by Julius's children who greeted us as if they had not seen us that day. At first, Julius remained inside his house and refused to take part, but changed his mind once two of his sons and Ludovic talked to him. However, he only agreed to sit on the veranda and watch the proceedings without being 'washed'. While the negotiations went on, a classificatory brother of Julius's whispered: 'He is the one who did this, so why does he refuse now?' The discussions were tense, as everyone shared an anxiety that the curse would not be removed but continue its work. Eventually a compromise was reached that an item of clothing would take Julius's place in the proceedings too. Yet there was one count on which Julius did not resist: he immediately handed over the Beretta semi-automatic shotgun that he said he had used to make the curse.[15]

Ludovic prepared to remove the curse by cutting down rolled-up *unanda* leaves from three *mnyengele* trees in the garden. He removed the metal blade from the curved tool called *ihindo* that is used for weeding the banana garden, and dug a shallow hole in the ground at the lower end of the courtyard, where it runs into the garden.[16] He lined this hole with the three *unanda* leaves, which he unfurled and placed on top of each other. From a plastic bag he had brought, Ludovic then produced the doughnut-shaped volcanic rock, a rusty cattle-bell and the head of an *iembe*, which he placed at the edge of the leaf-lined hole. He also took out a *Konyagi* bottle that contained the unfermented juice of boiled *mhoyo* bananas. The white liquid was poured on top of the leaves, while a green paste pounded from eight different kinds of leaves was stirred into the juice. Finally, he added cooking soda (*mbala*) from Julius's cooking hut and some tap water.

Julius's sons went with their wives and children into the cooking hut, where the *horo* goat was tethered to a post. An invocation was uttered over the animal by one of Julius's classificatory brothers before two of his sons led the goat behind the cooking hut, where it was suffocated, let of its blood and skinned.[17] Ludovic instructed that the *ikamba* section, which consists of a triangular-shaped piece of the breast and includes the throat, digestive tract, part of the breastbone and tips of the ribs, should be carved and presented to Julius.[18] The rest of the goat should be parted lengthwise. One half should be his fee and the other half should be cooked immediately. As the body was split in two, it inhibited the ordinary mode of butchering, where shares of meat that span both sides of the animal are presented to particular people on the basis of certain relationships. Halving the goat hence prevents the channelling of *horu* in specific directions for the purpose of compensating and extending certain relationships in particular ways. By contrast, the mode of butchering practised on this occasion contained and retained the animal's life force, which instead was channelled to remove the curse from those it entangled and affected.

Once the animal was halved, Ludovic removed two dewclaws and the tip of its tongue. He added these to the liquid contained by the banana leaves, along with a splash of its blood, some chyme from its reticulum stomach (*ngasuma*) and some dried sheep chyme he had brought.[19] A whisk called *mahande*, which is made from the stalk, leaves and flowers of three different plants called *ikavale*, *ibinu* and *makengera*, was used to remove the curse. Ludovic dipped the whisk in the liquid and tossed it onto his own cursing objects, and then onto the shotgun that Julius had used to make the curse.[20] He dipped the whisk again and tossed the liquid into the doorway of the cooking hut and that of the residential house, and then out along the auxiliary pathway and the *mengele*. Ludovic instructed Julius's sons and male grandchildren to stand in a line in the *sha* courtyard with the clothes of the absent men over their shoulders. They faced uphill or above (*fondoho*) and hence the doorway and interior of the cooking hut. Ludovic told them to raise their arms and spit lightly, while he stood at the lower end of the courtyard and tossed the combination of chyme, blood, banana juice and water onto their backs. The men then turned to face the plains, the graves and the homestead of Julius's son below (*siinde*), while the mixture was tossed onto their faces and chests. The men turned around once more, so that the *mahande* was tossed three times.

At this point, Ludovic interrupted the proceedings and asked if they wanted to finish that day or continue the next day. A short discussion ensued, but Julius's second-born son said he wished to return to his family in Moshi that evening, so they decided to finish. Accordingly, Ludovic told the men to walk out along the *mengele* all the way to the *shia* pathway, and return to the homestead. Ludovic explained that the liquid should ideally be tossed that afternoon, as well as the follow-

Figure 5.1. The whisk and liquid of Ludovic's *mahande* together with the stone, bell and hoe he uses for cursing.

ing morning and afternoon to make it three times in total. However, it is possible to truncate this by acting as if they leave the homestead be-tween each repetition.[21] He and I watched as the men walked back up the *mengele* and called *hodi*, as if they had arrived for a visit. Ludovic welcomed them in response and acted as if it was the following morn-

Figure 5.2. Ludovic tossing *mahande* on the shotgun used for uttering the curse.

ing, receiving them with the morning greeting *waamka*. They then resumed their positions in the courtyard, where Ludovic tossed the liquid onto them again before they walked out and came back in for a third repetition.

The same acts were performed for and by the women, who wore the clothes of the absent women over their shoulders. The only difference

Figure 5.3. Ludovic tossing *mahande* to wash the cooking pot and remove the curse.

was that the women turned around four times, and walked out and back to have the liquid tossed on them four times in total. As a result, the *mahande* was slung onto the men a total of nine times, while the women received it sixteen times. Throughout, Julius sat silently on his veranda and leaned on his cane. He did not betray any emotion, while the elders of the descent group observed and commented keenly from their position in front of the cooking hut.

The curse was now nearly removed from those who attached to the homestead. Julius's second-born son wanted to leave for Moshi immediately, worrying that it was getting too late to catch a bus. However, he was told that no-one could leave until they had eaten from the goat. We therefore sat down to eat the meat and drink some beer that had been bought at a nearby club. An act of commensality hence concluded and effectuated the cleaning of the cooking pot. It contrasted with the descent group's refusal to take part and claim their share of meat at the *ihora kaa* for Julius's son. Their refusal was due to a fear that the curse would affect them through eating or drinking at the homestead where it was uttered. Like the 'bad things' (*mawiishwa*) that result from death, the curse is contagious. But where the former is removed by eating or drinking before leaving the burial, the curse transmits through such consumption. The curse and its effects are hence conveyed along the channels and conduits of *horu*. However, the act of tossing a certain liquid enables people to partake in food-

stuffs at the *kaa,* and thus reconstitutes the transfers and transformations of *horu* in which the homestead entangles. Its ability to do so
stems from the fact that the tossed liquid combines various powerful
substances, such as banana juice, chyme, blood and cooking soda.
Indeed, as these combine in a leaf-lined hole in the ground, they manifest how fodder emerges from the land to yield chyme, banana juice,
blood and foods that are prepared by means of cooking soda, and thus
effectuate the transformations of *horu* that occur through dwelling
and life. It is underscored as the liquid is tossed through the doorways
and along the pathways that *horu* traverses as bridewealth prestations
in the form of powerful foodstuffs and children. The liquid is moreover tossed onto the chests and backs that persons employ to convert
and convey *horu* in sex, conception, birthing and childcare, which
the bridewealth prestations enable. The renewal and reconstitution
of these transfers and transformations was accentuated as the participants spat to clear their gullets and mouths, and thus made way for
the entry of *horu* in the form of foods. As the combination of animal
and vegetative juices was slung through and onto *moongo* and along
pathways of different kinds, it effectuated a human fluid that allowed
for capacity, health and well-being to course through the homestead
and its inhabitants. Like the ancestral backwash (*macha*) that Herman
drank after pouring beer on the ground, the participants' spit (*macha*)
entwined and combined with powerful substances to enable people to
partake in beer and meat at the homestead. By washing these various
in-betweens, it again became possible for the agnates to connect to
the homestead and its inhabitants through such transfers of *horu.*
These pathways, doorways, backbones and gullets could again facilitate connections and transformations that were actualized through
the act of commensality. As such, it simultaneously removed the curse
and allowed for the extension of dwelling and life.

The acts that followed our consumption of meat and beer underscored the contagious character of the curse and reveal how its removal constitutes a form of what Parkin (1995: 153) calls 'maladic
dispersal'. Before we left Julius's homestead, Ludovic placed an empty
oil drum over the hole in the ground, where the *mahande* whisk and
the bones of the goat were gathered on top of the banana leaves that
contained the remnants of the liquid he had tossed. According to
Ludovic, the drum was to ensure that no person or animal could access and remove the items, which would release and disseminate the
curse. The curse that had been removed from the houses and persons
now attached to the objects that had cleaned them, which were carefully gathered, emplaced and contained in this way.[22]

Ludovic was supposed to return a week later to remove the objects under the drum, but contracted malaria and was delayed several weeks. I therefore missed what he did, but tracked him down at his homestead, roughly ten kilometres away, where he described what he does when he returns to the cleansed homestead. To fully remove the curse, the client must provide a *suweni* or a female goat that has not yet borne offspring. Ludovic then enters every house of the homestead and removes an object, which must include some ashes from the hearth of the cooking hut. He adds these objects to the leaves, bones and *mahande*, which he referred to in combination as *seso*. He then fashions a rope from dried banana bark (*mdawi*), which he uses to wrap the objects and tie them on the back of the *suweni* goat. He departs the homestead just after nightfall and the owner walks him to the end of the *mengele* pathway. There he bids Ludovic farewell, turns around and picks up some soil from the *mengele*, which he tosses over his shoulder. Lest the curse returns, the owner neither speaks nor looks back in the direction Ludovic went, but walks straight to the cooking hut, where he sits down by the hearth. When he emerges from the doorway, he is free to talk and look in any direction he wants.

Ludovic for his part does not speak to anyone along the way, nor does he look back in the direction of the homestead he left. He walks straight to his own homestead, where he enters the cooking hut and unties the *seso* from the goat's back. Once he sits down by the hearth, he too is free to speak and look around without risk of the curse returning to where it was removed from. He hides the *seso* in a remote corner of his banana garden, and waits a day or two before he burns them by the side of a pathway at some distance from his home. When the objects are burnt, he returns to his cooking hut, where he again sits down by the hearth before he talks to anyone or looks back in the direction where the burnt-out *seso* remain. Ludovic claimed that the curse is finished when he re-emerges from his cooking hut, but said he nevertheless waits a month or more before he passes the place where it was burnt.

These practices entail that a curse is carefully gathered and gradually removed from the homestead, and then disposed of in an appropriate manner. The curse is washed off central features of the homestead and parts of the persons who attach to it, which include the multiple *moongo* that along with chests and pathways afford and engage reproduction. The curse is then contained and covered in a hole in the ground in the banana garden before it is removed from houses and hearth, and carried away. Once removed, it is first stored in a remote corner of the healer's banana garden, and then burnt at a

place where those affected by the curse and its removal are unlikely to
come. To be on the safe side, the *mwaanga* moreover avoids this place
and only passes there some time later to ensure that the curse is fully
displaced and dispersed.

The way in which the curse is gathered, displaced and emplaced
extends from and imbricates with the activities that occur during
burial, exhumation and reburial. It is underscored by the restrictions
on speaking and looking back, which also obtain when a deceased
person is moved in the form of a stone. They also enfold the activities that occur in connection with the bridewealth prestations, where
powerful foodstuffs emplace persons in relation to some of the same
architectural features. At least initially, the prestations moreover involve limitations on the use of language and the ability to be seen.
Speaking and seeing are directed at something or someone, so they
are intentional activities that imply relations along and through
which the curse can convey. As the curse is gathered and displaced,
its connections are cut to re-proportion relationships between persons
and things, among which life force may transfer and transform. It
effectuates and registers as an ability to talk and look around, in the
same way that the prestation of beer described by Gutmann enabled
a bride to speak to and see her husband's father after she had borne a
child (see chapter three). The removal of the curse thus also achieves
a subject transformation that affords or returns a capacity to engage
others by means of sight and sound.

The theme of dispersal was enunciated in the statement Ludovic
made when he tossed the liquid onto the homestead's inhabitants:

> Cooking pot I say, if it was a woman who hit you or if it was a man,
> today I make you cool (*ihoreria*). Be cool (*iholholhya*) as if you have been
> hit by the rain. Go to Taita, go to Kibo, go to Mawenzi, go to Upare, go to
> Chala, go to Jipe. When you leave here, go with the fog and go far. End –
> do not come back to these people. Whatever they eat, it shall enter their
> hearts, they shall not hurt again.

The places that Ludovic prompted the cooking pot to go to are geographical features that define the horizon for the people of Rombo.[23]
Kibo is the summit of Kilimanjaro that is located to the west or above
(*fondoho*), while Mawenzi is its second peak that is visible to the north-
west. Taita Hills are the easternmost point and the place where the sun
rises, while Lake Chala, Lake Jipe and the Pare Mountains are located
below (*siinde*) in a line to the south and southeast. Ludovic's statement
enunciated that he banished the curse by means of the *mahande* to the
furthermost points on the horizon or to the ends of the visible world. It
is reminiscent of Gutmann's (1924b: 47) *mhanga* who ceremoniously

stated that he removed objects from a bewitched person's body, which he gathered and deposited in rivers and lakes. They moreover recall Gutmann's (1924a: 135) account of how a man entered elderhood, as he was sprinkled with water in which several crops had been boiled, while Kibo, Mawenzi and other mountains were invoked together with *ndishi* banana trees and eleusine. Similarly, Nico made requests to the male elder of Murukuti and Kibo, when he rubbed eleusine onto the goat's back for the *mrina monikiwalo* in Herman's cooking hut (see chapter four). Again, Kibo is the summit above, while Murukuti is a standalone hillock in the plains below, where Horombo allegedly lost his life. Finally, the end of Ludovic's statement enunciated what we enacted at Julius's homestead, namely that the dispersal of the curse restores consumption and commensality to revive and ensure the capacity, health and well-being of those involved.

As the curse can transmit at various points during its removal, it validates Parkin's point that dispersal implies that maladic elements can reassemble and return to harm those who were cleansed. However, the curse does not transmit randomly, but disseminates along the lines and through the openings that channel *horu* through dwelling and life. Thus, the *mahande* is tossed through the doorways and out along the pathways that open the homestead beyond its confines. The curse hence contaminates these relational features, and thus attaches to and moves through and along them, like persons and prestations. Accordingly, the owner of the homestead walks Ludovic to the end of the *mengele*. As he turns around and tosses soil over his shoulder, he reveals how the curse may transfer and return along this conduit of *horu*. Its danger diminishes when the owner enters the doorway and sits down by the hearth, while the healer must walk through the doorway and rest by the hearth of his house. The result is that the curse not only transmits through consumption and commensality, but also transfers through and along the architectural features of the homestead that convey and convert *horu* to permeate dwelling and animate life.

The intimate links that the curse and its removal have to dwelling and life can be discerned from the objects they employ. One might surmise that hoes, bells and cooking pots are significant due to the fact that iron and clay were not available in Kilimanjaro, but were scarce goods only obtained through trade and exchange.[24] It arguably subtends Gutmann's (1909b: 169) claim that cooking pots had something 'mystical' about them, but it is belied by the role they play in cursing practices elsewhere in the region.[25] Cooking pots rather owe their significance to the roles they play in the transfers and transformation of *horu*. This gains support from Monica Udvardy's (1990) claim that cooking pots are among objects that are manipulated to facilitate a flow of life or life force among the Giriama. Conversely, Udvardy (1990: 145) claims that uttering a curse while breaking a cooking pot constitutes a disorderly engagement that harms fertility, so that the children of the accursed will not have children. In a related way, Marealle (1963: 87) claimed that women abstained from sex while making pots.[26] Pot-making – like planting, brewing and offering – is a powerful activity, whose result requires that its transfers and transformations of *horu* are channelled by sexual prohibitions. Like crops and powerful foodstuffs, pots too are effects of life force that must be directed to enable their emergence and subsequent deployment in cooking and consumption. This is enunciated by Marealle (1963: 87) in a statement that moreover entails how hitting a cooking pot is a dangerous proposition: 'If a pot breaks during the making it means a very bad omen, therefore the woman making the same would have to conduct a sacrificial ceremony to her ancestor so as to dispel the misfortune'.[27] The unspecified 'sacrificial ceremony' most likely involved an invocation and an offering of a powerful foodstuff that endeavoured to direct *horu*, and thus extend dwelling and life. In combination, this suggests that hoes, cattle-bells and cooking pots can be used to channel life force in both constructive and destructive ways, on the basis of the roles they play in the transfers and transformations of *horu* in dwelling. These transfers constitute people's capacity, health and well-being, so the objects they involve can be used both to heal and harm those whose existence entangles with them.

Contagion along the lines and through the openings that convey *horu* moreover accounts for the use of a *suweni* goat to remove the *seso*. The *suweni* lacks offspring, so it is devoid of relations that the curse can transmit through, after the *seso* is attached to its back. As the goat lacks kids, it also does not suckle and therefore cannot convey the curse through milk. The absence of offspring also means that the curse will not transmit to other homesteads through the lending relations (*ihara*) in which livestock partake. *Suweni* goats are moreover never used for *mrimwa*, so its meat will not be butchered and presented, and thus circulated through the relations that entangle persons and houses. Goat's milk is not used for human consumption, except as an occasional condiment for tea. There is nevertheless no risk that the *suweni* will convey the curse this way, as it does not produce milk. Its restricted involvement in the transfers of *horu* entail diminished relationality, which makes the *suweni* relatively safe as a vehicle for the curse. Ludovic moreover claimed that four bones from

a *suweni* must be added to the fire when he burns the *seso*. He is supposed to obtain these by slaughtering the goat that ferries the curse
and eating its meat in the period between its retrieval and destruction.
There is therefore no danger that the *suweni* is impregnated after it
arrives at his homestead. As the goat should not stay to reproduce,
it would not be inserted into transfers and transformations of *horu*
that could extend the curse. In fact, the goat may stay and bear kids,
which Ludovic considered the profit (*faida*) for his work. Occasionally,
however, he does slaughter a *suweni* and preserve its bones, which he
burns with the *seso*, as if he butchered every animal that removes a
curse.

However, the potential transfer of the curse through reproduction
extends beyond the goat. Ludovic therefore stressed how he abstains
from sex on the days that he removes a curse and engages its objects.
Sex would namely transmit the curse along with his semen, and thus
affect the person that receives it. Sex would moreover diminish the
power of his cursing objects, which underscores how they partake in
the transfer and transformations of *horu*. Indeed, it was in connection
with the cursing figurines that Gutmann (1926: 659) described the
breasts and penis as 'dispatchers of power' (*Kraftentsender*) or 'transmitters of force' (*Kraftträger*). Accordingly, the curse affects the banana garden, where it makes itself known through its effects on the
transfers and transformations of *horu*. If someone has hit a hoe or
uttered a cooking pot curse, it is namely shown (*ilhoria*) by a flower
spike or inflorescence (*sabo*) of a *mhoyo* banana tree aborting at your
homestead. In such an event, the *sabo* emerges from the top of the
tree as usual, but instead of peeling back and dropping its petals to
develop fruits, the flower spike falls to the ground and leaves the tree
barren and unproductive. In this way, the curse disrupts or halts its
horu to inhibit the growth of the bananas. *Mhoyo* owes its significance
to the role it plays in *mrimwa*, where it can always replace the fruits
and items from the *mnyengele* tree. *Mhoyo* bananas are furthermore
an important ingredient in the soft confinement foods, where they
contribute to the *mfee*'s *horu*, heat, blood and lactation. Their role in
this regard is justified with reference to the time the *mhoyo* tree takes
to produce its fruit, which coincides with the length of the human
pregnancy and the gestation of cattle. People thus stress how it takes
nine months from when the *sabo* appears until the bunch matures,
which contrasts with all other kinds of bananas that require a shorter
time, just as the gestations of other livestock are shorter than those of
cattle. To ramp up her lactation, a newly calved cow is furthermore fed
the stem of a *mhoyo* tree, which thus serves a purpose similar to the

soft foods. Human consumption and bovine reproduction moreover intertwine through *ikombia umbe* or 'to taste with the cow', where *kena* is made from *mhoyo* bananas and fed to the calf in order to afford the extraction and diversion of its mother's milk for human use (Myhre 2013b). People stress that the milk dries out prematurely if this is not performed. Gutmann (1924a: 137) recounted practices that concur with those of *ikombia umbe*, but claimed that the milk was first spat into the calf's maul by a young boy, who then could consume it himself. The practice recalls how adults spat foods into a newborn child, which in this context expands the range of body parts that convert and convey *horu* between humans and animals. The salient point is that these imbrications entail that an aborted *mhoyo* flower spike ramifies to disrupt the movements of *horu* between the living, their livestock and the dead, with the effect of halting dwelling and blocking life in the homestead.

The transfers and transformations are restored and dwelling resumed once the liquid combination of chyme, blood, *mhoyo* juice and water is tossed onto the hearth, through the doorways and along the pathways of the homestead, as well as onto the chests and backs of its inhabitants. These substances obviously feature in animal butchering, which not only everts blood and chyme, but deliberately deploys them to channel *horu* in certain ways. Thus, it is always ensured that the first blood to emerge when the animal is stuck falls onto the ground. People moreover pay close attention to the amount and appearance of the blood, as this together with the caul (*uanga*) shows (*ilhoria*) the health and *horu* of the animal. They emphasize that the first blood must fall on the ground to ensure that the homestead will succeed in holding livestock in the future. The chyme, meanwhile, figures when *ndaswa* meat is presented (*ichasa*) to the deceased, most commonly at the *mbuho*. The meat is always placed on top of the animal's chyme (*mooshe*), which is brought by the handful to the *mbuho*, if the animal was not butchered there. As the *ndaswa* pieces are made to rest on top of the chyme, it manifests how meat emerges as an effect of animal digestion and its transformation of fodder into foodstuffs and manure. The use of chyme as an intermediate form between fodder and manure underscores the pivotal role animal digestion plays as a transformational process that is central to dwelling and life, and the intensive form of horticulture they entail. The chyme and the meat moreover remain, at least until the following day, when the *ndaswa*'s disappearance demonstrates that the offering has been accepted. As this meat and *mooshe* are left behind, they – like the first blood – are forms of *horu* that are returned to the ground to ensure the future emergence of food and fodder, and hence the existence of human, animal and vegetative forms of life. Blood, meat and banana juice are hence transformations of chyme, which serves as a hinge in banana farming and livestock stall-feeding on which further transfers and transformations of *horu* turn.

According to Ruel (1997: 98), the Kuria speak of chyme as the life or well-being of the animal, which is removed and conveyed elsewhere, for instance for cleansing purposes. As mentioned in chapter three, the Kuria *obohoro* that designates life or well-being is a cognate of *horu*, while the Chagga term for chyme – *mooshe* – derives from *moo* or life, and is a cognate of the Kuria *omooyo*. I have also shown how *moo* is the root of *kumoosoni* and *moongo*, which are used to mean the left-hand side or that of the mother's brother, and the doorways and backs that feature in sex, conception, birthing and childcare. These conceptual links mean that when a man carves the *moongo* from an animal and sends it to replace the *horu* expended by the wife's parents or those of his children's left-hand side, the life of the animal is everted and conveyed elsewhere, in a similar way to what the Kuria do by means of chyme. Indeed, the way the different parts of the animal are claimed on the basis of past, present or future expenditures of *horu* entails that its different shares of meat evert from its chyme through different relationships that channel *horu* in certain ways. The animal body and its fluids are thus extroversions of chyme and different transformations of *horu* that occurred through the recipients' use of their corresponding anatomies. As a substance of life, *mooshe* can therefore be combined with other powerful substances to be tossed into and onto the body parts and architectural features that are conduits of life (*moongo*) for houses and persons, and facilitate the transfers and transformations that enable and constitute *moo*.

Ihora Kaa – Cooling or Cleansing the Homestead

Accordingly, chyme also plays a central role in *ihora kaa* or the cooling and cleansing of the homestead that allows its inhabitants to resume the activities that death disrupted. Such an event attracts many people and consists of proceedings that overlap with the 'washing of the cooking pot'. The main difference is that *ihora kaa* is performed for all to see, while *isambiya nungu* mainly involves those that attach to the homestead. The *ihora kaa* for Oswald's wife Valeria was conducted on the fourth day after she was buried in late 2000. On that occasion, we butchered a whole bull (*ing'uleta*) and a *mooma* goat in front of the doorway of Oswald's stable, where the animals were parted and the meat presented to be prepared and eaten by their rightful recipients. In the late afternoon, a dried cowhide was spread out (*iala*) in front of the doorway, right next to the fresh banana leaves where only the chyme remained of the two animals. The hide was placed so that its head faced uphill or above (*fondoho*), while four pieces of fresh *mnyengele* bark were cut and arranged in a square below (*siinde*) at its tail-end by Oswald's senior classificatory father, Constantine. Inside this square, Constantine unfurled and placed four *unanda* leaves, on which he combined some blood and chyme from the butchered animals. He also added some water (*mringa*) that Oswald had fetched the night before from a stagnant pool in a nearby riverbed.

While those in attendance gathered round, Oswald and his two sons took up position above the cowhide. They stood directly in front of the doorway, so that they faced the courtyard and the plains below. Constantine meanwhile faced them from below the hide, where he stood opposite the *moongo* of the house and the mountain above. He instructed Oswald and his sons to spit lightly towards the sky, while he dipped a *mahande* whisk in the liquid and tossed it onto their faces and chests. Once he had dipped and tossed the whisk four times, Oswald and his sons turned around to face the doorway, while Constantine tossed the liquid onto their backs. The procedure was repeated three further times, so that the liquid was tossed a total of sixteen times. It was then repeated for Valeria's three daughters before the *mahande* was tossed into the different doorways of the homestead's houses and out onto its *mengele*.[28] The tools used to dig Valeria's grave were gathered in a pile, and Constantine tossed the liquid onto them and the car that brought her body from Dar es Salaam. Constantine then shaved a tuft of hair from both the forehead and the nape of Oswald's head, which he added to the liquid on the *unanda* leaves. He handed the razorblade to Oswald, who cut hair in the same way from his sons' heads, which was also added to the liquid. One of Valeria's classificatory co-wives (*waeri*), who moreover is an immediate neighbour, similarly shaved some hair from the daughters' heads. These were only token gestures – or *mifano* in Swahili – performed in anticipation of their heads being completely shaved the following day. Removing his shoe, Constantine stepped on and broke the gourd that was used to fetch the stagnant water.[29] He took a sharp piece from the gourd and bore holes in the *unanda* leaves so that the liquid ran out and sank into the ground. He instructed Oswald to fold the leaves so they wrapped up the remains of the gourd, the *mahande* whisk, the hair and the bark. The parcel was placed on top of Valeria's grave, but this was only a preliminary step, as the two men returned after nightfall to retrieve and deposit the items in the same seasonal riverbed from which Oswald had fetched the stagnant water.[30]

Like the cleaning of the cooking pot, *ihora kaa* involves the gradual removal, careful gathering and eventual displacement of maladic effects. One could suspect that one practice is modelled on the other, but that which is dispersed is differentiated in these two cases. Where the cleaning of the cooking pot removes the curse that people term *seso* or *nungu*, the cooling of the homestead disperses bad things (*mawiishwa*) that result from a death at the homestead. In usual Bantu-language fashion, the adjectival root-form -*wiishwa* is prefixed according to the noun it qualifies, and thus forms different yet related family resemblance notions that figure in multiple language-games. These include witchcraft and theft, as well as homesteads where blood has been spilt or bones displaced.[31] In these language-games, the root-form -*wiishwa* imbricates with different activities and events, where *horu* is diverted in unproductive and harmful ways. As such, *mawiishwa* is an apt term for the effects of death, which interrupts dwelling and halts the transfers of *horu*.[32]

The disruption of dwelling that death involves is performatively recognized during *ihora kaa*, when a plank is removed from the bed of a deceased person who leaves a spouse behind. Depending on the gender of the deceased, this plank is split into three or four pieces, which are burnt in the homestead's hearth. If the bereaved is not able or willing to remove a plank from the bed, he or she will sleep with a piece of firewood in the days between the burial and *ihora kaa*. The piece of wood is then removed, and split and burnt in the same way. People say this practice stems from the days of the grass-houses, when one of the *isale* sticks that formed the bed was removed, split and burnt on this occasion. Its removal and destruction manifests how death disrupts sexual relations, and disables the surviving spouse from such engagements in the future. As such, it interrupts particular transfers and transformations of *horu* that permeate dwelling and animate life. The same act can moreover be performed to harm a living spouse, in a way that resembles and reiterates aspects of cursing. A female neighbour of Herman's, who lived with her husband's mother (*mamii*) while he worked in Dar es Salaam, was one day discovered splitting a plank from their marital bed and using it as firewood for the hearth. When her husband heard of this, he chased her away, which Herman explained was due to the fact that he would be harmed and eventually die if they had sex in the bed, which she had treated as if he were dead. Its gravity was underscored by the fact that the bed is where they had slept and had sex to conceive three children. Herman added that they could have been reconciled and continued life together if she had provided a *mooma* and he a *horo*, and these goats had been butchered and the *mahande* tossed on them and the house. In fact, this did occur in 2001, at a homestead that belongs to Boniface's descent group. In that case, the husband had dismantled the marital bed and placed it outside the house, after a row with his wife. As a result, she ran away to her natal homestead before she complained to the descent group, which ruled that the husband had to provide for the *mahande* to be tossed onto them, the bed and the house, which duly enabled the wife to return.

In a related way, Gutmann (1928: 441) described how a man who inherited the wife and house of a deceased brother lifted one of its hearthstones (*shia*) out of the ground together with the widow. While doing so, they swore to uphold all conjugal duties, which placed them under what Gutmann called the curse of the stone. Presumably this resulted from the fact that removing one of the three hearthstones inhibits cooking and consumption, and thus disrupts the transfer and transformations of *horu* that occur through dwelling. Accordingly, Gutmann (1928: 437) argued that the hearthstones were providers of power (*Kraftdarleiher*) and were even conceived of as the deliverers and bearers of generation (*Nachwuchs*). Like the plank from the bed, the removal of the hearthstone manifested how a person's death disabled and disrupted particular transfers and transformations of *horu* that these objects and their attendant activities involve. After swearing their oath, the man and the widow therefore replaced the stone so the hearth could again be used, but only after they put blood and chyme into the hole. As such, Gutmann's account provides another instance where these powerful substances facilitate dwelling and life, and the transfers and transformations of *horu* that they entail and involve.

Like the curse and its effects, the *mawiishwa* that are removed, gathered and displaced to cool or cleanse the homestead are contagious, and may transmit through and along the activities and relations of dwelling. The shovels, spades, hoes and pick-axes that are used for digging a grave will hence spread *mawiishwa* to the banana garden, where the trees will lose their *horu* and not yield fruit if the tools are not cleansed before they are used. Similarly, Gutmann (1909b: 133) described how the grave diggers rubbed their hands with the chyme of the butchered goat – a substance he moreover described as crucial in reconciliation and atonement ceremonies. Today, this extends to the car that transports a dead body, which is also cooled or cleansed with the *mahande*, lest it is bound for a lethal accident. It is such a serious concern that people toss *mahande* when they acquire a car, just to be on the safe side since they cannot know whether it has been involved in an accident. Like for the burnt *seso*, the place where the *mahande* is thrown is also avoided for some time afterwards. Care is taken not to cut grass in its vicinity to ensure that the bad things are not brought back to affect the livestock. Wittingly or unwittingly, the objects can reinsert the *mawiishwa* into the transfers of *horu* to divert dwelling and life. Conversely, tossing powerful substances, like chyme and blood, onto body parts and architectural features reanimates and redirects such transfers and transformations to revivify dwelling and life. A designated barrel of beer is accordingly brought out of the cooking hut and placed in the courtyard, once the *mahande* is tossed and *ihora kaa* nears its end. Those present are required to drink from this beer before they may depart. Otherwise, they risk contracting the *mawiishwa* that has been removed to allow the bereaved to resume dwelling. Consumption and commensality thus manifest how the transfers and transformations of *horu* are resumed within the homestead, and between its inhabitants and their neighbours and relations.[33] Indeed, it even entails that such controlled consumption banishes *mawiishwa* by means of *horu*, just like careless engagement with bad things can divert lifeforce in destructive ways. Life and death, growth and decline, healing and harming entwine and may turn from one to the other, depending on the ways and means by which *horu* transfers and transforms.

Speech and *Horu*

The verb to curse, or *iabisa*, is used to mean different activities, which span from *fyao* where only words are used, to *seso* and *nungu* which also involve objects of certain kinds. As I have shown, these objects are central for dwelling and owe their capacities to their engagement in practices that direct *horu*, and thus both enable and disrupt life. Language and *horu* similarly have a capacity to affect and effectuate each other, which is partly due to the fact that speech and foodstuffs enter through and emerge from the same openings and passages. Raimo Harjula (1989: 128) similarly argues that 'the Meru do not take a word as a mere signal or a symbol. Rather, a word is conceived of as an extension of one's personality, thus containing also the person's *finya*, power. This is especially the case with a blessing or a curse. Once uttered, such a word continues its existence and finally makes its original purpose come true'. The claim accords with Wittgenstein's idea that the meaning of a word is not its reference, but the use to which

it is put. But it surpasses this, as it entails that speaking is an intervention in the transfers and transformations of bodily power, which
is determined and made known through its effects in and on life and
the world. Accordingly, the curse is made known as it aborts a flower
spike and thus diverts the *horu* of the tree to affect the consumption
of the homestead's human and animal inhabitants. If the fallen *sabo*
is overlooked or not addressed, the curse will moreover result in the
illness and death of one or more persons in the homestead. Resulting
in swelling or emaciation of torsos and legs, it entails and manifests as
inabilities to consume and digest or toddle about (*itongoria*) between
homesteads.

Gutmann (1924b: 51) touched on these matters, as he described
the 'soul-power' (*Seelenkraft*) of the curser or *Beschwörer* (*mhanga*) and
his speech. He moreover claimed that it was this power that made the
newborn child sit or stick on the roof above the doorway, where it
was placed when it emerged with its mother from confinement (see
chapter three). The ability to make the child sit recalls the notion of
idamira, while the ability to do so by means of speech, which showed
and constituted the curser's capacity, is suggestive of the notion of
horu. It is underscored by Gutmann's claim that it was due to the
mhanga's head and speech lacking force (*Kraft*) if the child did not sit
on its own accord, but had to be supported by the curser's hand. In
light of this ethnography, it reveals that speech is a form of power or
force that emanates from a particular body part to affect beings and
thus is *horu* in another form. It is accentuated by the fact that the
capacity of speech to affect transfers and transformations of *horu* is
not restricted to *mwaanga*, but shared among all persons. Thus, Gutmann (1908: 298) argued that language (*Sprache*) is considered to
have a realizing force (*realisierende Kraft*), and is the most essential
faculty for demonstrating a person's soul, and a carrier and mediator
of beneficial and harmful influences, along with spit and other bodily
secretions. Accordingly, he described how people avoided quarrels and
conflicts as long as a cow was in milk, since this would irritate the
animal and make its lactation dry up (Gutmann 1924a: 138). Speech
is thus life force in another form, which hence not only has a capacity
to determine and effectuate transfers and transformations of *horu*,
but also has the power to affect persons, houses, crops and livestock,
along with their parts and substances that entangle in its conversions
and conveyances. It is for this reason that speech in the form of the
curse is counteracted by tossing powerful substances onto the aspects
of persons, objects and houses through which *horu* conveys to affect
its movements and currents.

Rene Devisch's (1998: 129) emphasis on the efficacy of speech is relevant in this regard: 'In oral culture, it is in the very saying of things that they are done and they are done by no other means: speaking is doing. Speaking, then, has its own finality'. Devisch moreover argues that 'speech weaves a tissue of life, rather than an exchange of information'. Where the first claim points to the idea that speaking is a kind of action or performance (Austin 1962; Barad 2003; Searle 1969), the latter moves beyond this to suggest that language and speech create a world of a particular kind. In Rombo, this occurs through the direction of the transfers and transformations of capacity of which speech and language constitute a particular form. Accordingly, Gutmann (1926: 659–60) described how the cursing stone was implored to well forth fury like a human being, and provide pain with its mouth and burn with its heat. It suggests that speech and language are not simply means for connecting a speaker and hearer, or a tool for associating words and things, but constitute life force in a particular form that is channelled in certain ways to realize particular forms. Gossip and rumours are therefore revealed in the intestines of animals and on *isale* leaves, where laypeople and diviners see and determine that 'there is a mouth' (*kure dumbu*) pertaining to particular persons or homesteads. Accordingly, Ludovic added the tip of the goat's tongue to the *mahande* liquid, so that speech and language would be channelled along with the other forms of *horu* it contained. Gutmann (1908: 300) moreover reported that 'beautiful tongue' was used to mean praise and blessings, while 'salty tongue' meant insincere praise uttered for ulterior motives, which along with curses constituted a form of 'violation by means of the tongue'. The persons who make village announcements in Keni are accordingly said to suffer harm (*imisha*) by this work, which occurs in the evening and early morning when it interrupts people who are asleep or engaging in sex.[34] The announcers therefore need to slaughter goats to counteract the destructive effects of these interruptions. As such, it underscores how speech and transfers and transformations of *horu* entwine, affect and effectuate each other. The entwinement of life force and language affords them a capacity to shift between cause and effect, which in turn provides each the ability to delimit the other. Speech and *horu* combine and disjoin, or cut and connect, to form and actualize relations of particular kinds that may be either constructive or destructive for those who entangle in them.

The account above shows how water features in both the washing of the curse and *ihora kaa*, where it combines and deploys together with the other powerful substances involved. Its use in this regard suggests a link with *horu* and provides an opportunity to consider more closely the event that took place in the plains in 2008 with the aim to bring rain to the area. This will be the topic of the next and final substantial chapter.

Notes

1. William's illness and the conflict with his wife and children are described more closely elsewhere (Myhre 2009).
2. *Ihora kaa* is termed *kuanua matanga* in Swahili, which means 'to break or remove the mourning'. It appears to be of long standing, as Gutmann, Raum and Dundas described activities following a funeral that strongly resemble what takes place today.
3. The only exception is one descent group that organizes *ihora kaa* the day after the burial regardless of the deceased's gender. This descent group originates from a man who migrated to Keni from Mashati to the north, which is provided as the reason why they do things differently.
4. *Machalari* consists of boiled meat and bananas, and is commonly prepared for the benefit of guests.
5. Harjula (1989: 128) describes a similar situation among the Meru.
6. Similarly, Schapera (1934: 302) and Wagner (1949: 103) describe how a curse can only be uttered by a senior over a junior relative. However, the curse must be uttered in Rombo and cannot stem from the 'unspoken anger' Schapera reports.
7. Mental illness is another frequent result.
8. It is possible that William cursed his wife and children in this manner because he perceived that they attempted to harm him, perhaps on the basis of two healers' claims that he had been bewitched (Myhre 2009). It is impossible to know, as it could not be ascertained at what point in time he conducted his curses, but the idea gains support from Msando's claim that one kind of curse was performed against unknown witches (Raum 1911: 210).
9. I am not sure if William's cooking hut contained a *kisumbadini* or whether Andrew used the term figuratively. It is possible he meant that his grandfather had poured milk next to the foot of a post supporting the attic.
10. Similarly, Gutmann (1908: 301) described how a man can curse his son by giving an offering of fluids to the ancestors.
11. Many *waanga* possess and use *mbelele* skins, which stem from what Raum (1907: 288) described as a 'holy animal'.
12. As another case described below reveals, any metal object can in fact be used as a means of cursing.
13. Therefore, while Ludovic showed me the other objects he uses for cursing, he could not show me these figurines.
14. *Kanzu* is a tunic of Arab origin that is commonly worn by men on the Muslim coast and islands. It is one of the items of clothing that according

to Widenmann (1899: 59) became popular in Kilimanjaro in the late 1800s. The *kanzu* is invariably white, so I suspect the emphasis on a black version was meant to underscore the extraordinary character of this event.

15. Again, accounts diverged with regards to how the curse had been performed. Some said that Julius had hit the barrel of the gun with another piece of metal, while others said that he had fired the gun while he uttered the curse.

16. Dundas (1924: 156ff) described a purification practice that resembles the one performed by Ludovic, which he claimed was performed for many different reasons that included both a curse and the event of a woman striking her husband with a cooking pot.

17. Similarly, in his description of the removal of the cooking pot curse, Gutmann (1926: 636) mentioned that the animal was not butchered in the courtyard as usual, but slaughtered behind the hut of the homestead.

18. The *ikamba* is considered one of the best shares of meat and is the claim of the male elders (Myhre 2013b).

19. Dried sheep chyme has potent cooling or cleansing capacities and is often used for such purposes, especially if one is not in a position to butcher an animal to obtain fresh chyme. Whenever a sheep is butchered, some of its chyme is therefore wrapped in dried banana bark and stored either under the eaves of the house or suspended from a corner of the cooking hut attic. It is kept apart from other objects and items due to its potency.

20. It is unclear whether *mahande* means the plant whisk or the mixture that is tossed by means of it (see note two in chapter three). The verb *ikulya mahande* is used to mean the act of tossing the mixture, but it can equally mean the tossing of the whisk or the tossing of the mixture by means of the whisk. This ambiguity or lack of clarification appears to be an abiding phenomenon of the regional ethnography. When Raum (1907: 288) briefly mentioned *mahande* in relation to oath-breaking, he claimed that the term referred to the liquid substance. This corresponds with Gutmann's (1913: 482; 1926: 641) references to '*ande*' or '*jande*' water. However, Dundas (1924: 156) claimed that *maande* were certain plants that formed part of the ingredients needed for purification, and Gutmann (1924a: 133) described how the *ikengera* plant and *isale* both had cooling powers. It is an intriguing possibility that *mahande* relates to the Nyoro term *mahano*, which Beattie (1960: 145) argued meant anything strange or marvellous, but in particular concerned conditions of ritual or magical danger. Many of the situations that Beattie described as occasioning *mahano* require tossing *mahande* in Rombo.

21. According to Gutmann (1926: 641), the *ande* was kept at the cleansed homestead for four days, where it was tossed every morning onto the cattle, the children and the central post of the homestead.

22. Similarly, Dundas (1924: 145) described an offering that ended in an act of purification performed by a 'medicine man', where the meat could not be taken away nor the bones disposed of randomly. It too suggests that

something contagious could be spread along with them, and thus resembles this current practice.

23. I return to consider the notions of *ihoreria* and *iholholhya* in chapter six.

24. Despite the fact that iron ore was not available in Kilimanjaro, Dundas (1924: 270ff) and Gutmann (1912) described how blacksmithing was well developed and passed on in certain descent groups. According to Dundas (1924: 272), smiths were greatly respected and feared, partly due to the curses they were able to invoke with their bells, which people who had been subject to theft employed them to perform on their behalf.

25. See, for instance, Udvardy (1990: 145) for the Giriama, Dundas (1924: 174) for the Pare, Feierman (1981: 355) for the Shambaa, and Hobley (1922: 103) for the Kikuyu.

26. Marealle's account must concern either Narumu in the extreme southwest or Ngaseni in the northeast, which were the only places where clay was available.

27. Dundas (1924: 174) too claimed that the breaking of a pot means bad luck.

28. At Oswald's homestead, the stable, the cooking hut and the residential house are separate buildings. These multiple *moongo* occasioned some confusion, as some acts were performed in front of the cooking hut, while others were conducted in front of the stable.

29. Sometimes it is the person most closely related to the deceased who breaks the gourd, rather than the elder who officiates at the proceedings.

30. Relatedly, Rigby (1968: 161) describes how an inauspicious ritual state (*ibeho*) is 'thrown away' in a pool or a swamp, and Parkin (1991a: 126) recounts how a homestead is cleansed and a death is banished by a river or a road junction. Beattie (1960: 150) meanwhile describes *mahano* as a 'power' that is physically contagious, but that can be 'left' or 'thrown'.

31. Witchcraft is euphemistically designated a 'bad thing' (*kindo kiwiishwa*), while the term 'bad person' (*mdu mbiishwa*) is used for someone who dabbles in witchcraft, as well as a thief and someone with a propensity to curse.

32. It is likely that the notion of *luswa*, which Wagner (1954: 44) translates as 'abnormal', relates to *-wiishwa*. There are at least many overlaps between the phenomena that give rise to *luswa* and those that occasion *-wiishwa*.

33. Similarly, Dundas (1924: 155) described how an evil was removed and sent elsewhere, when a person passing by a place where an offering was made was forced to eat of the meat and 'absorb its bane'. Gutmann (1909b: 147), meanwhile, described how an illness was transferred onto a goat and removed by the people who participated in eating its meat.

34. The notion of *imisha* is the same Herman used to describe the negative effect that an actual prestation of bridewealth milk and banana would have for their children (see chapter two). Like that prestation, the village announcements involve diversion of *horu* away from their creative and productive effects.

Chapter Six

NGAKUURIYA MOO

RETURNING LIFE, AFFORDING RAIN

When I returned to Rombo in August 2008, I quickly learnt of the visits that the Kamba-speakers had made to see the elders and leaders of the descent group that originates from Horombo and the last reigning *mangi* Tengia. I heard of the requests the people from Kenya had made that the chiefly descendants at Keni should return to Witini to alleviate the drought (*ukame*) and hunger (*njaa*) they suffered. The people on the mountain recognized that there was a drought, and knew that life was difficult in the plains, where they had hardly harvested from their own plots for several seasons. Nevertheless, the leadership of the descent group was reluctant to accommodate the request. They seemed fearful of the divisive effects the issue would have among its members and were concerned about the reaction from the church. They moreover wondered how they would obtain an animal to butcher. The last time they went, in November 2000, they had relied on contributions from people outside of their descent group that had enabled them to procure an animal. This time, however, they expected this would be even more difficult, given the seemingly ever-increasing demands for ever-decreasing amounts of cash.

Relying on the support of Peter, who is the first-born son of Tengia's first-born son and the descent group's male 'elder of culture' (*mzee wa utamaduni*), I attended their meetings over the following months. The meetings occur most Sundays right after Mass, in a designated place just behind the homestead where Tengia's grave is located. Many of his descendants live in the surrounding homesteads that are located near a cluster of tall trees that allegedly were planted by Horombo. In the shade of these trees is the building where Tengia arranged his *baraza* or public meetings whenever colonial officials were on *safari* in

the district. The building now stands empty, facing the office of Men-
geni Ward, where executive and public meetings take place.[1]

The issue of Witini was discussed in several descent group meetings.
There was surprisingly little opposition, as most attendants supported
the request of the Kamba. A collection of money to buy a bull-calf was
therefore initiated, while communication and coordination with the
Kenyans was left to an elder named Mamocha, who lives close to the
border. A date for the event was finally set and those who were to go to
Witini were called to a final meeting the afternoon before. Peter and the
descent group chairman made a final check to see whether those who
had been called to attend were present or if alternates were needed.
They were not concerned about individuals, but rather considered the
administrative sub-village (*kitongoji*) each person came from. In an indication that the event concerned space and place as much as people, it
was emphasized how each *kitongoji* where Tengia's descendants dwell
had to send two men. In addition, there were strict conditions that applied to those who would go. First, each person had to be circumcised,
and had to be able to walk the thirty-some kilometres to Witini and
back. The return moreover had to be made without turning around
and looking back in the direction of Witini, and, finally, the participants
had to abstain from sex for three days after the event. In a hint that the
ceremony concerned transfers and transformations of *horu*, it was repeatedly impressed on us that its success hinged on these requirements.

In this chapter, I describe the events that occurred over the following two days, and bring out how the ceremony concerned the transfers and transformations of *horu* that permeate dwelling and animate
life. In this way, the chapter deepens and accentuates the ethnography and arguments presented in the preceding chapters, and shows
how many of these literally came together over those two days. As
the account describes and determines how the event concerns and
furthers the recursive and transformational character of dwelling and
life, it also considers how rain and water form part of the transfers and
transformations of *horu*, and how Christianity inflects and affects the
notions and practices involved. Finally, it considers a set of cognate
notions that allows for a final regard and determination of the character of *horu* as a life force.

Removing the Bull

In the evening of that final meeting, the village criers walked through
Keni just after nightfall and broadcast that people would go to Witini
the next day, and that no-one therefore was allowed to farm in the

plains.[2] The event was now a common concern that regarded all the
people of the area and not just those of Horombo's descent group. The
event began for me at 3.30 the next morning, when soft knocks on my
door revealed two young men living nearby who had come to fetch me.
After exchanging greetings, we set off in the pitch-black night, scram-
bling down the rocky path towards the road that circles the mountain.
Only a sliver of a waning moon hung before us to the east, so we were
blinded by the outdoor lights of the occasional house with electricity.
There were no sounds except for our muffled voices and feet, and the in-
termittent crows of roosters. We stopped by Peter's homestead, but he
had already left. We therefore pursued him at Haula's – the homestead
of a long-deceased son of Tengia's, which is located not far from the tall
trees Horombo planted and across the path from the homestead where
his grave is found. Approaching the *kaa* through the *mengele*, we saw
Peter illuminated by the soft light of a paraffin torch (*mshumaa*) that
streamed out of the doorway of an old wattle-and-daub house. Over
his normal clothes, Peter had tied a woman's *kanga* around his waist
and over one shoulder, in a manner that to me resembled a Maasai
rubega or the blankets that people wear in the early photos from Kilimanjaro.[3] He had a woven basket at his feet and had thrust a spear into
the ground beside it. He used a torch to light up the leaves and trunks
of nearby banana trees, and told someone inside the house that he
searched for a *mnyengele* tree since he needed some dried bark – *mdawi*.
A middle-aged woman came out of the house and resolutely cut a piece
of bark in the dark from a tree close to the doorway. Peter received the
mdawi and went behind the house to fetch three *isale* leaves from a tree
growing close to the homestead's boundary.

At 4.30 a.m., one of Haula's sons arrived from the homestead located above (*fondoho*) or behind (*mma*) the one we were at. The house
in front (*mbele*) or below (*siinde*) was occupied by this man's youngest
brother, but had once belonged to their mother. Meanwhile, their eldest
brother lived at an adjacent homestead. Peter and Haula's son entered
the house, where the wife of the latter and the wife of his eldest brother
sat on a bed with a young girl between them. In a livestock pen opposite
the bed, Peter woke and raised a white and tan bull-calf. He tied the
strip of bark around its neck and instructed the women to pour curdled
milk from a gourd on the floor into a wooden *mboriko* bowl. He turned
the calf so it faced uphill and the back of the house, and then removed
his hat and one shoe. He dipped the stacked *isale* leaves in the milk and
tossed it onto the animal's head, back and rump, while saying:

> We are exhausted from the heat. We remember you Horombo. We
> remember you, give us some manure (*kaboru*) and something to eat.
> The children are dying from hunger (*nshaa*), *mangi*, they are dying of

hunger. Look for the person wherever he is (*naekeri ku*), sit together (*mutchamie*) and see what it is your children shall eat here at the homestead (*kunu mṛini*). We have made noise, we are exhausted, see how they make noise. May they remember you, like others remembered you in the past. We request very much, you great one (*hai sha moombe*). Whether he is by Murukuti, or wherever he is, we have provided this thing (*duwafuna kindoki*), we have provided this sacrifice (*duwafuna sadaka*), may he provide us with something to eat. Something to eat is what we seek, we seek nothing else.

Peter handed the *mboriko* to Haula's son, who gave it to the women, so they could share its contents. He tied the *isale* to the *mdawi* around the animal's neck and untied its rope, which he gave to Haula's son so that he could bring the calf out of the house. The women passed the emptied *mboriko* bowl through the doorway, along with a long-handled ladle (*kilikiyo*) and the gourd of milk. Peter placed all these items in his basket, where he already kept two drinking gourds (*shori*).

By tossing milk onto specific parts of its anatomy, the animal was hence detached from the house by a person who attaches to its doorway. Peter enunciated this as he used the verb *ifuna,* which means 'to take something out of someplace'. It was in other words an act of transfer or provision, where the animal was removed from the house to be brought someplace else. As the address was made to Horombo, it was a provision for the dead, which like other such aimed to make the deceased sit together (*mutchamie*). Here, however, it combined with the Arabic-derived Swahili notion of *sadaka* to suggest that the animal was an offering or a sacrifice. In return, Peter requested that they get manure and something to eat, and thus anticipated fodder and foodstuffs, and articulated how these turn on and emerge from bovine digestion. At the same time, milk along with the ladle and bowl that convey it were passed from hand to hand, and hand to mouth, and eventually through the doorway, to manifest how *horu* emerges from and enters into different body parts and architectural features. In this way, the preliminary address and activities already articulated and accomplished that the concern of the event was the recursive and transformational character of dwelling and life, where *horu* converts and conveys to further *ikaa* and *moo.*

Going to the Plains

We left Haula's homestead and walked to Horombo's tall trees by the road. While we waited for the other participants to arrive, Peter called out *kwakya* ('the day dawns') and *duenda Witini* ('we are going to Witini') at the top of his voice to broadcast that we were going to the plains. I thought he was calling those we waited for, but Peter explained it was to alert people to our activities so they would not go to farm in the plains. The bull began to eat the long grass surrounding the tall trees, which resulted in excited exclamations of encouragement, saying it was good the bull ate from this place before we set off. In line with the concern for transfers and transformations, its consumption meant that the animal contained parts of the area and conveyed its *horu* to the plains, where the chyme (*mooshe*) was to play a significant role later in the day.

Once everyone had arrived, we set off for the plains. At first, we used the remnants of the old cattle track (*shia ya umbe*) that was used in the past for herding and ferrying livestock between the plains and the mountain, but it soon merged with the road that descends towards the plains. Peter continued to call out *kwakya* and *duenda* along the way, even at the crossroads by the parish church, unperturbed by the presence of the priests nearby. As we walked downhill, the morning chorus rose and the moon paled to insignificance. The vegetation also changed, as the banana trees diminished and gave way to freshly tilled fields that awaited the rain before planting. When we reached the lower road that partly circles the mountain, the clear morning afforded vistas far into Kenya below and of Kilimanjaro's peaks above. At this point, we were joined by the final participants, who live in that area and were exempted from meeting us by the tall trees. From there, the road narrowed and deteriorated before we turned onto a path that was another remnant of the cattle track. It wended between uninhabited fields that mostly were tilled, even if some were covered in thin brown grass that resulted from the drought. We turned onto a track heading north, where Peter stopped to make sure that all were coming. It was the place of Tengia's old cattle *boma*, which now consists of bush and grassland. The place is called *manyatta*, which derives from the Maasai term for the ritual or warrior village (Århem 1991: 58; Spencer 1988: 86) and testifies to the close and enduring relations between multilingual peoples in this area along the Bantu-Nilotic interface.

At *manyatta*, Peter had thrust his spear into the ground and leaned on it in the morning sun, as he received a call on his mobile phone. It was just past 7 a.m., but already hot, and the flies settled on us in droves. We followed the track to the area named after Mamocha, the elder from the descent group who acted as a liaison with the Kamba-speakers. Some entered his homestead to fetch him, while the rest waited by his shop and beer club, which many visit from across the

border. It was pointed out how clever Mamocha had been in requesting land in the plains as a young man, at a time when no-one wanted
to move there. As a result, the land he received from Tengia was so
large that he had eventually taken four wives to be able to farm it.

Arriving at Witini

The road was covered in ankle-deep dust that together with the brown
grass betrayed the lack of rain. Small beacons marked where we
crossed the border, and not long after we encountered round wattle-
and-daub houses with thatched roofs that were surrounded by bare
earth. There was little sign of agriculture, but healthy-looking goats
roamed the area and browsed the brush. Peter, his younger brother
and Mamocha split off to meet the Kamba elders in a nearby homestead, while the rest progressed to Witini. As mentioned in the preface, the place consists of two small clearings on the outskirts of a
settlement that are surrounded by thick bush and shaded by a large
overgrown acacia tree. A little while later, Peter and the other two arrived with five Kamba elders. One of the latter led the well-fed *mooma*
goat by a rope, while another cradled a large gourd and a third carried
three drinking gourds that differed from those used in Rombo.

Once everyone had exchanged greetings, a Kamba elder took Peter
aside to discuss the proceedings. Due to the long hiatus, Peter admitted not fully remembering how and where they did these things. He
ordered some young men to remove the bushes that had sprouted in
the clearings, pointing out that we could cut the vegetation since we
were going to butcher there. First, however, we needed to pour beer
on the ground. Everyone therefore gathered in a circle underneath
the acacia, where the atmosphere became solemn and quiet as the
younger men paid close attention to the proceedings. Mamocha told
Peter to squat on his haunches (*utchamia ndolho*) and pour the beer
towards the mountain (*ukanda Kiboho*). Peter drew banana beer three
times into a drinking gourd from a disused cooking-oil can before
pouring it in front of him as he faced the mountain. While doing so,
he made the statements reproduced in the preface.

Once the invocation was over, Peter refilled the gourd and took
three sips before handing it to one of the Kamba elders to drink. Mamocha asked Peter to fill the second gourd and pass it in the other
direction, so everyone could drink the beer. Mamocha explained in
Swahili that everyone had to taste (*kuonja*) a little before passing it on.
Enunciating how this was an act of commensality between the dead

and the living, he added that if you give someone something without also eating, the recipients will think you deceive them. When everyone had tasted our banana beer (*wari*), it was the Kamba-speakers turn to pour their honey beer (*molatine*) on the ground. One of their elders changed places with Peter before he filled a vessel from the large gourd they had brought. The elder held the brimming drinking gourd between his hands, and while he addressed Horombo in the Kamba language, he tipped it forward, so the beer spilled in the direction of the mountain and hit the ground next to the beer Peter had poured. He then tipped the vessel towards himself, so the beer spilled away from the mountain, in the direction of the plains and the coast from where the rain was expected to come. In this way, the beer was made to flow and engage both the mountain and the plains where the different participants live. It moreover involved the directions from which the rain is anticipated and where it is hoped to arrive. Simultaneously, the beer was made to move from above (*fondoho*) to below (*siinde*), which relates to the homesteads of parents and sons, and those of older and younger brothers. At the same time, the flowing beer imbricated their statements, where Peter requested rain that would bring fodder and food to enable and extend dwelling and life for their children and livestock, which the drought imperilled. The pouring beer thus anticipated the movement of the rain, and evoked the topography and spatial orientations that dwelling and life entail and entangle. Simultaneously, it served to remember Horombo, *monikihamba* and the other deceased, whom the beer gathered in one place for communal consumption. The beer would enable Horombo to dwell in this particular place, while the rain would afford *ikaa* and *moo* for the living at their homesteads. The living thus returned life (*iuriya moo*) to Horombo and the deceased, as they poured and channelled a powerful substance in the form of beer and by means of requests and anticipation of rain. The statements hence reveal that rain forms part of the transfers and transformations of *horu* that constitute the existential debt relationship between generations. It is underscored by Peter's use of *iuriya*, which is the causative-prepositional form of the notions that designate recurring marital relationships across generations, the naming of second-born children and the return of a person who was buried away from the homestead.

After his address, the Kamba elder refilled the vessel and tasted the sweet, golden liquid before passing it to his neighbour. He filled their other gourds too and passed these in different directions for everyone to taste this beer as well. As on other occasions where powerful substances are presented with requests for the deceased to sit and eat, the living participants were required to join and partake in the *horu*. Our consumption was part and parcel of the transfers and transformations of *horu* between generations that afford dwelling and life, and that render the living indebted to the deceased.

Butchering at Witini

When beer from both the mountain and the plains had been poured and consumed, it was time to butcher the animals. Mamocha asked the Kamba for two men to assist with the bull, while they would provide two to help with the goat. Persons from both places should hence engage both animals, but difference in modes of butchering rendered this difficult in practice. The bull was first made to face the mountain before it was overturned and its legs tied. It was stunned by blows to the head with a large tree branch before its throat was cut with a machete. Some wanted to keep its blood, but Mamocha pointed out that there would be no broth for making *kisusio*. Most of it was therefore allowed to run into the dry soil, but a Kamba elder filled a drinking gourd with some that he put aside. At this point, the goat was wrestled to the ground beside the bull so that it too faced the mountain. A Kamba elder muttered a brief invocation, while stroking the goat's neck, back and rump, before younger men suffocated it and cut its throat to bleed it on the ground.

Skinning and parting the animals was left to younger men who worked in the hot sun, while the elders retreated to the shade. The Kamba elder who had addressed the goat explained that 'this work of culture' (*hii kazi ya utamaduni*) had been left to him and another man by his father. However, he also stressed that he was a Roman Catholic and a member of the Society of Saint Joseph (*shirika la mtakatifu Josefu*). He had also held an official position as a district elder (*mzee wa mitaa*), which seemed equivalent to a ten-cell leader (*balozi*) or hamlet chairman on the Tanzanian side of the border. His main achievement in this regard had been to evict the Maasai from the area, which the elders from Rombo acknowledged as a success. As they spoke, it emerged that Peter and this elder knew each other from their youth, when the latter had worked in Keni. In this way, their conversation testified to the circulation and engagement of people across borders and boundaries in this area. It was highlighted and facilitated by their above-mentioned use of language during the event, where the Kenyans conducted their activities by means of Kamba and those from Rombo used Chagga, while Swahili was the means of common communication and coordination. The event thus took place around and across national, ethnic and linguistic distinctions and boundaries, while Swahili and the concern for rain were connecting commonalities. Gathering across an international border, Swahili was used to connect and coordinate across different languages that were deployed to address the deceased and channel powerful substances in certain directions to secure rain and food. A common language and concern brought different people from their separate areas to conjoin in an uncultivated place (*sakeu*) to forge and reiterate a relation, whose anticipated result would enable and extend dwelling and life in their cultivated homesteads (*mdenyi*). The deployment and mutual transformation of cognate languages thus formed part of and facilitated transfers and transmutations of *horu*, of which rain is one form.

The directional and topographical nature of this relation reemerged when the hides were stretched on the ground. Peter asked a Kamba elder which direction the heads should orient, and was told they should point towards the mountain. This is how hides are stretched in Rombo too and the direction they face during *ihora kaa*. Peter's uncertainty was probably due to the fact that the hides could just as well point towards the coast and the east from where the rain was expected. His question was prompted by the fact that both the event and its effect concern and involve a relation that turns on and around the differences between the mountain and the plains, Chagga and Kamba, the sun and the rain from which dwelling and life emerge. These differences derive their importance from a mode of life, where the results of horticulture on the mountain combine through cooking and consumption with those of seasonal agriculture in the plains, and livestock and persons in the past circulated between homesteads and *boma*s, as well as through the wider region. The different activities convey and convert *horu* in different forms that combine and disjoin to enable and extend dwelling and life. *Ikaa* and *moo* remain the abiding concern, which both require and involve transfers and transmutations of life force that are sourced from and brought to different places to constitute a particular topography of *horu*.

While Peter and the Kamba elders chatted, Mamocha kept an eye on the butchering and instructed the men to divide the bull in the 'customary manner' (*kimila*). He asked the Kamba butcherers if they knew how to cut the pieces to place on the ground. They confirmed this and detailed how they include a piece from each joint (*kiungo*) and intestinal organ. Although the Kamba divided the animal differently from the Chagga, they cut meat for the deceased in the same way as *ndaswa*.

As the animal was divided and its shares of meat were placed along-side each other, the inside of the animal was uncovered to disclose the entrails. Mamocha balanced the smaller intestine on top of the large stomach for their inspection. Observing first the colon, which in Cha-gga is termed the arm (*koko*), he pronounced that it showed well, and added that it would have shown death or hunger if it were constricted (*imefungwa*). Turning to the spiral loop or courtyard (*sha* or *washa*), he pointed to purple dots and claimed that these showed rain. He felt and weighed the evenly filled jejunum, which is also called *koko*, and pro-nounced that this had strength (*ina nguvu*), which is wanted since this brings cattle (*inaleta ng'ombe*). Unfolding this arm, he pointed to white fibres that ran its length, which he deemed ropes for tying cattle. The young men paid close attention to what Mamocha showed and said, and expressed their admiration for what he could see. Since he used Swahili, his pronouncements were obviously meant also for the inter-est of the Kamba. As he stepped away from the intestines, he smiled and said he could also see a pregnancy, but he would not divulge the form it assumed or whom it concerned, even though he said it was one of those present.

Mamocha's pronouncements reiterate how the entrails enfold parts of persons and homesteads, and encompass the place, means, activities and results of dwelling. The animal thus carries inside the processes and topography on which capacity, health and well-being depend, and whose state and character its entrails show (*ilhoria*) and enable people to see (*ilholhya*), in the form of hunger and death, as well as pregnancies, rain and ropes for livestock. Reminiscent of this, Widenmann (1899: 34) described how a rainmaker (*Regenerzeuger*) could predict the rain for the *mangi* from the intestines of an animal, while Dundas (1924: 142) claimed that fatty strings showed cords for tying livestock. The animal's ability to encompass and enfold dwelling and its topography gives sense to the excitement when the bull-calf ate the grass by the tall trees before we left Keni. Its consumption and incorporation of the landscape on the mountain entailed that it con-tained and conveyed its *horu* to the plains, where they anticipated it would show the state and character of dwelling and life. As the intes-tines contain chyme, which is conceptualized as a substance of life (*mooshe*), they do not symbolize or signify dwelling and life. Instead, they enfold dwelling and life, which the butchering unfolds for harus-pication to show. Meanwhile, their ability to show rain reiterates how this meteorological phenomenon – on which dwelling and life rely – forms part of the transfers and transformations of *horu* that permeate and animate *ikaa* and *moo*.

Despite Mamocha's instructions, only the three first sections of the bull were carved in the customary manner before the remaining carcass was quartered. Aside from the removal of Julius's curse, this was the only time I saw an animal split lengthwise, rather than carved into sections comprising both sides of the animal. It was time that was the concern, so Mamocha asked the Kamba to proceed in the same way. When both animals were butchered, Mamocha and a Kamba elder counted how many persons were present from each party and divided the meat between the groups. We were more numerous than the Kamba, but Mamocha cut each section in two, which he placed in separate piles. Each share was then divided into more manageable parts that were thread on spits or placed on latticed branches over a large fire. Mamocha ensured the *ndaswa* was separated from the rest of the meat, along with the *sumbua* shares for those who butchered.

A handful of people tended the meat, while the rest chatted in the shade. The restrictions regarding the event and its participants were brought up. It was stressed that no-one may return here once we had left. If you forget something, it becomes the property or wealth (*mali*) of Horombo. It was also emphasized that no-one could bring any of the meat away from this place. If someone arrived after us, they could eat whatever remains, but it must be consumed there and not brought elsewhere. The event hence localized and emplaced the life force it involved in this particular spot. The Kamba elder who had poured the beer said that they are not allowed to turn around and look back until they have entered a house. If you need to turn around, you walk until

Figure 6.1. Roasting the meat and stretching the hides in the plains.

you reach a house and enter its doorway, he said. The claim echoed Ludovic's statement regarding the requirement for him and the owner of the homestead when he removes the remnants of a curse. As a conduit of life, the doorway secures the outcome of these events, which concern and facilitate transfers of life force that include rain.

When the meat was ready, everyone gathered underneath the acacia tree. The two groups sat opposite each other, with those from Rombo on the side of the mountain and the Kamba on the side of the plains. The meat that was earlier divided between the groups had been recombined over the fire, but was now divided again and placed on branches and brambles on the ground. Before we ate, Mamocha used a euphemism to warn that if someone has something at home, god shall see to him, and if someone looks askance at another while he eats, god shall see to him. To explicate, he added that some are able to bewitch you with their eyes when you swallow, but that god shall see to him, if such a person is present. The concentration of people eating in close confinement and within sight of each other provided an opportunity for someone to transform a prospectively beneficial event into a destructive one by means of witchcraft (Myhre 2009). We all responded to Mamocha's statement by repeating 'then god shall see to him' before chunks of meat were carved and handed around. Each person used his own knife to cut the chunks into smaller pieces. Meat that was found to be uncooked was returned to the fire. Mamocha and Peter ensured that everyone ate meat from both animals. In this way, all shared and consumed meat from the plains and the mountain, and from both the male and the female animal. As in the *irukwa* exhumation, we gathered the bones on the stretched hides to reassemble the remnants of the animals, after they had been disassembled and the different sections circulated and consumed by those present. The meat we were unable to eat was finally placed on top of the bones for someone else to consume later.

Finishing at Witini

Preparations began for the final act after we had eaten. This was to take place in the adjacent clearing, and would include Peter and the senior Kamba elder, along with three others from each group that they would select. Peter picked his brother, Haula's son and Mamocha, while the Kamba man chose their most senior elders. The rest were left to peer through the bushes. Peter and a young man first fetched large handfuls of chyme (*mooshe*) from both animals, which they placed in a large heap in the middle of the clearing. They also brought the *ndaswa* meat and Peter's basket, which contained the beer, drinking gourds, spoon and milk gourd. The Kamba elder meanwhile fetched the vessel containing the blood that he had reserved from the bull. He stuck his fingers into the coagulated blood and dug out three globs that he placed on top of the *mooshe*.[4] While he did so, Mamocha said in Chagga: 'You (singular) eat Horombo, eat blood and mix it with meat. Drink (plural) Horombo, eat (plural) Horombo and mix blood and meat. Give this to your wives, may they drink and eat, it is indeed this we request of you'. As Mamocha switched from the singular to the plural, his statement enunciated that Horombo should gather and eat with his wives and the other deceased, and thus reiterated how these acts concern congregation and commensality.

Peter and the Kamba elder cut six substantial pieces of the *ndaswa* from the bull, which they placed on top of the chyme, next to the blood. The use of only this meat accorded with a claim Peter had made earlier that only the bull had *mrimwa*. The number of pieces meanwhile revealed how the practice entailed that both groups provided three pieces for Horombo. When the meat was in place, Mamocha said in Chagga:

> You elder, we request very much, you life-elder (*hai na hai sha moombe*), we request rain (*duiterewa mfua*), you life-elder. We have given you this meat, Horombo, we request strongly (*duiterewa hai na hai*). The cattle are finished, the children are finished, and the banana trees are finished. This is indeed why we have given you this meat. Eat Horombo and give it to your wife who is named Mashine. You great one, we request, you male elder of the children. We request very much, Matoni, *hai na hai*, Kiboho, and Mawenzi and there at Murukuti. We only request rain, there is nothing else we request, you great one. We request rain, we request very much, elder of the children and whomever else is there with him. Give us just even some drizzle, we are finished, people, the children are finished and the banana trees are finished and the cattle are finished. What shall we go and place on the ground (*dueshe itchasa na kyoki*), Horombo? Another day, what shall we place on the ground?

Mamocha ended his statement by spitting lightly towards the sky in the direction of the mountain.

After some debate regarding the next step, it was agreed that we should pour beer on the ground for the deceased to swallow the meat they had been provided. An additional gourd was needed for this, and while that was being fetched, Mamocha spoke into the air that they requested god (*mungu*) for rain. He asked Horombo to talk to god, if he has seen him, and tell god to bring us rain. He was interrupted when the gourd arrived and Peter began to pour beer on the ground. Peter

began to make an address in Chagga, but Mamocha intervened and
instructed him to pour the beer below or downhill (*wawike kusoswa*),
using a locative adjective that derives from the verb 'to descend or go
downhill' (*isoka*). In response to this, Peter poured the beer further
down, right at the edge of the *mooshe* towards the plains. At the same
time, the Kamba elder poured their beer at the opposite end, just above
the pile of chyme towards the mountain. Peter thus used a *shori* to
pour *wari* away from the mountain and towards the plains, while the
Kamba elder poured *molatine* by means of their drinking gourd away
from the plains and towards the mountain. While doing so, both made
statements in their respective languages to address Horombo and request rain. The concurrence meant that different powerful substances
moved in separate directions from the pile of chyme to engage the different directions and ecologies involved. As the Chagga poured below
and towards the plains, and the Kamba poured above and towards
the mountain, they switched these directions and ecologies around
to manifest and show how dwelling and life concern and result from
movements between them. At the same time, their cognate languages
intertwined and overlapped to reveal how both kinds of beer and language emerge from chyme as transfers and transformations of *horu*.
As these material and linguistic flows combined at and bifurcated
from this substance of life (*mooshe*), they instantiated a relation between different substances, peoples and ecologies to constitute a particular topography of *horu*. Peter's statements underscored this, as he
reiterated that they requested and anticipated rain to emerge as an
effect of this to extend dwelling and life, and afford future generations
and prestations:

> You Horombo Ukoni, we request some rain, we request some rain, those
> children have died and we do not even have bananas, and your cattle
> are finished. We do not know how we shall dwell, if you know how to
> dwell with your children then protect them, you great one. Let us get
> some light drizzle.

After refilling the gourd, he continued:

> We also request the owner of your homestead (*monikiwaloki kunu kaa
> kwaffo*), we request nicely, request on our behalf, we request rain, we
> request food, what shall we come and place on the ground another
> time? If you encounter rain, it has finished and the people are finished,
> what shall we come and give you another time? The livestock are also
> finished, we request very much.

While Peter refilled his gourd for the third time, Mamocha resumed
his earlier appeal, interleaving the Swahili term *mungu* that the Cath-

Figure 6.2. Different kinds of beer being poured by means of different kinds of gourds in different directions above and below the pile of chyme.

olic Church uses with the pre-Christian notion of *ruwa*: 'Talk to god (*mungu*), you Horombo, talk to *ruwa* and give us some rain. The one with the rain is god (*mungu*)'. Mamocha was interrupted again, as Peter continued: 'I have returned life to you, father, you life-elder, I have returned life to you, I have returned life to you Horombo, I have returned life to you Ukoni, and all the children. You (singular) have summoned us, we have summoned them, may they summon some water for us and some rain. May we get even some beer like this one'. Then Mamocha interjected: 'We are finished, you great one. Look for god and virgin Mary, look for us, Horombo, if you get there, talk to god and virgin Mary, may he summon some rain for us'.

Peter and Mamocha spoke in a call and response that lent the address a dialogic character, where statements by one effectuated complementary pronouncements by the other. At the same time, the Kamba made their address, which gave the occasion a polyphonic character, where similar statements in cognate languages moved and intertwined with the powerful substances that streamed in different directions from the chyme. *Horu* and language in different forms thus bifurcated and flowed from the substance of life (*mooshe*) to be channelled in particular directions for the purpose of affording rain, and extending dwelling and life. As the beer emerged from chyme, the act showed how consumption and production nest as transformations of each other and cascade as *horu* in different forms, which language entwined to channel in specific directions. Peter's statement at Haula's that they have made noise, yet Horombo has failed to see them and how they suffer, entails that the event involved a deliberate deployment and direction of language. Cognate languages and powerful substances in different forms were thus engaged, combined and made to move in separate directions with the hope of eliciting *horu* in the form of rain, which in turn would make them quiet. In this way, these acts and statements concern how language and life force are transformations of each other that can afford, channel and delimit each other through dwelling and life. It was underscored as the gourds were filled a final time, and the beer tasted and sent around with the emphasis that everyone drank both kinds. It reiterated the form of the event, as life force in different forms was deployed and channelled along with language to constitute a relationship from which further life-giving movements were anticipated.

The Kamba elder asked Peter to place blood on the chyme for the deceased women, which he did while he repeated his request for life and rain, and the appeal for Horombo to congregate and eat with his wives. Peter then shook out the *kanga* he had worn on his way down the mountain, and tied it around his waist in the manner women do. He declared that he had become a woman, in order to pour milk on the ground. No women are allowed at Witini, so men must assume their role and position, which requires a transformation by means of clothing. In this connection, he emphasized the act of shaking out the *kanga* four times, which is the number pertaining to women. As a piece of fabric, the *kanga* can be used by different people for multiple purposes, but by shaking it out four times and tying it around his waist, he made it clear that it was worn as if by a woman. Combined with this act, the fabric transformed Peter and enabled him to assume a subject position and act as a woman. Squatting, he poured milk from the gourd into the spoon, which he used to convey the liquid on the ground next to the beer. Meanwhile he said:

> This milk, female elder, this milk, wife of Horombo, this milk *msheku* Matoni, this milk, my mother cook *kena*, cook *kena*, give to your husband, we request some rain, let us get some rain, cook *kena*, eat all of you with your husbands, your grandchildren and great-grandchildren remember you, my mother.

He refilled the spoon and poured more milk, while saying:

> And the married daughters of the homestead (*wana wa kaa*) shall cook here, and the married daughter of the homestead and the owner of this place (*monikiwalo*) sit together, female elders cook *kena*, eat and get completely full. We remember you, may you remember us the same way. We only request some rain, let it not be rain that kills, let us get some rain to cause the grass to sprout. And the cattle are finished now, what shall the cattle eat now? The place is finished (*kuwasia*), the place is exhausted (*kuwaiya*), the place is completely finished.

Peter filled the spoon a third time and said:

> With this, my mother, we request very much, female elder of the children, I have returned life to you, I have returned life to you, children of Tengia and whomever else, all of you sit and eat *kena* with the great-great-grandchildren, get completely full.

Peter poured milk into the spoon a final time and declared that he would finish it all. Mamocha supported this, adding that the rest is for cooking *kena* the following day. It was received with laughter, but Peter said as he poured it on the ground:

> This is for *kena*, my mother, and for *kena* to be placed at the corner of the bed and the hearth (*kishiini*), cook it and serve it so your neighbours (*wamamrasa*) can eat.

Peter poured the remaining milk from the gourd and took four small sips from the spoon before passing it to the others to taste. His statements bore significant similarities to the ones MaShirima made, when she poured milk in connection with Herman's bridewealth prestation (see chapter two). Here too, the milk is for a named deceased female elder to cook *kena*, which she is requested to share with her husband,

the other deceased women and their husbands. The *wana wa kaa* who
detached from the house in marriage are also requested to cook *kena*
and share it with the person who established the homestead – *moniki-*
walo. As Peter stated, it is an act of remembrance where the dead are
named and provided with a powerful substance that they are asked
to convert and gather around to consume as a soft food. In return for
this, the living request that the deceased shall remember the living and
provide *horu* in other forms to enable dwelling and life in particular
places. The recursive and mutual character of these transactions was
enunciated by Peter, who declared that they have been summoned to
summon the deceased, who they request to summon the rain. The locative constructions *kuwasia* and *kuwaiya* that Peter employed when he
stated that the place is finished and exhausted underscore how these
transfers and transformations of *horu* concern, occur between and
are constitutive of places. It thus enunciated what was enacted when
the beer was poured in separate directions to move from the mountain
to the plains. Meanwhile, his reference to *kishiini* revealed how these
transfers of *horu* that the prestations activate and achieve form part of
those that pass through houses and homesteads.[5]

The deployment of certain effects of dwelling with the hope of
bringing rain to enable future dwelling furthermore engaged the recurring temporal figure described in chapter three. In particular, it
was enunciated as Peter repeatedly claimed that their existence depends on preceding generations. The living owe their existence to the
deceased, and therefore are obliged to extend dwelling into the future,
with the hope and expectation that their successors will remember
them and do the same. In this way, the prestations are transfers between the living and the dead that form part of the topographical
movements of *horu* that occur through dwelling and life, and that
constitute persons, houses, livestock and crops as their effects, which
extend through time and space. In line with this, the different addresses reiterated that it was the land and its drought that compelled
them to deploy livestock and foodstuffs with the aim of its regeneration and continued dwelling.

Preparing for departure, Peter placed the gourds and spoon back in
his basket. The Kamba wanted to retrieve their vessel, so the elder told
him to get rid of the rest of the blood. Peter therefore dug out three
further globs and placed them on the *mooshe.* There was an accent on
finishing what we had brought through mutual prestations for the deceased and consumption by the living. All that remained when we left
the clearing was therefore a pile of chyme with six pieces of roasted
meat and ten globs of coagulated blood on top, and trails of beer at

both ends with a blotch of milk below or to the east. It was the result
of two groups of people gathering in one place to locate and leave *horu*
in multiple forms for Horombo and the other deceased with a hope to
elicit rain and extend life in their homesteads. Thus, in his final address, when all the substances were in place, Peter said:

> We keep your homestead, Horombo Ukoni, we keep it. We are leaving
> here, we are going to wait and see if you remember us. *Hai*, Ukoni,
> gather (*msase*) with your wives and your children. See us (*mdulholhye*)

Figure 6.3 The pile of chyme topped with blood and meat, and surrounded
by beer and milk, as a result of the proceedings at Witini.

how we suffer, we have suffered, we are finished. Even when we climb back from the plains, we ask if we will arrive but say we will never arrive. Give us some rain, do not give us rain that kills. Just give us some for growing crops. We request very much, you great one.

Peter enunciated how the requested outcome of the event was uncertain and therefore something for which they would wait and see (*ilholhya*). In fact, his two uses of *ilholhya* entail that the event shows the deceased the state of life and the land, while the uncertain effect they anticipate to remedy the situation will show the character of their relationship to Horombo. The event thus served as a double mode of determination that deployed *horu* and language to ascertain the state of dwelling and channel life force in particular ways to afford its extension into the future. In a twist on the time figure of dwelling, the event thus deployed its past effects to show its present state with a hope for its future extension, which in turn reveals the character of the relationships that entangle the dead and the living.

Leaving Witini

It was time to leave, so everyone was told to ensure they had all their belongings. The poles that had supported the spits over the fire were pulled up and placed on the embers, so nothing remained except a heap of ash and two animal hides that contained the bones, scraps of meat and roasting spits. There was also a pile of chyme containing and surrounded by different powerful substances. We gathered in a circle around this pile, as Mamocha reminded everyone not to turn around once we had left, and not to have sex once we got home. He said the Kamba know when they may turn around, but those of us from Rombo could not look back until we reached the intersection by the parish church. Peter added that we should run from Witini in different directions, with each person pursuing his own path before gathering by the road near the settlement. No person was allowed to follow in the footsteps of another, but needed to trace his own avenue through the landscape. Each person thus became a vector of *horu*, energized by the meat, beer and milk we had consumed. As such, we were manifestations and iterations of the lines of *horu* that we had occasioned, and that in everyday dwelling render persons as well as crops, livestock and houses as their effects. We would thus course through the landscape to elicit rain in our wake, primed to dwell and extend life in the plains and on the mountain. Mamocha also told us to lift our gaze and spit lightly towards the sky. Some spat to the east where the rain is anticipated before turning around to spit towards the mountain where it is expected to arrive. Meanwhile, Peter implored: 'Walk around, Horombo' (*utchambuka Horombo*), and Mamocha repeated recurring phrases from the addresses, such as 'we request rain', 'the grass is finished', 'the goats are finished', 'the children are finished' (*duterewa mfua, mara yasia, mburu sisia, wana wasia*). Our expectorations were afforded by the powerful substances we had consumed, which imbricated with those we had poured and placed on the ground to create a confluence that released Horombo and enabled him to move around. These final acts and statements thus reiterated the form of the event, as *horu* in different forms emerged from each other to enable persons to move around and channel life force to extend dwelling and continue life.

Finally, Peter counted to three and we all ran in different directions amid calls and ululations from the elders. We did not run far before we slowed to a walk in the general direction of the mountain. After fanning out across the neighbouring fields, we gradually re-formed into one long line of people. The effect was perhaps to make us look like a war party, which re-created the situation that occasioned Horombo's death. When we reached the nearby road, those in front were told to stop, so that everyone could gather. No-one could turn around, so it was difficult to determine if everyone was present. However, Peter had fallen back and was shouting instructions to one person who was astray, so he would join us. When he and Peter arrived, we continued in a single file to the international border, where the Kamba and Mamocha bid farewell. This too was a tricky proposition, but eventually they walked to the person in front and turned around to return along the line and shake our hands. Despite earlier admonitions, the Kamba thus turned around and looked back even though they had not yet entered a house. Mamocha was furthermore exempted from returning to the tall trees with the rest of us, even though he belonged to Tengia's descent group. Instead, he counted as a plain-dweller in this particular situation and was allowed to go home.

The rest of us pressed on, with Peter and his spear at the rear. He ensured that no-one turned around, while we took turns at the front to set the pace through the blistering sun. When the path reached the road, we walked in two lines side by side, but changed to three abreast when the road widened. Everyone we met was forced off the road with calls to step and stay aside. At first, it only concerned pedestrians and cyclists, but later it included motorcycles and cars, as we progressed up the mountainside. Most stopped or slowed down, as we shouted and shook our walking sticks, but some forced us to jump aside. We were aided by two strangers, who walked ahead and signalled that people should lower their speed and keep aside. Even a lorry was forced to stop for us in this way. Nothing was to impede or halt our progress, as we moved up the mountain. Instead, we displaced everything in our way, to hopefully bring rain in our wake. The sense of force and purpose was exacerbated by the four songs of a call and response variety in which the elders led us. These concerned how the cattle only ate banana stems without leaves (*tenge*) and therefore bellowed (*iyamia*) from hunger; how the cattle were finished so we went to place meat on the ground (*itchasa*); how we herded cattle in the past; and how the cattle are in the plains where we protect them. The songs concerned the cattle herding of the past that had been displaced by stall-feeding, and which the drought imperilled. Accordingly, the situation necessitated provisions of powerful substances from which we emerged as a force to propel the rain. In addition, we were carried forth by the cheers, salutations and applause from those we encountered along the way, who congratulated us on what we had done. Their calls imbricated with our *horu* to power us along, while the rain would hopefully follow in our wake.

At the junction by the parish church, Peter told us to stop and turn around, and look in the direction from which we came. Some trees by the roadside prevented us from seeing the plains, but we faced that way for a minute or so before we turned and continued uphill. We were now free to look in any direction. Our singing escalated as we approached the main road, eventually emerging from the cattle track to reach Horombo's tall trees. We circled one tree below the road three times before Peter told us to spit three times towards the plains and three times towards the mountain, while he said: 'Horombo, we have arrived' (*Horombo duwashika*). As we sat down in the shade of the tree, those from the descent group who had come to receive us shook our hands and uttered their commiserations for our exertion. They served us beer in drinking gourds from a wooden barrel that was kept at the foot of the tree. More descent group members arrived, including the chairman who shook our hands and congratulated us. Everyone was served, but the others sat at a little remove from those who had gone to Witini. Peter rose and announced in Swahili that everyone had acted appropriately and that no-one had turned around or done anything to ruin the *mila* or custom. He reminded us that we should not have sex for three days, and one elder warned that the penis now has fire (*ire motcho*) and power (*ire ngufu*), and that sex therefore was dangerous (*hatari*). His statement enunciated how the event deploys and channels *horu* to concentrate heat and life force in a specific place from which it aims to attract rain. Those who conveyed this *horu* took part in its directed flows, and were therefore hot and powerful from its concentration. The sexual prohibitions ensured that this *horu* was not diverted or dissipated, but also protected others from the harm it could inflict. The fact that we contained abundant heat and life force underscores how the event is a prestation of *horu* that is channelled in certain directions to afford rain, which the participants share in and attract through their consumption of the powerful substances.

Darkness approached, but before we could leave we had to plan for the following day. The chairman suggested that those who went to Witini should perform the next day's *mila* without interference. If we allowed others to be involved and the rain failed, it would only lead to mutual suspicion and accusations that one or the other group did something wrong. It was therefore best that those who started also finished, and then we would see if they had done a meaningful thing (*kitu cha maana*), he argued. Everyone agreed, so we trickled out. Most people we encountered on the way home congratulated us and expressed their excitement and support for what we had done. Many pointed out that the conditions had already changed in the plains, where we could see dark clouds gathering and flashes of lightning.

By Horombo's Tall Trees

The following morning, the participants gradually gathered by the house where Tengia conducted his *baraza* and meetings in the past. We discussed the lightning the evening before and looked at the overcast sky, expressing confidence that the cloud cover would burn off, so the sun would emerge and the heat rise, and the rain arrive. At 8 a.m., Peter limped in, visibly sore from the exertions the day before. He apologized for being late, but suggested we start even though everyone had not yet arrived.

We returned to Haula's homestead, where Peter asked me and two others to join him behind the house. He sifted through the leaves of an *isale* tree that forms part of the homestead's boundary, until he found four unbroken leaves. He pulled these out, just like people do before divination, and as he had done the previous morning before taking the bull out of the house. Back in the house, Haula's son turned the *mooma* goat we had come to fetch so that it faced the mountain, while Peter asked his wife to bring him some milk in an *mboriko*. She first poured it from a plastic bottle into the gourd we had used the previous day, and then poured it from the gourd into the *mboriko*. Like the day before, Peter stacked the *isale* leaves and dipped them in the milk, which he tossed onto the goat with a flick of his wrist. He tossed milk onto its back, head and rump, ensuring that it hit both its right and left hind legs, and thereby the parts of the animal that are claimed by the male elders, affines, female elders and mother's brother. Meanwhile, he announced to Horombo and his child that we had arrived safely, and that we provided this goat that resulted from dwelling at the homestead for the purpose of securing rain:

> *Hai* Horombo, *hai* Horombo Ukoni, we have arrived safely (*duleokia*), you great one, we have arrived safely and the *washeku* have ululated, so we have recovered. We have arrived safely, we request rain, we do not request rain that kills, we request rain for growing crops, and the cattle are finished, you great one, and in the plains we have not received anything, you great one. This goat has emerged with good health, it agrees in the same manner we used to give things in the past, it has emerged here at Mrau, child of *mangi*.

Peter returned the *mboriko* to the woman, who drank the milk while he tied the *isale* to the twine around the goat's neck. She asked if we were not to take the rest of the milk, which Peter denied. He led the animal out of the house and as we walked up the road bordering the homestead, she ran through the banana garden with the gourd, begging us to take it anyway. Peter's brother received it and explained that some fear using *mrimwa* milk for cooking, lest they suffer from eating it. He shrugged and said you can never know, possibly hinting at its *horu* rendering it harmful to those not taking part in the event.

We returned to the tall tree below the road, where we tied the goat to an adjacent tree. Peter fetched the *kanga* he wore the day before, shook it out four times and tied it like a skirt around his waist. He removed leaves and debris to expose the ground at the foot of the tree, and poured milk four times from the gourd into the spoon he had brought to Witini. Pouring the milk on the ground below (*siinde*) the tree, he said:

> This milk Matoni, this milk mother of Horombo, this milk you elder of this homestead (*mṛi shu*). Yesterday we came to the plains, we came to the requesting place (*kutereweni*), we requested you and they received us and the female elders ululated. Give us, we request some rain. Do not bring us rain that kills, but rain that brings a little plenty (*kambora*). Let the children eat and get full, let the children eat and get full, you female elder of this homestead (*we msheku wa mṛi shu*).

Peter refilled the spoon and continued:

> And you female elder of this homestead, cook *kena*, eat all of you. And married daughter of the homestead (*mwanamkaa*), give them in the

same way you drank the beer. Eat all of you, cook *kena*, eat and get completely full. And those who are wherever, give them and they shall say it is the great-grandchildren of Horombo who remember them. The thing we request is some rain, not rain that kills, but that brings grass for those cattle. If people farm, let them get something to eat.

He filled the spoon again and proceeded:

Dwell here (*kaa haa*), search for each other and eat everyone, men and women, we remember you, you life-elder, we remember you, we have been called (*duwalaukiwa*) because regardless of what we do, we do not get anything. Even if the crops flower (*dukivika*), we get nothing. Rain we request for grass and food. It is indeed the thing we request. We are dying from hunger (*duwafa nshaa*), we are dying, we are finished.

Peter filled the spoon a fourth time to hold forth:

Hai msheku Matoni, owner of this homestead (*monimri shu*). We do not know anything, it is you who shall see those who know more, those you met in this homestead, it is you who know who they are, we do not know them. We have returned life to you, we request life my mother, we have returned life to you, my grandmother, we have returned life to you, female elders of this homestead and female elders of all the homesteads, all of you of Horombo, we have returned life to you, you great one.

Peter's statements reiterated the earlier invocations and enunciations, but added some significant elements that undergird earlier claims. The locative construction *kutereweni* states that Witini is a requesting place and enunciates how prestations occur between homesteads or other sites, and thus unfold topographically to constitute and form part of the landscape. Similarly, the recurring address of the female elder as the 'owner of the homestead' reiterates how women attach to houses between which husbands merely circulate. It moreover entails that the living are temporary caretakers, who owe the presented foodstuffs to the deceased for their homesteads, which they maintain as places of dwelling. This was enunciated in the final address, where Peter articulated that they present milk to the female elder they knew, while she should present it to those she encountered when she arrived at the homestead. The statement implies that dwelling is a continuous process that is maintained by those who pass through and attach to the homestead through *ikaa*. It moreover turns on the practice of requesting someone by means of something (*iterewa mdu na kindo*), where you approach those you have a relationship to, so they can bring it to others they relate to and know. Relationships to and knowledge of people fade with time, so the living may neglect someone who wants his or her name carried forth or a prestation

made, thus occasioning problems for the living. Peter's use of the concept of *ilaukiwa,* which concerns ancestral problems, reveals that the
drought formed part of the same relationships and processes. Meanwhile, his claim to ignorance constituted the event as a form of determination, where the outcome resolved the state and character of their
relationships.

Figure 6.4. Peter wearing a *kanga* and pouring milk at the foot of one of
Horombo's tall trees.

Peter placed the spoon upright along the trunk of the tree with the tip of its handle next to the white remnants of the milk on the ground. Smiling, he untied his *kanga* and said that he was now a man again. Seizing a *shori* from his basket, he drew beer three times before pouring it next to the milk at the foot of the tree. While doing so, he said:

> This beer Horombo, this beer Horombo, we came yesterday, we arrived home safely (*duwashika kaa ung'usha*), there is no problem, you protected us well, do not forget the thing we requested, we request some rain, we do not request rain that kills, we request rain to bring some crops, we request rain to bring some grass for the cattle in the plains, we request some well-being (*kausima*), may illness not come to the place (*kutashe nduari*), this is the thing we went downhill for yesterday, you great one. Gather (*msase*) all you male elders of this homestead with Horombo and Horombo Ukoni, protect us, your children are finished, your great-grandchildren are finished, we are finished, we are finished, we are exhausted from the heat, we are finished. We request with *mangi* Augusti, gather all of you here, mother of Ndeserua, say to them, why do you leave the children so that they die from hunger, why, bring your younger siblings from the old days and just see (*telholhieni*) the children of your great-grandchildren, what shall they eat, you great one?

Peter refilled the gourd and continued:

> You *msheku* Matoni, gather with all the female elders of Horombo, all of Horombo, we request you, the thing we request you, my mother, is some rain, we just request, your children, grandchildren, and great-grandchildren, may they get something to eat, and may the cattle get something to eat, now if we do not get this, yesterday we gave you meat, if there was no grass we would not have had that bull, we request, and we have a goat here, without grass we would not have this goat, we request you, may you give us more like you gave us this here, you great one, we request rain, we do not request rain that kills, but that brings food, *hai* my female elder, *hai* you great one.

Peter filled the gourd a final time before pouring the beer and saying:

> We have returned life to you Horombo, we have returned life to you, Horombo Ukoni, we have returned life to you, we have returned life to you elder Tengia, we have returned life to you female elders and youths, we have returned life to you. The thing we request is rain, do not give us rain that kills, we request rain that brings food and grass for the cattle and goats, it is indeed the thing we request you, you great one. I have returned life to you *mangi*, I have returned life to you Horombo, I have returned life to you Horombo Ukoni and all the female elders and anyone who is wherever, seek them all, this is the thing I request you.

The significant addition to this address was Peter's use of *kausima*, which is a diminutive form of the Swahili *uzima* that means 'life', 'health', 'completeness', or 'wholeness', but that I have rendered as 'well-being'. His request that illness (*nduari*) should not come implies that illness involves diversions of *horu* with concomitant transformations or disruptions of dwelling and life. Its use in this context accentuates how drought involves similar diversions and disruptions that threaten dwelling and life, and jeopardize future prestations. Combined with Peter's statement that the two animals were the result of grass and feeding that the deceased enabled, it underscores the recursive character of these proceedings, where *horu* is provided in different forms to facilitate rain and enable dwelling that may result in further prestations.

Peter placed the gourd alongside the tree trunk beside the spoon he used for the milk. The goat was untied and suffocated below the tree, close to the remnants of the milk and beer, with its head oriented uphill towards the tree and these powerful substances. It was suffocated by a young man, but raised for Peter to stab its chest. Its first blood was made to fall on the ground, while the rest was gathered in a *sufuria*. Peter removed its platelets with his hand, which he shaped into a ball that he placed at the foot of the tree, next to the beer and milk. He put the gourd and the spoon back in the basket, and returned the leaves to cover the ground. Now no-one could see what had occurred and remained there. However, the blood, milk and beer that he placed at the roots (*mri*) of the tree to attract rain are *horu* in different forms that circulate through and emanate from the veins (*mri*) and other body parts of humans and animals. In this way, the proceedings deployed and directed *horu* to conjoin the vein-roots of different beings to extend dwelling and life. The tall trees are moreover said to have been planted by Horombo, who allegedly buried one person alive underneath each one to provide them with a particular position and power. The trees can therefore not be cut, but are left to grow so their branches tangle to form a tunnel across the road. Each falling bough anticipates a death in his descent group that can only be prevented by butchering an animal at its foot, which in turn enables its use as firewood in a homestead.[6] The claims entail that these trees contain abundant *horu*, due to the persons buried underneath them, which renders harmful their involvement in dwelling. Like the tree of the barren at Shimbi and the overgrown acacia at Witini, these are repositories of *horu* that cannot be cut and engaged in the transfers and transformations of life force unless an animal is butchered. Such deployment of powerful foodstuffs and substances interlocks the veins (*mri*) of those involved with the roots (*mri*) of trees, which in this case extend to Horombo who planted the trees and those he buried underneath them. These acts are hence further events where persons be-

Figure 6.5. Horombo's tall trees lining the road in Keni-Mengeni.

come extended (*ialika*) and emplaced (*idamira*), as their veins interlock with the roots of these trees.

We carried the dead goat across the road and up to the nearby meeting place of the descent group, where we placed it on the ground so that its head pointed uphill. Peter made a first cut through the fur on its breastbone, which was followed by a few cuts from his younger brother. The rest of the skinning was left to younger men. Fresh banana leaves were cut in the surrounding gardens and care was taken to include four *mnyengele* leaves since this was a *mooma* goat. The leaf is distinguishable by the red colour along its stem, whose term – *samu* – derives from the word for 'blood'. While *mhoyo* derives its significance from maturation that coincides with the gestation of humans and cattle, *mnyengele* obtains its importance from circulating *samu* through its body. Both accentuate how *horu* permeates humans, livestock and crops, which makes them amenable for the manipulation of life force, dwelling and life.

Peter seized control of the butchering once the animal was skinned. Cutting out the internal organs, he proclaimed the presence of a cooking pot curse (*kure nungu*) and pointed to a white, nearly transparent bulge on the liver. It was about five centimetres long and three centimetres wide, and he took special care in slicing it off. By carving shares of meat that manifest different relationships, butchering unfolded the state and character of the homestead to which the animal attached, whose relations it enfolds. It moreover contained and showed relations beyond the homestead, as Peter also claimed to see rain from the reddish colour of the small intestine. His claim reiterated how rain forms part of the transfers and transformations of *horu*, where chyme plays a pivotal role and thus enables the animal to enfold and reveal this meteorological phenomenon.

Once the animal was parted, Peter prepared the few different parcels of meat that were to be presented and eaten by specific people. There was *sumbua* for those who butchered, and *molisa* for the person who kept the animal. He stressed that the latter should be generous since the bull and the goat, as well as the beer and milk, emerged from (*ifuma*) one homestead. Haula's son came forth to receive this share, which was presented on the goat's hide. He carefully wrapped the meat in the skin, which he tied up with the rope. Although this parcel is usually handled as such, he placed it in a plastic carrier bag so that no-one could see the contents when he brought it home. The *molisa* included the *itasura* stomach, which is presented full of chyme to the person who swept the animal's manure to show the recipient how well they cared for the animal (Myhre 2013b: 117). The rest of the meat was then divided into two shares – one for the men and one for the women.

While we butchered, people who had not accompanied us to Witini trickled in and were told to find hearthstones, firewood and a *sufuria* for a makeshift hearth. It proved a particular challenge to find suitable hearthstones, which indicated how long it was since this event last occurred. The *sumbua* was roasted and eaten while the men's meat boiled in a large *sufuria* covered with fresh banana leaves. As we chatted and dozed in the shade, Peter sent for the barrel with the remaining beer since it too had to be finished. People came and went, while others passed by since we were seated at a busy intersection of footpaths. Some stopped in their tracks, concerned about intruding, but were told they could pass. Most greeted us and walked on, but they were mainly members of Horombo's descent group, who live in the surrounding homesteads. Some women made a throwaway remark to which Peter's brother responded. This elicited an angry reaction, as Peter told him we were at an *mbuho* and should sit in silence (*dukeri mbuhoni dutchamia sii*). In light of the relationship between language and life force, it seemed that the use of speech to engage outsiders would divert *horu* and jeopardize the anticipated outcome.

Peter was concerned that no women had arrived to receive their meat and worried it would remain raw, while the men's share was ready to be eaten. Asking the advice of other elders, he shook out and wore his *kanga* again to drop the meat in the *sufuria*. His need to transform and assume the subject position of a woman entails that the women's claim to their share of meat is absolute and that the men may not handle it beyond presenting it. It was underscored when the female elder of culture arrived, and Peter immediately felt compelled to explain what he had done to their share of meat. His need to account was perhaps motivated by the fear and suspicion that accompany people's engagement with food, and especially that which others shall consume (Myhre 2009).

When the descent group chairman arrived, we sat down to eat in a large semi-circle that counted more than twenty-five persons. Peter cut the men's share of meat into pieces and placed them on a metal tray, which a young man brought around for us to help ourselves. The women's share, Peter re-presented undivided to the most senior woman present, who delegated its division to the female cultural elder. Broth or *supu* was ladled out, but there was not much, so we were encouraged to mix it with the blood to make *kisusio*. Afterwards, the remaining beer was served, and while we drank, Peter rose to give the chairman a briefing of the day before. He reiterated that everything had gone according to plan and that nothing had been done to imperil the outcome. He also expressed his pleasure with the preparations for the event. The chairman thanked Peter for his account and those who went to Witini for what they had done. He added that the descent group had resolved to resurrect custom (*kufufua mila*), and that he regarded this event as an important step in this regard. A middle-aged man who works as a tailor by the main road asked to speak. He wanted to inform Peter that the people working in the shops and stalls along the main road supported what we had done and had been very excited the day before. He wanted Peter to know this and to tell him that he should not have any concerns over this. The conversation, which largely took place in Chagga while we butchered, cooked and ate, had imperceptibly switched to Swahili as the interaction assumed the form of a descent group meeting. Moreover, the concern was to remove any lingering doubts over what we had done and thus aimed to achieve a determination of this as an event of a particular kind. Here too, language was hence deployed to determine the transfers and transformations of *horu* that the event involved, and to channel these in particular directions for specific purposes.

At this point, the meat, broth, blood and beer were gone. It was therefore suggested that those who were not directly involved in the *mila* should leave, so that we could finish. Soon, only those who went to Witini remained, together with the female elder of culture and the most senior female elder. The elder of culture was handed the spoon and the milk gourd that Peter so far had handled on their behalf. However, she said she was not able to pour milk on the ground (*iwikiya marua sumbai ngidima ku*). Peter and the others pressed her and asked her how she can be *mzee wa utamaduni* if she cannot do this. In her defence, she said that she had been appointed and had not volunteered for that role. Peter asked if she wanted him to do it for her, but she had the senior female elder in mind. There was also discussion regarding where the milk should be poured. Peter suggested it should be at the lower end of the blood-smeared banana leaves on which the pile of chyme rested, but the senior female elder asked which direction the goat's head had been oriented. When Peter pointed uphill, she replied that the milk should be poured above the leaves (*iwikiya kudoswa*). The milk should hence be poured above or uphill (*fondoho*) to flow downhill or below (*siinde*), and thus move from where the rain is wanted to where it is expected to arrive from. The final act of the event thus reiterated how *horu* in one form was made to flow in a particular direction from where life force is hoped to arrive in another form.

The elder of culture crouched at the left-hand side of the butchering remains, while Peter and his brother hunched on the other, and the senior female elder stood below. She transferred milk from the gourd to the spoon, which Peter instructed her to pour on the ground while addressing *msheku* Matoni. She knew little of what to do and say, and Peter even accused her of sabotaging the event. She firmly denied this, but replied that said she was afraid (*ngihowa*), probably of the clergy and their reaction, if they found out. Nevertheless, she made the following address:

> You *msheku* Matoni, I have given you this milk, give it to the wife of Moonde and of Tengia and of Ndeserua and of Horombo and all the other female elders. We have made you sit in a place (*duwakudamira*) like we have done before, *hai na hai*, and the female elders of the homestead we request you (plural) see us (*mudulholhye soso*), your grandchildren and great-grandchildren, help us and heal (*mukire*) your grandchildren, *hai na hai*. We request rain for cultivation and *msheku* Matoni and wife of Moonde and other female elders, we request rain to bring cultivation, we do not request rain that kills.

She looked relieved when the ladle was empty, thinking she was done. Accordingly, she was not pleased when she was told to continue, but refilled the spoon and said:

> And if there are generations (*rika*) and if there is anything else, then this thing has come to make you sit here (*kishakudamira hadi*), and those of that generation shall say that the goats are finished, the cattle are finished, I request you elder Horombo and elder Matoni, help us, that

means the hunger has increased, the banana trees are finished, the goats are finished, we have nothing, *hai na hai*, request on our behalf with god (*uduiterewe kwa mungu*) that we get rain, let it not be rain that kills, but that brings food, give us food.

When she filled the spoon again, she was instructed to return life (*urie moo*):

Hai na hai and you the brides of the children (*waliawana*) of *msheku* Matoni, help us and we will help you, may we get a little something to

Figure 6.6. Female elder pouring milk on the ground.

multiply the grandchildren of that female elder, *hai na hai*, the owner of this place of Ndeserua (*monikiwaloki kwa Ndeserua hadi*) and you Ndeserua and *mangi* Augusti, father of my husband, and you *msheku* MaKimario and you of this place and that, and you male elders in the ground (*wameku wa sumbai*), help us, let us get a little something, may the rain come, may it not come to kill us, *hai na hai*.

At first, she spoke in a low voice and seemed uncomfortable with what she did. During the second statement, the others provided clues for what to say, which nearly drowned out her voice. It gave this event a polyphonic or cacophonous character too, which thus resembled what occurred around the chyme in the plains. Later, however, she spoke more clearly and her voice emerged as a singular force that entwined and accompanied the milk she poured. Her use of the notion of *idamira* entailed that the act enabled and occasioned the deceased to stay or sit in one place, while the verb-form she used (*ki-*) underscored that this is a process to which the powerful substance subjects the person. Her request that the milk should heal (*ikira*) the living entailed that the act of pouring it extends out of or unfolds from language-games that concern health and well-being, while her appeal that the living shall multiply echoed MaShirima's request that the homestead shall grow (see chapter two). In combination with the crops, livestock and food she mentioned, she thus requested and anticipated multiple outcomes from pouring the milk that would enable and effectuate the extension and continuation of dwelling and life. As she specified phenomena and processes that constitute dwelling and life, no-one was compelled to add the phrase 'I have returned life to you', despite her failure to utter those exact words. Instead, the powerful substance she poured and that intertwined her requests sufficed to channel *horu* so as to enable the continuation of dwelling and life for which they hoped.

The female elder of culture moved aside so Peter could pour beer beside the milk that was visible as a white blotch on the ground, above the leaves that contained the traces of butchering. While doing so, he said:

> This beer Horombo, this beer of the fields that have been opened or released (*kishamba kiharauka*), this beer Horombo Ukoni, we have ascended from the plains, you made us arrive safely, you woke us up well Horombo, we request some rain, do not give us rain that kills, give us rain to raise something to eat (*yedosa kando kelya*), the cattle are finished, the goats are finished, the banana trees are finished, and we the children of the grandchildren of Horombo and of Ndeserua do not dwell (*dukaa ku*), this is the only thing we request Horombo Ukoni, we request you sit with your wife and tell her that this is how the children

have cried to you, what shall they eat, see us at the homestead (*udulhol-hye na kunu kaa*), you *mangi* Tengia, let us be helped.

He poured beer into the gourd three additional times before he continued:

You have given us power (*ngufu*), today we sat again there by your trees, there where we sat yesterday, we went to rest and we woke up, if there is a bad thing (*kindo kiwiishwa*) let us know, but we encountered a good place (*kuusha*), give us again some power so that we can dwell again like we dwelled yesterday and dwell today (*duininge se kangufu dukae shali dulekaa iwo shali duwakaa lunu*), *hai* elder Ndeserua, you Maunga owner of this place, owners of the homesteads (*weniwamṛi*) and *mangi* Augusti and you who got lost and you who are wherever, it is you who know them so search for them, you have been given milk, go and eat *kena* now, if we do not get some rain, when the cows eat grass it gives birth and gets milk, where shall we get grass, where shall we get a thing like this one here?

He refilled the gourd and held forth:

We request you, protect us so your grandchildren and those who are wherever may eat and get full, we remember you today, and you remember us like we remembered you yesterday, you (plural) remember grass for us, *kena* and milk you have drunk, and beer you have drunk, and meat you have eaten here.

He filled the gourd a final time and ended by saying:

I have returned life to you Horombo, I have returned life to you Ukoni, I have returned life to you *mangi* Tengia, I have returned to you cattle and property or wealth (*mali*), my grandfather and you Ndeserua, I have returned life to you Matoni, the thing we request, we shall exert ourselves like we do here today, we remember you, so do remember us, we are dying, we are finished, we request god, you talk to him, may he bring us rain, you great one.

As Peter stated that the beer resulted from fields that were opened for cultivation, he enunciated how it was the effect of their horticultural and agricultural activities. He did so by using the notion of *iharauka*, which features when the person is opened or released during the *matanga*, as a prelude to and part of the discharge of the name that enables its extension into the future. Herman and MaLasway used the same notion, when they once complained about the exhausting heat and looked forward to the rains that 'will loosen or enliven the bones' (*mafuha neharauka*) and enable them to work.

Peter moreover requested rain to raise food in return for the beer. He thus reiterated that rain affords food to emerge, which in this case would result from the presentations of *horu*. He made the request by means of the causative form (*idosa*) of the verb 'to climb', 'ascend' or 'rise' (*idua*) that concerns the act of going up the mountain. Similarly, the female elder fashioned the preposition 'above' from a locative construction of the passive-causative form of the same verb (*kudoswa*), when she told Peter that the milk should be poured above the chyme. The implication was that the powerful substance would emanate from *mooshe* to flow downhill. These statements thus entailed that foods should rise and powerful substances flow as the effects of us climbing back up the mountain from the plains. In this way, it will enable them to dwell in the future, like they dwelled in the past to effectuate the powerful substances they presented. The use of *idosa* furthermore entailed that crops would rise from the resulting rains, just like houses emerge from each other to enable and require persons to climb or ascend (*idua*) the mountain as they toddle (*itongoria*) between homesteads.

Peter moreover reiterated a form employed in previous addresses, where questions are posed for the deceased and answers are hoped for in the form of rain and growth of fodder and foodstuffs. As the emergence of *horu* in different forms is anticipated in reply to the questions posed, the form underscores how language and life force entwine and transform. At the same time, the deceased are implored to see the living and look after them at the homestead. The statements and the substances they involve are hence another form of showing or making visible that enables the deceased to see the living and their situation, at the same time as their effects enable the living to see the capacities of their dwelling. As such, the addresses and prestations are requests, provisions and transformations of *horu* or *ngufu* in different forms that effectuate determinations of dwelling and life to enable their continuation and extension through time and space.

At the end, Peter took three small sips from the gourd and passed it on for the rest of us to taste. The *mrimwa* was over and the atmosphere elated, as people were eager to leave after two long days. We returned the benches and chairs to a nearby homestead, and the rest of the paraphernalia was carried away. The senior female elder shook our hands and commiserated with our effort before we left. An hour later, it rained heavily until darkness fell.

Waves of *Horu*, Waves of Rain

The statements and activities that occurred over those two days were efforts at enabling *horu* in different forms to move downhill, in anticipation that rain would arrive and move uphill to afford the growth of food and fodder, and allow production, reproduction and consumption. In the form of beer, meat, milk, blood and chyme, *horu* moved in one direction to attract rain in the other direction and facilitate transfers and transformations of *horu*. By deploying the effects of past dwelling and life, *kaa* and *moo* could in this way continue into the future to manifest as homesteads extending uphill.

However, the event at Witini and by Horombo's tall trees is just one of many occurrences that take place at other similar features that dot the mountainside.[7] Like the trees of Horombo, these are also called *kiungu* or *fiungu* in the plural and are left to grow, as their branches may not be cut for firewood or fodder. They are also often located beside or at the junction of the footpaths (*mko*) or roads (*shia*) that crisscross the area. As one walks through the landscape, one encounters these *fiungu*, which are immediately recognizable from their contrast to the cultivated trees that mark the boundaries (*mrasa*) between homesteads.[8]

The neighbours (*wamamrasa*) surrounding each *kiungu* gather irregularly to butcher an animal or pour beer and milk at its base with requests for rain to the *monikiwalo* and deceased relatives. It varies how often this occurs, depending on the inhabitants of the area. There has for instance been no activity at the *kiungu* near Ngufumari's homestead for a long time, while Lasway described how they gather each year to provide powerful foodstuffs by the *kiungu* near

Figure 6.7. *Kiungu* located beside a footpath on the mountain. Note its stark contrast to the pruned and slender character of the trees marking the boundary of the banana garden in the background.

their homestead. Such practices are in fact more prevalent in Shimbi, where traces of beer and milk or piles of chyme are frequently seen by the *fiungu*. However, I did participate in one such event in Keni in 2000, around the time Horombo's descent group went to Witini. On that occasion, the men from Boniface's descent group suffocated and butchered a small male *horo* goat beside a large stone at their meeting place, which is surrounded by their homesteads. The meat was cooked on a makeshift hearth next to the stone and *ndaswa* was placed at its foot with requests to their apical ancestor for rain. This event only involved the members of a single descent group, but they more commonly engage people from different *ukoo* who address each other as neighbour (*mamrasa*) and occupy the homesteads surrounding the *kiungu*. Like at Witini, the event gathers the participants around a particular geographical feature, where they deploy and channel *horu* in different forms to attract rain. When this replicates at multiple *fiungu* across the mountainside, the events serve to expand and amplify the wave of *horu* that is released in the plains below, where the rain is expected. When this occurs before and after the event at Witini, the rush of life force it sets in motion extends up and across the mountainside to afford a surge of *horu* in the form of rain without which dwelling and life are impossible.

Early ethnographic sources describe similar practices, which thus appear to have a longevity and temporal extension. Gutmann (1909c: 87) claimed that 'sacrifices' (*Opfern*) were conducted concurrently throughout the land at the order of the chief, when war threatened, hunger was to be avoided, a general misfortune haunted the land, or for events of general significance, such as the investiture of chiefs. These sacrifices took place at large stones that marked the graves of particular deceased persons, where goats were killed for those who were considered the founders of particular districts (*Bezirke*) and the originators of specific clans (*Sippe*). The Chagga term Gutmann translated as *Bezirke* was *mungo*, of which *kiungu* appears to be a diminutive form. Meanwhile the places where the events took place were called *fifu finini* or large or venerable tombs (*Grabmäler*). In addition, Gutmann (1909c: 87ff) claimed there were 'sacrificial centres' (*Opfermittelpunkte*) that concerned the entire land, where beer was poured at the grave of a particular person from whom the land derived its name and blood. This preceded the animal sacrifices by the *fifu finini* and involved two representatives from each district of the land. In accordance with this, our trip to Witini involved two persons from each administrative sub-village and was conducted for the sake of Horombo, who lent his name to Rombo District and shed his blood to defend the land, and was the originator of the former chiefly descent group. Finally, the event at Witini also occasioned a series of powerful prestations that multiplied at different locations to wash over the land.

Raum (1911: 171–72) also argued that 'sacrifices' on behalf of the apical ancestor of a clan were made by its living members on particular occasions. These occurred at the homestead the ancestor once occupied, which was called *kjungu* or *mungu*. No human dared fell a tree in such a homestead for fear of retribution, but if one were to topple, people realized that the deceased were angered, which occasioned deliberations by the chief and elders about whether a sacrifice was needed.[9] Moreover, when eleusine fields were to be cleared, if an epidemic occurred, or a war party was planned, the chief consulted a diviner to determine whether an offering was required for the 'spirits of the land' (*Landesgeistern*). According to Raum, these were the first settlers on the mountain or the ancestors of the chiefly clans, whose 'places of worship' (*Verehrungstätte*) were clusters of trees. Some of these were located in the plains, at the places the settlers first ascended and where the mountain-dwellers descended to present cattle, smallstock, beer, eleusine, honey, milk or tobacco. Raum's claim regarding the first settlers recalls the notion of *monikiwalo*, while the items presented are powerful substances that result from current dwelling and life. In accordance with the notion of 'returning life', both Gutmann's and Raum's accounts therefore suggest that these prestations were debts that the living owed the deceased for their existence, and that they provided in order to secure and extend dwelling and life for the future.

Raum's claim that these prestations were made when eleusine fields were cleared recalls and is reiterated by Peter's statement that the beer results from fields that had been opened (*kiharauka*). His diminutive term *kishamba* concerns the eleusine fields of the plains, while the statement entails and enunciates that such provisions of powerful substances enabled further agricultural activities. Relatedly, Gutmann (1909c: 96–97) described how the ground was 'pacified' (*befriedigt*) when the creation of a furrow required the construction of a dam to supply water. Such pacification was done by means of a concoction made from dried sheep chyme, banana flowers, a banana offshoot, honey and hyrax (*mbelele*) hair, as well as plants resembling those of the *mahande* whisk. However, the mix was not tossed or sprinkled, but scattered on the ground, which was implored to 'be cool like a hyrax'. The retention and direction of water was hence enabled by an act of cooling. While Gutmann does not provide the vernacular term, it seems likely that this concerned and involved the concept of *ihora* and substances and practices that resemble the *mahande*, which cool the homestead – *ihora kaa*. The claim gains support from Gutmann's (1909c: 93) account of how famine occasioned that the unopened stomach and intestines of a butchered animal were thrown in a water source with requests for rain, and his claim that such a source was known as *kjore* or 'place of life' - *Stätte der Lebenssetzung* (Gutmann 1926: 332).[10]

Once the furrows were constructed, beer was poured into them with requests for the person who first dug the channel to 'give us our water'. Moreover, when the furrow was reopened after its yearly cleaning and maintenance following the rainy season, an elder poured beer at the head of the furrow that diverted water from the river. The beer was poured just before the water was led in to wash the *wari* down the canal. The beer thus facilitated the diversion and direction of water towards people's homesteads for the purpose of irrigating the banana gardens to obtain fodder and foodstuffs. The provision of *horu* in one form afforded the elicitation and channelling of life force in another form to facilitate its transfers and transformations through dwelling and life. In this regard, it is significant that the Chagga term for water – *mringa* – also appears to derive from the term for vein and root – *mri*. The conceptual link accentuates how water is *horu* in another form that circulates through the veins and roots of persons and crops. These descriptions not only provide a historical depth to current practices, but furnish additional detail that deepens and underscores how water is *horu* in one form, whose flow and direction are facilitated by prestations of life force in other forms.

Raum (1911: 172) claimed that the chiefly prestations by the tall trees in the plains were 'political affairs', by which he meant that they transcended the concerns of the individual person. In a related vein, Steven Feierman (1990) explores the shifting ways in which political discourse of the nearby Shambaa revolves around the capacities of the chiefs and others to heal or harm the land by bringing or stopping the rain. These constitute the grounds for political power, as the capacity to extract tribute rests on the ability to facilitate or impede fertility. The fact that the event at Witini was conducted by the descendants of the former *mangi* who trace their ancestry to Horombo suggests that it too formed part of political power and privilege. It gains support from the way people contributed to the procurement of a bull for the same event in 2000, which could be understood as a form of tribute. Moreover, the term Feierman translates as political power is the Swahili term *nguvu*, whose vernacularized form – *ngufu* – Peter employed in one of his addresses and that sometimes substitutes for *horu*. In

2006, when the rains got off to a good start before they stopped early, people moreover attributed this to the newly elected President Jakaya Kikwete. Many contrasted the situation with the reign of the previous president Benjamin Mkapa and argued in Swahili that the rain showed that Kikwete had power (*ana nguvu*) and that the country was governed well (*nchi inatawaliwa vizuri*). In Chagga, meanwhile, others claimed that the rain showed that Kikwete was a 'true man' (*msoro lhoy*).

However, the idea that the event at Witini pertains to political power and affairs restricts the reach and import of these notions and practices. As I have shown, they rather concern the discharge and direction of *horu* for the purpose of affording and regulating rain, which is conceptualized as life force in one specific form. The power of the *mangi* and his descendants is hence not an ability to coerce subjects to do something they otherwise would not, but rather the ability to unleash and channel capacity (*horu*) for the purpose of enabling health and well-being. These phenomena extend beyond the domain of politics to encompass and concern life (*moo*) and the world with all its contents. Accordingly, Moore (1978: 40) argues that 'the Mangi was not only a secular head of the political system, but also responsible in mystical and religious ways for the well-being and perpetuation of his people'.[11] All persons channel and direct *horu* in different forms through different body parts, but the *mangi* could convey life force in the additional form of rain. He was thus a person writ large who like the precolonial Rwandan 'king' earned his legitimacy 'from his capacity to control the flows of substances along hierarchically defined trajectories' (Taylor 2005: 148). Along similar lines, Devisch (1988: 261) argues that 'the chief acts as the *supreme mediator* of the (re)generative processes in and between the cosmos, the land, the society and man: his solemn title is *kyaambvu*, "the bridge"', and de Boeck (1994b: 457) holds that the Luunda paramount is 'the lord of the soil' who 'enables the fertility and fecundity, the social and biological reproduction, and the material welfare of the community as a whole'. Like these, the *mangi* was a conduit that facilitated the health, well-being and fertility of people, livestock and crops, as he afforded the transfers and transformations of life force that permeated the cosmological realm, including meteorological phenomena like the rain and the sun. The Shambaa notion of 'covering the land' can thus be understood as the chief's ability to funnel and regulate the flow of capacity to ensure that it spans and contains or encompasses the land.

The idea that rain is *horu* in one form, whose movements and transformations these events facilitate, gains support from Sanders's

(2008: 153) claim from among the Ihanzu that 'water is said to be cooling, a life force, and something without which women could not give birth. In the form of rain, water allows crops to grow. As fertilizing fluid, it produces children'. In contrast to Ihanzu, however, the affordance of rain does not involve the conjunction of masculine and feminine forces, but the manipulation of a singular ungendered life-force, which is conveyed and converted in different forms to enable rain. It occurs for instance by means of the recurring gendered numbers, which channel and determine the uniform prestations of life-force that are placed or poured on the ground. Similarly, the way Peter wore and removed the *kanga* for the purpose of pouring *horu* in different forms did not concern the gendered character of these substances. Rather, it revealed that gender is the effect of the deliberate retention, release and direction of *horu* in specific forms for particular purposes. Gender is therefore not a basic character and aspect of the world, but a further effect of the transfers and transformations of a uniform life-force that permeates dwelling, animates life and constitutes the world.

The argument that rain is *horu* in one form that pervades the landscape gives new sense to the report by the Leipzig Mission Inspector Martin Weishaupt (1912: 431) that drought was blamed on the telegraph lines between Tanga and Moshi, which restricted the rain from reaching Kilimanjaro. In Hasu's (1999: 190) view, this was an example of how modern technological devices were seen as the origin of misfortunes that imperilled fertility. By contrast, this ethnography suggests that the telegraph lines were an impediment across the horizon that inhibited the movements of *horu* between geographical locations. These would have involved the places invoked by Ludovic when he cooled or cleansed the cooking pot curse, and by Mamocha when we placed meat on the chyme at Witini. Significantly, both included in this regard Murukuti, where Horombo was killed. The idea that language-games concerning rain and fertility entangled new phenomena gains support from Gutmann's (1926: 307–8) report of how people complained that the ground or soil (*Erdboden*) had no nourishment (*Nahrung*) after European rule (*teri ja maheri ha Wasungu ikiwodese kandofo*). The vernacular phrase involves and concerns the concept and substance of soil (*teri*), while the verb *iwodese* appears to be a dialectical version deriving from *idua* – to climb, ascend or rise – meaning that colonial rule inhibited crops from rising or emerging from the ground. Combined with current claims regarding Kikwete, the accounts are not primarily proof that the event at Witini is a political concern. Instead, they reveal how the grammars of *horu*, dwelling and life provide resources for conceptualizing and addressing national politics and calamitous events, like the colonial conquest (see also Vokes 2009).

Precolonial Power, Christian Gods

The conception of these events as processes that discharge and direct life force, which permeates corporeal, social and cosmological phenomena, allows for a reconsideration of the Chagga concept of *ruwa* that the early ethnographers translated as 'god'. Raum (1911: 171) for instance speculated that the notion of *kjungu* derives from the Bantu word for 'god' (*mungu*), which the Chagga had replaced with *ruwa*. Apparently in line with this, Peter and Mamocha used both terms interchangeably at Witini, where they asked Horombo to intercede on their behalf with *mungu* and *ruwa* before our trip ended at the *kiungu*, where additional requests were made.

However, the translation of *ruwa* as 'god' is the result of peculiar colonial interpretations and projections, where the early ethnographers played a part. Dundas (1924: 107) thus opened his chapter on 'religion' by arguing: 'The Chagga name for God is *Ruwa*, identical with their word for the Sun. But whether the God and the Sun are identical, or whether the Sun is the dwelling-place of the God, is a question they do not seem to be clear on themselves'. Raum (1911: 193), meanwhile, claimed: 'The Chagga speak in the same breath about *Ruwa* as the sun – *Ruwa* goes up, *Ruwa* goes down, *Ruwa* is shining strong – and of *Ruwa* as a godly being: *Ruwa* has created the humans, etc.'. The Judeo-Christian influence is evident in accounts of *ruwa* as an unknowable and indeterminate transcendent being: 'Though the God takes little part in the lives of humans, he is yet supreme above all other powers and the ultimate arbiter of fate' (Dundas 1924: 107). Relatedly, Raum (1911: 194) claimed that 'obviously there are certain traits that *Ruwa* is equipped with. But they give forth a shadowy sketch, not a picture', before he proclaimed that *ruwa* is great and his powers boundless. The biblical influence persists in contemporary accounts that rely on these missionary and colonialist tales, like in Anza Lema's (1999: 41–43) description of *ruwa* as an omniscient, omnipotent supreme being, and his claim that 'his infinite greatness was revealed in his work as Creator, Sustainer and Judge of all'.[12]

In contrast to elsewhere, the conception of *ruwa* as a 'god' and a subject of a 'religion' did not result from attempts to discover a 'native religion' that the missionaries could denounce in opposition to Christianity (Green 1995: 40). Instead, it formed part of Protestant *Volks-*

mission efforts to discover a vernacular concept by means of which the Christian god could be translated and proselytized. For Gutmann at least, the vernacular notion of *ruwa* was not a matter for rejection, but proof of a primordial religion based on organic sociality. He thus argued that the sacrificial centres were 'places where the general interests of the land also found a general religious centre' (Gutmann 1909c: 88). The Protestants therefore co-opted the concept of *ruwa*, which remains the term for the Christian god in the areas where these missionaries settled in central Kilimanjaro. As the Catholics relied on Swahili for their work, they employed the term *mungu* instead.

However, an alternative conception of *ruwa* that concerns the transfers and transformations of *horu* can be gleaned from the early ethnographic descriptions. Raum (1911: 194), for instance, argued that 'atmospheric effects' were the only area where *ruwa* could not be confused with the ancestors: 'Rain and drought, that occasion famine, obviously come from above'. Mareale (1965: 58), meanwhile, claimed: 'A sacrifice was also made to Ruwa during a famine or an epidemic, when sacrifices by the witch-doctors to the other gods had failed. On these occasions, the Mangi (chief) would join in praying to Ruwa to remove the calamity from the land'. Like Gutmann (1909c: 88), Dundas (1924: 150) argued that it was the generalized nature of epidemics, droughts and famines that summoned offerings for the land as a whole: 'Now there is only one spirit or ancestral line with whom the whole country has any tie, and this is the ancestral line of the Chief. Any epidemic, famine, drought or other general calamity, may be attributed to the anger of the Chief's ancestors who have not been given the animals sent on Earth by them'. Dundas's claim suggests that this involves a form of debt, where the living return livestock that the deceased provided. The living thus return life, which they owe the *mangi* and his ancestors whose position turns on the ability to convey and control the movement of beings and substances, and redress epidemics, famines and droughts (cf. Taylor 2005: 148).

In line with this, Gutmann (1913: 486) claimed that the *mangi* was the 'master of the weather', but also described how the chief requested a rainmaker to provide rain by sending gifts of meat and beer. His description of the latter's activities resembles the 'washing of the cooking pot' and the 'cooling of the homestead', as stagnant water, specific wild plants and blood from a sheep were mixed in a cooking pot with an ostrich feather, while the rainmaker spat and uttered a statement that included the names of the surrounding hills and mountains. If these efforts failed, the rainmaker approached the *mangi* and urged him to make an offering to his ancestors, or divination could reveal that the absence of rain was due to an envious 'rainbinder', whom the *mangi* could grant the rainmaker permission to curse by means of a *nungu* (Gutmann 1913: 487; see also Widenmann 1899: 34).

As a last resort, the rainmaker could instruct the *mangi* to make an offering to *ruwa* for which a goat was provided by one of his subjects. At the chiefly homestead, this goat was hoisted onto the roof of the house, so its back was directly above the doorway. The rainmaker kneeled over the goat and took a mouthful of beer from a gourd, which he spat four times towards the sky with the words: 'Sun, my chief, let the rain come down on us here below' (Gutmann 1913: 487). He repeated the request by means of milk, before he stabbed the goat in the heart and the carcass was brought down to the courtyard. The animal body was halved; one half belonged to the rainmaker and the other was the share of the old man assisting him. An animal was thus placed on its back (*moongo*) and aligned with the doorway (*moongo*) of the house before the rainmaker spat powerful substances towards the sky and stabbed the animal, whose blood presumably trickled down over, into and out of the doorway. Different powerful substances were hence made to move out of and into the doorway of the *mangi*'s house, at the same time as a request was made to *ruwa* for rain to flow from above (*fondoho*) and onto the people below (*siinde*). Like in various contemporary practices, *horu* in certain forms were directed out of the doorway of the house, in return for which *ruwa* was requested and anticipated to provide rain. The actions thus reiterate how rain is *horu* in one form that partakes in the transfers and transformations that occur through different *moongo* in dwelling and life.

In this respect, it is intriguing that the noun *ruwa* appears to derive from the verb *iruwa*, which means 'to be open'. *Ruwa* then does not designate a heavenly being, as the early ethnographers maintained, but an opening that facilitates the movement of rain, as an effect of powerful substances that move through doorways and down the mountainside. It gains support from Dundas's (1924: 168) description of how the rainmaker employed a particular pot that enabled the rain to fall, as long as its mouth was turned towards the sky. Just as *horu* emerges as soft foods from the mouths of cooking pots, so it comes forth as rain from cosmological openings (*ruwa*) that imbricate the *nungu*. Moreover, the term *uřuka* that Gutmann (1909c: 89) translated as 'land', and which he claimed the deceased gave the *mangi* on the basis of the offerings by the *fifu finini*, appears to derive from the stative form *iruka* of the verb *iruwa*. If so, this means that the land itself concerns a state of openness, across and through which *horu* may move, so that crops can rise and persons extend in time and space.[13]

Accordingly, Gutmann (1913: 505) described atmospheric phenomena like the sun and the moon as 'growth-enhancing powers' (*wachstumsfördernden Mächte*) that relate to the life forces (*Lebenskräfte*) of livestock and crops. Broadly in line with this, Ruel (1997: 237) argued that the sun (*irioba*) is a 'force of life' and that the central concern of Kuria religion is with 'the life or well-being given by the Sun, figuring deity; or, more directly, the relationship between people and ordered growth'. Sanders (2008: 120), meanwhile, describes how the Ihanzu notion of *mũnyankalĩ* was used to mean either god or a spirit, but its manifestation was the sun, which in invocations was implored to receive offerings on its journey between the houses of his two wives in the east and the west. In return, those making the offerings requested rain to afford the growth of crops and the birth of children (Sanders 2008: 130). *Mũnyankalĩ* appears to be a cognate of *monikiwalo* and *ruwa* appears to relate to *irioba*, which not only designates the sun but also means 'the above' and the sky. Even if they rely on Judeo-Christian notions and suppositions, Ruel and Sanders nevertheless reveal regional resonances and cognate forms.

The notion of opening was underscored, as Dundas (1924: 108) claimed that *ruwa* had released humans from a mysterious vessel from the aperture of which they presumably emerged. Combined with the notion of *horu*, it accords with the idea that persons exist as life force in a certain form and become as the effects of its movements and transformations that issue from and occur between openings of different kinds. Indeed, the vectorial character of the person entails that it has the form of a vessel that gains and releases *horu* in different forms through different parts of the body. Accordingly, Raum (1911: 197) and Marealle (1965: 57) described how the homestead's owner gave thanks to *ruwa* by uttering a statement and spitting towards the sky every morning and evening.[14] Elders and adults in present-day Rombo recount how their fathers performed such practices in the past, when they were children. In light of the above, such spitting concerns and constitutes an activity where persons insert themselves in and direct the movements of *horu* that permeate dwelling and animate life to constitute the world. It is underscored by the example Widenmann (1899: 32) gave of such a 'morning prayer' (*Frühgebet*), which resembles and reiterate Peter's invocations, as *Erua* is thanked for his protection and requested to provide something to eat. Meanwhile, Gutmann (1926: 114) described how the bride's first menstruation at the marital homestead compelled her groom's mother to spray water with her mouth onto a child, while saying: 'Pooh, the rain'. The practice accentuates how rain and water are *horu* in one form, whose movements involve the transfers and transformations of other powerful substances. The mouth and gullet thus imbricate other openings, like those of cooking pots and houses, which hence may be manipulated to afford the rain. The role of these anatomical features in relation to rain reveals how the entrails may manifest this meteorological phenomenon and chyme can afford its arrival (Dundas 1924: 142; Gutmann 1909c: 93; Widenmann 1899: 34).

The interchangeable use of *mungu* and *ruwa* by Peter and Mamocha does not corroborate colonial claims that *ruwa* was a pre-Christian deity. It rather suggests that Christianity became entangled in existing language-games concerning the transfers and transformations of *horu* that occur between heaven and earth, and the dead and the living, through dwelling and life. Christopher Taylor (2005: 145) similarly describes how the Catholic missionaries appropriated a Rwandan term and thereby substituted a notion of 'diffuse fecundating fluid' with the Christian God. Something similar occurred in Kilimanjaro, but there 'God' appropriated and transposed the concept of an opening through which life force flows in the form of rain. The imbrication between the grammar of dwelling and that of Christianity subtended Peter's use of the term *sadaka* to mean the bull we removed from Haula's house, and the verb *kubariki* in his request that Horombo should bless those who had come to Witini. It is also evident from the way people argue that the altar of the church is like the *mbuho* since both contain relics in the form of bones. These claims form part of further comparisons between deceased relatives and Catholic saints, who both act as intermediaries for the living. The deceased intercede through requests, prestations and commensality, whose terms, practices and material forms people compare with prayer, Collect and Holy Communion. Thus, in 2001, the outstation choir had prepared and practised a Chagga hymn, in which they sang that the congregation was gathered at the *kiṛaoni* or the place in the house where milk and beer are poured on the ground. When Nico removed the stone from the *mnyengele* that Herman had fetched to bury at his homestead, he made a statement that started in Swahili with a clear resemblance and reiteration of church prayers before it lapsed into Chagga and the form of an ancestral invocation, where notions like *idamira, kaa, iira* and *hai na hai* featured. These imbrications also underpin the enthusiasm for holy water, which was tossed on Valeria's grave and occasionally may replace *mahande.* They were also activated when the Kamba departed in the plains, and we shook hands and said 'peace of the lord' (*amani ya bwana*) and 'peace of Christ' (*amani ya Kristo*). These acts and statements reiterated the Catholic sign of peace that follows the

Eucharist prayer, and thus tapped into the language-game of the Mass to bolster the family resemblances between Catholic practices and ancestral prestations. The sign of peace succeeds the Collect in church, where people provide something prior to communal consumption, which they claim resemble *mrimwa*. For *mrimwa*, you first present and then consume powerful foodstuffs of different kinds, while in church you chiefly provide money and then eat the Communion wafer.[15] The perceived and emphasized similarities hinge on the transfers and transformations of life force, as money is an effect of *horu* you provide with your hand for which you receive something to ingest through your mouth. Like dwelling, Christianity turns on a concept of transformation, where a transcendent deity assumes a human form, whose death affords eternal life on those who follow. Moreover, the funeral liturgy proclaims that the earthly life of those followers arises from and reverts to ashes and dust, or the soil (*udongo*) as it is rendered in Swahili, from which food and fodder rise. Transformation is particularly acute in connection with Communion, where Catholics hold that the priest transubstantiates bread and wine into flesh and blood. Both *mrimwa* and Communion thus involve the deployment and transformation of *horu* for the purpose of extending dwelling and life. These similarities and differences incited the clergy and evangelicals to decry the activities at Witini as the worship of other gods or the devil, while others praised it as an appeal to the Christian god. Regardless of whether this god is conceptualized as a supreme being or a conduit of life force, many argue that the deceased can mediate with it better than the Catholic saints because their existing relationships make them amenable 'to request someone by means of something' (*iterewa mdu na kindo*). The complex relationships between these notions and practices occasioned conflicting claims, where even church stewards enabled and praised those who went to Witini, while others like the female elder of culture experienced doubt and insecurity, as they feared the priests and their reactions.

A Cool State, a Clean State, a State of Plenty

When Peter poured milk at the foot of Horombo's *kiungu*, he requested rain that would bring *kambora*, which I translated as 'a little plenty'. *Kambora* is the diminutive form of *mbora*, which is used in the plural to mean 'plenitude' or 'abundance', and often features as an exclamation concerning an affluence of crops, livestock or children. However, *mbora* is also used to mean a fecund unmarried woman and the stem of a banana tree, which each have a capacity to occasion additional iterations, and further the growth of humans, homesteads, livestock and crops. Relatedly, *mbora yasha* – plenitudes have come – is uttered when rain falls in abundant amounts that allow fodder and crops to grow, and animals and people to be fed.

The concept and state of *mbora* is a cognate of the Sukuma-Nyamwezi notion of *mhola*, which Per Brandström (1990: 167–68) describes in terms that recall and reiterate many elements from this ethnography:

> Most important, to secure life and its various demands, the state of *mhola* must be attained, maintained, and, over and over again, reattained ... *mhola* is the 'cool' state, the state of peace and good relations between the living and between the living and the dead, where the women conceive, the herds and flocks multiply and the land yields fruit. *Mhola* carries a notion of wholeness and completeness and refers to the desirable state of life in a most comprehensive sense. Health, prosperity, peace and everything good in life belong to the realm of *mhola*.

Brandström's account evokes the notions of *ikaa* and *moo*, as *mhola* concerns a state where different activities nest as transformations of each other to afford the becoming and constitute the being of persons, livestock and crops. Moreover, the idea that *mhola* is to be attained and maintained recalls Gutmann's (1935: 8) claim that 'all the ingredients of community life grow out of undivided protoplasm. But without the stimulus to activity they wither away'. As argued earlier, Gutmann's claim most likely concerns the notion of *horu*, while Brandström's claim that *mhola* is a 'cool' state connects to the concept of *ihora*, which features when the homestead is cooled or cleansed after burial.

The idea of cleansing moreover occurs in the notion of *isambiya nungu*, which Ludovic performed at Julius's homestead by means of substances and activities that also feature in *ihora kaa*. Their link was underscored when Ludovic tossed the *mahande* on the participants and used the concepts of *ihoreria* and *iholholhya*, which also derive from *ihora*. *Ihoreria* is a causative-prepositional form that can be rendered as 'to make cool or clean by or for something or someone', while *iholholhya* is an intensive or double prepositional form that means 'to cool or cleanse intensively' or 'to cool or cleanse with and for something'.[16] *Iholholhya* is furthermore used regarding a sick person to mean that his or her state has improved, but that he or she is not fully recovered.[17] It is an active form that concerns a process the person goes through, while the passive form *ihororwa* is used in the same way to mean a process he or she is made to go through. Both forms concern how the recovered person is a transformed subject, who undergoes a process to achieve a state of health and well-being.

Herman moreover used the causative form *ihorera* in the imperatives *ahorere* and *wohorere*, when he poured beer on the ground after bringing the stone to his homestead, and when he pronounced that his son carried the name of his wife's father's deceased older brother. By means of these terms, Herman implored the deceased to be cool and to cool the problem that stemmed from the name without a bearer. Meanwhile, Nico used the imperative *mohorere* as he urged the dead to sit and eat and cool the homestead, when he rubbed eleusine onto the goat that we then butchered. *Ihorera* is in addition used for the removal of any kind of curse, and occurs in situations where 'bad things' are removed by tossing the *mahande*. *Ihorera mawiishwa* is therefore occasionally used instead of *ifuna mawiishwa*. One example would have been the tossing of *mahande* that Herman and MaSway deemed necessary if the adulterous couple had had sex in the banana garden. Another would have been the tossing of *mahande* after the woman split and burnt a piece of wood from the marital bed or when the husband dismantled it and placed it outside the house. Like when Herman poured beer on the ground, *ihorera* is also used to mean the act of presenting powerful substances to the deceased in more or less ceremonial settings and forms, which otherwise is indicated by the phrase *irunda mrimwa*. People render *irunda mrimwa* in Swahili as 'to perform customs' (*kufanya mila*), but Herman's and Nico's uses of the imperative – *horere* – reveal that the act of pouring a powerful substance serves to cool the deceased and their problem, as well as the homestead they share with the living. In return, they request *horu* in other forms that will realize *mbora* or a cool state of health and well-being, where beings of different kinds emerge and reiterate to extend dwelling and life through time and space.

Ihora and its derivative forms hence concern states and processes of cooling, cleansing, curing and ceremoniality. Like many notions considered in this book, these are also to be found in the early ethnographic sources, where Gutmann and Raum variously translated *yolora* as 'to atone', 'to make good' and 'to calm', but also acknowledged that it means 'to cool'. Raum (1907: 287) recognized that *yolora* was derived from the notion of *yora*, and his informant Yohane Msando described the *mhanga* as a person who possessed 'magic' that 'calms' and 'cools' (*yolora*) illness (Raum 1911: 203). Redolent of what occurred when Ludovic banished the cooking pot curse, he moreover described how the 'medicine man' spat water onto the head of a person suffering from headache and implored it 'to be cool' like the hyrax or *mbelele*, while he listed the rivers and mountains of the area (Raum 1911: 204).[18] Meanwhile, Gutmann (1913: 480) hinted at the notion of *horu* when he described how the inhabitants of a dwelling owed a libation to the 'master of the homestead' (*menikihamba*) who calmed or cooled the life forces of the ground (*Lebenskräfte der Erde*), and were required to soothe the 'terrestrial soul-power' (*irdische Seelenkraft*) by interspersing the banana trees with certain calming plants, such as dracaena, *ndishi* or the short *mhoyo* bananas, and *mnyengele*.[19] According to Gutmann, people described these activities with the words: '*Ngaolora idema il i l ilawave*: "I cool this plot, in order that it does not bring forth pain"'. Such cooling was hence an act of *yolora*, which involved prestations of powerful foodstuffs and the planting of cultivars that play integral parts in *mrimwa* and divination. It resembles Herman's act of *ihorera*, while the exhortation that the land shall not bring forth pain reiterates MaShirima's request that fever (*homa*) shall be turned away from the homestead as a result of pouring milk on the ground. Some of the calming plants Gutmann mentioned feature destructively in cursing, where they occasion and register diversions of *horu* to harm the inhabitants of a specific homestead, which in turn require interventions like *ihora* or its derivate forms. It underscores how these notions and practices pertain to the ambivalent and ambiguous transfers and transformations of *horu* that permeate dwelling and animate life.

Gutmann (1926: 425ff.) moreover revealed how these phenomena encompassed barter and trade, as the market-place needed to be 'cooled' (*entsühnt*), if business was hindered for one or more days. A ewe was then butchered and the entire market-place 'cleansed' (*gereinigt*) by means of the animal's blood and chyme, which were mixed and sprinkled as 'cooling water' (*Sühnewasser*). Redolent of how spouses are reconciled after a fight in present-day Rombo (see chapter two), such cooling was especially important when blood was spilled at the market-place. For such a 'bad thing' (*böse Ding*), a goat had to be butchered, and all the people and the goods cooled, before they could leave and the items be used for food. The notion of a 'bad thing' recalls the concept of *mawiishwa*, while the way in which *ihora* thus also concerned barter and trade evokes how cars are currently cooled and cleansed, and the notion of *horu* extends to encompass money as one of its forms.

According to Gutmann (1926: 430), even more extensive and serious cooling was required, if a woman gave birth or aborted at the market-place. A milk cow was then butchered and both the market-place and the *mangi*'s homestead were cooled, and *Jande* was sprinkled on all the women district by district. Similarly, Raum (1911: 163) described how *yolora* also featured in connection with pregnancy out of wedlock, which required that the male lover provide two goats 'to cool' the situation. Unfortunately, he did not describe the proceedings, but the conjecture that it involved blood and chyme gains support from his account of a peace-making oath (Raum 1907: 287). The oath was made by tying the parties together with a rope, which was placed across the stomach of a goat and cut in a sudden movement to bring forth blood that was sprinkled onto the participants. Breaking the oath could occasion an epidemic, which a diviner determined and prevented by smearing and 'cooling' the rope with blood and chyme from a slaughtered sheep (Raum 1907: 288). The offending party was also cooled with an 'atoning liquid' called *mande*, which a 'medicine man' tossed on them with a whisk, while saying: 'Today I atone you, so that you shall be clean (cool) like the *mbelele*'. The *mande* did not consist of blood and chyme from butchered livestock, but blood from wild animals and certain dried plants that were reconstituted in beer. Differences obtain, but the similarities to the tossing of *mahande* belie an intervening century and its demographic and social changes. Moreover, the imbrications of similarities and difference are amenable to description in terms of language-games involving family resemblance notions that derive from *ihora* and regard states and situations of health and well-being.

The depth and significance of these phenomena are underscored by the very first sources from this area. Thus, Rebmann described how he was kept waiting for days, until he was permitted to see *mangi* Mamkinga: 'The sorcerers were the cause of this delay. I was told, that on the arrival of a stranger a medicine must be compounded out of a certain plant, or a tree fetched from a distance, mixed with the blood of the sheep or the goat, from which the king himself makes the Kishogno for his guest. And what is to be done with this mixture? The stranger is besmeared or besprinkled with it, before he is allowed to come into the presence of the king' (Krapf 1860: 251).[20] Von der Decken similarly described how Munie Wesiri cleansed the path leading into his camp before the *mangi* could meet him: 'Holding a dark tube or bottle made from leather, he approached and sprayed a dirty liquid onto the tents, huts, and people by means of a cow's tail he dipped into it' (Kersten 1869: 293). If the Baron had reservations, the people around him stretched out their hands to receive some of the 'blessing mixture' (*segenbringenden Mischung*).

While neither Rebmann nor von der Decken mentioned the use of chyme, it features in Charles New's (1873: 371ff) account of his reception at the boundary of Old Moshi. He refused to undergo the *ku hossa* ceremony that would allow him to enter the area, so the female *mganga* or 'sorceress' who met his entourage suggested they submit to *uvumba*, 'a potion she had prepared from various herbs'. New refused this too, so 'all but our party were well christened with the liquor, whatever it was; the paths were treated in the same manner, and then we were led forward. A little ahead we found that a sacrifice had been performed, a goat having been killed, and its entrails strewn on the path. At this point I received a christening *nolens volens*, the people imagining, no doubt, that it warded off some evil from them' (New 1873: 372). Chyme or *mooshe* was hence used at the boundaries to cleanse people arriving from outside, in order to remove or prevent bad things that could emerge or arrive along the paths to affect the *mangi*, the people and the place in which they dwell. Similarly, Gutmann (1909b: 98) reported that the threat of war was countered by animal offerings on the pathways leading into the area to prevent the enemy from entering. These accounts suggest notions and activities that resemble *ihora* and its derivatives, yet also mention phenomena like *mrasa*, *mawiishwa* and *shia* that remain prevalent for the transfers and transformations of *horu*, and hence dwelling and life.

In this regard, it is significant that Raum (1907: 275) called attention to rain, as he recalled von der Decken's account of how the Taita wished to butcher a goat and make a *kishong'u* to rectify the rain that they claimed had stopped due to the arrival of the Europeans. Rebmann also considered rain, as he related: 'I was commanded to remain in my dark hut, whilst out of doors the victim was being strangled, not only for my behoof, but to serve in the production of rain. And in very deed it so fell out that the sorcerer had scarcely completed his ceremonial, when amid thunder the rain began to fall in torrents, and the deluded spectators were excited to honour the fortunate magician with the words: "Hei muanga wa Mangi! hei Muanga wa Mangi!" – Well done, O sorcerer of the king! Muanga (sorcerer) is a title of honour in Jagga' (Krapf 1860: 252). Rebmann continued: 'When the rain began to fall I was summoned to leave my hut, and while I stood beneath its lower opening, the sorcerer without asking my permission bespattered my face and the front part of my body with this filthy mixture, using a cow's tail for the purpose'. Rebmann hence watched how an animal was strangled in front of the doorway to make rain, before he was made to stand in front of the doorway and be besprinkled with a liquid that most likely contained chyme and blood. He thus witnessed how an animal was brought out of the house and the blood and chyme everted from its body, so they could be tossed onto him when he emerged from the doorway.[21]

The prefix of New's term *ku hossa* suggests that it is either a locative construction of a dialect form of *ihora* or a notion encountered en route to Kilimanjaro, where cognate notions use the infinitive marker *ku-* rather than *i-*. Thus, Parkin (1991a: 257) reports that the Giriama verb *kuhasa* translates as 'to bless', even though it also means 'to repair' and 'to heal', and yields the noun *muhasa* which means 'medicine'. Cognates of *ihora* and its derivatives have even wider geographical distribution, as Agnes Hoernlé (1937: 233) shows, when she describes similar practices from southern Africa on the basis of Henri Junod's (1927) ethnography:

> Among the Shangana-Tonga, the final ritual in connection with the possessed diviners is the *hondlola* (purification rite) which takes place after any severe illness. The body is 'cleansed' from top to toe with the stomach contents of the sacrificed animal, with which have been mixed drugs of all kinds, and the particles which drop off on to the mat are carefully collected and hidden in some place. This finally buries the sickness, as it were.

Hondlola appears to derive from *hola*, which in Luc de Heusch's (1980: 30) view concerns both the recovery of a sick person and the cooling down of a newly fired cooking pot.[22] Similarly, Jean Comaroff (1985: 68) draws on Willoughby (1928) to argue that the Tshidi term *go hodisa* means both 'to cool' and 'to heal', and concerns an acquired skill that tempers the contagious heat of illness. Indeed, Adam Kuper (1982: 20) claims the entire region is marked by the fact that 'the same word means "to cool" and "to heal" (*hola* in Tswana, *phola* in Zulu, etc.)', and that 'cattle dung is a cooling and healing agent, and the chyme and gall-bladder of a sacrificed beast have powerful beneficent properties'. His claim is supported by Malcolm Guthrie (1970: 163), who argues that the proto-Bantu form *-pód-* has yielded root-forms like *-hor-*, *-hol-*, *-holer-*, *-pol-* and *-phol-*, which variously mean 'to become cool or cool down', 'to become cured, get well', and 'to become quiet'. But where Guthrie's argument concerns different languages, the ethnography from Rombo reveals how several of these forms and meanings occur in the same place, where they variously concern cooling, cleansing, curing and ceremonial activities that include pouring powerful foodstuffs on the ground. Moreover, Guthrie's claim that one meaning is 'to become quiet' gives sense to Peter's repeated assertions that they had made noise regarding the drought, which implied that they would become quiet if the rains arrived. Similarly, we sang on our return from Witini that the cattle bellowed due to the drought, and thus implied they would become quiet if the rains arrived. Furthermore, Nico requested that the person we brought and emplaced at Herman's homestead should dwell quietly, and Peter admonished his brother that we should sit quietly by the *mbuho*. As both the latter events involved pouring and placing powerful substances on the ground, they suggest that dwelling and life both involve and facilitate a cool, clean and calm state of plenty where *horu* converts and conveys to constitute capacity, health and well-being, and manifest and emplace persons, houses, livestock and crops.

As the least elaborate verb-form, *ihora* is most likely the root that forms the basis for the adjective *-holo* or 'soft' and the noun *horu* or 'life force'. It is most likely also the root for other notions that also concern or involve movements of life force, such as *msoro* or 'man', *horo* or 'whole male goat', *ioru* or 'stream', and its related term *kjore* or the 'place of life' that is a source of water (Gutmann 1926: 332). It is also at the root of *boru* or 'manure', which according to Moore (1976: 363) 'had peaceful, cooling, fertility-causing, life-bringing in it', and is strikingly similar to the Kuria notion of *obohoro*. If the verb *ihora* means 'to cool or cleanse', and the noun *horu* does not concern some*thing* but transfers and transformations that allow something to be, then it concerns cool or clean movements or interactions that afford beings of different kinds in a calm manner that quiets people and livestock and actualizes a state of plenty – *mbora*.

Notes

1. Executive meetings take place within the ward offices, while public meetings are conducted on the open space outside the building. This is adjacent to and overlaps with the space where people used to gather for the *baraza*, facing Tengia and the colonial officials who were seated on the small veranda in front of the doorway.
2. The village criers normally announce public meetings of different kinds, most commonly for the village or the ward.
3. A *kanga* is a printed piece of fabric, which women wear in pairs throughout eastern Africa.
4. The Kamba elder said he knew it had to be three globs of blood because the event was on behalf of a man. His statement suggests either that the same gendered numbering obtains among both Kamba and Chagga, or that he wanted to demonstrate that he knows Chagga *mrimwa*. In either case, the statement testifies to the contact and circulation of persons and ideas across ethnic and linguistic boundaries in this area.
5. *Kishiini* is a diminutive form of *ushiini*, which is another term for the *mbaariko* area, where the gourds were kept and the milk curdled in the grass-houses. As described in chapter four, this is where informants claim that women were buried inside the house.

6. Gutmann (1909c: 90) described similar phenomena.
7. In some areas, they are performed near large stones instead of tall trees, but these are exceptional cases rather than the rule. However, Widenmann (1899: 35) described offerings at the foot of large trees or stones in particular locations, often by streams or crossroads.
8. To give a sense of their frequency, Herman and I passed between five and ten such trees on the roughly seven-kilometre walk along the footpaths between his homestead and that of the diviner MaKawishe at Mkuu.
9. Horombo's descendants today say exactly the same thing regarding the tall trees he allegedly planted.
10. According to Gutmann (1926: 334), the initiates moreover received their new names from such a source, which underscores how language entwines and flows along with *horu* in the form of water.
11. I hasten to add that this in my view is neither mystical nor religious, but concerns material transfers and transformations that are conceptualized in terms of *horu*.
12. In earlier sources, both Rebmann (Krapf 1860: 239) and Widenmann (1899: 31) reported that *rua, irua, erua* or *eruwa* meant god, which the Chagga identified or equated with the sun. Widenmann moreover argued that *ruwa* was omniscient and all-seeing. Sanders (2008: 118) makes a surprisingly similar argument, claiming that the Ihanzu *itunda*, which supplanted a cognate of *ruwa* (*lyoa*), is an omnipresent and determining, yet elusive and inscrutable presence that created the world and all it contains.
13. In a manner that relates to this claim and the activities at Witini, Widenmann (1899: 34) described an apparently vernacular understanding of rain, as emerging or originating from the sea, from which it extends across or over the land, and falls when god wishes.
14. Ruel (2000:82) describes a similar practice from among Kenyan Kuria.
15. I say chiefly, since crops and sometimes even goats are included in the Collect.
16. The same verb-form is involved in 'to see' – *ilholhya*.
17. *Ngaholholhya* is rendered in Swahili as *nimepata nafuu*.
18. He claimed that the blood of the hyrax has a cooling capacity.
19. Gutmann translated the possessive noun *menikihamba* as *Heimstätten-herr*, which is best rendered as 'master of the homestead'.
20. Similarly, Johnston (1886: 90) reported that a goat was slaughtered and a skin-ring fashioned when he arrived at the boundary of Mandara's chiefdom, while Thomson (1885: 88) and Rebmann had similar experiences with the *mangi* of Shia and the 'King of Kilema' (Krapf 1860: 238).
21. In this regard, it is significant that the mixture was tossed onto Rebmann's face and front, and that chyme was flung onto pathways, and thus was applied to parts of the body and the landscape through and along which *horu* enters and emerges in different forms.
22. De Heusch also draws on Henri Junod (1910).

CONCLUSION

This book opened with an episode from October 2008, when Chagga-speakers from Tanzania and Kamba-speakers from Kenya gathered in the plains below Kilimanjaro to return life to the long-dead *mangi* Horombo, and request rain to alleviate the drought and hunger they suffered. The ensuing ethnography has combined contemporary field-work material and historical sources to fill in a background and provide additional detail to this event. It has considered changes and varia-tions in modes of production and habitation, and explored the role and significance of bridewealth prestations and marital relations for the homestead – *kaa* – and the activities that occur within and around it. The account has shown how these transactions and relations in-volve processes of attachment and detachment that suspend persons between multiple homesteads, and render them in a state of extension that the notion of *ialika* or marrying concerns. Central in this regard are sex and reproduction, where persons convert and convey *horu* or life force in different forms by means of different body parts through different activities that moreover constitute and shift persons between different subject positions. In fact, the ethnography discloses how all engagements involve such transfers and transmutations, which en-compass the living and the dead, and include speech or language and the rain that we requested in the plains. On this basis, it emerges that the notion of *ikaa* or dwelling concerns how different activities nest as transformations of each other, and how *horu* moves through them in different forms.

The activities that constitute dwelling moreover involve a set of no-tions that derive from the concept of *moo* or life. These notions regard persons and animals of reproductive merit, as well as the left-hand side, the doorway, back, chyme and fire. As such, they concern the beings, places, conduits, substances and processes whereby *horu* con-verts and conveys to afford the becoming and constitute the being of persons, houses, livestock and crops. In combination, they enunciate how life and the world in which it occurs are effects of material transfers and transformations that take place through parts of persons, houses, animals and crops in dwelling. These notions that derive from *moo* are means of connection and distinction that amount to vernacular versions or re-descriptions of the anthropological relation (Strathern 1988, 1995, 2005). It is most evident in the case of *moongo*, as the doorway affords entry to facilitate the initial bridewealth prestation, and thus provides a point of contact between prospective affines who are reproductively unrelated. However, the doorway later serves to distinguish the bride from her parents, as she may not use a bed in their house but instead sleeps on a hide by the door once she has borne children at her marital homestead and her husband has presented 'the goat of the child's mother'. Her transformation from daughter to bride bars her from sleeping in one bed, but enables her to occupy another. It manifests her gradual detachment from one house and growing attachment to another through the use of her back in sex, conception, childbirth and care.[1] But while she detaches from the parents' house through the doorway, she remains connected through their reproduction, which engaged her mother's back. Thus, where the doorway connects, the backbone separates, and where the backbone conjoins, the doorway distinguishes.

The relational capacities of *moongo* were enhanced and multiplied by the polygynous homestead of the past. Each house then was inhabited by one woman and her children, who connected through her back but became distinguished by different doorways. When a son received his mother's house, its doorway separated him from his brothers, who had either received their own homesteads or relocated with their mother to a new dwelling. These doorways furthermore distinguished brothers from sisters, as they attached to other houses in marriage. At the same time, the doorways connected the houses of the different wives, whose inhabitants were distinguished by conception and childbirth, and hence the women's backs. The husband's circulation between these houses made the singular doorway his means for connecting to a particular wife, while it separated him from the others. As he went out of one house and into another, the different doorways connected and separated husband and wives, who also conjoined and disjoined by means of the women's backs through sex and reproduction.

The children of a single house are furthermore said to be of 'one womb' – *ndeu imu* – which articulates how they are born of and connect through the same uterus, where the parents' *horu* combined as semen and blood. However, *ndeu* also means 'stomach', so it equally enunciates how the inhabitants of the same house connect through consumption, and thus are of 'one stomach'. The foodstuffs consumed chiefly derive from the livestock and the banana garden they manure, and are therefore effects of chyme (*mooshe*) that combine over the hearth where they are prepared by its fire (*motcho*). The chyme and the hearth-fire thus connect the inhabitants of the single house through cooking and consumption, yet simultaneously distinguish them from the other houses and their inhabitants, who eat foods that emerge from other animals, gardens and hearths. However, they all connect through the bridewealth prestations that brought the houses into being, and that actualized from the chyme and hearth-fire of the husband's father and those of their agnates' homesteads. These prestations were made to and consumed in different homesteads, which hence share a common 'place for eating' (*kulo*), yet each is a 'place of life' (*kumoosoni*) for a different *kaa* with its own doorway, hearth and livestock, and where the bride employs her back in sex and reproduction.[2] Like the doorways and the backs, so the chyme, the fire and the left and the right simultaneously connect and separate persons and places. They are relational facilities of different kinds that enable the permutations of relationships and subject positions that constitute life.

The different notions that derive from *moo* share a concern for how beings of different kinds detach and attach for the purpose of enabling further beings of the same kind. Some concern how foodstuffs emerge from livestock, gardens and hearths, and others regard how persons present these substances through doorways to forge relationships that allow them to reproduce. Others still concern how children emerge through or by means of the backs of women, who in the past extended existing homesteads, while they currently enable new dwellings. The different notions and their usages hence concern how persons use parts of houses and homesteads to reproduce, and how houses and homesteads use parts of persons and their co-inhabitants to reproduce. The different notions 'cut' or 'sharpen' (Holbraad and Pedersen 2009: 381) persons, houses, livestock and crops to reveal them as the effects of and the conditions for the transfers and transformations of *horu* that occur between places and through doorways, as well as by means of backs, intestines and hearths. As different 'in-betweens' (Patton 2000: 10), they are openings and lines through and along which persons, houses, livestock and crops become and transform, as *horu* converts and conveys to actualize beings of different kinds. To paraphrase Rupert Stasch (2009: 16), they are 'concrete channels of communicative contact and separation' that afford dwelling and life, and at the same time channel, determine and enunciate the move-

ments of *horu* that permeate and animate them. Like the anthropological relation, they are both conceptual and interpersonal facilities that
constitute different tools for life (Strathern 2005: 6ff).

As the notions that derive from *moo* involve actions and engage objects, their usages can be considered what Ludwig Wittgenstein calls
language-games. Meanwhile, the concern they share for the transfers
and transformation of *horu* means that *moo* and its derivatives can be
regarded as family resemblance notions. Like these notions, Wittgenstein's descriptive tools are also means for connection and distinction,
or channels of communicative contact and separation. Thus, the notion of family resemblance reveals similarities or points of contact
between the multiple uses of a term, while the idea of language-game
illuminates them by way of their differences. Accordingly, the tools
both attach to and detach from that which they concerns, as Wittgenstein states on the one hand that 'one must look from close to' (PI
§51), yet on the other argues: 'If we look at things from an ethnological point of view, does that mean we are saying that philosophy is
ethnology? No, it only means that we are taking up a position right
outside so as to be able to see things *more objectively*' (CV: 37). The
description thus proportions a relation to provide a perspective on a
particular segment of language.

In fact, Wittgenstein's emphasis on difference entails that his approach amounts to an otherness-oriented conception of language
and meaning. While such conceptions date back at least to Ferdinand
de Saussure's ([1916] 1983) approach to linguistics, Wittgenstein's
differ as he does not conceive of and trace systematic contrasts or
structural oppositions between signifiers and the signified. In fact,
he rejects the relationship of reference that undergirds this conception and instead pursues the multifarious uses of language that its
uniform appearance belies: 'It is like looking into the cabin of a lo-
comotive. We see handles all looking more or less alike. (Naturally
since they are all supposed to be handled.) But one is the handle of a
crank which can be moved continuously (it regulates the opening of a
valve); another is the handle of a switch, which has only two effective
positions, it is either on or off; a third is the handle of a brake-lever,
the harder one pulls on it, the harder it brakes; a fourth, the handle
of a pump: it has an effect only so long as it is moved to and fro' (PI:
§12). His simile brings out how language involves a diversity of uses
and effects, which create a braid of similarities and differences between multiple relationships, including many of an analogue kind
(Myhre 2012). His tools are thus devices for eliciting the similarities
and differences internal to a language through descriptions of its con-

crete instances of use (cf. Englund and Yarrow 2013; Myhre 2013a). To paraphrase Holbraad and Pedersen (2009: 381), Wittgenstein's notions 'cut' or 'sharpen' the uses of words to reveal their peculiar characteristics, and unfold the activities and objects they involve and engage. His tools depart from the direction and impetus of conventional analysis, as they deploy description to allow concepts to emerge. As objects of comparison that elicit difference, language-games moreover depart from conventional anthropology, where comparison commonly charts the commonalities between different contexts, cultures or societies (Segal 2001). Thus, where the notions that derive from *moo* concern how *horu* converts and conveys to actualize beings of different kinds, so 'family resemblance' and 'language-game' regard how language and meaning involve and realize a multitude of uses and concepts. As their similarities and differences are traced across and between different situations of use, so language and meaning are revealed as the effects of and conditions for linguistic and conceptual transfers and transformation. As such, it attends specifically to a multilingual situation where cognate concepts proliferate throughout a region, like they do in and around Kilimanjaro.

Since the drought that occurred in 2008 inhibited the growth of fodder, it imperilled the chyme and the foodstuffs that are presented, prepared and consumed to enable dwelling and life. It thus jeopardized the transfers and transformations of *horu* that take place between persons and homesteads of the right and the left, and that occur by means of doorways, backs, intestines and hearth-fires. Consequently, the drought resulted in an event that set in motion movements and transmutations that engaged most – if not all – of the phenomena that derive their terms from *moo*. Thus, animals that included a female *mooma* goat had milk tossed onto their backs (*moongo*), so they could be removed through the doorway (*moongo*) of the house to be butchered. The resulting meat was cooked over a fire (*motcho*) before it was consumed and presented to Horombo the 'life-elder' (*moombe*) on top of the chyme (*mooshe*), while milk, beer and blood were poured and placed around it. In this way, the house yielded animals and their bodies everted chyme, which in turn rendered meat, milk, beer and blood. The event thus effectuated how beings and substances of different kinds turn into and out of each other through dwelling, at the same time as the notions of *mooma, moongo, mooshe, moombe* and *motcho* turn into and out of each other to enunciate how life becomes as the effects of these transfers and transformations. The event did not assign priority among these beings and notions, but instead allowed forms of *horu* to emerge from each other, and *moo* to contort and yield the notions that regard the means through or by which it occurs. In this way, the event captured and conveyed life *as* transfer and transformation, and thus revealed the form life has in this part of the world. Indeed, it was this life we returned, as Peter wielded and everted *horu* in different forms, and engaged the life of which he spoke to facilitate and channel the transfers and transformations that *moo* involves. Like the acts of 'opening' described by Ruel (1997: 69), Peter created the condition on which life depends by affording the conversions and conveyances of *horu*. As he engaged and addressed life to facilitate its flourishing, the words he used neither referred to nor signified something, but combined with his acts to participate in that which they concerned. It echoes Wittgenstein's use of language to describe language and underscores how these phenomena constitute language-games that involve family resemblance notions.

Indeed, the notion of *moo* and its derivatives can shed light on Wittgenstein's concept of form of life, and the idea that language-games extend into and out of each other. As mentioned in the introduction, the common interpretation is that the form of life constitutes an extensive web or encompassing system that connects or integrates a plurality of language-games. The understanding is supported by Wittgenstein's simile of the ancient city and his claim that 'language is a labyrinth of paths' (PI: §203), which both suggest a phenomenon that extends in time and space. Elsewhere, however, he argues: 'What has to be accepted, the given, is – so one could say – *forms of life*' (PI: p. 226). Its given character entails that form of life is not the result of language-games combining as so many parts of a whole, but rather that language-games arise or emerge from the form of life as elaborations or constructions that determine particular aspects pertaining to it.[3] The idea accords with the claim that language-games are descriptive means that elicit the similarities and differences between situations of use, and unfold the activities and objects they involve and engage to allow concepts to emerge. It furthermore gains support from Wittgenstein's use of the notion of 'background' against which one distinguishes between true and false, and something appears as significant and meaningful (OC: §94, 461). It also concurs with the ethnography presented in this book, where language shapes, determines and effectuates the transfers and transformations of *horu* that animate *moo* and occur by means of lines and openings that derive their terms from it. *Kumoosoni, mooshe, moongo, mooma, moombe* and *motcho* thus arise or unfold from *moo* to grasp and specify transfers and transmutations that afford and regard the emergence, existence and evaporation of beings of different kinds. As these notions employ prefixes and suffixes to embellish or elaborate the root-form *moo*, they create concepts that involve actions and engage objects to constitute a multitude of language-games. The event that occurred in 2008 reveals how only a single concept and language-game features at a time, and then is displaced by another to capture and convey how notions and beings turn into and out of each other. As the concepts and language-games unfold from the form of life, they emerge and exit as multiples of 'one', which eventually fold back into the form of life. Concepts and language-games are therefore self-similar iterations that become and occur in the same way as persons, houses, livestock and banana trees. Like them, each 'one' contains and retains connections to the other 'ones', which constitute the background or life from which it emerges and returns.

Like *moo*, the verb *ihora* also yields a multitude of derivative forms that concern cooling, cleansing, curing and ceremoniality, which afford and constitute health, well-being and capacity. Accordingly, it gives rise to the nouns *horu* and *mbora*, which underscore how the event that occurred in 2008 created the condition on which life depends. Like those that derive from *moo*, the notions that originate from *ihora* emerge and exist as multiples of 'one' to form part of distinct language-games that moreover involve different body parts. When the different notions and language-games give way to each other, the different body parts also yield to each other to equally emerge as multiples of 'one'. Thus, hands or arms actualize foodstuffs that enter mouths, which enable the renewed use of arms and hands, as well as of chests and backs, penises and vaginas, wombs and breasts, in the different activities that constitute dwelling and life. As *ikaa* and *moo* concern how production, reproduction and consumption nest as transformations of each other, so the different body-parts presuppose and contain each other as *horu* moves through them in different forms. In this way, *horu* folds back on itself to afford the becoming and constitute the being of persons, houses, livestock and crops that manifest as lines of homestead, where alternate generations extend dwelling and life. These processes moreover give rise to gender categories and positions, which equally emerge as 'ones' and that yield to each other as persons move through them due to the transfers and transmutations of the uniform life force. At the same time, the notions that emerge from *moo* and *ihora* fold back on each other and their respective root-forms to effectuate a multitude of concepts and language-games that articulate how dwelling and life involve both expansion and reiteration. Like Wittgenstein's notions, they are topological phenomena that concern the shapes and surfaces of beings and concepts, and regard the movements and distortions of life force and meaning. As these personal, material and conceptual beings ramify and replicate through time and space, they realize temporal and spatial forms that manifest as lines of houses and trees, and give new directions to the recurring debates regarding demography and development in Kilimanjaro.

How *horu* folds back on itself to realize beings of particular kinds was enunciated by the elder who responded to the announcement of the newborn's name by saying: 'The spider's silk knots itself, the name of the grandfather has returned to our land. We shall not become extinct' (Gutmann 1926: 315). Like Peter's invocations in 2008, this statement implies a past and anticipates a future, and thus constitutes the present as a process of emergence and becoming, or ever-present forthcoming. It recalls Sally Falk Moore's concern with the production of the present from the past, and their links to overarching structures and events. But where her task is to integrate events in a larger process, my concern is to let the event emerge and unfold the past and the future it entails and contains. It reiterates how other beings come into existence as the effects of material transfers and transformations, and thus allows the event to become another 'one'. As it too contains and retains connections to other 'ones', it is also burdened with a past yet pregnant with a future, as it emerges from and eventually sinks back into life.

These relations received articulation in Gutmann's (1932: 65) account of how a head of livestock was butchered to thank the deceased and a skin-ring (*kishong'u*) was fashioned for both mother and child three to four months after its birth. Before the animal was killed, a male elder bent its head towards the child that rested in its mother's lap inside the house. He then spat between its horns and said: 'You apical ancestor, who begot this new generation (*Nachwuchs*), so that we came to be here and be named after you and be called your discharge (*Ausfluß*) for which you care, we tell you: request the heavenly person (*mdu tšu o ruwa*), who assisted you in creating us, so that we were named after you. We say to you: here is the fat of the child, which lets us grow at this place (*olufumbutsa kuḏi*)'. The statement entails that the past projects into the future to constitute a present, as it enunciates how generations emerge from and care for each other, and how they enable each other's growth and reiterate each other's names. At the same time, *horu* conveys as the animal's head is bent and spat upon, and prestations of fat or meat are made to replace the life force others expended on your behalf, and to secure future growth. It resembles events that I have described from present-day Rombo, and even involves a dialectical version of the notion that MaShirima used in her address to the homestead's deceased relatives that the place and its inhabitants shall grow.[4] The recurring use of the same notion over a century reveals how a conceptual past projects into the future to constitute a present. And it emerges from an approach that manifests the same relation, as it combines historical sources and contemporary ethnography to describe and attain concepts that may extend into the future.

As cognates of these concepts proliferate, their similarities facilitate engagements and transfers around common concerns, while their differences allow those involved to emerge and interact as distinct beings. It was this that occurred in 2008, when the people from the mountain and those from the plains met and interacted as different 'ones' to return life to Horombo and request rain. The distinctions between them did not coincide with those of 'culture' and 'society', but were the effects of a particular moment where people gathered and engaged in activities with a long history and significance in the area. As language-games that unfold from life and displace each other, their meaning resides in a patchwork of similarities and difference that extends laterally through time and space, and recedes towards a conceptual and topographical horizon. Considered as such, they open for an ethnography that returns life to old accounts and anthropological concerns that perhaps may affect future trajectories.

Notes

1. It is her growing attachment to the *moongo* of her marital house through the use of her back in sex and reproduction that gives sense and urgency to MaShirima's recurring emphasis on the bed as central for the marital relationship.
2. Arguably, it is because the different houses and their inhabitants share a right-hand side and chest through agnatic relationality and paternity that the emphasis is placed on the left-hand side and the back, which distinguish them.
3. Charles Taylor (1995:96) touches on this, when he points out that for Wittgenstein 'language is rather something in the nature of a web, which, to complicate the image, is present as a whole in any one of its parts'.
4. *Ifumbuka* and *ifumbutsa* are dialectal variations of each other.

GLOSSARY OF CHAGGA TERMS

Boru – manure.

Fondoho – above

Fyao – curse made by means of words only

Horo – male goat

Horu – life force, bodily power

Iabisa – to curse

Ialika – to marry, literally 'to be in a state of extension or unfolding'

Idamira – to cause or make someone sit, used especially in connection with burial practices

Ihara – to lend livestock, livestock lending

Ihora – to cool or cleanse

Iira – to seize, take or stick

Ikaa – to dwell, dwelling

Ikariya – to be brave, powerful or mature

Ikeri – to be

Ilauka – to be in a state of calling, used when the deceased cause problems for the living

Ilaukiwa – to be in a state of being called, used when the living suffer problems caused by the deceased

Ilholhya – to see

Ilhoswa – to dream, be shown or instructed, literally 'to be made to see'

Iruu – banana, used to variously mean a single fruit, a bunch of fruits, or the entire tree carrying a bunch.

Irukwa – to be in a state of openness

Iruwa – to open or be open

Isale – dracaena

Isasa – to gather or congregate

Itchamia – to sit

Itchasa – to place meat on the ground for the deceased

Itchema – to cultivate or farm

Iterewa – to request or ask someone for something

Iumba – to conjoin

Iuriya – to return, make something return

Iwikiya – to place or put

Kaa – homestead

Kaandeni – open area located behind the house

Kali – attic

Kelya kiholo – soft food of a semi-liquid consistency that is commonly made from eleusine, milk, meat, blood and bananas in different combinations

Kilikiyo – ladle or spoon

Kishong'u – skin-ring fashioned from a butchered animal

Kiungu – tall tree that is left to grow wild, at the foot of which beer, milk and meat are placed with requests for rain

Koko – arm or hand

Kulo – right-hand side, literally 'the side for eating'

Kumooso – left-hand side, literally 'the side of life'

Lhoy – truth

Makosha or *machawa* – green leaves of the banana tree

Mamrasa – neighbor, literally 'person of the boundary'

Matonga – stumps

Mashia – hearthstones

Marua – milk

Mawilho – dried banana bark

Mba – house

Mbala – cooking-soda, used as a substitute for salt

Mbora – stem of the banana tree, fecund woman and a state of plenty

Mboriko – wooden bowl used for storing and serving certain soft foods and liquids.

Mbuho – tall and large *isale* tree where the dead are gathered after exhumation

Mdawi – dried banana bark

Mdenyi – banana garden, literally 'cultivated place'

Meku – male elder

Mengele – pathway leading into the homestead

Mfee – confined woman

Mfele – wife or woman

Mii – husband

Mkara – intermediary, literally 'person who enables dwelling and the homestead'

Mko – footpath

Monikiwalo – owner of the place or homestead

Moo – life

Mooma – female goat that has born offspring, literally 'mother of life' or 'life-mother'

Moombe – term of address meaning great one, literally 'life-elder'

Moongo – doorway, back or backbone, here transcribed as conduit of life

Mooshe – chyme, here transcribed as substance of life

Motcho – fire

Mrasa – boundary between homesteads

Mri – vein or root

Mṛi – homestead, town or city

Mrike – bodily heat

Mringa – water

Msheku – female elder

Msoro – man

Mwaanga – healer, diviner

Mwali – bride

Mwana mbele – first-born son, literally 'child in front'

Mwana wa kaa – daughter, literally 'child of the homestead'

Mway – plains

Nanua – banana blossom

Ndaka – offshoot of the banana tree

Ndaswa – meat that is placed on the ground for the deceased

Nungu – cooking-pot, can also mean a particular kind of curse

Riko – hearth

Rina – name

Sabo – flower stalk of banana tree

Sakeu – bush or wilderness, uncultivated place

Samu – blood

Seso – curse made by means of words and metal objects

Sha or *sha nduwe* – courtyard in front of the house, literally 'outside' or 'big outside'

Shia – pathway or road

Shori – drinking gourd

Siinde – below

Siinde ya kaa – area located below the homestead where the dead are buried and the first-born son is provided land

Sumbay – down

Uli – bed

Unanda or *urongo* – rolled-up emerging banana leaf

Wafije – mother's brother

Wari – banana beer

Warimu – the deceased

Watoi – terms of address between people whose children have married

-wiishwa – adjectival root-form, meaning 'bad'

BIBLIOGRAPHY

Allen, N. 2000. *Categories and Classifications: Maussian Reflections on the Social.* Oxford: Berghahn Books.

Allen, R., and M. Turvey. 2001. 'Wittgenstein's Later Philosophy: A Prophylaxis against Theory', pp. 1–35 in R. Allen and M. Turvey (eds), *Wittgenstein, Theory and the Arts.* London: Routledge.

Anon. 1990. *The Catholic Church in Moshi: A Centenary Memorial 1890–1990.* Moshi: Ndanda Mission Press.

Århem, K. 1990. 'A Folk Model of Pastoral Subsistence: The Meaning of Milk, Meat and Blood in Maasai Diet', pp. 201–31 in A. Jacobson-Widding and W. van Beek (eds), *The Creative Communion: African Folk Models of Fertility and the Regeneration of Life.* Uppsala: Acta Universitatis Upsaliensis.

Århem, K. 1991. 'The Symbolic World of the Maasai Homestead', pp. 51–80 in A. Jacobson-Widding (ed.), *Body and Space: Symbolic Models of Unity and Division in African Cosmology and Experience.* Uppsala: Acta Universitatis Upsaliensis.

Ashton, E.H. 1943. 'Medicine, Magic, and Sorcery among the Southern Sotho', *Communications from the School of African Studies University of Cape Town.* Cape Town.

Ashton, E.H. 1952. *The Basuto: A Social Study of Traditional and Modern Lesotho.* London: Oxford University Press for the International African Institute.

Austin, J. 1962. *How to Do Things with Words.* Cambridge, MA: Harvard University Press.

Barad, K. 2003. 'Posthumanist Performativity: Toward an Understanding of How Matter Comes to Matter', *Signs: Journal of Women in Culture and Society* 28(3): 801–31.

Beattie, J. 1960. 'On the Nyoro Concept of *Mahano*', *African Studies* 19(3): 145–50.

Beidelman, T.O. 1961. 'Right and Left Hand among the Kaguru: A Note on Symbolic Classification', *Africa* 31(3): 250–57.

Beidelman, T.O. 1963. 'Witchcraft in Ukaguru', pp. 57–98 in J. Middleton and E.H. Winter (eds), *Witchcraft and Sorcery in East Africa.* London: Routledge and Kegan Paul.

Beidelman, T.O. 1986. *Moral Imagination in Kaguru Modes of Thought.* Bloomington: Indiana University Press.

Beidelman, T.O. 1997. *The Cool Knife: Imagery of Gender, Sexuality, and Moral Education in Kaguru Initiation Ritual.* Washington: Smithsonian Institution Press.

Bouveresse, J. 2007. 'Wittgenstein's Critique of Frazer', *Ratio (new series)* 20(4): 357–76.

Brain, J.L. 1973. 'Ancestors as Elders in Africa – Further Thoughts', *Africa* 43(2): 122–33.

Brandström, P. 1990. 'Seeds and Soil: The Quest for Life and the Domestication of Fertility in Sukuma-Nyamwezi Thought and Reality', pp. 167–87 in A. Jacobson-Widding and W. van Beek (eds), *The Creative Communion: African Folk Models of Fertility and the Regeneration of Life.* Uppsala: Acta Universitatis Upsaliensis.

Broch-Due, V. 1990. 'Cattle Are Companions, Goats Are Gifts: Animals and People in Turkana Thought', pp. 39–58 in G. Pálsson (ed.), *From Water to World-Making.* Uppsala: Nordic Africa Institute.

Broch-Due, V. 1993. 'Making Meaning out of Matter: Perceptions of Sex, Gender and Bodies among the Turkana', pp. 53–82 in V. Broch-Due, I. Rudie and T. Bleie (eds), *Carved Flesh/Cast Selves: Gendered Symbols and Social Practices.* Oxford: Berg.

Comaroff, J.L. 1980. 'Introduction', pp. 1–47 in J.L. Comaroff (ed.), *The Meaning of Marriage Payments.* London: Academic Press.

Comaroff, J. 1985. *Body of Power, Spirit of Resistance: The Culture and History of a South African People.* Chicago: Chicago University Press.

Comaroff, J., and J.L. Comaroff. 1991. *Of Revelation and Revolution: Christianity, Colonialism, and Consciousness in South Africa,* vol. 1. Chicago: Chicago University Press.

Comaroff, J., and J. Comaroff. 1993. 'Introduction', pp. xi–xxxvii in J. Comaroff and J.L. Comaroff (eds), *Modernity and Its Malcontents: Ritual and Power in Postcolonial Africa.* Chicago: University of Chicago Press.

Comaroff, J., and J. Comaroff. 1997. *Of Revelation and Revolution: The Dialectics of Modernity on a South African Frontier,* vol. 2. Chicago: Chicago University Press.

Corsín Jímenez, A., and R. Willerslev. 2007. '"An Anthropological Concept of the Concept": Reversibility among the Siberian Yukaghirs', *Journal of the Royal Anthropological Institute (N.S.)* 13(4): 527–44.

De Boeck, F. 1994a. '"When Hunger Goes around the Land": Hunger and Food among the Aluund of Zaire', *Man (N.S.)* 29(2): 257–82.

De Boeck, F. 1994b. 'Of Trees and Kings: Politics and Metaphor among the Aluund of Southwestern Zaire', *American Ethnologist* 21(3): 451–73.

De Heusch, L. 1980. 'Heat, Physiology, and Cosmogony: *Rites des Passage* among the Thonga', pp. 27–43 in I. Karp and C.S. Bird (eds), *Explorations in African Systems of Thought.* Bloomington: Indiana University Press.

De Heusch, L. 1985. *Sacrifice in Africa: A Structuralist Approach.* Manchester: Manchester University Press.

Deleuze, G. 2006. 'Immanence: A Life', pp. 384–89 in G. Deleuze (ed.), *Two Regimes of Madness: Texts and Interviews 1975–1995.* Cambridge, MA: MIT Press.

Deleuze, G. and F. Guattari. 1994. *What is Philosophy?* New York: Columbia University Press.

De Saussure, F. [1916] 1983. *Course in General Linguistics.* London: Duckworth.

Devisch, R. 1988. 'From Equal to Better: Investing the Chief among the Northern Yaka of Zaïre', *Africa* 58(3): 261–90.

Devisch, R. 1991. 'Mediumistic Divination among the Northern Yaka of Zaire: Etiology and Ways of Knowing', pp. 112–32 in P.M. Peek (ed.), *African Divination Systems.* Bloomington: Indiana University Press.

Devisch, R. 1993. *Weaving the Threads of Life: The Khita Gyn-Eco-Logical Healing Cult among the Yaka.* Chicago: University of Chicago Press.

Devisch, R. 1998. 'Treating the Affect by Remodelling the Body in a Yaka Healing Cult', pp. 127–57 in M. Lambek and A. Strathern (eds), *Bodies and Persons: Comparative Perspectives from Africa and Melanesia.* Cambridge: Cambridge University Press.

Drury, M.O. 1996. *The Danger of Words and Writings on Wittgenstein.* Bristol: Thoemmes Press.

Dundas, C. 1924. *Kilimanjaro and Its People: A History of the WaChagga, Their Laws, Customs and Legends, Together with Some Account of the Highest Mountain in Africa.* London: H. F. & G. Witherby.

Dundas, C. 1955. *African Crossroads.* London: Macmillan & Co.

Englund, H., and T. Yarrow. 2013. 'The Place of Theory: Rights, Networks, and Ethnographic Comparison', *Social Analysis* 57(3): 132–49.

Evans-Pritchard, E.E. 1956. *Nuer Religion.* Oxford: Clarendon.

Feierman, S. 1981. 'Therapy as a System-in-Action in Northeastern Tanzania', *Social Science and Medicine* 15(3B): 353–60.

Feierman, S. 1990. *Peasant Intellectuals: Anthropology and History in Tanzania.* Madison: University of Wisconsin Press.

Ferguson, J. 1997. *Expectations of Modernity: Myths and Meanings of Urban Life on the Zambian Copperbelt.* Berkeley: University of California Press.

Fiedler, K. 1996. *Christianity and African Culture: Conservative German Protestant Missionaries in Tanzania, 1900–1940.* Leiden: E.J. Brill.

Fortes, M. 1962. 'Introduction', pp. 1–13 in M. Fortes (ed.), *Marriage in Tribal Societies.* Cambridge: Cambridge University Press.

Gausset, Q. 2002. 'The Cognitive Rationality of Taboos on Production and Reproduction in Sub-Saharan Africa', *Africa* 72(4): 628–54.

Geissler, P.W., and R.J. Prince. 2010. *The Land is Dying: Contingency, Creativity and Conflict in Western Kenya.* Oxford: Berghahn Books.

Gell, A. 1998. *Art and Agency: An Anthropological Theory.* Oxford: Clarendon Press.

Gill, J.H. 1991. *Merleau-Ponty and Metaphor.* New Jersey: Humanities Press.

Glock, H.J. 2001. 'The Development of Wittgenstein's Philosophy', pp. 1–25 in H.J. Glock (ed.), *Wittgenstein: A Critical Reader.* Oxford: Blackwell.

Gluckman, M. 1950. 'Kinship and Marriage among the Lozi of Northern Rhodesia and the Zulu of Natal', pp. 166–206 in A.R. Radcliffe-Brown and D. Forde (eds), *African Systems of Kinship and Marriage.* London. Oxford University Press.

Green, M. 1995. 'Why Christianity is the "Religion of Business": Perceptions of the Church among Pogoro Catholics in Southern Tanzania', *Journal of Religion in Africa* 25(1): 25–47.

Green, M. 1999a. 'Procreation Theories and Their Implications: Overcoming the Absent Father in Southern Tanzania', pp. 47–67 in P. Loizos and P. Heady (eds), *Conceiving Persons: Ethnographies of Procreation, Fertility and Growth.* London: The Athlone Press.

Green, M. 1999b. 'Women's Work is Weeping: Constructions of Gender in a Catholic Community', pp. 255–80 in H.L. Moore, T. Sanders and B. Kaare (eds), *Those Who Play with Fire: Gender, Fertility and Transformation in East and Central Africa.* London: Athlone Press.

Gulliver, P. 1963. *Social Control in an African Society.* London: Routledge.

Gupta, A., and J. Ferguson. 1997. *Culture, Power, Place: Explorations in Critical Anthropology.* Durham, NC: Duke University Press.

Guthrie, M. 1970. *Comparative Bantu: An Introduction to the Comparative Linguistics and Prehistory of the Bantu Languages,* vol. 2. Farnborough: Gregg.

Gutmann, B. 1907. 'Die Frau bei den Wadschagga', *Globus. Illustrierte Zeitschrift für Länder und Völkerkunde* 92(1): 1–4, 29–32, 49–51.

Gutmann, B. 1908. 'Fluchen und Segnen im Munde der Wadschagga'. *Globus* 93: 298–302.

Gutmann, B. 1909a. 'Geburt und Heirat bei den Wadschagga', pp. 163–88 in *Jahrbuch der Bayerischen Missionskonferenz.*

Gutmann, B. 1909b. *Dichten und Denken der Dschagganeger.* Leipzig: Beiträge zur ostafrikanschen Volkskunde.

Gutmann, B. 1909c. 'Die Opferstätten der Wadschagga', *Archiv für Religionswissenschaft* 12: 83–100.

Gutmann, B. 1911. 'Ostafrikanischer Animismus und Totenkult', *Evangelisch-Lutherisches Missionsblatt* 23: 546–50, 568–73.

Gutmann, B. 1912. 'Der Schmied und seine Kunst in animistischen Denken', *Zeitschrift für Ethnologie* 44: 81–93.

Gutmann, B. 1913. 'Feldbausitten und Wachstumsbräuche bei den Wadschagga', *Zeitschrift für Ethnologie* 45: 475–511.

Gutmann, B. 1923. 'Die Kerbstocklehren', *Zeitschrift für Eingeborenensprachen* 13(4): 260–302.

Gutmann, B. 1924a. 'Die Ehrerbietung der Dschagganeger gegen ihre Nutzplannzen und Haustiere', *Archiv für die gesamte Psychologie* 48: 123–46.

Gutmann, B. 1924b. 'Der Beschwörer bei den Wadschagga', *Archiv für Anthropologie* 20: 46–57.

Gutmann, B. 1926. *Das Recht der Dschagga.* Arbeiten zur Entwicklungspsychologie. Munich: C.H. Beck'sche Verlagsbuchhandlung.

Gutmann, B. 1928. 'Der Steinahne', *Archiv für die gesamte Psychologie* 52: 424–44.

Gutmann, B. 1932. *Die Stammeslehren der Dschagga*. Arbeiten zur Entwik-
lungspsychologie. Munich: C.H. Beck'sche Verlagsbuchhandlung.

Gutmann, B. 1935. 'The African Standpoint', *Africa* 8(1): 1–17.

Gutmann, B. 1966. *Afrikaner-Europäer in nächstenschaftlicher Entsprechung*.
Stuttgart: Evangelisches Verlagswerk.

Hacker, P.M.S. 2001a. 'Developmental Hypotheses and Perspicuous Repre-
sentations: Wittgenstein on Frazer's *Golden Bough*', pp. 74–97 in P.M.S.
Hacker (ed.), *Wittgenstein: Connections and Controversies*. Oxford: Clarendon Press.

Hacker, P.M.S. 2001b. 'Wittgenstein – an Overview', pp. 1–33 in P.M.S. Hacker
(ed.), *Wittgenstein: Connections and Controversies*. Oxford: Clarendon Press.

Håkansson, T. 1989. 'Family Structure, Bridewealth, and Environment in
Eastern Africa: A Comparative Study of House-Property Systems', *Ethnology* 28(2): 117–34.

Hanfling, O. 1989. *Wittgenstein's Later Philosophy*. Basingstoke: Macmillan.

Hanfling, O. 2000. *Philosophy and Ordinary Language: The Bent and Genius of
Our Tongue*. London: Routledge.

Harjula, R. 1989. 'Curse as a Manifestation of Broken Human Relationships
among the Meru of Tanzania', pp. 125–37 in A. Jacobson-Widding and
D. Westerlund (eds), *Culture, Experience and Pluralism: Essays on African
Ideas of Illness and Healing*. Uppsala: Acta Universitatis Upsaliensis.

Harris, G.G. 1962. 'Taita Bridewealth and Affinal Relationships', pp. 55–87
in M. Fortes (ed.), *Marriage in Tribal Societies*. Cambridge: Cambridge University Press.

Harris, G.G. 1978. *Casting Out Anger: Religion among the Taita of Kenya*. Cambridge: Cambridge University Press.

Hassing, P. 1979. 'Bruno Gutmann on Kilimanjaro: Setting the Record
Straight', *Missiology* 7(4): 423–33.

Hasu, P. 1999. *Desire and Death: History through Ritual Practice in Kilimanjaro*.
Helsinki: Transactions of the Finnish Anthropological Society.

Heald, S. 1999. *Manhood and Morality*. London: Routledge.

Heidegger, M. [1954] 1978. 'Building Dwelling Thinking', pp. 347–63 in D.F.
Krell (ed.), *Basic Writings: Martin Heidegger*. London: Routledge.

Helmreich, S., and S. Roosth. 2010. 'Life Forms: A Keyword Entry', *Represen-
tations* 112(1): 27–53.

Herbert, E.W. 1993. *Iron, Gender, and Power: Rituals of Transformation in African Societies*. Bloomington: Indiana University Press.

Hirsch, E. 2014. 'Melanesian Ethnography and the Comparative Project of
Anthropology: Reflection on Strathern's Analogical Approach', *Theory,
Culture and Society* 31(2/3): 39–64.

Hobley, C.W. 1922. *Bantu Belief and Magic, with Particular Reference to the Kikuyu and Kamba Tribes of Kenya Colony; together with Some Reflections on
East Africa after the War*. New York: Barnes and Noble.

Hoernlé, A.W. 1937. 'Magic and Medicine', pp. 221–45 in I. Schapera (ed.),
The Bantu-Speaking Tribes of South Africa. London: George Routledge &
Sons.

Holbraad, M., and M.A. Pedersen. 2009. 'Planet M: The Intense Abstraction of Marilyn Strathern', *Anthropological Theory* 9(4): 371–94.

Hunter, E. 2009. 'In Pursuit of the "Higher Medievalism": Local History and Politics in Kilimanjaro', pp. 149–67 in D. Peterson and G. Macola (eds), *Recasting the Past: History Writing and Political Work in Modern Africa.* Athens: Ohio University Press.

Hunter, M. 1936. *Reaction to Conquest: Effects of Contact with Europeans on the Pondo of South Africa.* London: Oxford University Press.

Hutchinson, S.E. 1996. *Nuer Dilemmas: Coping with Money, War, and the State.* Berkeley: University of California Press.

Hutchinson, S.E. 2000. 'Identity and Substance: The Broadening Bases of Relatedness among the Nuer of Southern Sudan', pp. 55–72 in J. Carsten (ed.), *Cultures of Relatedness: New Approaches to the Study of Kinship.* Cambridge: Cambridge University Press.

Hyman, J. 2001. 'The Urn and the Chamber Pot', pp. 137–52 in R. Allen and M. Turvey (eds), *Wittgenstein, Theory and the Arts.* London: Routledge.

Iliffe, J. 1979. *A Modern History of Tanganyika.* Cambridge: Cambridge University Press.

Ingold, T. 2000. *Perceptions of the Environment: Essays on Livelihood, Dwelling and Skill.* London: Routledge.

Ingstad, B. 1989. 'Healer, Witch, Prophet, or Modern Health Worker? The Changing Role of *Ngaka ya Setswana*', pp. 247–76 in A. Jacobson-Widding and D. Westerlund (eds), *Culture, Experience and Pluralism: Essays on African Ideas of Illness and Healing.* Uppsala: Acta Universitatis Upsaliensis.

Jacobson-Widding, A. 1990. 'The Fertility of Incest', pp. 47–74 in A. Jacobson-Widding and W. van Beek (eds), *The Creative Communion: African Folk Models of Fertility and the Regeneration of Life.* Uppsala: Acta Universitatis Upsaliensis.

Jaeschke, E. 1985. *Bruno Gutmann: His Life – His Thoughts – His Work: An Early Attempt at a Theology in an African Context.* Erlangen: Verlag der Evangelisch-Lutherische Mission.

Japhet, K., and E. Seaton. 1967. *The Meru Land Case.* Nairobi: East African Publishing House.

Jennings, M. 2008. *Surrogates of the State: NGOs, Development, and Ujamaa in Tanzania.* Bloomfield: Kumarian Press.

Johnson, F. 1939. *A Standard Swahili–English Dictionary.* Nairobi: Oxford University Press.

Johnston, H. 1886. *The Kilima-Njaro Expedition.* London: Witherby.

Junod, H. 1910. 'Les Conceptions physiologiques des Bantous Sud-Africains et Leurs Tabous', *Revue d'Ethnographie et de Sociologie* 1: 126–69.

Junod, H. 1927. *The Life of a South African Tribe.* 2 vols. London: Macmillan.

Karp, I. 1978. 'New Guinea Models in the African Savannah', *Africa* 48(1): 1–16.

Kenyatta, J. 1938. *Facing Mount Kenya.* London: Secker & Warburg.

Kersten, O. 1869. *Baron Claus von der Decken's Reisen in Ost-Afrika in den Jahren 1859–1861.* Leipzig and Heidelberg: C.F. Winter'sche Verlagshandlung.

Kopytoff, I. 1971. 'Ancestors as Elders in Africa', *Africa* 43(2): 129–42.

Krapf, J.L. 1860. *Travels, Researches, and Missionary Labours during an 18 Years' Residence in Eastern Africa*. London: Trübner and Co.

Kuper, A. 1982. *Wives for Cattle*. London: Routledge.

Lan, D. 1985. *Guns and Rain: Guerrillas and Spirit Mediums in Zimbabwe*. Oxford: James Currey Press.

Latour, B. 2000. 'A Well-Articulated Primatology: Reflections of a Fellow-Traveller', pp. 358–81 in S.C. Strum and L.M. Fedigan (eds), *Primate Encounters: Models of Science, Gender, and Society*. Chicago: University of Chicago Press.

Latour, B. 2005. *Reassembling the Social: An Introduction to Actor-Network Theory*. Oxford: Oxford University Press.

Law, J. 2009. 'Actor Network Theory and Material Semiotics', pp. 141–58 in Bryan S. Turner (ed.), *The New Blackwell Companion to Social Theory*. Oxford: Wiley-Blackwell.

Lehmann, F.R. 1941. 'Some Field-Notes on the Chagga of Kilimanjaro', *Bantu Studies* 15(4): 385–96.

Lema, A.A. 1999. 'Chaga Religion and Missionary Christianity on Kilimanjaro', pp. 39–62 in T. Spear and I. Kimambo (eds), *East African Expressions of Christianity*. Oxford: James Currey.

Levi-Strauss, C. 1969. *The Elementary Structures of Kinship*. London: Eyre and Spottiswoode.

Levi-Strauss, C. [1979] 1982. *The Way of the Masks*. Vancouver: Douglas & McIntyre.

Levi-Strauss, C. [1984] 1987. *Anthropology and Myth: Lectures 1951–1982*. Oxford: Basil Blackwell.

Lienhardt, G. 1961. *Divinity and Experience: The Religion of the Dinka*. Oxford: Oxford University Press.

Marealle, P.I. 1963. 'Notes on Chagga Custom', *Tanganyika Notes and Records* 60: 67–90.

Marealle, P.I. 1965. 'Chagga Customs, Beliefs, and Traditions', *Tanganyika Notes and Records* 64: 56–61.

Marealle, T.L.M. 1952. 'The Wachagga of Kilimanjaro', *Tanganyika Notes and Records* 32: 57–64.

McCall, J.C. 1995. 'Rethinking Ancestors in Africa', *Africa* 65(2): 256–70.

Mendonsa, E.L. 1976. 'Elders, Office-Holders and Ancestors among the Sisala of Northern Ghana', *Africa* 46(1): 57–65.

Merker, M. 1902. *Rechtsverhältnisse und Sitten der Wadschagga*. Gotha: Justus Perthes.

Merlan, F. 2016. 'Women, Warfare, and the Life of Agency: Papua New Guinea and Beyond', *Journal of the Royal Anthropological Institute* 22(2): 329–411.

Moore, H.L. 1986. *Space, Text and Gender: An Anthropological Study of the Marakwet of Kenya*. Cambridge: Cambridge University Press.

Moore, H.L. 1999. 'Gender, Symbolism and Praxis: Theoretical Approaches', pp. 3–37 in H.L. Moore, T. Sanders and B. Kaare (eds), *Those Who Play with Fire: Gender, Fertility and Transformation in East and Central Africa.* London: Athlone Press.

Moore, H.L., and M. Vaughan. 1994. *Cutting Down Trees: Gender, Nutrition, and Agricultural Change in the Northern Province of Zambia, 1890–1990.* Oxford: James Currey.

Moore, S.F. 1976. 'The Secret of the Men: A Fiction of Chagga Initiation and Its Relation to the Logic of Chagga Symbolism', *Africa* 46(4): 357–70.

Moore, S.F. 1977. *The Chagga and Meru of Tanzania.* London: International African Institute.

Moore, S.F. 1978. 'Old Age in a Life-Term Social Arena: Some Chagga of Kilimanjaro in 1974', pp. 23–76 in B.G. Myerhoff and A. Simić (eds), *Life's Career – Aging: Cultural Variations on Growing Old.* London: Sage Publications.

Moore, S.F. 1981. 'Chagga "Customary" Law and the Property of the Dead', pp. 225–48 in S.C. Humphreys and H. King (eds), *Mortality and Immortality: The Anthropology and Archaeology of Death.* London: Academic Press.

Moore, S.F. 1986. *Social Facts and Fabrications: "Customary" Law on Kilimanjaro, 1880–1980.* Cambridge: Cambridge University Press.

Moore, S.F. 1987. 'Explaining the Present: Theoretical Dilemmas in Processual Ethnography', *American Ethnologist* 14(4): 727–36.

Moore, S.F. 1993. 'The Ethnography of the Present and the Analysis of Process', pp. 362–76 in R. Borofsky (ed.), *Assessing Cultural Anthropology.* New York: McGraw Hill.

Moore, S.F. 1996. 'Introduction', pp.ix-xix in O.F. Raum *Chagga Childhood: A Description of Indigenous Education in an East African Tribe.* Hamburg: Lit Verlag.

Moore, S.F. 2005a. 'Part of the Story: A Memoir', *Ethnos* 70(4): 538–66.

Moore, S.F. 2005b. 'From Tribes and Traditions to Composites and Conjunctures', *Social Analysis* 49(3): 254–72.

Myhre, K.C. 1998. 'The Anthropological Concept of Action and Its Problems: A "New" Approach Based on Marcel Mauss and Aristotle', *Journal of the Anthropological Society Oxford* 29(2): 121–34.

Myhre, K.C. 2006. 'Divination and Experience: Explorations of a Chagga Epistemology', *Journal of the Royal Anthropological Institute* 12(2): 313–30.

Myhre, K.C. 2007a. 'Family Resemblances, Practical Interrelations and Material Extensions: Understanding Sexual Prohibitions, Production and Consumption in Kilimanjaro', *Africa* 77(3): 307–30.

Myhre, K.C. 2007b. 'Om ritualer og sosial relasjoner: Refleksjoner rundt et kraftfullt bytte', *Norsk Antropologisk Tidsskrift* 18(3–4): 253–65.

Myhre, K.C. 2009. 'Disease and Disruption: Chagga Witchcraft and Relational Fragility', pp. 118–40 in L. Haram and C. Bawa Yamba (eds), *Dealing with Uncertainty in Contemporary African Lives.* Uppsala: Nordic Africa Institute.

Myhre, K.C. 2012. 'The Pitch of Ethnography: Language, Relations and the Significance of Listening', *Anthropological Theory* 12(2): 185–208.

Myhre, K.C. 2013a. 'Cutting and Connecting: "Afrinesian" Perspectives on Networks, Exchange, and Relationality', *Social Analysis* 57(3): 1–24.

Myhre, K.C. 2013b. 'Membering and Dismembering: The Poetry and Relationality of Animal Bodies in Kilimanjaro', *Social Analysis* 57(3): 114–31.

Myhre, K.C. 2014. 'The Multiple Meanings of *Moongo*: On the Conceptual Character of Doorways and Backbones in Kilimanjaro', *Journal of the Royal Anthropological Institute* 20(3): 505–25.

Myhre, K.C. 2015. 'What the Beer Shows: Exploring Ritual and Ontology in Kilimanjaro', *American Ethnologist* 42(1): 97–115.

Needham, R. 1960. 'The Left Hand of the Mugwe: An Analytical Note on the Structure of Meru Symbolism', *Africa* 30(1): 20–33.

Needham, R. 1967. 'Right and Left in Nyoro Symbolic Classification', *Africa* 37(4): 425–52.

New, C. 1873. *Life, Wanderings, and Labours in Eastern Africa.* London: Hodder and Stoughton.

Ngeze, P.B. 1994. *Bananas and Their Management.* Kagera: Kagera Writers and Publishers Co-Operative Society Ltd.

Oboler, R. 1994. 'The House-Property Complex and African Social Organization', *Africa* 64(3): 342–58.

Odner, K. 1971. 'A Preliminary Report on an Archaeological Survey on the Slopes of Kilimanjaro', *Azania* 6: 131–49.

Parkin, D. 1989. 'The Politics of Naming among the Giriama', pp. 61–89 in R. Grillo (ed.), *Social Anthropology and the Politics of Language.* London: Routledge.

Parkin, D. 1990. 'Eastern Africa: The View from the Office and the Voice from the Field', pp. 182–203 in R. Fardon (ed.), *Localizing Strategies: Regional Traditions of Ethnographic Writing.* Edinburgh: Scottish Academic Press.

Parkin, D. 1991a. *Sacred Void: Spatial Images of Work and Ritual among the Giriama of Kenya.* Cambridge: Cambridge University Press.

Parkin, D. 1991b. 'Simultaneity and Sequencing in the Oracular Speech of Kenyan Diviners', pp. 173–89 in P.M. Peek (ed.), *African Divination Systems.* Bloomington: Indiana University Press.

Parkin, D. 1995. 'Latticed Knowledge: Eradication and Dispersal of the Unpalatable in Islam, Medicine, and Anthropological Theory', pp. 146–66 in R. Fardon (ed.), *Counterworks: Managing the Diversity of Knowledge.* London: Routledge.

Parkin, D. 2000. 'Invocation: *Salaa, Dua, Sadaka* and the Question of Self-Determination', pp. 137–68 in D. Parkin and S. Healey (eds), *Islamic Prayer across the Indian Ocean: Inside and Outside the Mosque.* Richmond: Curzon Press.

Patton, P. 2000. *Deleuze and the Political.* London: Routledge.

Paul, S. 2003. 'Nachrufe: Otto Raum (1903–2002)', *Anthropos* 98(1): 198–201.

Pietilä, T. 2007. *Gossip, Markets, and Gender: How Dialogue Constructs Moral*

Value in Post-Socialist Kilimanjaro. Madison: University of Wisconsin Press.

Piot, C. 1999. *Remotely Global: Village Modernity in West Africa.* Chicago: University of Chicago Press.

Raum, J. 1907. 'Blut- und Speichelbünde bei den Wadschagga', *Archiv für Religionswissenchaft* 10: 269–94.

Raum, J. 1909. *Versuch einer Grammatik der Dschaggasprache (Moschi-Dialekt).* Berlin: Georg Reimer.

Raum, J. 1911. 'Die Religion der Landschaft Moschi am Kilmandjaro. Originalaufzeichnungen von Eingeborenen', *Archiv für Religionswissenschaft* 14: 159–211.

Raum, O.F. [1940] 1996. *Chagga Childhood: A Description of Indigenous Education in an East African Tribe.* Hamburg: Lit Verlag.

Rigby, P. 1966. 'Dual Symbolic Classification among the Gogo of Central Tanzania', *Africa* 36(1): 1–17.

Rigby, P. 1968. 'Some Gogo Rituals of "Purification": An Essay on Social and Moral Categories', pp. 153–78 in E.R. Leach (ed.), *Dialectic in Practical Religion.* Cambridge: Cambridge University Press.

Riles, A. 2001. *The Network Inside Out.* Ann Arbor: The University of Michigan Press.

Rodima-Taylor, D. 2016. 'Gathering Up Mutual Help: Relational Freedoms of Tanzanian Market-Women', pp. 76–94 in K.C. Myhre (ed.), *Cutting and Connecting: 'Afrinesian' Perspectives on Networks, Exchange and Relationality.* Oxford: Berghahn Books.

Ruel, M. 1962. 'Kuria Generation Classes', *Africa* 32(1): 14–37.

Ruel, M. 1997. *Belief, Ritual and the Securing of Life: Reflexive Essays on a Bantu Religion.* Leiden: E.J. Brill.

Ruel, M. 2000. 'The Kuria Homestead in Space and Time', *Journal of Religion in Africa* 30 (1): 62–85.

Sanders, T. 1999. '"Doing Gender" in Africa: Embodying Categories and the Categorically Disembodied', pp. 41–82 in H.L. Moore, T. Sanders and B. Kaare (eds), *Those Who Play with Fire: Gender, Fertility and Transformation in East and Central Africa.* London: Athlone Press.

Sanders, T. 2008. *Beyond Bodies: Rainmaking and Sense-Making in Tanzania.* Toronto: University of Toronto Press.

Schapera, I. 1934. 'Oral Sorcery among the Natives of Bechuanaland', pp. 293–305 in E.E. Evans-Pritchard, R. Firth, B. Malinowski and I. Schapera (eds), *Essays Presented to C.G. Seligman.* London: Kegan Paul, Trench, Trubner & Co.

Schapera, I. 1940. *Married Life in an African Tribe.* London: Faber & Faber.

Searle, J. 1969. *Speech Acts: An Essay in the Philosophy of Language.* Cambridge: Cambridge University Press.

Segal, R. 2001. 'In Defense of the Comparative Method', *Numen* 48(3): 339–73.

Setel, P. 1999. *A Plague of Paradoxes: AIDS, Culture, and Demography in Northern Tanzania.* Chicago: University of Chicago Press.

Snyder, K. 1999. 'Gender Ideology, and the Domestic and Public Domains among the Iraqw', pp. 225–53 in H.L. Moore, T. Sanders and B. Kaare (eds), *Those Who Play with Fire: Gender, Fertility and Transformation in East and Central Africa*. London: Athlone Press.

Sommerfelt, T. 2016. 'From Cutting to Fading: A Relational Perspective on Marriage Exchange and Sociality in Rural Gambia', pp. 58–75 in K.C. Myhre (ed.), *Cutting and Connecting: 'Afrinesian' Perspectives on Networks, Exchange and Relationality*. Oxford: Berghahn Books.

Southall, A. 1972. 'Twinship and Symbolic Structure', pp. 73–114 in J.S. La Fontaine (ed.), *The Interpretation of Ritual*. London: Tavistock.

Spencer, P. 1988. *The Maasai of Matapato: A Study of Rituals of Rebellion*. Manchester: Manchester University Press.

Stahl, K.M. 1969. 'The Chagga', pp. 209–22 in P. Gulliver (ed.), *Tradition and Transition in East Africa: Studies of the Tribal Element in the Modern Era*. London: Routledge and Kegan Paul.

Stambach, A. 2000. *Lessons from Mount Kilimanjaro: Schooling, Community and Gender in East Africa*. London: Routledge.

Stasch, R. 2009. *Society of Others: Kinship and Mourning in a West Papuan Place*. Berkeley: University of California Press.

Steiner, F. 1954. 'Chagga Truth: A Note on Gutmann's Account of the Chagga Concept of Truth in *Das Recht der Dschagga*', *Africa* 24(4): 364–69.

Stoll, A. 2007. *Wittgenstein*. Oxford: One World.

Strathern, M. 1984a. 'Marriage Exchanges: A Melanesian Comment', *Annual Review of Anthropology* 13: 41–73.

Strathern, M. 1984b. 'Subject or Object? Women and the Circulation of Valuables in Highlands New Guinea', pp. 158–75 in R. Hirschon (ed.), *Women and Property – Women as Property*. London: Croon Helm.

Strathern, M. 1987a. 'Out of Context: The Persuasive Fictions of Anthropology', *Current Anthropology* 28(3): 251–81.

Strathern, M. 1987b. 'Producing Difference: Connections and Disconnections in Two New Guinea Highland Kinship Systems', pp. 271–300 in J.F. Collier and S.J. Yanagisako (eds), *Gender and Kinship: Essays Toward a Unified Analysis*. Stanford: Stanford University Press.

Strathern, M. 1988. *The Gender of the Gift: Problems with Women and Problems with Society in Melanesia*. Berkeley: University of California Press.

Strathern, M. 1995. *The Relation: Issues in Complexity and Scale*. Cambridge: Prickly Pear.

Strathern, M. 1996. 'Cutting the Network', *Journal of the Royal Anthropological Institute (N.S.)* 2(3): 517–35.

Strathern, M. 1999. *Property, Substance, and Effect: Anthropological Essays on Persons and Things*. London: Athlone Press.

Strathern, M. 2005. *Kinship, Law and the Unexpected: Relatives Are Always a Surprise*. Cambridge: Cambridge University Press.

Sutton, J.E.G. 1969. 'The Peopling of Tanzania', pp. 1–13 in I.N. Kimambo and A.J. Temu (eds), *A History of Tanzania*. Nairobi: Heinemann Educational Books.

Taylor, C. 1992. *Milk, Honey, and Money: Changing Concepts in Rwandan Healing*. Washington: Smithsonian Institution Press.

Taylor, C. 1995. *Philosophical Arguments*. Cambridge: Harvard University Press.

Taylor, C. 2005. 'Fluids and Fractals in Rwanda: Order and Chaos', pp. 136–65 in M. Mosko and F.H. Damon (eds), *On the Order of Chaos: Social Anthropology and the Science of Chaos*. Oxford: Berghahn Books.

Thomson, J. 1885. *Through Masailand*. London: Sampson Low, Marston, Searle, and Rivington.

Udvardy, M. 1990. '*Kifudu*: A Female Fertility Cult among the Giriama', pp. 137–52 in A. Jacobson-Widding and W. van Beek (eds), *The Creative Communion: African Folk Models of Fertility and the Regeneration of Life*. Uppsala: Acta Universitatis Upsaliensis.

Viveiros de Castro, E. 2003. *And*. Manchester: Manchester Papers in Social Anthropology.

Viveiros de Castro, E. 2013. 'The Relative Native', *HAU: Journal of Ethnographic Theory* 3(3): 473–502.

Vokes, R. 2009. *The Ghosts of Kanungu: Fertility, Secrecy and Exchange in the Great Lakes of East Africa*. Oxford: James Currey.

Von Clemm, M. 1962. 'People of the White Mountain: The Interdependence of Political and Economic Activity amongst the Chagga in Tanganyika, with Special Reference to Recent Changes', unpublished D. Phil Thesis. Oxford: Oxford University.

Wagner, G. 1949. *The Bantu of North Kavirondo*, vol. 1. Oxford: Oxford University Press.

Wagner, G. 1954. 'The Abaluyia of Kavirondo (Kenya)', pp. 27–54 in D. Forde (ed.), *African Worlds: Studies in the Cosmological Ideas and Social Values of African Peoples*. London: Oxford University Press for the International African Institute.

Walther, K. 1900. 'Beiträge zur Kenntnis des Moschi-dialekts des Ki-Chagga (Kilimanjaro, Deutsch-Ostafrika)', *Zeitschrift für Afrikanishce und Oceanische Sprachen* 5(19): 33–43.

Wayne, H. 1995. *The Story of a Marriage: The Letters of Bronislaw Malinowski and Elsie Masson. Vol. 1 1916–20*. London: Routledge.

Weiner, A.B. 1980. 'Reproduction: A Replacement for Reciprocity', *American Ethnologist* 7(1): 71–85.

Weishaupt, M. 1912. 'Überblick über unsere Missionsstationen in Ostafrika', *Evangelisch-Lutherisches Missionsblatt* 67(18): 430–33.

Weiss, B. 1996. *The Making and Unmaking of the Haya Lived World*. Durham, NC: Duke University Press.

West, H. 2005. *Kupilikula: Governance and the Invisible Realm in Mozambique*. Chicago: University of Chicago Press.

Whyte, S.R. 1997. *Questioning Misfortune: The Pragmatics of Uncertainty in Eastern Uganda*. Cambridge: Cambridge University Press.

Widenmann, A. 1899. *Die Kilimanjaro-Bevölkerung: Anthropologisches and Ethnographisches aus dem Dschaggalande*. Gotha: Justus Perthes.

Willoughby, W.C. 1928. *The Soul of the Bantu.* London: Student Christian Movement.

Winter, J.C. 1977. 'Kinship Terms of Address (Old Moshi)', pp. 37–41 in S.F. Moore (ed.), *The Chagga and Meru of Tanzania.* London: International African Institute.

Winter, J.C. 1979. *Bruno Gutmann 1876–1966: A German Approach to Social Anthropology.* Oxford: Oxford University Press.

Wittgenstein, L. 1953. *Philosophical Investigations.* Oxford: Blackwell.

Wittgenstein, L. 1958. *The Blue and the Brown Books.* Oxford: Blackwell.

Wittgenstein, L. 1969. *On Certainty.* Oxford: Blackwell.

Wittgenstein, L. 1980. *Culture and Value.* Oxford: Blackwell.

Wittgenstein, L. 1993. 'Remarks on Frazer's *Golden Bough*', pp. 115–55 in L. Wittgenstein, *Philosophical Occasions.* Indiana: Hacket Publishing Company.

INDEX

www.ingramcontent.com/pod-product-compliance
Lightning Source LLC
Chambersburg PA
CBHW070907030426
42336CB00014BA/2324